Street Style in America

Street Style in America

AN EXPLORATION

Jennifer Grayer Moore

An Imprint of ABC-CLIO, LLC

Santa Barbara, California • Denver, Colorado

FEB   '18

Library of Congress Cataloging-in-Publication Data
Names: Moore, Jennifer Grayer.
Title: Street style in America : an exploration / Jennifer Grayer Moore.
Description: Santa Barbara, California : Greenwood, [2017] | Includes bibliographical
    references and index. |
Identifiers: LCCN 2017007824 (print) | LCCN 2017010522 (ebook) |
    ISBN 9781440844621 (ebook) | ISBN 9781440844614
Subjects: LCSH: Exoticism in fashion—United States—History—20th century. |
    Urban youth—Clothing—United States—History—20th century. | Fashion
    merchandising—United States—History—20th century. | Lifestyles—United States—
    History—20th century. | Expression.
Classification: LCC GT615 (ebook) | LCC GT615 .M66 2017 (print) |
    DDC 391.00973/0904—dc23
LC record available at https://lccn.loc.gov/2017007824

ISBN: 978-1-4408-4461-4
EISBN: 978-1-4408-4462-1

21   20   19   18   17   1   2   3   4   5

This book is also available as an eBook.

Greenwood
An Imprint of ABC-CLIO, LLC

ABC-CLIO, LLC
130 Cremona Drive, P.O. Box 1911
Santa Barbara, California 93116-1911
www.abc-clio.com

This book is printed on acid-free paper ⊗
Manufactured in the United States of America

Contents

Preface

In the early spring of 2015, just as I was in the process of completing my first book, *Fashion Fads through American History: Fitting Clothes into Context,* my former editor Rebecca Matheson approached me with the daunting prospect of writing a book on "street style." As an avid reader of fashion periodicals and fashion trade publications, I was keenly aware that the concept of street style was incredibly "hot." It seemed that everywhere I turned in contemporary fashion media the term "street style" was being used—to promote trendy fashion concepts, to sell merchandise by connecting it to a sense of freshness and innovation, to celebrate celebrities and thereby promote the brands and designers they wear—yet even a fleeting consideration of this omnipresent concept revealed a great disparity in terms of *meaning*. I was left to wonder, what *is* street style? What do we mean when we use the term?

This is a book about dress styles, a visual language that is rich, complex, and not as univocal as some have made it out to be. Part of what this book strives to accomplish is the presentation of an orderly and cohesive discussion of what street style has been over the course of American history and what it is today. It is clear that it is a concept that has evolved over time. There is a large body of literature, primarily from the field of sociology, that has investigated the realm of subcultural style (an important subgenre of street style) through various kinds of fieldwork including interviews and observations. Much has been accomplished in terms of understanding why individuals participate in these kinds of street styles; however, research and theory building about style, coming from the social sciences, generally give only the most cursory attention to the style itself. This work draws upon the rich body of literature generated in the social sciences and augments it by delving into the specifics of dress practices.

The documentation of specific street styles (including cut, fit, materials, brands, do-it-yourself techniques, specific innovators, and retailers) is lacking. Few texts written by an historian and devoted exclusively to this subject exist. Many of the important texts are outdated, and one of the most widely read books deals with the subject from a distinctly British point of view, thereby giving short shrift to some important aspects of American dress history. This work deals primarily with street styles as they existed and continue to exist in the United States, while also discussing the variations that have existed over time and around the world. The effort to go beyond a simplified, homogenized, even stereotyped depiction of street styles is consequently also a focus of this text, a focus that is indebted to the theory building of authors like Dr. David Muggleton, whose work is referenced in several places in this text.

This book contributes to the field of dress studies and fashion history as it undertakes the subject of street style simultaneously on a theoretical level, on a documentary level, and on a broadly historical level. The overall landscape of the fashion industry—the respective roles of producers and consumers—is integral to this discussion. The specific social contexts, considered in light of economics, politics, communication, and technology, are summoned to cast light on the emergence, diffusion, and interpretation of sartorial choices. Thus the content in this text is designed to fill many gaps in the fashion-historical record, and my aim is to create a resource that both fills a need in the existing body of literature and elucidates points where clarity is required.

Writing this book has necessitated an omnivorous approach to research, one that I must admit I greatly enjoy. Primary-source materials (old newspapers, magazines, and photographs) were indispensible sources of information and insight. Theoretical discussions, academic papers, and historical texts also informed this work. Among the most evocative sources used to develop a robust picture of the aesthetics of street styles from the past and the historical context in which they thrived was the use of autobiographies, some of well-known rockers and artists, others of lesser-known witnesses and participants in cultural milieus that have largely faded away. For the benefit of the reader I have included many of the really provocative and compelling sources in the Further Reading sections of many entries included in Part 2 of this book.

This text can readily be used as a reference book. The Table of Contents clearly directs the reader to specific topics such as Zooties, Goths, Punks, Surfers, Beats, Grunge rockers, Modern Primitives, or Hippies, and the index and in-text citations both make plain where topics overlap and cross-reference. The introductory chapters in Part 1 incrementally build the picture of the history, meaning, and importance of street style, while the A–Z chapters documenting specific street styles in Part 2 provide specific examples of street-style phenomena. Cross-referencing shows how one street style evolved out of (or in some way interpreted or responded to) a street style that preceded it. However the reader chooses to use this book, it is my sincere hope that it will prove to be both interesting and useful.

Acknowledgments

I would like to give my most heartfelt thanks to the countless students at the Art Institute of New York City and Pratt Institute who assisted me by engaging in spirited debates about the nature of contemporary street style and who weighed in on the nuances of identification with contemporary style groups and subcultures. Your thoughtfulness and introspection have contributed to the richness and depth of this work. I would also like to thank my husband, Jason Moore, for being a constant source of support and insight for this project and for all things. Finally, I must acknowledge the countless people who agreed to speak with me about their personal style, their identification with subcultural groups, or their relationships to street-style phenomena in their roles as fashion professionals. For both your time and your openness I am thankful.

How to Use This Work

This text is divided into three distinct sections. Part 1 consists of several chapters that explore the history, meaning, and importance of street style. The chapters within this section provide the reader with background that will enrich his or her understanding of the style groups that are discussed in detail and depicted in full-page photographs in Parts 2 and 3 of this volume. In Part 1, the concepts of street style and subcultural style are carefully defined, and their importance as driving forces in the inspiration of fashion design and product development is introduced. Part 1 also develops the historical context for the evolution of street styles, including both the social contexts for their emergence as well as the landscape of the fashion industry that facilitated the movement of style from the street to the fashion industry and ultimately to large numbers of consumers. Finally, Part 1 explores the importance of modes of communication with regard to developing and spreading street styles. The roles of print media, moving images, celebrities, new media, and retailers (both brick-and-mortar and virtual) are all considered as important components in the development and diffusion of street style.

Part 2 explores specific style groups that have existed or are currently visible in the United States. Each entry within this section develops the time, place, and social factors surrounding the emergence of the style and carefully describes aspects of the street style from its origin through widespread adoption, considering both variations and stereotypes. These entries explore the symbolic interpretations of the sartorial choices both from within the group that adopted the look and by outsiders. Additionally, each entry discusses representations of the look in literature, film, and television. Finally, the entries provide an exploration of the commodification of each street style and the trickle-up effect to designers and other commercial entities.

Part 3 is dedicated to visual representations of the street styles discussed in Part 2. Each entry is complemented by a full-page photograph that captures and characterizes key elements of the style. A brief analytical description accompanies each picture. Part 3 both reinforces the information in Part 2 and provides a useful visual reference source.

Part I

Exploring the Historical Context for
the Development of Street Style

Chapter 1

Introduction

What is "street style"? The quick answer to this question is that the term means different things to different people, and its referent varies greatly depending upon the interests of whomever one asks. For some, street style is about *fashion,* the new, the constantly changing, that which the masses will emulate. For others, street style is about *antifashion,* that which remains largely unchanged year after year and which seeks to affront the mainstream rather than spawn emulation. A discussion of street style may revolve around what Ted Polhemus has termed a "style tribe," a recognizable sartorial expression situated within a group that may have some sort of shared interest such as music, gaming, or literature. In some instances these style tribes may appropriately be labeled subcultural groups, factions of people who are united socially because of a shared vision of mainstream society's shortcomings. Subcultural groups utilize style as both personal expression and visible rejection of mainstream codes of conduct. Beginning in the 1990s the term "street style" routinely came to be used to refer to urban (usually African American) dress, which is now commonly referred to as hip-hop style. This application of the term may have paved the path for its use in common parlance today. Since the early 2000s the term "street style" has been used as a general descriptor of dress assemblages seen most anywhere other than a runway or a fashion editorial, and the prevailing implication of the term is that street style is an expression of personal style. This text investigates both recognizable style groups (including subcultural styles) and 21st-century personal style.

A note of caution is necessary before proceeding. Street style, even the street style of recognizable social groups, is neither static nor homogenous. Street style is constantly evolving and is subject to an infinite number of personal interpretations that written documentation may inadvertently belie. One critique that emerges again and again in the study of subcultural groups and their styles is that authors (whether they are sociologists or fashion historians) try to make tidy, linear, grand narratives of these groups, their dress, and the meaning inherent in it. I have tried to avoid such generalizations about people, meaning, and intentions; and where styles are described I have tried to make clear that I am documenting distinctive elements, not exhaustive permutations. Labels such as "leathermen" or "cholo" are labels utilized to describe appearance, not a person's individual character or personal identity. How a person looks cannot automatically be construed as who or what a person is.

Street style, unlike fashions presented in a designer collection, isn't monolithic, organized, or finite. We cannot turn to a runway or lookbook to see exactly what was offered and in what combinations in a given season. Additionally, the modification of street style is not subject to seasonal change but rather to changes that respond to culture, collective selection, and whimsy, and some street style is definitively a form of antifashion, and as such it maintains certain tropes with little variation over an extended period. This work will seek balance in each of the descriptions of specific street styles by offering details ranging from obscure to commonplace, prototypical to stereotypical, with discussions including both evidence of personalized creations and products of commodity culture. Describing and discussing a workable sample of the variations of stylistic expression is an effort to give a well-rounded portrayal of the many possibilities of a given street style. Describing and discussing the stereotypes that mass media have arranged and packaged are also relevant as it is often these tropes that have come to have lasting importance and influence in the larger universe of fashionable dress. Considering iconic visual language side by side with lesser-known variations is part of the effort to provide an authentic picture of each sartorial style.

The A–Z entries in this text discuss the various street style groups in terms such as subcultural, post-subcultural, style tribe, and street style of the new millennium; therefore, these introductory remarks will now turn to a discussion of what these categories delineate.

Subcultural Style

A subculture is defined as a group that differentiates itself from the mainstream or "parent" culture. Differentiation takes the form of ideology, lifestyle, cultural production (music, graphic design, dance), and dress practices. The study of subcultures and their styles emerged in the middle of the 20th century, and the theoretical constructs that are applied to understanding subcultures and their practices have changed substantially in the past 60 years. Theories of subcultures have generally become more grounded in the realities of subcultural lives as they are actually lived. Initially, subcultural theorists who were a part of the "Chicago school" of thought posited subcultural groups as universally deviant and their members wholly united in terms of needs, outlook, and the circumstances surrounding each individual's motivation to join the unified, homogenous group (see Cohen 1955). Thus, dress practices were dealt with in a cursory way that failed to recognize diversity and individualization and were exclusively viewed as a direct response to mainstream dress practices. Some 15 years later the writings of the Birmingham Center for Contemporary Cultural Studies (CCCS) came to dominate the discussion surrounding subcultures and their style. Scholars coming out of CCCS, including Dick Hebdige, who wrote the seminal work *Subculture: The Meaning of Style* (1979), suggested that all subcultures were working class, politically oriented, and defined in contrast to the parent culture. In addition, the characteristics of the parent culture and its hegemonic power were essentially viewed as causal factors that produced the subcultural response, including dress practices. CCCS writers generally conceived of subcultural groups as virtually unchanging, and members of subcultures could be labeled as authentic or inauthentic, insiders or hangers-on. Finally, CCCS scholarship viewed the symbolism of dress as purposeful and fully conceived. Hebdige in particular wrote of subcultural style as having subversive implications and semiological potency capable of signifying revolt, refusal, defiance, and contempt. Hebdige also pointed out that subcultural group members were not designers of symbols but rather were masterful appropriators of existing visual culture. He noted, "'Humble objects' can be magically appropriated; 'stolen' by subordinate groups and made to carry 'secret' meanings: meanings which express in code a form of resistance to the order" (18). Thus the CCCS approach was more nuanced than that of the Chicago school but still viewed subcultures and their styles as homogenous, unchanging, and operating exclusively in response to the mainstream.

In the past 30 years or so sociologists and cultural theorists have both modified and moved beyond the theories developed by the Chicago school of thought and the CCCS. In some instances modern writers have abandoned virtually all tenets of the early writings, while others have sought to temper and improve upon statements that are now deemed too broad and sweeping. For example, drawing from the social theory of Pierre Bourdieu (1984), Sarah Thornton (1997) has argued that membership in a subcultural group has much to do with the development of specific tastes, insider knowledge, and specific social capital (what she calls subcultural capital). This approach allows that dress styles may be adopted for social rather than political reasons. Other writers have drawn on gender theory as it is elucidated by Judith Butler and have argued that subcultural membership is largely performative. This approach separates subcultural practice from some essential characteristic or deeply held belief of the person who participates in the subculture. Still other authors have sought to redefine subcultural groups as "neo tribes" (see Maffesoli 1996) and have argued that consumption patterns largely define modern sociocultural groups and that attachment to groups is both ephemeral and superficial— more akin to a lifestyle choice than to a deeply rooted set of convictions born out of a specific cultural upbringing. Others have largely ignored the matter of whether subcultures are actual groups and instead have focused on how individuals may use "radical style as a way to draw social boundaries in a way that relieves them from the pressure or expectations to interact with unfamiliar peers" (Bešić and Kerr 2009, 114).

Understanding what has been written about subcultures in general is useful to developing a honed understanding of subcultural style. Subcultural styles do manifest widespread tropes and trends, but this does not imply a singular use or message. Shared or overlapping interests among individuals who dress similarly are likely, as dress is at a minimum an expression of a momentary taste; however, some modicum of shared interest does not imply a profound solidarity aesthetically or ideologically. This is true of late-20th-century style groups (i.e., of the postmodern era), and it is also clear from a diverse and robust variety of historical records that the singularity implied by early theorists never existed. Given that this is a text that is primarily concerned with style, commodities for creating any given street style are crucial to understanding it. In early writings on subcultural dress, commodified subcultural style was treated as a clear indication that the purchaser of such products was undoubtedly a poseur. The act of purchasing dress-related items was considered antithetical to core membership (as it marked engagement in the mainstream commodity culture) and a clear indication that a person was not a true member of a subcultural group. Since this is a text about style, the aim here is not to grapple with what makes one an *authentic* member of a given group. Indeed, to argue about whether style communicates a fixed essence of someone's character seems to rely on an outdated notion of how dress is used from at least the late 20th century onward. Style does have communicative properties, but they are neither fixed nor unified to express a singular idea.

Post-Subcultural Style

There is a large body of work that draws from postmodern philosophy and argues that subcultural style is (to varying degrees) pure veneer—a meaningless display (see Muggleton 2000). This branch of theory has led some sociologists and cultural theorists to posit a new category referred to as post-subcultural style. Theories of post-subcultural styles push beyond the notions that subcultural identity is varied and in flux and, in essence, posit a use of style that is superficial and completely individualized. This theory of post-subcultural style is rooted in the tenets of postmodernism, a rich and varied field of inquiry. A few key points pertaining to postmodernism itself can provide context for a meaningful discussion of the theory of post-subcultural style.

The reworking and revisiting of old ideas in fashion are often cited as revelatory symptoms of postmodernity. According to Frederic James (1985), one attribute of late-20th-century culture onward is the waning of an elite or "high culture" authority. One result of this, he posits, is that art and design have come to be defined by "pastiche"—meaning the imitation and repetition of past designs. For James, the reworking of old styles points to a sort of void in late-20th-century culture, in which neither new design nor new meaning is created. James is not alone in his concern about the revisiting of past designs. Professor of Cultural Studies Elizabeth Wilson (1992) has noted that postmodern cultural products demonstrate an interest on the surface, but they have no symbolic value or meaning and are disconnected from a greater cultural narrative. Wilson points to the fact that designs revived from the past may look interesting, but they will fail to recapture the meaning they originally had. Finally, postmodern theorists indicate that from the late 20th century onward the speed of life has quickened to an extraordinary pace due to the speed of technology and mass communication. Jean Baudrillard (2005) has suggested that the speed of life is such that our ability to gain historical perspective and construct an historical narrative has collapsed, and he sees part of the problem therein as the inability to dispose of old ideas. For Baudrillard, the inability of a culture to pause and assess itself will ultimately lead to cultural stagnation and reliance on reworking ideas that should have been relegated to the dustbin.

Post-subcultural groups (essentially postmodern subcultural groups) rely heavily on recycling old styles, do not manifest a true divide between high and low or mainstream and deviant culture, and are not explicitly connected to a sociocultural context (i.e., they are not a response to widespread or important phenomena in society). Furthermore, many members of post-subcultures do not identify as members of a group, a clear indication that what is shared among individuals who appear to be similar may not be a reflection of their core values. Thus their style is likely not a form of resistance. David Muggleton posited the essence of post-subculturalists succinctly when he wrote, "They do not have to worry about contradictions between their selected subcultural identities, for there are no rules, there is no authenticity, no ideological commitment, merely a stylistic game to be played" (2000, 47). Muggleton, writing with Rupert Wienzierl in the introductory essay of *The Post-Subcultures Reader,* notes that any subversive quality that may seem to be a part of post-subcultural style is a mere illusion (2003, 5). Furthermore, the ubiquity of so many of the tropes of post-subcultural style means that aspects of dress that were once revolutionary, shocking, and deviant have largely lost their incendiary power as they have been reused and recycled by generations of individuals who have sought some form of personal expression through their iconic stylistic features. Importantly, wearers of post-subcultural styles are incredibly varied in their approaches to dress, their use of commodities, their identification with the social group that their dress relates to, and their reasons for dressing as they do. Thus post-subcultural dress styles relate in many superficial ways to subcultural styles while lacking any pretense to true or authentic communicative power.

Street Style in the New Millennium

The final category of street style that is dealt with in this text is the early-21st-century application of the concept. Open any mainstream fashion magazine or peruse the multitude of fashion websites and blogs that exist on the Internet and one is bound to find fashion editors, fashion retailers, and photographers ranging from part-time amateurs to professionals at the top of the industry documenting outfits as they are worn on the street. Thus a preliminary working definition of the contemporary notion of street style is personal style. Contemporary street style is often about the styling or combining of various pieces of apparel into a specific, unique look. Contemporary street style often incorporates current fashion trends and designer brands but also routinely utilizes vintage items and do-it-yourself techniques. Thus contemporary street style walks a line between fashion and anti-fashion as it both embraces the contemporary and eschews any fixed notion of how contemporary dress should be worn. The root of contemporary street style is the celebration of sartorial individualism, though the involvement of stylists in crafting street style "looks" for both celebrity clients and the press clouds this issue. Furthermore, many fashion commentators have sought to find common threads or tendencies in street-style aesthetics in fashion capitals of the world including New York, Tokyo, and Paris. Chapter 4 of this text scrutinizes this effort to create order and communicative power out of individual efforts to dress fashionably. Despite some murkiness with regard to street style as a referent, what is abundantly clear about street style in the new millennium is that it is a powerful vehicle for the communication of fashionable ideas and is an important part of the commercial fashion landscape. Much has been written about street style, but little has been done to investigate what it really is and why it is important. This work will undertake that task.

Street style, whether it is subcultural, post-subcultural, or individualistic, is an important part of both fashion and antifashion. It is a powerful expressive tool for individuals, regardless of whether it is an effort to communicate a shared ideal and spirit of the time or simply an expression of a fleeting whim or personal taste. Street style is also important to the fashion industry. Subcultural and post-subcultural styles have been profoundly influential to designers. Most of the A–Z entries in this text include references to examples of specific designer collections that have taken the aesthetics of the street and interpreted them, often elevating the street aesthetics for the high-style collections. Street styles have also stimulated the development of commodities. Aesthetic choices that have originated as do-it-yourself modifications have been mass produced and have thereby impacted commodity culture. In some instances the translation of dress practices from do-it-yourself to commercially made designs has inspired the development of new technologies in the fashion industry, a further indication of the importance of street style to the business of fashion. Street style is also part of the story of how the fashion industry has undergone a dramatic reorientation from the latter half of the 20th century onward. Whereas there was a time when fashion designers (especially couturiers) and their elite clients established fashion, the emergence of street styles in the wake of World War II has dramatically impacted the power structures and the currents of trickle-up and trickle-down, a story that is told in detail in chapters 2 and 3. Finally, street styles of all kinds are important sociocultural markers of attitudes, tastes, and even current events. The act of getting dressed is a practical consideration that is required by societies that frown on public nudity, but it is also a vehicle for expression, which is sometimes conscious, planned, and targeted and other times undertaken with only subconscious reflection upon current norms. However, dress is always a symbol of the times in which we live and, therefore, worthy of careful investigation.

Further Reading

Baudrillard, J. 2005. *The Intelligence of Evil or the Lucidity Pact.* Translated by James Benedict. New York: Verso.

Bešić, N., and M. Kerr. 2009. "Punks, Goths, and Other Eye-Catching Peer Crowds: Do They Fulfill a Function for Shy Youths?" *Journal of Research on Adolescence* 19 (1): 113–21.

Bourdieu, P. 1984. *Distinction: A Social Critique of the Judgment of Taste.* New York: Routledge.

Butler, J. 1993. *Bodies That Matter: On the Discursive Limits of Sex.* New York: Routledge.

Cohen, A. 1955. "A General Theory of Subcultures." In *The Subcultures Reader,* 2nd ed., edited by K. Gelder and S. Thornton, 50–59. New York: Routledge.

Hebdige, D. 1979. *Subculture: The Meaning of Style.* New York: Routledge.

James, F. 1985. "Postmodernism and Consumer Society." In *Postmodern Culture,* edited by Hal Foster, 111–25. London: Pluto Press.

Maffesoli, M. 1996. *The Times of the Tribes: The Decline of Individualism in Mass Society.* London: Sage.

Muggleton, D. 2000. *Inside Subculture: The Postmodern Meaning of Style.* New York: Berg.

Polhemus, T. 1994. *Streetstyle: From Sidewalk to Catwalk.* London: Thames and Hudson.

Polhemus, T. 1996. *Style Surfing: What to Wear in the 3rd Millennium.* London: Thames and Hudson.

Thornton, S. 1997. "The Social Logic of Subcultural Capital." In *The Subcultures Reader,* 2nd ed., edited by K. Gelder and S. Thornton, 184–92. New York: Routledge.

Wienzierl, R., and D. Muggleton. 2003. "What Is Post-Subcultural Studies Anyway?" In *The Post-Subcultures Reader,* edited by R. Wienzierl and D. Muggleton, 3–26. New York: Berg.

Wilson, E. 1992. "Fashion and the Postmodern Body." In *Chic Thrills,* edited by Juliet Ash and Elizabeth Wilson, 3–16. London: Pandora.

Chapter 2

The Sociocultural Context for the Development of Street Style

The entries in this book document the wide variety of street styles that have populated the history of American dress across the last 90 years. Many of these styles originated in the United States and have influenced global dress practices, while some originated abroad and consequently developed and changed through their adoption into American culture. One notable point about the A–Z street and subcultural style entries in this volume is that none of them predates the 20th century. In fact, the earliest example included in this comprehensive text, "Zooties" (marginalized youths, especially African American and Latino individuals who wore zoot suits), emerged only at the very end of the 1930s. The failure to document earlier street styles in the United States is not an oversight, but rather it speaks to the essential nature of dress practices in the social, cultural, and commercial context prior to the second quarter of the 20th century. Clearly there is a lengthy time frame preceding the emergence of consumer-driven styles.

This chapter explores key aspects of the landscape of sartorial and social practices in the United States and how they changed from the first decades of the 20th century through the post–World War II period. Two prongs of inquiry frame this endeavor. First, the evolution of the commercial fashion marketplace is fundamental to the emergence of street styles. I will demonstrate how mass production, which facilitated mimicry of high-style fashion trends, ultimately eroded the long-lived principle of sartorial distinction and thereby paved the way for new modes for sartorial expression that were consumer driven. Second, this chapter will show that the development of street style is a radical expression of youth culture and that social change and development in American society engendered unique expressions of youth only in the 20th century. In order to fully understand street style one must understand the fundamental sociocultural characteristics within American culture and the American fashion system that provided the fertile context for its development.

Street style in its most extreme subcultural forms is essentially a rejection of mainstream sartorial values. It can be a strong countercultural statement. However, street style in its less organized, less political, and less subversive forms is, at a minimum, expressive of personal taste, individuality, disdain for the homogenous mainstream, and defiance of conventions. The inclination to express oneself and stand out in a crowd through sartorial practices is an important form of self-expression within a given social milieu. Importantly, this is an impulse that has not always been widely enacted. The context in which street and subcultural styles began to emerge is predicated on two factors. First, the existence of and widespread emulation of an existing dress standard by the majority of individuals, and second, both the willingness and the ability to defy the relevant dress standard. These are not minor points of predication as notions of fashionable and appropriate dress and grooming are both culturally and institutionally formed and have long exerted powerful sway within the general populace. Understanding this part of the story is fundamental to fully grasping the importance of all kinds of street style.

Part 1: Evolution of the Fashion Marketplace

In order to properly situate the advent of sartorial experimentation and dissension from the mainstream that began in the United States in the 20th century, it is important to provide a brief sketch of what preceded the development of these oppositional dress styles. Having a grasp of what the mainstream looked like and how it changed over time is important, and for some readers the next few paragraphs will mark a return to "Fashion History 101." To begin, a point must be made about the broad history of Western fashion—a point that takes us far beyond the advent of any kind of American fashion, but that explores a relevant phenomenon and sets the stage for understanding the critical tensions, the push and pull, that exist between the dual impulses of conformity and individuality in fashionable dress.

Fashion: A Delicate Balance between Conformity and Originality

It is undisputed among fashion historians that the cycle of fashion change began in the 12th century in Europe among aristocrats and landed gentry who innovated original concepts and emulated and competed with one another (Norris 1927; Tortura and Eubank 2015). It is generally argued that early in the history of fashion, to be *in fashion* was to follow the tastemakers and style setters who routinely changed their appearances when the legions of copycats reached a critical mass that eroded the style innovator's distinction. This game of follow-the-leader fueled fashion change. The basic principle outlined here is still an important part of fashion today. A sartorial idea is introduced; it is first adopted by style leaders, then it diffuses throughout the general population where it is widely adopted; it is ultimately abandoned once the novelty of the stylistic ideal has faded. At some point within this progression yet another sartorial innovation is introduced so that the cycle of stylistic change is never at a standstill.

The ability to follow the leader is predicated on the ability of individuals to access stylistic ideas and make copies. From the late 19th century onward, the replication of a new mode could be achieved with a great degree of similarity to the original (a topic that we turn to in due course). However, with regard to eras predating the Industrial Revolution, the historical record that has thus far been unpacked is not detailed enough to fully show how *slavishly and precisely* styles were followed throughout the first 500 or so years of the fashion cycle, nor exactly *how* the tipping point that precipitated evolution of new styles was reached. Although specific, comprehensive details are often lacking and conclusions must be drawn from scattered examples, the general notion that scholars accept is that early in the history of fashion the underclasses participated in fashion through emulation *to the best of their abilities* (Roche 1994; Styles 2007). Although copious and specific evidence from early in the history of fashion as to the quality and similarity of interpretations and the length of the delay between style introduction, style emulation, and style change is largely unavailable, deductions can be made based on general knowledge of the technology, economy, and marketplace. Notably, in eras predating mass-production techniques for apparel (including devices like the sewing machine and standardized patternmaking techniques) and photo-realistic reproductions of imagery for the communication of fashionable ideas, a great deal of variety must have existed in terms of quality, extravagance, and similarity to the trendsetting style. This leaves room for the idea that elite individuals could still distinguish themselves sartorially even though a dress idea had diffused to a larger population. This point is crucial as it speaks to the degree of uniformity that may or may not have existed, and I ultimately argue that cookie-cutter uniformity on a mass scale, which became easily obtainable in the 20th century, is part of what led to the development of street and subcultural styles.

Fashionable Conformity in the Age of Mass Production

Ample evidence of mass participation in fashion and the mass emulation of style setters becomes more copious and varied as we draw closer to the present. Primary-source materials, including newspaper advertisements, dry goods and department store ephemera, mail-order catalogs, and photographs of all kinds (posed, snapshots, professional, and amateur), all provide evidence that from the middle of the 19th century onward, people had increased access, in a more timely manner, to fashionable clothes that followed styles established by elite individuals. Improved access in terms of variety, quality, fidelity to the original, and rapidity of emulation can be attributed to the ongoing development and refinement of the ready-to-wear industry as well as the dissemination of images through the increasingly diversified realm of mass media, including the reproduction of photographs beginning at the end of the 19th century. The source material from the mid-19th century to the mid-20th century indicates silhouette similarity between society mavens and school-girls, titans of business and humble shopkeepers. Comparisons made between the apparel offerings in the Sears mail-order catalog and nearly contemporaneous designs developed by Parisian couturiers or Savile Row tailors of the early 20th century show a quick and literal interpretation and dissemination of fashion from the high end to the mass market. However, in the first decades of the 20th century, within this context of timely and faithful copying, there was still ample room for making points of distinction in terms of the quality of materials and fabrication that kept fashion interesting and competitive. Of particular importance was the distinction of *who* designed and made one's clothes, a distinguishing factor that became especially perceptible in the domain of women's fashions toward the end of the 19th century.

Fashion designers represented a new kind of leader to follow. Most fashion historians concur that the fashion industry as we conceive it today was formed in 1858 when Englishman Charles Frederick Worth first opened the doors to his Parisian atelier (Aspelund 2009, ch. 1; De La Haye and Mendes 2014, Introduction). Prior to Worth's enterprise, dress styles emerged through networks of taste-makers who instructed professional tailors, dressmakers, cobblers, wigmakers, and clothing decorators to do their bidding, thus making the origins of specific style ideas difficult to trace. The lack of a discernible point of origin for a style idea undoubtedly also impacted copying, influencing the varying degrees of fidelity that existed throughout the population. Worth, *le père de la haute couture* (the father of haute couture), fundamentally changed the garment-making industry by wresting much of the creative control out of the hands of the taste-making elite consumer and gripping it in his own. Design innovation and the exertion of a specific taste level and point of view were fundamental to the move from garment maker to fashion designer—the move that Worth pioneered by designing seasonal collections, controlling the selection of textiles and trim, and formalizing the creation of patterns. Equally important, however, was the fact that Worth's name became synonymous with good taste and an enlightened sense of fashion.

In the ensuing decades, Worth commanded a large retinue of prestigious clients who were lured to his atelier by virtue of his streamlined system of production (that manufactured garments much more rapidly than other ateliers), by his evolving styles, but also, undeniably, by the innate value of his name. The Worth label was elite, and the cachet associated with having Monsieur Worth create a garment on one's behalf was enviable and evocative of a high level of status, taste, and social capital. Legions of other designers sprouted up in the wake of this sea change, and a thriving couture industry was in evidence by the end of the 19th century. The evidence shows that design innovation and designer "genius" came to define fashion, and following the leader came to mean following the lead of Parisian couturiers. For the fashionable, elite sartorial distinction came to be identified in large part by the stylistic ideas propounded by a specific fashion professional.

By the turn of the 20th century the authority of the individual designer was such that not only did a vast field of individuals find substantial enough client bases to thrive, but more importantly, that unique and conflicting design visions existed coevally. The aesthetic agendas of designers as diverse as Mariano Fortuny, Paul Poiret, and Gabrielle Chanel commandeered legions of followers whose sensibilities could be met, identities could be proclaimed, and taste levels could be distinguished through their designer of choice. Designers created and innovated with wealthy and elite target clients in mind, and importantly, design ideas were carefully guarded secrets that were shared with both the fashion press and the general public only on carefully arranged dates on the fashion calendar. The privileged few purchased couture originals, and exclusive manufacturers, who had purchased the rights to make line-for-line replicas, produced a few dozen to a few hundred copies. The press lauded the genius of each individual designer, which, in turn, the public internalized in some form. In this context a new balance was struck between the polarities of conformity and individuality. An individual client commissioned clothes that were personalized to her specifications but that were also produced for other customers with subtle variations. Garments were also reproduced for retail sale, but for only a short time and in relatively small quantities. In this context the exclusivity of the designer label, in addition to the design and construction of the garment, was an important point of distinction that was part of what elevated it above the fashionable apparel of other consumers in the marketplace.

From the inception of the formalized haute-couture industry in the 19th century, high-quality line-for-line reproductions of couture models were made in small numbers through licensed (legally contracted) foreign entities, especially in America. However, this carefully regulated part of the business had always "facilitated foreign copying on a far grander scale than couturiers intended," and as mass-production technologies improved, they increasingly enabled the quick, unauthorized replication of couture designs in large numbers. This became a pervasive phenomenon by the 1920s. Capitalizing on the fact that dress styles simplified in the second decade of the 20th century and the fact that laws protecting intellectual property were especially weak in the United States, manufacturers found a wide array of ways to copy designs without the permissions of designers (see Stewart 2005 for a thorough discussion, especially 106, 109). Although a great deal of variety existed among copies, which varied in quality and similarity to the original based on how the garment had been copied (i.e., by lifting a pattern from an authentic dress or relying on a surreptitiously rendered sketch), designers clearly felt the threat of mass production and sought ways to compete in that sector. In an effort to capitalize on the importance of authenticity and the power of the designer name, designers including Paul Poiret, Elsa Schiapparelli, and Jeanne Patou all dabbled in the ready-to-wear market in the first decades of the 20th century, but it was largely through unlicensed ready-made interpretations of designer concepts that the American middle class was able to follow the leader. Although the quality and origin of one's clothes still maintained some distinction between innovators and followers, the middle market progressively produced copies and interpretations that were increasingly fine and that gradually eroded this distinction. Additionally, after World War II, amidst a burgeoning consumer culture, the media facilitated the modification of middle-class consumers' attitudes toward fashion, until there was a sense that everyone had a "right to fashion." This attitude quickly gained a real foothold in the mass market (Lipovetsky 1994, 63). The spending power of the middle class was outpacing that of the upper classes, and, importantly, the needs, desires, and habits of this large and powerful consumer base were different from those of the elite fashion consumers that their pecuniary might replaced. The masses required quantity, easy access, and economy in their fashions, eschewing the rarefied requirements of distinction and originality. Thus the postwar years mark a culminating point in which a shift to a mass-market model and mentality was imminent.

Mid-Century Shifts in the Fashion Industry

By the late 1950s, there is ample evidence in the press to show that taxes and a diminishing elite clientele were causing major disruptions amongst couturiers and that "more and more they [were] looking to professional buyers . . . to keep their houses going" ("Yield from High Fashion" 1957, 69). Furthermore, these mass-market buyers were no longer obtaining exclusive rights to a design (meaning more than one manufacturer could produce a given look), thereby allowing the fashion of the moment to fully permeate the marketplace. There was a substantial supply of line-for-line copies in addition to the interpretations that less ethical manufacturers were making (many buyers used buying trips to gain access to the collections so as to copy the looks without permission). By the spring of 1958 couture houses were showing their collections to retailers like R. H. Macy and Sears, Roebuck & Company who replicated the looks in the thousands ("Bringing Paris Fashions" 1960, 75). By the 1970s many Parisian leaders of high style were faced with such financial challenges that they sold their companies, and thus the coterie of elite designers found themselves having to follow directives from managers who were not a part of the intimate circle and having to pay close attention to the financial bottom line. With increased attention to fiscal responsibility, designer collections began to demonstrate a move from seasonal design and inno-vation to long-term marketability. As a result, in the latter half of the 20th century the elite fashion innovators whose names had been the hallmarks of sartorial dis-tinction were active participants in the erosion of stylistic individuation. The cru-cial point here, with regard to the trajectory of street style in the United States, is that by the late 1950s the American marketplace was saturated with sameness, and this context is coeval with the emergence of a long line of highly individuated street and subcultural styles. Thus, it may be argued that the evolution of the com-mercial fashion marketplace, which included the widespread ability to closely mir-ror the most elite fashion trends, and which thereby eroded the long-lived principle of sartorial distinction, paved the way for new modes of sartorial expression that were consumer driven (and that in many cases ultimately informed and inspired the mass market).

Part 2: Social Change and Development in American Society

Shifts in cultural standards and worldview must also be considered as part of the trajectory that led Americans to use dress as a way to both self-differentiate and dissent from the mainstream. The propensity to self-differentiate points to homog-enizing influences in American culture that extend far beyond those discussed in reference to the apparel industry, while the desire to dissent visibly and publicly from mainstream standards points to waves of dissatisfaction that have rolled through a variety of demographics throughout the 20th century. This portion of the chapter aims to elucidate some of these cultural factors.

The Rise of Youth Culture in the United States

Street and subcultural styles are intimately linked with youth culture, which is generally viewed as rebellious, experimental, iconoclastic, and imbued with enough energy to "spark a social revolution" (Palladino 1996, 37). However, this was not always the case. Prior to the 1930s in the United States, there existed re-markably little in the way of a unique or influential youth culture. Grace Palladino, writing about teenage culture in the United States, noted that in the "decade or so" prior to World War II, "most teenage children had worked for a living. In fact, some had been required to pay back the debts they had incurred in childhood before they were able to leave the family home" (1996, xiii). With the majority of adolescents toiling through the day in agricultural or industrial labor, and only a minority at-tending and completing high school, prior to the 1930s there was little opportunity for young people to congregate, share ideas, develop their own unique cultural standards, and develop dress styles.

In the 1930s and 1940s the number of adolescent Americans attending high school increased dramatically, and coincident with that social shift came increased independence and opportunities, along with specific "teenage notions of propriety and style." Attending classes and teen-centric social events like football games, dances, and trips to the local soda counter all required "in fashion" wardrobes in order to run with the "in crowd," a factor that shaped the lives of teens living during the privations of the Great Depression and the shortages of World War II. Many teens undoubtedly experienced social turmoil and exclusion based on their inability to keep up sartorially (Palladino 1996, 8, 10, 40). Thus the emerging teen culture, which made dress a point of distinction as well as exclusion that impacted a young person's potential for social prosperity, was the perfect incubator for street styles that functioned outside of the normative, fashionable mode of dress. *Time* magazine contributor John Lacayo (Lacayo and Bellefonte 1994) once aptly summed up the situation, noting that for youths, "style is the best defense against anxiety and alienation is the natural state." As the A–Z entries in this text demonstrate, a great deal of American street style emerged out of youth culture and relied on do-it-yourself techniques, secondhand clothes, and body modifications, many of which can be attained or accomplished with little financial capital. Additionally, many of the street and subcultural styles developed in groups that formed in part out of a spirit of disenfranchisement and, therefore, reflect a solution to feelings of anxiety and alienation.

Another factor that contributed to the rise of street styles in youth culture relates to economics and the marketplace. Beginning in the war years of the 1940s in the United States, marketers were increasingly attuned to teenagers as a unique demographic with spending potential that could be primed for better financial times. Indeed, in the midst of World War II more and more young people were earning enough to enjoy readily expendable income. Writing about the "Beatlemania" of the postwar years, André Millard noted, "It was the Americans who created the idea of a 'teenager' and built the industries that provided goods and services to them," and this leisure class of affluent teens was unique to the United States at that time. Industries that catered to teens included the mass media, which produced magazines, movies, and television shows (as well as the advertisements that were connected to these outlets). The mass media catered to the "stifled" teenager with ideas for how to enact a "rock and roll" lifestyle (Millard 2012, 122, 123, 134) and gave youths across the nation an "express route" to subculture and its style (Lacayo and Bellefonte 1994).

If the American economy created the context within which the American teenager could exercise his or her tastes through spending, there were manifold aspects of American culture that created the context for American teens to develop and exercise a taste for rebellion. Historian of the 20th-century United States William

Tuttle Jr. points to two phenomena that shaped the teenage rebellion impulse in the 1950s. First was the "psychic havoc" (2001, 15) that was wrought on young minds during the war. Images of atomic bombs, the Holocaust, and Pearl Harbor that were printed in *Life* magazine and graphically portrayed on newsreels that screened before movies targeted at teen audiences undoubtedly left American youth with feelings of despair, dismay, and disillusionment at the world that civilized adults had created. Secondly, Tuttle notes that beginning in the late 1930s, psychologists and pediatricians had published research that the populace at large had absorbed. Among the seminal texts were Mary McAldrich's *Babies Are People Too* (1938) and Dr. Spock's *The Common Sense Book of Baby and Child Care* (1945). Tuttle argues that both of these texts inculcated a new sense of permissiveness among parents that encouraged a new sense of entitlement for exploration, freedom, and rebellion among American youth. Such impulses are easily expressed in response to the mainstream culture and are readily manifested in sartorial expressions. The "cultural goal of assimilation and homogenization [that] left little room for dissent" (Breines 1992, 1) also incubated rebellion in youth culture. This last factor, however, was not strictly a quandary among American *youth*; thus the context for rebellion and the embodiment of dissent must also be considered in light of American culture at large.

Homogeneity and Discontent in Postwar American Mass Culture

It was not only teen culture that was incubating dissatisfaction and seeking differentiation and a way to voice dissension in the postwar era. Nostalgic depictions of the 1950s often focus on the happy nuclear family, with each member well situated in his or her roll and gratified by the abundance of the postwar economy. However, historical and sociological studies have revealed that anxiety, tension, stultifying homogeneity, and pressure to conform were hallmarks of the era that impacted husbands and wives as well as children and teens.

Homogeneity in American culture was created in a variety of ways, a phenomenon that was aptly captured in a 1963 song recorded by Pete Seeger. In "Little Boxes" Seeger sings about uniform houses and uniform adults, children, and recreational activities, and he notes that they are "all made out of ticky tacky and they all look just the same." Homogeneity in housing was facilitated in postwar suburban housing developments created by companies like Levitt and Sons (known for erecting Levittown, Long Island). Housing developments of this kind were often created all at once by a single builder using assembly-line techniques that resulted in rows and rows of uniform structures. Populations of (typically white) middle-class Americans were enticed to move from the cities to these developments, resulting in communities of aesthetic, economic, and social "sameness" (Freeman 1999, 24). Along with suburban housing developments came the development of suburban shopping centers that were orderly, clean, comfortable, and *curated* by management. Stores had standardized designs, and malls were populated by a "preponderance of chains and franchises over local independent stores." Thus not only did every store in a single shopping center look the same, but merchandise was markedly similar from mall to mall across the expanse of sprawling suburbs. Notably, the products themselves often lacked revolutionary features. In the 1950s marketers, advertisers, and merchandisers conceived of "average" American consumers, and products were designed to meet the "middle of the middle"—resulting in bland, undifferentiated patterns of consumption (Cohen 2003, 263, 295).

Social conformity with regard to behavior was also a notion that was stressed in the decade following World War II. The perpetuators of American culture instructed men and women alike in the correct ways to act, think, and dress. William Whyte's 1956 book *The Organization Man* observed the postwar push for conformity among men: advertisements geared at men stressed correctness and conservatism in dress and behavior, and mass media in the form of television and movies instructed men regarding their roles as providers, dutiful husbands, and fathers. Writing about postwar women, historian Wini Breines observed that the 1950s was a period in which "façade," "pretense," and "dissimulation" were emphasized, and "a fixation on grooming, cleanliness [and] controlling the body thrived" (1992, 1, 149). Linda Eisenmann noted that postwar women faced conflicting and competing ideologies about the correct state of womanhood. Whether to conform to cultural standards of appropriate work or stay home and conform to prescribed maternal roles was a primary source of conflict that led to confusion and "unprecedented insecurities" that ultimately fueled deeply felt dissatisfaction (2002, 134, 137). Eva Moskowitz's survey of postwar women's magazines from 1945 to 1965 found women felt great pressure to live up to cultural standards of marriage and motherhood but ultimately felt dissatisfaction and discontent, envy of their husbands, regret, and resentment. She further observed that the magazines' writers "contributed to the discourse of discontent" (1996, 78)—an observation that reinforces the notion that the American mass media fueled conformist and suppressive ideologies. Perhaps the most notorious revelation of conformist ideologies being applied to American womanhood was Betty Friedan's seminal book *The Feminine Mystique* (1963), which was first published in serialized installments in *McCall's* magazine and which identified American cultural practices as a kind of mandate to deny women a true identity.

Nonconformist Tendencies in American Dress Practices: A Breakdown of Authority

It was inevitable that homogeneity and conformity would lead to widespread disaffection, and the ability of disaffection to lead to sartorial rebellion had already been demonstrated in the United States in the late 1930s. The zooties, who were largely disenfranchised racial and ethnic minorities (predominantly African American and Latino), predate by more than a decade the onslaught of the street and subcultural styles that cascaded through the postwar period. The zooties were the first American hipsters or "hep cats" whose street style was the embodiment of supreme hipness. Notably, being hip may be construed as a rejection of the mainstream, as a defense mechanism, and as the product of "special insights of life under pressure" (Lacayo and Bellefonte 1994). Disaffection, alienation, and the urge to rebel were part and parcel of the lived experiences of minority groups in the pre–Civil Rights era but did not reach critical mass within mainstream, white American culture until the changes in the mass-fashion marketplace, the rise of teen culture, and the sociocultural factors of the postwar period collided. Notably, the rockabilly street style of the 1950s borrowed heavily from the attire of the zooties, repurposing it as a form of white sartorial rebellion, which first emerged in the segregated South.

Developing an exhaustive context for the emergence of sartorial rebellion in American culture may well be a topic better explored in a text of its own, one that analyzes all we know about American culture in the early 20th century. The arguments presented here are designed to give the reader adequate context for understanding the emergence of street style in general, while each of the A–Z entries provides specific information about the historical context in which individual styles emerged.

Concluding Thoughts

The *fashionably* dressed body—one that follows the contemporary mode—is at its most fundamental level a body that conforms to cultural standards at large (Entwistle 2000, ch.1) and to the ephemeral standards of good taste and contemporaneity that cultural tastemakers form and promulgate. Thus street and subcultural styles, which purposefully flout, rework, and undermine fashionable standards, are at their root embodiments of nonconformist impulses, which exist on a spectrum from revolutionary and countercultural to whimsical and countertrend. Such subversive tendencies that arose in dress practices around the middle of the 20th century can be connected to three strands of sociocultural change: changes in the fashion industry, the rise of youth culture, and the sociocultural context of conformity in the postwar period.

The advent of street and subcultural styles in the United States is indicative of a confluence of larger sociocultural trends. The democratization of fashion through mass production has typically been interpreted as a generally positive phenomenon that broke down many of the visible boundaries of taste and class. However, the evolution of the fashion industry also created a context in which it became increasingly difficult to express and differentiate oneself. Within the sea of sameness that had been created through rapid mass production of both legal line-for-line copies and illegally produced replicas, self-expression and differentiation through contemporary apparel had been curtailed as they pertain to mainstream fashion. However, the A-Z entries demonstrate that the fashion marketplace also provided many of the building blocks for creating subversive dress practices that were crafted by youth cultures within a context of widespread social disaffection. Out of this context emerged consumer-driven styles that asserted sociocultural and aesthetic difference through sartorial choices that broke with the widespread norms. Out of this context emerged the first American street styles.

Further Reading

Aspelund, K. 2009. *Fashioning Society: A Hundred Years of Haute Couture by Six Designers.* New York: Fairchild Books.

Breines, W. 1992. *Young, White, and Miserable: Growing Up Female in the Fifties.* Chicago: University of Chicago Press.

"Bringing Paris Fashions Down to the Mass Market." 1960. *Business Week,* August 20, 72–77.

Cohen, L. 2003. *A Consumer's Republic: The Politics of Consumption in Postwar America.* New York: Alfred A. Knopf.

De La Haye, A., and V. Mendes 2014. *The House of Worth: Portrait of an Archive.* London: V&A Publishing.

Eisenman, L. 2002. "Educating the Female Citizen in a Post-war World: Competing Ideologies for American Women, 1945–1965." *Educational Review* 54 (2): 133–41.

Entwistle, J. 2000. *The Fashioned Body: Fashion, Dress and Modern Social Theory.* Cambridge, UK: Polity Press.

Freeman, T. 1999. "Post-war America Hitches Up and Heads for the Burbs." *NREI,* 20–26.

Gaddis, J. L. 2005. *The Cold War: A New History.* New York: Penguin Books.

Kuznick, P. J., and J. Gilbert 2001. "U.S. Culture and the Cold War." In *Rethinking Cold War Culture,* edited by P. J. Kuznick and J. Gibert, 1–13. Washington, D.C.: Smithsonian University Press.

Lacayo, R., and G. Bellefonte 1994. "If Everyone Is Hip . . . Is Anyone Hip?" *Time* 144 (5): 48.

Lipovetsky, G. 1994. *The Empire of Fashion.* Translated by C. Porter. Princeton: Princeton University Press.

Meyerowitz, J. 1994. "Beyond the Feminine Mystique: A Reassessment of Postwar Mass Culture." In *Not June Cleaver: Women and Gender in Postwar America 1945–1960,* edited by J. Meyerowitz, 229–62. Philadelphia: Temple University Press.

Meyerowitz, J. 1994. "Introduction: Women and Gender in Postwar America 1945–1960." In *Not June Cleaver: Women and Gender in Postwar America 1945–1960,* edited by J. Meyerowitz, 1–16. Philadelphia: Temple University Press.

Millard, A. 2012. *Beatlemania: Technology, Business, and Teen Culture in Cold War America.* Baltimore: Johns Hopkins University Press.

Moskowitz, E. 1996. "It's Good to Blow Your Top: Women's Magazines and a Discourse of Discontent." *Journal of Women's History* 8 (3): 66–98.

Norris, H. 1927. *Medieval Costume and Fashion.* Mineola, NY: Dover Publications.

Palladino, G. 1996. *Teenagers: An American History.* New York: Harper Collins.

Roche, D. 1994. *The Culture of Clothing: Dress and Fashion in the Ancien Regime.* Translated by Jean Birrell. Cambridge, UK: Cambridge University Press.

Stewart, M. L. 2005. "Copying and Copyrighting Haute Couture: Democratizing Fashion, 1900–1930." *French Historical Studies* 28 (1): 103–30.

Styles, J. *The Dress of Everyday People: Fashion in the Eighteenth Century.* New Haven: Yale University Press.

Tortura, P. G., and K. Eubank 2015. *Survey of Historic Costume.* New York: Fairchild Books.

Tuttle, W. M. 2001. "An Era of War, Hot and Cold." In *Rethinking Cold War Culture,* edited by P. J. Kuznick and J. Gibert, 14–34. Washington, D.C.: Smithsonian University Press.

"Yield from High Fashion Is Low." 1957. *Business Week,* February 16, 69–71.

Chapter 3

The Flourishing of American Street Style: The Clothing Industry, Mass Media, and Its Consumers, 1930 to the Age of the Internet

Chapter 2 laid a foundation for understanding when and why street and sub-cultural styles began to develop in the United States. By tracking changes in the fashion industry as well as fundamental changes in American youth culture, a context was created for understanding the new fertile landscape in which dress that marks dissension and difference could develop. This chapter constructs a context for *how* the many postwar street styles developed. The first part of the chapter discusses key concepts pertaining to apparel manufacture and distribution from the postwar period onward. Additionally, this section reviews in detail media outlets that aided the communication of subversive styles. This chapter then considers the consumer of subcultural and street styles from the postwar period to the end of the 20th century and theorizes the motivations for dressing in opposition to the mainstream.

The American Apparel Industry: Manufacture and Distribution in the Postwar Period

Street and subcultural styles emerge beyond the boundaries of the traditional fashion system, but that does not mean that they were ever wholly independent of the system that commercially produces textiles and apparel. Review of the topical entries included in this text shows that the majority of these styles were initially created through the use of basic, often inexpensive ready-to-wear that already existed in the marketplace. However, those apparel basics were styled on individual bodies in a manner that created a striking and sometimes subversive sartorial effect. Thus understanding how the American marketplace came to have such a wealth of options is important. Additionally, with regard to the production of apparel and accessories, do-it-yourself techniques including the modification of existing apparel and home sewing were also a part of the history of the vast majority of street and subcultural styles. Thus exploring the resources that were available to do-it-yourselfers also reveals how American street styles flourished. Notably, almost all of the stylistic categories that are documented within this text ultimately evolved so that apparel with the specific characteristics of a street or subcultural style could be purchased with the unique characteristics in place (the sale of preripped jeans is a case in point). In some instances, boutique or mail-order collections were curated so that a certain look could easily be purchased via one-stop shopping. Therefore, this chapter engages the available evidence from designers who worked to produce products for youth and street cultures and explores the types of retail outlets that sold street-style–influenced apparel as a way to understand how these styles were perpetuated. The mass and long-lived appeal of many of these styles and the homogeneity that often is in evidence late in their evolution indicate increased reliance on a mass-production infrastructure and professional retailing. How these facets of the apparel industry evolved to enable quick and cheap production to facilitate street and subcultural style is key to understanding their development and proliferation.

American Manufacturing

The ability to produce ready-made clothes had been developing in the United States since the latter part of the 19th century. Apparel basics including work clothes and undergarments were among the first kinds of clothes that were mass-produced, and by the final decade of the 19th century, fashionable garments including women's shirtwaists and skirts and men's shirts and pants could be purchased ready-made. Documents like the Sears catalog provide evidence of the wealth of fashionable, practical, and widely affordable ready-made apparel for men, women, and children that was available in the marketplace from the last decades of the 19th century. However, the profound impact that World War II had on the American economy and manufacturing infrastructure cannot be understated.

American manufacturing had switched into high gear years before the United States entered the war in response to the bombing of Pearl Harbor in Hawaii on December 7, 1941. That act of Japanese military aggression precipitated the mobilization of American military personnel and the formal entry into the war that necessitated outfitting millions of American men; however, American factories had already been supplying all kinds of American-made necessities to foreign allies. World War II created massive demand for American manufacturing of all kinds of goods including armaments, vehicles, apparel, and packaged comestibles. Distinguished professor and policy analyst Vaclav Smil has succinctly noted of American manufacturing, "In the 1940s the United States was the world's leading industrial power and the largest producer of goods in virtually every manufacturing sector" (2011, 67). Notably, great advancements in the streamlining of mass-production techniques for apparel were an important part of this manufacturing boom and helped pave the way for the production of increasingly inexpensive apparel and accessories designed to suit mass-market consumers in the postwar period.

Journalist Bernard Roshco, writing in the early 1960s, documented both the volume and the speed of production that typified the New York apparel industry in the decades following the end of the war. He noted in his text *The Rag Race* that much of Seventh Avenue was, in the 1950s and 1960s, still concerned with copying high-style clothes, especially European models, and that a copy could reach the mass market in as little as a month, in part because of assembly-line-style modes of production. With his attention focused exclusively on fashions generated by the fashion *industry,* he went on to note that fashion diffusion had become so rapid that it often had the adverse effect of "blurring the social distinctions that are one of the most important stimulants for the acceptance and diffusion of a new fashion." Roshco also noted the amazing homogeneity in the marketplace, citing the fact that juniors' clothes took details from popular adult fashions and that, in fact, a few basic styles, largely denuded of the "complicated cutting and construction" found in the high-style original, flooded the marketplace (1963, 6, 46, 47). Thus Roshco's observations about the speed of production bolster some of the assertions about sameness in the marketplace that were discussed in chapter 2 as a relevant catalyst for the emergence of street and subcultural styles in the United States. However, mass-production techniques were also being employed to address new and creative styles that were emerging from the streets.

Exploring the evolution of specific popular dress practices reveals that mass-production techniques could be harnessed, modified, or innovated in order to meet new stylistic demands. For example, having developed an interest in non-Western techniques and handicrafts in general, the hippie subculture developed the taste for tie-dyed fabric (a technique that traditionally requires binding cloth with strings or rubber bands by hand before submerging the bundled cloth in one or more dye baths). The widespread cultural and sartorial influences of the hippies are discussed in the entry dedicated to their style, which was widely interpreted through a variety of products in the marketplace. Notably, a new, specialized technique for mimicking tie-dye was developed to facilitate mass production, thus helping to spread this particular subcultural aesthetic. Similarly, the style embodied by hippies in the late 1960s and early 1970s included a tendency to personalize denim with handwrought patchwork and embroidery. This aesthetic was also created through mass-production techniques that brought the street style to the population at large. Mass-production capacities coupled with low-wage/low-cost production in places like North Africa and Central Asia also facilitated the diffusion of street and subcultural style in the postwar period. Once again, the specific dress practices of the hippies provide rich examples of how the marketplace at midcentury was able to diffuse style. Specifically, there is evidence that long, flowing robes called caftans and strings of beads, customarily given as gifts and referred to as "love beads," could be acquired through trade with Asia and Africa and thereby made available to American consumers at low cost (Moore 2015, 13, 180–81, 182, 273–74). These examples from the 1960s demonstrate that the landscape of manufacturing and trade had developed by midcentury to facilitate the mass diffusion of street styles.

American manufacturing also contributed to the widespread availability of consumer goods to facilitate home sewing and other kinds of do-it-yourself techniques. Hand and machine sewing, knitting, embroidery, patchwork, and crochet had for centuries been an important part of the creation of both fashionable and functional clothes and an important part of consumer culture; and in the latter half of the 20th century this kind of handiwork contributed to the development of street and subcultural styles. For example, there is ample evidence that people used the products of the paper-pattern industry to make unique apparel styles that skirted the boundaries of contemporary fashion. Both Vivienne Westwood and Mary Quant, who helped dress punks and mods (a primarily British street style), respectively, both began designing clothes for the youth cultures with which they were involved by purchasing commercial patterns from companies like Butterick, McCall's, Simplicity, and Vogue and modifying them to suit their visions and tastes. In fact, advertisements from the 1960s and 1970s in particular show paper-pattern companies specifically representing versions of hippie street style on the sleeves of patterns that were sold in North America. In addition to utilizing commercial patterns, do-it-yourself guides also provided simple instructions for creating street style looks. Texts like *Clothing Liberation: Out of the Closets and into the Streets* (1973) and *Superjeans: Easy Ways to Recycle and Decorate Your Jeans* (1974) provided readers with simple line drawings and descriptions of styles seen in the streets and included written directions for creating bell-bottom jeans by adding panels of fabric and for converting overalls into dresses with a bohemian flair.

Companies like Coats & Clark and Dritz, sellers of sewing notions like threads, buttons, trims, and iron-on patches and letters, also emerged as important contributors to the personalization of apparel and the creation of dress that were part of contemporary street and subcultural styles. In some cases, notions companies retailed items that were simply adopted by individuals who dressed in a specific style (i.e., a punk's purchasing of studs and grommets or a b-boy's purchasing of iron-on letters that were readily available in the marketplace), while in other cases, notions makers began to produce trims or patches with a specific aesthetic that was in line with contemporary street-style trends. There is also evidence that suggests that both paper-pattern companies and notions companies ran advertisements for their products that aligned them with countercultural movements. For example, a Simplicity advertisement from 1969 suggested that one could obtain a "nonconformist" look by using the company's patterns, and a Coats & Clark advertisement from 1973 evoked hippie ideals of self-expression and individuality (see Heinmann 2006 and 2007, unpaginated).

The historical record also reveals that some individuals who went on to become professional and successful commercial fashion designers began their careers by catering to a subcultural milieu. As noted, British designer Mary Quant, who did not pursue a formal education in design, began by modifying Butterick patterns and sewing garments for the swinging London mod scene. Quant, who co-owned a boutique called Bazaar, encapsulated the success of her youthful street-style designs when she noted, "The shop was constantly stripped bare. . . . There was a real need for fashion accessories for young people chosen by people of their own age. The young were tired of wearing essentially the same as their mothers" (1966, 41). Tommy Hilfiger, living in upstate New York in the 1960s, was similarly inspired by youth culture and similarly understood that young people craved a way to buy into the look and feel of 1960s counterculture. His shop in Elmira, New York, sold items like bell-bottom jeans and decorated denim. Vivienne Westwood, who like Quant was working in England, was connected to the rock and roll and *avant-garde* scenes through her art-school-trained, band-promoter boyfriend, Malcolm McLaren. They opened a series of stores, including Seditionaries, Sex, and World's End, that catered to rockabillies and punks and sold apparel that evoked the spirit of those musical and subcultural scenes. Like Quant's early work, much of Westwood's early production was made by modifying paper patterns. Additionally, Westwood, who was not trained as a fashion designer, also used the technique of making a pattern from an existing garment (Westwood and Kelly 2014, 144). Notably, Westwood and McLaren also routinely utilized the mass-production technique of silk screening to create T-shirts with provocative graphic prints, thereby facilitating the quick and inexpensive transmission of elements of the developing punk look to an expanding, international audience.

The boutiques that were run by individuals like Quant, Westwood, and Hilfiger were important to street style and subcultural milieus both for the items that were sold and for the space they provided to young men and women to see and be seen and share information and interactions. The autobiographies of Westwood, Hilfiger, and Quant position their shops as hubs for their respective social scenes: places to drink, smoke, dance, and listen to music. Retailers of all kinds—many of which sold an eclectic mix of apparel, accessories, albums and cassettes, and paraphernalia as diverse as tambourines, handcuffs, and hash pipes—developed to cater to subcultural groups. For example, in the 1960s the hippie subculture was retailed at places like Psychedelicatessen, Electric Lotus, and Tribal Connection in New York City, Psychedelic Shop and Wild Colors in San Francisco, and People's Place in Hilfiger's hometown of Elmira, New York. Over time, some boutiques evolved into national chain stores that were important meet-up spots in shopping malls across the United States. Merry-Go-Round, founded in 1968, was "one of the first hippie-style shops to build a cross-country chain" and was doing $75 million per annum by 1975 (Sullivan 2006, 156). Merry-Go-Round ultimately evolved in the latter decades of the 20th century to provide parachute pants for aspiring b-boys, studded garments for second-generation punks and new wavers, and apparel that mimicked the looks of celebrities like Michael Jackson and Madonna.

Mail-order catalogs and listings in the back of various kinds of magazines and newspapers have also functioned as an important way to disseminate street and subcultural styles, especially prior to the widespread adoption of Internet communication and retailing. Specialty items ranging from T-shirts branded with the names of surfboard or skateboard manufacturers, to tiny string-bikini posing suits marketed to bodybuilders, to leopard- and zebra-print spandex pants listed in the back of heavy-metal magazines have been offered via mail order. In many cases, full-color advertisements of a vast array of products included small order forms that could be snipped out and sent away. Also common were tiny, postage-stamp-sized black-and-white advertisements that either listed a small array of products with sizes, prices, and an address to which one could send money, or requested a single dollar be sent in order to obtain a catalog of items. For example, an advertisement that ran in *Creem* magazine (a popular music fan magazine) in 1983 promised all aspects of new-wave dress could be obtained from Diana's, located on lower Broadway in New York City. Notably, mail-order catalogs—like the *Good Earth* catalog, which conveyed information of interest to the hippie subculture—were vehicles for spreading products through commerce but also functioned as an arm of the alternative press, as retail products have the ability to convey a vision of an alternate lifestyle.

In the postwar period, the United States became the "first true mass consumption society" (Smil 2011, 69). Consumer products of all kinds filled stores, American income was rapidly rising, and advertisers were spending in an effort to create desire and demand. The surfeit of consumer products including apparel may be linked to the development of street and subcultural styles in two ways. First, the emphasis on constant consumption, keeping up appearances, and conforming to an ideal vision of prosperity undoubtedly alienated some Americans who, in turn, sought out alternative modes of expression and alternative communities of consumers (or anticonsumers). Second, and perhaps more importantly, the profound quantities of merchandise available in the marketplace provided the building blocks with which to subvert the fashionable standard.

Streamlined mass production, easy access to do-it-yourself materials—which were sometimes advertised in direct relationship to groups like the hippies—and specialty boutiques, and mail order made street and subcultural styles readily available and were all important conduits for the flourishing of the style groups detailed in this book. A point of explanation should be made with regard to the spread of style through commercial products. While some individuals who identified with a subcultural group or established street style may have chosen to develop their looks through the use of commercially available goods, it is also important to note that the availability of commercial products undoubtedly functioned as a sort of recruitment tool. Consumer scientists have pointed out that "people identify with certain objects or consumption activities and through those objects or activities, identify with other people" (Schouten and McAlexander, 48). Thus, gravitation toward and purchase of goods help to develop a social network. Furthermore, "It is possible for a marketer who understands the structure and ethos of a subculture of consumption to cultivate a lasting, symbiotic relationship with it" (Schouten and McAlexander, 57). Essentially, makers of commercial goods that are targeted toward a specific group may form a bond with that group (e.g., Doc Marten boots and punks, or Harley Davidson apparel and motorcycle enthusiasts). Such a relationship can involve facilitating communication, providing activities, and creating *new* symbols that thereby change the appearance of a given street style. Thus, examining the role of producers and retailers is another way to explore style development, diffusion, and change over time.

The Mainstream Fashion Press and Beyond: Communication of Street and Subcultural Styles

The dissemination of subcultural and countercultural content is an important part of the history of these kinds of street styles in the United States. The printing press had, of course, been around for hundreds of years by the time the first American street style emerged in the 20th century, improving since the invention of moveable type in the 15th century. However, professional, traditional printing presses have always presented hurdles to individuals interested in disseminating information that goes against the grain of mainstream society. First, professional printers fetch professional fees, and cash-richness is not common in subcultural milieus. Second, professional printers both employ their own standards of propriety and are subject to legal guidelines that may amount to censorship. Certainly the historical record demonstrates that subversive printers have existed over the centuries, but it is still fair to say that the reliance on a professional to disseminate subcultural information presents a hurdle to individuals wishing to share a subcultural message.

From the late 19th century onward a variety of techniques for reproducing text developed. Among them were the hectograph (1869) and spirit duplicator (1923), which was more commonly known in the United States as the Ditto machine, named for the company that made it. Both of these devices used alcohol solvents, which were slow and messy and could produce only a limited number of duplicates. The mimeograph machine (1886) was used well into the 20th century but also presented production problems. Mimeograph reproduction was fairly slow and required the creation of a stencil that was used to make the copies. All of these kinds of duplicating machines were used to make early fanzines and counter-cultural publications as they could readily be set up in a private residence and did not require professional oversight. Still, their limitations meant that the production of copies remained fairly limited. Photostatic copying that uses light, static, and dry toner powder was invented in 1907, and it was used in offices around mid-century, but it truly came to impact everyday consumers beginning in the late 1960s when Xerox machines began to proliferate. The technology became increasingly inexpensive and exponentially faster as the decade progressed. The ability to quickly and cheaply photocopy material facilitated the development of a whole universe of "alternative" publications.

Fanzines, consumer-created serial publications devoted to a specific topic, were first seen in notable numbers in the 1940s in the United States. In this period fanzines were largely dedicated to the topic of science fiction fandom and the publication of short stories, and they provided a way for individuals who were interested in the genre to share literature, communicate information about conventions, and also provide information about commercial products of interest to other science-fiction fans. In the late 1960s fanzines, which were largely produced on photostatic copiers, were an important part of the hippie scene and were an iconic element of the 1970s punk scene as these homespun publications not only shared information but evolved a new graphic style (see Berniere and Primois 2012 for extensive examples). Underground newspapers, which relied on varied modes of print reproduction ranging from archaic devices that produced primitive and smudged copies to neatly rendered multicolored productions, were also an important tool for conveying subcultural information. Notable serials included publications like *Lesbian Connection* (1974–1980), the *Berkeley Barb* (1965–1980), alternative weeklies like the *Village Voice* (1955–), the *East Village Other* (1965–1972), the *Chicago Reader* (1971–), and the *San Francisco Bay Guardian* (1966–). Commercial publications that targeted topics of interest to young people (especially popular music) were also increasingly widespread from midcentury onward and were also an important conduit for conveying information about evolving music scenes, the musicians who shaped them, and the ways in which those musicians presented themselves. Among the publications in this genre were *Creem* (1969–1989), *Tiger Beat* (1965–), and *Bop* (1983–2014). Localized music-scene publications like *Screamer* (1987–), which documents the Los Angeles heavy metal scene, also represent an important way in which specific cultural content can be conveyed.

Notably, from the 1960s onward mainstream publications began to give increased focus to the dress of everyday life. For example, beginning in the 1960s

Women's Wear Daily began to print images of fashionable women on the street and at social events. Additionally, American *Vogue,* under the leadership of Grace Mirabella, strove to convey "a sense of ease, a sense of motion, a sense of life" (Mirabella 1995, 145) and included both fashion editorials that recreated the street as well as images of noteworthy women in their own clothes. While publications like *Women's Wear Daily* and *Vogue* were largely dedicated to showing *fashion,* their focus on the street and the sartorial realities of real people at least inadvertently reflected issues of contemporary dress culture. Additionally, at midcentury mainstream publications like *Time, Life, Newsweek, Look,* and *The New Yorker* routinely contemplated fashion as a "social factor" and reported on it. The extensive documentation of youth culture, including the dress practices of groups like "sidewalk surfers" (skateboarders), bobby soxers, and flower children, is reflected in the bibliography of this text, which relied extensively on such detailed contemporary accounts.

The evidence connecting the publication of printed images and the diffusion of an idea through commerce is vast and multifaceted. Former *Vogue* editor Jessica Daves provided extensive documentation of the link between the publication of fashion images and sales in her 1967 text *Ready-Made Miracle* (161). Additionally, the dissemination of images and text is the foundational concept of traditional advertising and catalog retailing. Thus it is simple to extrapolate that the publication of all kinds of street and subcultural images, in a wide variety of publications, would similarly spawn interpretations both through do-it-yourself techniques and via traditional retail outlets.

By the middle of the 20th century, printed imagery was but one conduit through which information could be conveyed to the population. There had been a rapid expansion of television-set ownership through the 1950s, and by the 1960s 90 percent of American households had a television set (Smil 2011, 94). The broadcasting of subcultural and countercultural imagery was fairly limited in the 1950s, 1960s, and 1970s (largely restricted to images in the news and narrative fiction that included stereotypical characters representing countercultural types). Public-access television, which was pioneered in the late 1960s (Linder 1999, 6), was one portal for the exchange of information from outside mainstream culture. Public-access television facilitated the broadcast of largely uncensored material including poetry readings, political commentary, and musical performances. The development of cable television in the 1980s opened up new portals for the communication of ideas from beyond the mainstream. The cable television channel that has had perhaps the most profound impact on youth culture is MTV. The music television channel, which launched in August 1981, was originally dedicated to showing music videos and sharing music news. Thus the channel functioned as a 24-hour-a-day conduit for the communication of popular culture. It has been suggested that, especially early in the history of the station, the demands of filling broadcasting hours outstripped the supply of music videos from major labels and well-known acts, and as a result the channel showed an unusually large number of British new-wave bands (Majewski and Bernstein 2014, 12). Later the station evolved to dedicate blocks of time to musical styles that were not mainstream pop, including rap and heavy metal. The increasing importance of the visual representation of musical acts undoubtedly spread across genres but is especially evident with regard to the evolution of the heavy metal scene and its sartorial style.

Just as the mass production and retailing of street and subcultural styles have changed their visual aesthetics, so too have the mass media impacted the dissemination of these styles. The mass media facilitate a style's mass adoption outside of the social milieu in which it developed, and thus as styles diffuse, their meanings change in tandem with stylistic shifts and in tandem with the myriad mindsets of new adopters who understand the aesthetics in varied ways. These many forms of mass communication have facilitated both the assimilation and the mixing of the many street and subcultural style genres. This in turn has created new understandings and meanings for American street and subcultural styles while also stripping most street styles of a greater, universalizing narrative about American culture and identity formation. This latter point is one that Ted Polhemus takes to a nihilistic extreme in his 1996 text (51–56) and that is raised in each of the entries on individual street and subcultural style. These styles were originally created to communicate some specific thing, but over time, as styles diffused throughout American culture and beyond, meaning became both diffuse and varied, and thus to dress in a certain way does not necessarily mean to *be* a certain type of person.

Dissension, Distinction, and Tribe Formation: Exploring the Communicative and Social Allures of Antifashion

Developing a picture of the conditions of the American fashion marketplace and media landscape provides two concrete paths to understanding how American street and subcultural styles flourished in the latter half of the 20th century. However, the critical components of American *culture* that created a context in which the desires to dissent from the mainstream, distinguish oneself from others, and form tribes of like-minded individuals are more amorphous, but they are critical to knowing how (and why) street and subcultural styles proliferated. Thus the following paragraphs present a number of angles from which the social context may be considered, and while this portion of the text strives to offer a variety of applications and interpretations of the historical record, it may be open to the criticism of omission, as most certainly the development of an American society in which dissension, distinction, and tribe formation became commonplace is the result of complex intersections in the culture of the middle 20th century.

Cultural shifts were afoot in the postwar period. In the 1940s urban populations increased by 22 million people, almost four times the increase of the previous decade (Smil 2011, 75). Importantly, the concentration of individuals in an urban space has, since the beginning of the fashion cycle in the medieval period, been an integral part of fashion development and change, as the actual concentration of individuals provides a context in which communication and competition naturally flourish, and the dressed body is a convenient site for that exchange. One major difference between the urban context of medieval times and that of the middle of the 20th century has to do with the composition of the urban populations. Notably, a large part of the new urban demographic was African American, as waves of migration out of the South, to the North and West, had taken place in the 1940s, having peaked in 1945 with an estimated 700,000 individuals relocating (Smil 2011, 75). Throughout much of the United States, African American culture began to permeate the mainstream, creating points of conflict, contrast, excitement, and intrigue. Early subcultural and youth groups, which were predominantly white, including the Beats, rockabillies, and hippies, both engaged in and responded to African American culture and channeled the tastes, lifestyle, and the ethos of these marginalized *others*. Notably, the perception, both real and imagined, that a dominant culture was politically, socially, or economically repressing others is a theme that runs through the origin stories of many of the groups discussed in this text; included among them are both skinheads and punks. This tension became more visible given urbanization and the increasingly heterogeneous mix of people in American cities.

Heterogeneity also resulted in the loss of a singular narrative or universalizing point of view in American culture. Cultural shifts facilitate the disruption of norms, and distinguishing oneself from the norm for pleasure and for power is a theme of American culture in the 1950s. In the second chapter of this book, groundwork was laid for understanding the mainstream impulse to attain homogeneity in the wake of World War II, but there is also evidence that conformist inclinations were challenged on a variety of levels. The perception of a repressive dominant social structure may have been part of the catalyst, but a search for personal fulfillment may have also influenced postwar individuals. In the 1950s popular interpretations of texts like Abraham Maslow's "A Theory of Human Motivation" (1943), which presented the tenets of self-actualization, encouraged individuals to seek personal fulfillment, pleasure, and knowledge. Although the 1950s are often cited as a period of extraordinary conformity in fashion, there is evidence that self-actualizing motivations explicitly influenced the way people dressed. For example, fashion designer Elizabeth Hawes published an entire book in 1954 that drew upon self-actualization theory and encouraged readers to express themselves in order to attain more satisfying lives. In *It's Still Spinach* Hawes advised her readers to take control of their personal appearance and to "start looking at fashion through your own eyes rather than at second hand through the eyes of some fashion reporter, style commentator, or adviser" (10). Hawes further noted that taking control of one's dress could have broader implications for happiness and fulfillment. She wrote, "Anyone who wants life to be more amusing, free, interesting, peaceful, and exciting can start right now to dress as most pleases him or her—at least part of the time" (233). The latter part of this thought seems to imply that dressing to please one's self might not always jive with widespread notions of social acceptability and might have a positive impact only in specific contexts.

A psychological study published in 1958 partially buttressed Hawes's perception that full unbridled self-expression through dress could function as a positive force in one's life. Edwin Hollander presented research that explored conformity, status, and the social "credit" that is sometimes received for "idiosyncratic" behavior. Hollander concluded that individuals in a given reference group could actually improve their social standing by exhibiting nonconformist behaviors in certain contexts. While one study cannot provide universalizing conclusions about the perception of nonconformity at large in the United States in the postwar period, the study does hint at a trajectory in American culture. Notably, numerous studies conducted in the 21st century indicate that nonconformity can have social costs but can also be used as a provocative tool for challenging hierarchy and marking affiliation (see Bellezza, Gino, and Keinan 2014 for their research and a comprehensive literature review of psychological and consumer science studies). Thus the desire to dissent and to flout conformity may speak to changes in the psychology of some Americans in the postwar period.

A further indication of shifts in American psychology relates to the celebration of youth culture and its emulation by American adults. The shift in some aspects of cultural authority and in the touchstones of beauty and good taste from the wise and worldly parental figure to the precocious neophyte marks a shift that seems to go beyond mere admiration for the beauty associated with youth. Evidence of adult emulation of youth style dates to the early 20th century when collegiate men and women began to "dress casual" by subverting dress conventions and showing insubordination with regard to widely accepted conventions of propriety (Clemente 2014, 23). The emphasis on freedom and comfort (which included young college women's wearing of pants and men's work shirts) and the collective destruction of long-lived sartorial codes gradually transferred beyond the gated communities that constituted many early-20th-century campuses. Historian Deirdre Clemente noted, "Initially, gym clothes as street clothes rattled the sensibilities of the unconvinced," but "by the 1960s, nearly everyone under the age of sixty owned a sweatshirt" (4). In fact, according to Clemente, by the 1960s, 90 percent of shoppers for casual "college clothes" were not college students, or even college aged (40). In his 1932 text *The Psychology of Clothes* psychologist J. C. Flugel noted this interest, which was cultivated among mature adults, in the expressive practices of youth culture, observing that mature people wanted to share in "the appearance and activities of youth" (115). There is evidence that producers of apparel recognized the importance of youth styles at a variety of levels. Notably, since at least the 1930s, garment manufacturers had sought the assistance of college-aged students and used their ideas about dress to create designs for production (Clemente 2014, 29–30). In 1965 the "cult of youth" was such that at least three couturiers created collections inspired by youth apparel: French couturier Andre Courreges offered the "Little Girl Look"; his compatriot in couture Yves Saint Laurent designed the "Baby Girl Look"; and American designer and iconoclast Rudi Gernreich offered the "Kiddo Look" (Meehan 1965, 26–30). Writing in 1967, Iowa State professor Karlyn Anspach noted the tendency among adults to "alter their image in an attempt to prove they are not old" (278) and observed that the fashion industry was widely interpreting the style of "long haired rock and roll singers" and "mods" (281). The widespread interest in youth culture and youth aesthetics and an emphasis on comfort and rule breaking may be considered as the culmination of a collection of factors that shows the breakdown of social control through dress and that contributed to the flourishing of American street and subcultural styles.

Finally, the breakdown of social control evidenced by changing dress practices is just one symptom of the widespread change and fragmentation that was taking place in American society as the population grew larger and more diverse. With the fragmentation of the population and of a cohesive American narrative came a need to form meaningful groups, many of which embodied a unique sartorial style. Writing in 1978, anthropologist Ted Polhemus noted of late-20th-century culture that individuals had "unprecedented freedom" as well as a general lack of "sociocultural identity," and he concluded from these observations that people were increasingly using style to create social groups (2011, 62), even though visual identification with a social group through dress practices (even permanent ones such as piercing and tattooing) might not indicate full or deeply felt commitment to the way of life associated with that look (Polhemus 1996, 50). Regardless, street and subcultural styles can often provide a way to socialize, incubate ideas, and react to the dominant culture from a unique point of view, and thus the flourishing of American street and subcultural styles is indicative of the independent spirit of American culture at large.

Further Reading

Anspach, K. 1967. *The Why of Fashion.* Ames: The Iowa State University Press.

Bellezza, S. M., F. Gino, and A. Keinan. 2014. "The Red Sneaker Effect: Inferring Status and Competence from Signals of Nonconformity." *Journal of Consumer Research* 41 (2): 35–54.

Bernierè, V., and M. Primois. 2012. *Punk Press: Rebel Rock in the Underground Press, 1968–1980.* New York: Abrams.

Clemente, D. 2014. *Dress Casual: How College Students Redefined American Style.* Chapel Hill: University of North Carolina Press.

Daves, J. 1967. *Ready-Made Miracle: The Story of American Fashion for the Millions.* New York: G. P. Putnam's Sons.

Flugel, J. C. 1932. *The Psychology of Clothes.* London: Hogarth.

Hawes, F. 1954. *It's Still Spinach: How American Men and Women Can Have More Satisfying Lives by Dressing to Suit Their Individual Personalities.* Boston: Little Brown and Company.

Heinmann, J. 2006. *70s Fashion: Vintage Fashion and Beauty Ads.* Los Angeles: Taschen.

Heinmann, J. 2007. *60s Fashion: Vintage Fashion and Beauty Ads.* Los Angeles: Taschen.

Hilfiger, T., and P. Knobler. 2017. *American Dreamer: My Life in Fashion & Business.* New York: Ballantine Books.

Hollander, E. P. 1958. "Conformity, Status, and Idiosyncratic Credit." *Psychological Review* 65 (2): 117–27.

Lawson, D. 1974. *Superjeans: Easy Ways to Recycle and Decorate Your Jeans.* New York: Scholastic Book Services.

Levi's Denim Art Contest: Catalogue of Winners. 1974. Mill Valley, CA: Squarebooks.

Linder, L. R. 1999. *Public Access Television: America's Electronic Soapbox.* Westport, CT: Greenwood Publishing Group.

Majewski, L., and J. Bernstein. 2014. *Mad World: An Oral History of New Wave Artists and Songs that Defined the 1980s.* New York: Abrams.

Meehan, T. 1965. "Where Did All the Women Go?" *The Saturday Evening Post* 238 (18): 26–30.

Mirabella, G. 1995. *In and Out of Vogue.* New York: Doubleday.

Moore, J. 2015. *Fashion Fads through American History: Putting Clothes into Context.* Santa Barbara: ABC-CLIO.

Polhemus, T. 1994. *Streetstyle: From Sidewalk to Catwalk.* London: Thames and Hudson.

Polhemus, T. 1996. *Style Surfing: What to Wear in the Third Millennium.* London: Thames and Hudson.

Polhemus, T. 2011. *Fashion and Anti-fashion: Exploring Adornment and Dress from an Anthropological Perspective.* Lexington, KY: Open Source.

Quant, M. 1966. *Quant by Quant.* London: Cassell and Company, Ltd.

Roshco, B. 1963. *The Rag Race: How New York and Paris Run the Breakneck Business of Dressing American Women.* New York: Funk and Wagnalls Company, Inc.

Schouten, J. W., and J. H. McAlexander. 1995. "Subcultures of Consumption: An Ethnography of the New Bikers." *Journal of Consumer Research* 22 (1): 43–61.

Smil, V. 2011. *Made in America: The Rise and Retreat of American Manufacturing.* Cambridge, MA: MIT Press.

Sullivan, J. 2006. *Jeans: A Cultural History of an American Icon.* New York: Gotham Books.

Torbet, L. 1973. *Clothing Liberation: Out of the Closets and into the Streets.* New York: Praeger Publishers.

Westwood, V., and I. Kelly. 2014. *Vivienne Westwood.* London: Picador.

Chapter 4

Street Stylin': Personal Style, Self-Expression, and the Importance and Impact of Street Style Photography on the Fashion Industry

In roughly the last 15 years the concept of "street style" has become a guiding idea in American dress practices and both a fixture of and focal point in social media, fashion advertising, retailing, and reporting. Street-style pictures have become a mainstay of fashion photography from start-up blogspots to *Vogue, Women's Wear Daily,* and *Harper's Bazaar* and have profoundly impacted the language of contemporary "fashion." Importantly, this phenomenon has reoriented many sectors of the apparel, accessories, and beauty industries. Novices and fashion professionals alike have come to use the expression "street style" with unfettered abandon. The term is used to sell apparel and accessories, beauty products, magazines, and books, and it is also used as a tool for self-promotion—which has proven to be quite lucrative for some enterprising individuals who now find themselves in the front row at major fashion shows and in a position to weigh in on the current state of fashion and style. However, despite the widespread promotion of the concept, what is currently implied by the use of the expression "street style" is not always clear and is not always the same. Thus it would, it seems, be quite easy to make a case asserting that this trendy linguistic terminology is an empty set, a mere turn of phrase that adds contemporaneity and pizzazz to long-lived fashion concepts and dress practices. In truth, asserting that something is "street style" is a technique that is used to up-sell the mundane, but there is more to the story.

This chapter engages the concept of unique personal stylishness outside of the boundaries of shared cultural interests like music or sports, and in so doing does not focus on core, identifying stylistic aspects in the same way that a discussion of Dead Heads or skateboarders would. In addition, the focus in this chapter sets aside subcultural alliances and countercultural impulses that informed the dress practices of groups like the Black Panthers and the Beats. In essence, the main focus here is on the concept of street style as personal style or as simply being stylish on the street. Again, on the surface, this might seem like a nonstarter for a provocative investigation; however, this chapter shows that the concept has an historical trajectory that illuminates critical notions about fashionable dress and that, more recently, the concept has evolved to have specific commercial implications that reveal much about the current state of fashion design, retail, communication, and consumption.

This chapter begins by demonstrating that the essential and largely equivalent concepts of personal style and street style have been part of American dress practices for more than a century, and that for many decades the concept was clearly and unambiguously couched within the dictates of *mainstream* fashion. Tracing the historical discussion of personal style and street style shows the evolution of the concept itself and helps make sense of the fragmented meaning of the concept in contemporary dress. Next the discussion moves to an examination of why and how the concept has recently been applied and interpreted in both commercial and noncommercial contexts. The chapter explores the importance of the street-style phenomenon with regard to communicating dress concepts, advertising, merchandising, and retailing and concludes with theorizing about the widespread interest in the phenomenon and the reasons it has gained such cultural currency.

The Evolution of the Street Style and Personal Style Concepts in the United States

Chapter 1 detailed key tenets of the history of Western fashion in an effort to build a context for understanding the proliferation of street and subcultural styles. That chapter discussed the guiding concepts of copying, keeping up, and competing within the greater narrative of fashion as a long-lived game of follow-the-leader. As also noted, within this context the concept of personal distinction was an important factor, which began to break down only in the middle decades of the 20th century. The pages of American *Vogue* provide a record of the move from personal distinction within the realm of fashion to iconoclastic, individualistic, radical dress practices in the mainstream. *Vogue* has long been the leading voice in American fashion and has enjoyed readership that far surpasses that of other fashion publications. Thus the longevity, popularity, and reputation of the magazine mark it as a reliable touchstone.

Both photographic and written evidence clearly demonstrates that distinction and individuation through dress were carefully guarded concepts in the first half of the 20th century. The most finely dressed individuals, people who cared about both fashion and stylishness, walked a thin line between asserting personal taste and running afoul of established conventions. For example, an article from 1900 entitled "The Well-Dressed Man: Some Observations on the Ways of Smart Men" indicated that smartly dressed men should pay little attention to fashion and rely instead on the advice of their tailors and their own, well-informed personal opinions "as to what is good style and becoming" (334). However, the article also clearly implied that a fixed cannon of acceptable, widely known and understood dress practices absolutely shaped such personal opinions. The negative implications of being an iconoclast were unambiguous in the first decades of the 20th century. An article from 1908 directly asserted that "originality" was "frowned on" in fashionable circles and noted, "If a human being cannot be classified as belonging to a certain cut of trousers, coat, or waistcoats, let him beware, for he is a misfit human being and we all know the cheap end of all misfits" ("As Seen by Him" 1908, 288). Thus, expressing individual style while demonstrating taste and knowledge that were bound by the prevailing cannon of fashion was an idea that was clearly expressed for men and women throughout the early decades of the 20th century. Expressions of individual taste and stylishness were thus largely subtle inflections in dress selection, color, cut, and fit—finely honed choices that improved one's overall appearance.

This general conception of personal style continued well into the middle of the 20th century. For example, a 1933 pamphlet by fashion professional Alma Archer entitled *The Secrets of Smartness and the Art of Allure* aptly captured the contemporary tone of the 1930s as it encouraged smartness and the prevailing notion of individuality, yet also included a "personal style test" designed to pinpoint mistakes in dress (which was meant to encourage the purchase of the Alma Archer Method, a program designed to help women achieve stylishness within acceptable boundaries). Notably, taking proactive measures to ensure one's own stylishness was deemed important in the first half of the 20th century. The agency of the wearer was clearly accorded high status, and individuals were advised to take responsibility for their personal appearance. A 1933 article observed an often-repeated notion when the writer stated, "No matter how brilliant a gown a designer may create, it is the woman who wears it who makes the gown a fashion" ("As They Wear It" 1933, 32). Investing thoughtfulness into the creation and selection of clothes, cultivating a personal style, and understanding the importance of following only the fashions that fit or benefited the wearer were routinely stressed into the postwar period (see "Made for You" 1948, 136–41, for a lengthy exposition of this idea).

The first hints that personal style could be something more than the careful selection of fashionable apparel and the certain *je ne sais quoi* that a person could imbue in a carefully chosen outfit were first glimpsed in mainstream fashion in the early 1970s. A *Vogue* article from 1972 noted that fashionable women largely had the same things in their closets as other women but advised readers, "Never feel locked-in by fashion" as there would always be "another way around" ("Personal Style" 1972, 91), implying that fashionable clothes could be worked with and around to make a suitable personal statement. Women and men of the 1970s were heirs to almost two decades of street and subcultural styles and had witnessed the myriad do-it-yourself techniques, crosscultural borrowings, and reimaginings of existing apparel; thus, while *Vogue* writers did not overtly encourage dissent from the fashion system, "finding another way around" was most certainly open to this kind of interpretation.

In the 1980s the concept of personal style gained increased attention in the high-style fashion press. It was routinely used to sell both beauty products and apparel and was a term that was regularly applied to the point of view expressed by individual designers like Halston and Zoran. Under the stewardship of editor in chief Grace Mirabella, American *Vogue* increasingly focused on "real life dressing," and street photography became more common. Importantly, by the middle of the 1980s there was some attention paid to women who wore things that were definitively not part of the fashion cannon. "Close-ups" (short, focused articles) of women wearing things like men's apparel or vintage and non-Western clothes, or affecting a distinctly disheveled look, appeared in the 1980s, while the old narrative of picking things that suited the wearer and expressed personality continued to be the mainstay of the conversation about personal style ("Vogue's View" 1984, 168). While American cultural currents in the 1980s were engendering a variety of street and subcultural styles, aesthetic decisions by important mainstream designers were also facilitating a shift to a more overt personalization of dress. By the late 1980s many fashion designers were offering "classic" clothes, which were stylistically unremarkable and essentially *made* for personalization. Fashion designers understood that contemporary dress was becoming more individualized; Michael Kors captured this idea succinctly when he quipped, "The days of wearing something because it's 'in' are over" (Schecter 1989, 59).

By the 1990s American *Vogue* had seemingly embraced the breakdown in sartorial authority and ran countless articles that featured irreverent juxtapositions, the mixing of high style and mass-market and flea-market finds, and celebrated individuals who flaunted their iconoclastic personal style. What was once viewed as the mark of a "misfit" had emerged as a point of distinction and even empowerment ("Vogue Point of View" 1991, 259). By the end of the decade the cult of personal style held such sway that a *Vogue* writer declared, "The fashion uniform is dead. Personal style reigns supreme" ("Cult of Personality" 1997, 108).

Although the terms "street style" and "personal style" are now generally construed as synonymous, the evolution of the former term requires some examination. The term "street style" first appeared in American *Vogue* in the early 1980s and was generally applied to the exceptionally personalized, unique dress of regular people, and it was routinely applied to snapshots taken in foreign cities including Paris. The transition to the widespread use of "street style" as a preferred synonym for a more generalized "personal style" began in the late 1990s and seems to be related to myriad factors. First, there is evidence of institutional interest in street and subcultural style by at least 1994. In that year the Victoria and Albert

Museum in London presented its seminal exhibition entitled *Streetstyle, from Sidewalk to Catwalk, 1940 to Tomorrow,* which considered examples of street and subcultural styles on aesthetic par with traditional fashion design. At the same time, Christie's auction house in London presented its first "street style" sale. Notably, auction houses and museums have the ability to elevate both the commercial and cultural value of objects by placing them in important institutional settings and, in the case of sale at auction, by assigning and recording a monetary value.

Street-style photography was also evolving in the latter part of the 1990s. The genre of street-style photography had existed since the camera became widely available at the end of the 19th century, but it had become an institutional fixture of mainstream publications only in the 1960s. Perhaps the most widely recognized examples of this photography can be found in *The New York Times.* Beginning in the early 1970s the late Bill Cunningham began his "On the Street" column, which captured almost 50 years of New York City street style. By the 1980s, similar columns were mainstays of subcultural papers like *The Village Voice,* which began its weekly column in 1980 under the authorship of Amy Arbus. However, in the 1990s street photography embarked on a new course as paparazzi photographs of celebrities were published in the newly launched *In Style,* which began publication in 1994. Images of this kind seamlessly merged the celebrity snapshot with commentary that elevated the image to the realm of fashion photography and consequently created a new source of inspiration for consumers. By the middle of the aughts, new fashion-media outlets including fashion blogs were also developing the genre of street-style photography while applying the "street style" label to highly varied images. Innovators in this category include Scott Schumann, who launched his blog *The Sartorialist* in 2005, and Yvan Rodic, whose influential *Facehunter* site started in 2006. Within the span of just a few years this phase of the personal-style/street-style evolution took on widespread cultural and commercial currency that is still significantly impacting the fashion industry as the second decade of the 21st century nears its end. However, with widespread interest in the phenomenon came commercial applications and a fragmentation of the meaning of the genre.

Street Style in the 21st Century: Street-Style Photography's Mixed Messages and Meanings

In the 21st century, in the age of Internet communication, the publication of street-style photography has blossomed while the meaning of street style has fragmented. Some street-style photographs document profoundly distinct and creative dress, while many images document and comment upon incredibly subtle nuances of mainstream fashionable dress. Thus, close examination of street-style images and the text associated with them reveals that contemporary street-style photography and commentary remain true to the core ideas about personal style that have existed and evolved over the course of the past 100 years. This phenomenon creates confusion and denudes the meaning of the term for contemporary observers. It seems safe to say that the mixed messages and meanings are not purposeful reflections of the historical nuances of the personal-style concept but, rather, are evidence of the co-opting of the term to meet a variety of needs and goals. Taking as a given that the street-style/personal-style concept is important to 21st-century conversations about stylish dress (an issue returned to toward the end of this chapter), it is important to note that this multivalence has the potential to undercut both the expressive potency and implicit hierarchy of contemporary dress practices. Three distinct categories of street-style photography and commentaries seem to exist in the 21st-century fashion press; therefore, three working definitions of street style itself seem to exist.

First, some street-style photographs document highly personalized assemblages of dress. Images of this kind may be posed or snapshots (or posed to look like snapshots), and they generally show women and men dressed in combinations of high-style and mass-market apparel, contemporary designs and vintage pieces, clothes worn as they were intended to be worn and clothes worn in unique, personalized ways. Pictures of this kind may be of celebrities or regular women and may depict the personal style of the person depicted or the style envisioned by a stylist (which is often the case with celebrity street-style pictures in this category). Images of this kind reflect the notion of street style as innovative, iconoclastic personal style—a notion that we have seen has been widely visible in the mainstream fashion press from the 1980s onward. This category of street style is the highest order of personal style as it has the ability to break down barriers of high and low, masculine and feminine, dated and contemporary. Personalized assemblages in this category may be both iconoclastic and trend setting, and they mark the zenith of the trajectory of personal style from a concept bound by rules of decorum to one in which personal expression is largely unfettered.

A second category of street-style photography is largely focused on celebrities and fashion models who are "off duty," implying they are wearing their own clothes on the street. These images, which are usually true snapshots, have a tendency to depict mundane articles of clothing such as jeans, hoodies, sweatpants, and T-shirts paired with one or more branded luxury items such as a Chanel bag, a Hermes belt, or Christian Louboutin high-heeled shoes. Images of this kind largely intermix pricey fashion-forward and fashion-branded items with basics and conflate groundbreaking or unique stylishness with status dressing and the promotion of contemporary trends. While images that conform to these specifications may show currently fashionable pieces of apparel or accessories, they tend to be basic, staple, classic pieces and, therefore, often do not communicate a unique or innovative contemporary fashion idea. Furthermore, these assemblages of basics tend to conform to existing ideas for pairing—meaning that they do not express a new or noteworthy point of view, creativity, or personality. Thus images of this kind fall sartorially short of the aesthetic standard of rebellious personal expression that was set in the first group—a standard that, importantly, is routinely stated or implied in street-style commentary *regardless of what is depicted*. Arguably, street-style pictures of this kind would never be taken of a regular woman because the style itself is generally unremarkable, though the person depicted is often exceptionally attractive or is bedecked in exceptionally trendy or expensive items. In a sense, images of this kind may be understood as reverting to early-20th-century conceptions of personal style whereby the individual has dressed to please himself or herself, while conforming to fashions of the day. A generous reading of images of this kind could explore nuances of color and texture that are becoming to the wearer and could seek out fine points of cut and fit that flatter the figure, though notably such features are almost never the focus of editorial comments that accompany this kind of image. Indeed, it is the editorial commentary that creates confusion as images of this kind are frequently described as interesting, inspiring, and standard setting. The same kind of language that is used to assess the iconoclast in his or her eclectic assemblage is routinely used to describe a famous beauty in jeans and a T-shirt.

The last category of street-style photography is less common than the first two and essentially depicts a person (often a recognizable personality from film, television, or popular music) wearing apparel almost exactly as it was presented on the runway. The person depicted may or may not have made aesthetically impactful choices for hair, makeup, and accessories. In general, pictures of this kind simply show a contemporary person wearing a contemporary fashion as it was conceived by the designer and his or her team of stylists. In images of this kind, "street style" simply means fashion being worn in the street. On one level this is again a reversion to the early-20th-century interpretation of personal style as the dress of an individual person; however, the wholesale adoption of a runway look has the potential to invite criticism about wearing what becomes or flatters an individual and opens the door to the criticism of becoming a fashion "victim." When recognizable personalities adopt runway looks wholesale, there exists a strong chance that the sartorial decisions are the result of promotional considerations. Celebrities who are brand ambassadors generally have complex contracts that detail specific responsibilities for representing the brand corporeally, while an up-and-coming designer may strike a deal with a person of note for a one-time-only turn on a red carpet or other public event. In essence, the runway look on the street may be just as orchestrated as the runway look on the runway itself.

It is important to note that the careful orchestration of many street-style images is a phenomenon not glimpsed in the 20th century when the concept was gaining cultural currency. Although photo shoots were staged on the street, as were posed photographs of individuals with unique personal style, a clear distinction between snapshots and posed shots was always evident, even if the distinction was not made explicit. Street-style photography in the new millennium often makes indistinct the line between personal expression and commercial construction. Across the three categories of street-style photography, for various reasons, it is seldom clear whether the person in the image is expressing personal taste and preference, or if the person depicted is showcasing an ensemble crafted to promote a brand or sell a specific item.

The fact that this line is blurred is an important point. The presentation of a commercial vision in the guise of personal expression muddies the communicative and expressive power of dress in the 21st century. A true, unorchestrated expression of street style should by nature reflect elements of the zeitgeist as it is channeled through an individual's sartorial selections. Although one may argue that this is true in the case of a stylist at work, the commercial implications of styled photographs (the applications of which are discussed in the following section) temper true unfettered expression with the demands of revenue generation and other business interests like development of brand identity. Furthermore, the multivalent nature of the "street style" label, coupled with the cloudy provenance of the style expressed in street-style images, has the potential to undercut the implicit hierarchy of contemporary dress practices. If all things are stylish (for different but undisclosed reasons), then ultimately nothing is exceptionally stylish. The indiscriminate application of this trendy nomenclature to highly varied images and intentions makes for a sort of fashion vacuum in which standards of taste are siphoned out of contemporary dress.

Fashion Media and the Street-Style Phenomenon: Bloggers, Fashion Publications, Retailers, and the New Media Hybrids

Since roughly 2007, a variety of Internet media outlets has used the different kinds of street-style photography. These websites employ the street-style concept to express myriad sartorial tastes and to document contemporary dress practices, but they are also generally designed to make retail sales. Street-style blogs are perhaps the most focused conduit for the communication of street style. Among the most noteworthy examples are *Man Repeller, Facehunter, The Sartorialist,* and *Tommy Ton.* Street-style blogs emerged as websites that featured snapshots of individuals who were spotted on the street. Originally, the photographer may or may not have posed and styled those individuals (asked them to add or remove a jacket or hat). Over time, however, it has become increasingly clear that many street-style blogs feature pictures that are highly editorial and art-directed. In fact, a book entitled

Street Fashion Photography: Taking Stylish Pictures on the Concrete Runway was written solely for the purpose of instructing aspiring street-style bloggers in the subtle arts of styling street-style "models" and crafting well-composed pictures. Additionally, street-style blogs have evolved so that they may feature the work of a fashion professional like a designer or model. For example, in the spring of 2016 blogger Garance Dore featured photographs of the designer Racil wearing her own clothes and clearly posed and styled in a manner that recalled mainstream fashion editorials. Some street-style blogs also feature the blogger as a model who shows outfits that presumably reflect his or her personal style but may also reflect a commercial contract or consideration that has been arranged between the designer and blogger. *Harpers Bazaar* documented 19 such bloggers, many of whom had model looks and figures (some of whom work as professional models), in a 2016 article (Pieri). Thus in many cases, street-style blogs function exactly as fashion editorials do, though many of them retain a sort of outsider status that makes them appealing to some demographics. While blogs represent a formal platform for individuals to share street-style photographs, various forms of social media are also used (sometimes in conjunction with a blog) to share images. Instagram, Pinterest, and Facebook are all portals through which one can share images of oneself, a fashionable stranger, or a product that one wishes to promote.

Serialized publications have also become portals for communicating concepts of street style. Both *Vogue* and *Harpers Bazaar* feature street-style pages and posts in their traditional print and online formats. In both cases, images are generally linked to buying information including the name of the designer and the price, while street-style pictures posted online frequently include digital links that direct the reader directly to retail websites. Notably, general-interest publications like the *New York Post* and *People* magazine also routinely feature street-style pictures with retail information. Internet concerns that largely function like traditional magazines or newspapers by regularly posting articles, images, and advertisements are also important conduits for promoting the street-style concept. The Refinery29 website routinely posts groups of street-style pictures, which are often organized around an upcoming seasonal trend. Images provide readers with ideas for how to wear current fashions, regularly list the designer's name, and often provide links to sites like Pinterest, which often links directly through to a designer's social-media platform or business website. Refinery29 has also posted articles to help individuals achieve a specific street-style aesthetic. For example, "Cool-Girl Outfits to Copy This Summer" was crafted to help readers achieve the Coachella look. H&M copresented the article, which included links to "shop the look" (Ives 2015). Similarly, Maybelline sponsored a series of street-style images featuring "beauty lessons" from New Yorkers, with links to "shop the slideshow" included (Wong 2015). WhoWhatWear.com also routinely provides commercial links through its street-style images. Often an image photographed in the street is followed by a series of product pictures and links to retailers like Barneys, Nordstrom, and Net-a-Porter.com.

Some retailers have embraced the street-style phenomenon and the "selfie" (a picture taken by oneself) craze by encouraging customers to upload images of themselves wearing an item that is currently available for purchase. Disturbingly, retailers also routinely access and use street-style images that consumers have taken of themselves and uploaded to social media, including Facebook and Pinterest, without the consent of the people in the photos. When "consumer engagement," a broad industry term that implies consumer reference of brands in social-media posts or through the use of hashtags, is evident, companies like Piqora and Olapic help brands select images that capture an interesting consumer-driven concept or authentic personal expression for commercial use. Many companies use one or both of these practices, and links that invite consumers to share pictures they have posted on Facebook and Twitter appear on retail sites like Aerie; however, many apparel companies including Crocs and American Eagle Outfitters have come under scrutiny for using images (especially of minors) without the appropriate consent. Regardless of how the street-style image is acquired, the use of such pictures for commercial means impacts the way in which the public at large understands and interprets street style.

Some Internet-based outlets defy traditional categories with regard to their missions, content, and use of street style. The website StealHerStyle.net is interesting in that it posts seemingly candid snapshots of notable women including film and television celebrities, musicians, and fashion-industry professionals like models, designers, and bloggers. Images are then captioned with a thorough list of the items being worn by the person depicted, and links to retail websites are provided. StealHerStyle has a tabloid tenor and trades in paparazzi pictures and social-media "selfies" but is solely devoted to facilitating the copying of celebrity style. Polyvore .com is a unique platform that is a robust and diverse website functioning as a clearinghouse for fashion trends. The website is structured in part like most retail websites, with categories devoted to clothes and accessories; however, within a category such as dresses, each image is a link to a distinct retailer. Polyvore.com's use of street-style photography is one category within the site and is similar to StealHerStyle.com in that candid snapshots are presented. However, Polyvore.com has a more professional look and tone and presents the snapshots along with collages of items that are the same or similar to what is depicted. These collections of pictures are presented like a magazine page but include links to the products used to achieve the look.

The large number of websites and printed publications that make street style a focal point is evidence of the importance of the concept in contemporary dress practices. However, close examination of the various sources that highlight street style reveals images that conform to all three of the categories described above as well as varied reasons for promoting the concept. Thus the images themselves seem to be functioning and influencing in a variety of ways. Some street-style pictures operate largely as a document of individual taste and promote contemporary dress ideas, whereas many street-style pictures create or promote a commercial vision and specifically function as a conduit for selling apparel and accessories. Importantly, the boundaries of each role are not always clear.

Theorizing the Importance of the Street-Style Phenomenon

Whether a street-style picture is posted on a blog, an online publication, or a retail website, the ubiquitous presence of these kinds of images reinforces the fact that celebrating personal style has become increasingly important in the first decades of the new millennium. This phenomenon points to several key characteristics of consumers in the 21st century.

First, individuals have a desire to see themselves. Obsessive picture taking, editing, and posting are widespread phenomena that transcend the demographic boundary of millennials. Consumer psychologist Kit Yarrow, writing in *Decoding the Consumer Mind: How and Why We Shop and Buy,* noted that there is an intensified emphasis among consumers to revel in their own individuality and perceive others as audience members. Thus taking pictures that highlight some special personal characteristic or accomplishment and posting them for feedback feed this need. This is a new degree of narcissism that, at its extreme, finds individuals taking countless dozens of pictures, applying filters, and editing images in order to make a single social-media post of a seemingly unstudied moment (see Garcia 2015). Not only does peeling back the reality of image making reveal the characteristics of contemporary consumers, but it also reveals a change in the essence of street-style photography at the personal, noncommercial level. Importantly, there is discernible evidence that individuals wear things in social-media street-style posts that they would never wear beyond the bounds of the image frame, a point of interest revealed by Instagram star Essena O'Neil (Garcia 2015). Thus even the individual need to proclaim and celebrate personal style is fraught with layers of contradiction and inauthenticity as expressions may be motivated not only by personal taste but by the desire to get "likes" and develop a social-media presence (which has the potential to be monetized).

Second, seeing oneself as unique, creative, and original is important to people in the new millennium, and eschewing the runway in either word or deed is a point of pride for many individuals. Making a proclamation that one has somehow circumvented the fashion system is an important concept in 21st-century dress practices and is at the root of authentic street-style image making. However, many brands have realized that consumers have a desire to express individuality and difference and are "dazed and cynical about ads" (Voight 2000), and thus marketers accommodate this need by showing their products being used in a "real" life context, in "authentic" expressions of unstudied individuality. Mari Cortizo, a former account-planning chief at the Chiat Day London office, noted as early as 2000, "As the Internet and other advances open up communications between marketers and the public, people will get bolder in questioning everything that the marketing world is feeding them" (Voight 2000); thus, concealing marketing within the guise of uniqueness, novelty, and personal authenticity is a key strategy. Tapping into the cultural zeitgeist has the ability to boost sales. As a result, 21st-century brands customize products, communicate individually with customers through social media, create specialized URLs for curated shopping experiences, and make consumers feel as if they are "respected and connected" to brands ("Extreme Individualism" 2016). Making consumers feel as if they are engaging in something unique, personal, and noncommercial and reflecting images of consumers in the marketing itself are ways to tap into the desire to be unique while still selling commodities. Street-style and personal-style imagery and rhetoric tap into key components of the psychology of our time but do not necessarily offer anything new or revolutionary.

The fast pace of fashion, the omnipresence of information, and the rapid-fire diffusion of new ideas make being unique, in the know, and in the *avant-garde* difficult, as constant change and instantaneous communication make it challenging to stand out for more than a moment. The deep need to be unique, independent, and free-spirited is truly difficult to satisfy. However, it is clear that various arms of the fashion system are harnessing the street-style concept, promoting a hodgepodge of ideas that construes personal style as virtually anything and ultimately nothing. The fact that we can all be street-style stars—and that we can buy personal style— is psychologically satisfying but calls into question the present state of sartorial innovation.

Is There Novelty in 21st-Century Dress?

Street-style images and text typically function together to highlight uniqueness, opposition to the mainstream, and even subversive aesthetics; however, in roughly the last decade a disproportionate number of street-style pictures have taken on decidedly mainstream characteristics and have been harnessed to prop up the fashion industry. Many street-style images serve the fashion marketplace in a fairly traditional manner as they promote interest in contemporary fashions, are positioned to stimulate sales, and potentially contribute to interest in apparel and accessories brands. Contemporary street-style images and commentary routinely support the traditional fashion industry in the guise of creativity, iconoclasm, and self-expression, and notably, discussions in the mass media "produce meaning" (Woodward 2009, 84), impacting conceptions and perceptions in the culture at large. The questions now become: Is the street-style category noteworthy, and is anything at risk?

Fashion photography has traditionally highlighted the aesthetics of taste-makers; however, under close examination it becomes clear that the valorization of street style is often done not to assert standards or ideas but to create a valuable marketing and retailing concept. Given that the mainstream fashion press, including *Vogue, Women's Wear Daily,* and *Harpers Bazaar,* promotes images from all three contemporary street-style categories without clarification, it is possible that street-style photography as it is currently conceived and utilized has the ability to further erode the power of the fashion press—and what remains of a hierarchy of fashion and stylishness—by routinely presenting images that show fragmented, contradictory, and banal ideas. That said, historically, fashion photography has captured the zeitgeist and has expressed a refined taste. Contemporary street-style photography considered as a whole captures two important factors: the heterogeneity of dress practices in the 21st century and the acceptance of complete relativism with regard to what constitutes stylishness. It remains to be seen if the commercial applications of street style will diminish over time, thus allowing the truly creative and expressive examples (see category one) to take center stage and recoup the significance of the street-style moniker. This correction would mark an important point of distinction in conversations about contemporary dress, as it would contribute to clarifying the important hierarchies of fashion and stylishness that have long functioned within fashion. Without these hierarchies and standards, without levels of taste and stylishness, the expressive and communicative powers of dress are diminished; and such a loss is, in essence, a loss of an important cultural touchstone.

Further Reading

Archer, A. 1933. *The Secrets of Smartness and the Art of Allure.* N.p.: N.p.
"As Seen by Him." 1908. *Vogue,* February 27, 288.
"As They Wear It—Seen by Him." 1933. *Vogue,* November 1, 32.
Barberich, C., and P. Gelardi. 2014. *Refinery29: Style Stalking.* New York: Potter Style.
Caplan, J. 2005. "Messengers of Cool." *Time* 166 (17): 98.
"Cult of Personality." 1997. *Vogue,* January, 108–21.
"Extreme Individualism." 2016. WGSN, April 27. Retrieved May 1, 2016, from www.wgsn.com.
Garcia, P. 2015. "Instagram Star Quits Social Media, Says It's Not Real Life." *Vogue,* November 2. Retrieved November 15, 2015, from www.vogue.com.

Hill, A. 2005. "People Dress So Badly Nowadays: Fashion and Late Modernity." In *Fashion and Modernity,* edited by C. Breward and C. Evans, 66–77. Oxford, UK: Berg.

Ives, A. 2015. "Cool-Girl Outfits to Copy This Summer." *Refinery29,* April 17. Retrieved May 31, 2015, from www.refinery29.com.

Jarrett, M. S. 2006. *Street: The Nylon Book of Global Style.* New York: Universe Publishing.

"Made for You: Made to Order by a Great House, Made Your Own by Your Own Ideas." 1948. *Vogue,* October 1, 136–41.

"Personal Style." 1972. *Vogue,* March, 91.

Pieri, K. 2016. "The 19 Fashion Blogger Instagrams You Should Follow Now." *Harpers Bazaar,* June 13. Retrieved November 12, 2016, from www.harpers bazaar.com.

Rodic, Y. 2010. *Face Hunter.* New York: Prestel.

Rodic, Y. 2013. *Travels with Facehunter: Street Style from around the World.* Philadelphia: Running Press.

Schecter, L. 1989. "Vogue's View: Antifashion Fashion." *Vogue,* June, 59.

Schuman, S. 2009. *The Sartorialist.* New York: Penguin Books.

Sims, J. 2014. *100 Ideas that Changed Street Style.* London: Laurence King Publishing.

Singer, M. 2015. "Fashion in the Age of the Selfie: Looking at the Spring 2016 Collections from a New Angle." *Vogue,* October 14. Retrieved October 21, 2015, from www.vogue .com.

Taschen, A., and A. von Hayden. 2014. *Berlin Street Style: A Guide to Urban Chic.* New York: Abrams Image.

Thomas, I., and F. Veysset. 2012. *Paris Street Style: A Guide to Effortless Chic.* New York: Abrams Image.

"Vogue Point of View: Daring to Be Different." 1991. *Vogue,* October, 259.

"Vogue's View: Close-ups, Personal Style." 1984. *Vogue,* July, 168, 170.

Voight, J. 2000. "The Consumer Rebellion." *Adweek* 50 (2): 46.

"The Well-Dressed Man: Some Observations on the Ways of Smart Men." 1900. *Vogue,* November 15, 334–35.

Wong, J. 2015. "13 Beauty Lessons from the Streets of NYC." *Refinery29,* May 15. Retrieved May 31, 2015, from www.refinery29.com.

Woodward, S. 2009. "The Myth of Street Style." *Fashion Theory* 13 (1): 83–102.

Yarrow, K. 2014. *Decoding the Consumer Mind: How and Why We Shop and Buy.* San Francisco: Jossey Bass.

Part II

A–Z Listing of American Street Styles

Introduction to the Entries

The entries in this section are designed to give the reader an understanding of American street and subcultural styles. Each entry will situate the style in its time period, its geographical location, and the cultural movement that the style emerged from or was connected to. The sociocultural context is always presented in connection to each style, and key historical events, influential people, and places of note are discussed in conjunction with seminal works of art, music, or other cultural productions that stimulated the development of the street style. For many of the street styles discussed in detail in the entries that follow, a message, mission, or point of view could be embedded in the sartorial choices; thus the contextual information that is supplied is critical to understanding these larger themes.

A detailed analysis of each style is at the heart of each entry. In some cases the roots of one street style may be found in another, and this connection is made whenever it is relevant. Each entry also maps the evolution of a street style from its earliest stage through broad adoption. An effort is always made to show the myriad ways in which a street style could be interpreted and modified on an individual level, while attention is also given to the core attributes that are the hallmarks of a given street style. Media stereotypes are discussed whenever possible as a point of comparison and contrast to what authentically was worn in the street. It cannot be overstated that while every effort has been made to provide a wide range of details regarding each style group, a work of this kind cannot help but make generalizations and will undoubtedly fail to capture every regional nuance. Additionally, although many of these style categories are attached to subcultures or lifestyles, and certainly street styles have communicative power and may relate strongly to personal identity, I have tried to craft the language of this text so that it is clear when I am describing groups like cholos or leathermen, I am describing a visible aesthetic category and am not making assertions about individual people, nor broad strokes about beliefs, behavior, or lifestyle.

The diffusion of street style to the mainstream and commercial culture is an important part of the trajectory of a consumer-driven style and is also typically important to the apparel industry as many street styles trickle-up to mass production. Thus the roles of celebrities and mass media, including movies and television, are discussed along with important books and magazine articles that communicated key aspects of a street style or street culture through images and text. Additionally, influential retailers who sold apparel and accessories to innovators of a street style and the designers who sampled from the street-style aesthetics are discussed, though given the number of times that street styles from groups like punks, Goths, and hippies have served as sources of inspiration, the examples given are certainly not exhaustive.

In some cases the entry concludes with a discussion of when and why a street style disappeared; in other cases the street style is still in use, and its current state is detailed. In all cases, however, a discussion of why the style is socially, historically, and aesthetically important for both the individuals who wore it and for the individuals who study it is a point of conclusion.

The Further Reading section that follows each entry includes texts cited in the entry as well as those that will advance the reader's study of the topic. Many of the readings are primary-source materials that echo the voice of the time period. Memoirs and autobiographies are important sources for descriptions of clothes and the contexts in which the clothes lived and moved. Anthologies, scholarly papers, and historical texts round out the reading lists. Thus this text provides the reader with substantial foundational knowledge and easy access to additional source material to advance his or her inquiry.

American Street Gangs (19th Century–Present)

Street gangs in the United States are a constantly evolving phenomenon that have been in existence in some form since the late 18th century but burgeoned in the 19th century when waves of immigration created racial and ethnic tensions in a context of socioeconomic hardships (Howell and Moore 2010, 1). American street gangs function as a solution to the demands of urban life and help people to adapt amidst social disorganization, by forging familial bonds and finding strength in numbers, facing racial or ethnic discrimination in groups, and staking claim to a "turf." Many street gangs also provide a source of income for members, who may be involved in petty crimes like robbery or more organized endeavors like narcotics trafficking or prostitution. Notably, while street gangs are socioculturally and economically different from national or international organized-crime syndicates or mafias, this chapter will discuss both kinds of street gangs as the interest here is how apparel is used to represent gang affiliation rather than how gangs may be structured for illegal commercial enterprises. Additionally, it must be noted that traditional street gangs operate on a level as local as a neighborhood bound by a few square blocks and, therefore, are subject to incredibly localized points of distinction that are informed by a regional culture and immigrant or migrant populations. Additionally, gang membership changes over time, sometimes rapidly, further impacting sartorial differentiation. Thus this chapter provides only an introduction to a topic that is highly diverse and constantly evolving.

Modern gang membership is marked through apparel cut and color, insignia (sometimes also referred to as colors), argot (slang), hand gestures, and graffiti. Earning the right to wear colors is often a rite of passage that is restricted during a probationary period (Klein 1995, 177) and may require the initiate to commit a criminal act. Making gang membership visible is important as the negative response to a gang can help to "crystalize" a group (Covey 2003, 42), while animosity toward other groups is part of the glue that binds street gangs together (Sanders 1994, 140). American street gangs largely use contemporary apparel to dress themselves and to mark their group affiliation; thus most of the evidence of unified street-gang dress practices comes from the 20th century onward, when the proliferation of mass-produced ready-made apparel allowed greater uniformity to be quickly, easily, and cheaply obtained. However, some information is available regarding the unique sartorial practices of gangs in the 19th century.

It has been estimated that in the 19th century hundreds, perhaps thousands, of gangs formed amidst the tides of immigration, first on the East Coast in cities like New York, but ultimately spreading westward with waves of immigration (Howell 2015, chapter 1). These populations of marginalized people, unified by their ethnicity and poverty, formed groups including the Bowery Boys, the Roach Guards, the Plug Uglies, and the Dead Rabbits. Many gangs were formed of working-class youths who worked as longshoremen, butchers, carpenters, and varied manual laborers. Thus as street-gang members, youths generally wore their working-class clothes. Notably, throughout the 19th century the wardrobes of the great masses of working-class people were neither large nor differentiated, and unmarried young men were forced either to save to have a set of clothes made or left to attire themselves in "slops," the earliest form of ready-made apparel that were as stylish and finely tailored as their name suggests. The Bowery Boys were unusual in that they dressed in elegant apparel (Andrews 2013), but notably this related not to some whim of personal expression but rather to the fact that the members of this gang held jobs that both required finer clothes and facilitated their purchase. Most of the discussion of American street-gang style in this entry will focus on men, who across the centuries have been the predominant demographic in street gangs. However, there is evidence that women were involved in street gangs as early as the 19th century. One notable example was "Hell-Cat Maggie," a member of the

Dead Rabbits, who was renowned for wearing brass fingernails to street brawls (Andrews 2013). The use of specialized apparel or accessories as a device for surviving street brawls seems to have been a point of sartorial differentiation among early street-gang members. A gang member of the Whyos, who were "named for a bird-like call the members used to alert one another" (Howell and Moore 2010, 3), named "Dandy" Johnny Dolan reportedly wore shoes that were weaponized with an axe blade (Andrews 2013).

Evidence suggests that some early-20th-century youths who began in local street gangs ultimately graduated to more organized crime families that had national and even international influence. Among the individuals who experienced this trajectory was Al "Scarface" Capone, who began in the streets of New York as a member of the James Street Gang but ultimately became a notorious figure in the Sicilian mafia, based out of Chicago (Howell and Moore 2010, 3). Early-20th-century gangsters who were part of organized crime seem to have dressed differently from their less-organized street-hood counterparts. Among the apparel commonly worn by Capone and his fellow gangsters were three-piece suits, two-tone spectator shoes, fancy silk neckties with bold patterns or hand-painted effects, and broad-brimmed fedora hats. It has been suggested that the selection of this "business-like garb reflected their aim to legitimize their status as businessmen" (Beshears 2010, 197), despite their heavy connections to activities like illegal bootlegging and extortion. While the finery of early-20th-century mafiosos establishes a link with the 19th-century Bowery Boys, their sartorial selections also linked them to the more base instincts of people like Hell-Cat Maggie and Dandy Johnny Dolan. An article in *The New York Times* from 1926 pointed out that rakishly tilted fedoras served to shield the eyes and identity of the wearer, while voluminous overcoats could conceal a large gun. It was also noted in this contemporaneous account that gangster clothes, though made of fine fabrics and cut in current styles, subverted widespread cultural tendencies with their gaudy aesthetics ("Crime Gangs Organized as Big Business" 1926).

Major changes in street-gang style were under way at mid-century, and many of the attributes that developed in this period have become iconic markers of American street gangs. Journalist Harrison Salisbury noted diversity in the way gang members dressed in the 1950s in New York City. In some instances he observed "slick" dress including pegged pants, felt hats, and velvet-collared top coats, all of which created an overall impact of the "cool, cultured, beat the rap type" (Salisbury 1958, 28–29). Another writer for the *The New York Times* (Schumach 1956) noted flashy blazers, and it may be suggested that these sartorial choices may have purposely been chosen to echo the look of notorious gangsters. A more slovenly, down-market look was also noted in the 1950s. Schumach recorded street-gang members wearing sneakers and long hair, while Salisbury observed leather jackets paired with blue jeans in New York City and noted that this look was typical gang apparel across numerous cities (197). Notably, while most street gangs were incredibly insular in the 1950s, staying within the bounds of tightly controlled neighborhoods (Salisbury 1958, 197), the similarity across gangs and across cities could be observed, and Salisbury attributed this similarity to mass communications including records, comics, advertising, television, and movies (204). Mid-century street gangs also evolved increasingly specific techniques for marking gang membership. "Colors" is the term that is frequently used to refer to specific insignia that is typically attached to the back of a leather or denim jacket or vest. The wearing of colors first developed among members of motorcycle clubs and gangs in the post–World War II period and by the 1950s had impacted the dress practices of pedestrian street gangs. In the 1950s gang jackets were often satin with embroidered colors (Hager 2014, 13). Importantly, some gang members in the 1950s simply dressed in the "convention of the high school adolescent" (Salisbury 1958, 29), and interestingly, there was evidence of gang members working within these mainstream conventions to mark gang membership. For example, Salisbury remarked upon the wearing of letterman-style sweaters adorned with a letter used to designate a gang rather than a school (68). "Auxiliary" girl gangs were also reported in the 1950s (Schumach 1956), though their numbers were small and their look was not recorded with regularity or detail.

In the 1960s and 1970s American street gangs increasingly derived their sartorial aesthetics from American motorcycle clubs and gangs. In particular, the practice of tattooing seems to have become more common among street-gang members, and the wearing of colors based off the jean vests pioneered by the Hell's Angels became standard practice for marking gang membership (Hager 2014, 13). Writing about the birth of hip-hop, Steven Hager noted that there were hundreds of street gangs in New York City in the 1970s, totaling perhaps 20,000 members (22), and that "every gang had the same uniform: jean jackets with insignias on the back, Lee jeans, Garrison belts, and engineer boots" (17). Notable New York City gangs included the Black Spades, the Savage Skulls, the Savage Nomads, and the Royal Charmers, all of which clearly marked their group affiliation with hand-stitched, painted, and later iron-on images and text. Female participation in street gangs continued to be relatively rare, comprising roughly 5 to 10 percent of all gang members (Covey 2003, 133); however, the first all-girl gangs were documented in the 1970s (Howell 2015, 10). Female gang members generally adopt the characteristics of their male counterparts and wear basic apparel like jeans and sneakers and gang colors. However, the way in which these pieces are styled tends to go in two markedly different directions. Some female gang members adopt an aggressively masculine aesthetic that may include wearing clothes that are loose or oversized.

Conversely, female gang members may adopt an overtly sexual presentation that includes tight pants and low-cut shirts. These differences may be accounted for by the cultural or ethnic background of the gang members or by how the gang functions, either independently or as an auxiliary to a men's gang. However, while these factors may be used to offer an explanation for masculine or feminine aesthetics, sociocultural factors are merely explanatory and neither causal nor universal.

In the 1980s a shift away from clearly marking gang membership with insignia that definitively declared the name of the gang was evident. The Crips and the Bloods are both predominantly African American street gangs that emerged in the Los Angeles metropolitan area in the early 1970s. Over time these gangs have evolved so that dozens of chapters or "sets" have developed throughout the United States. Regional differences are found among the sets; however, the wearing of a hue that marks gang membership is a critical element of dress. Blue and black dominate the Crips's gang apparel, while the Bloods wear apparel that is predominantly red. Contemporary dress, particularly bandanas, T-shirts, baseball caps, professional sports team jerseys, and in the 1990s branded hip-hop apparel were important markers of membership, while the wearing of traditional colors (insignia) seems to have become less common. In the 1980s there was a florescence of gang activity in Los Angeles, with roughly 600 gangs aligning with either the Crips or Bloods (Reinhold 1988). The use of gang hues and symbols was so powerfully entrenched that "parents carefully dress[ed] their children in brown, yellow, or other 'neutral' colors and avoid[ed] buying British Knights brand sneakers because the initials [had] come to mean 'Blood Killer'—a sign of disrespect in a Blood hood" (Reinhold 1988). Over time the wearing of outfits dominated by gang colors seems to have become less common, as they are easily observed by police. Notably, this sartorial move echoes the decision among members of the Black Panther party to abandon the Afro hairstyle in the late 1960s (Moore 2015, 46). Additionally, Herbert Covey has noted that the adoption of Crips and Bloods subcultural dress is so widespread that true gang activity and membership is "impossible to accurately estimate" (2003, 41).

The Almighty Latin King and Queen Nation (ALKQN) is an organization that was originally formed in the middle of the 20th century as a group committed to expressing a collective Latino identity, originally functioning primarily as a vehicle for empowerment and an outlet of ethnic pride. Over time, however, the ALKQN has evolved into a more typical street gang with chapters throughout the United States. Like the Crips and the Bloods, the ALKQN uses identifying colors, which are black and yellow or black and gold. All kinds of contemporary apparel are worn in these distinctive hues as a marker of membership. Additionally, symbolic stones or beads that show membership as well as specific roles in the organization are worn. For example, green beads or stones indicate that one is a peacemaker, whereas amber is the color of an adviser (Brotherton and Barrios 2004, 186). Latin kings and queens may also wear a crown insignia as a marker of membership. The ALKQN is an organization that openly and equally accepts both male and female members; however, the attire of female Latin queens is strictly regulated, especially at meetings where tight clothes, short skirts, bare stomachs, and cleavage are restricted (Brotherton and Barrios 2004, 195). In its finest moments the ALKQN organization taps ethnicity as a source of strength that aids agency and morality (Brotherton and Barrios 2004, 265); however, law enforcement routinely indicts the organization for typical street-gang behavior including trafficking in illegal or stolen property and street violence.

Notably, the sartorial practices of American street-gang members have been made fashionable through the mass media. A vast array of representations in the media have served to communicate the aesthetics of gang dress, ranging from a depiction of 19th-century gangs in *Gangs of New York* (2002), organized crews from the 1920s in the series *Boardwalk Empire* (2010–2014), mid-century street toughs in the musical *West Side Story* (1957), and late-20th-century street gangs in the television series *The Wire* (2002–2008), the narrative movie *Colors* (1988), and the documentary *80 Blocks from Tiffany's* (1979). Sociologist Malcolm W. Klein noted in 1995 that film, television, and press coverage has educated American youths about gang names, colors, symbols, attitudes, and behaviors. "In short they learn to walk gang, talk gang, and act gang" (1995, 90). Undoubtedly, the proliferation of gang imagery in the media has impacted gang-related dress in two ways. First, it has affected how real gang members dress. By making the visual language of gang membership widespread, it diffuses the power and meaning to insiders. Additionally, the promotion of gang-related imagery through the mass media has developed the image's cultural cachet and inspired the interpretation of gang aesthetics as fashion. This phenomenon was most notable in the hip-hop style from the 1980s and early 1990s. Some rappers of this era had ties to local gangs, wore the clothes as performers, and inspired copycats who may or may not have had knowledge of the symbolism. Mass-market apparel companies in turn created apparel that further proliferated the style, moving it further away from the street-level symbolism.

The ubiquity of some street-gang symbols (like the color blue), and a fear of gang growth and development, has led a variety of institutions to implement wholesale bans on certain kinds of apparel basics including hoodies, sports jerseys, and bandanas in specific color combinations. Bans are justified in schools as a way to prevent harm and to protect individuals who are too young to understand the consequences of their actions (Gereluk 2006, 108). Public spaces like the Maplewood Mall and the Mall of the Americas (both in Minnesota) have issued bans on "gang related clothing" but have not specifically elucidated all that is included under such a ban. Gang colors and hoodies in general are often cited, and some people have argued that bans on gang clothing amount to bans on hip-hop apparel and are thus veiled techniques for banning minority youths (McGuire and Serres 2016).

The use of clothing among members of American street gangs functions as a way to show group affiliation, which in turn shows strength in numbers. Gang colors or insignia may galvanize members and may be a source of pride and a symbol that is vigorously protected. Gang members may also use their apparel to make proclamations about their prosperity and economic power. Street-gang membership and the apparel that marks it fulfill specific needs for members, including "status, sense of identity, and perceived protection from rival groups" (Klein and Maxson 2006, 165). The allure of street-gang symbols is such that members of a given community may wear the symbols without actually being a member of a gang. Given that street gangs largely use mass-market apparel and accessories and contemporary dress to create their symbols, falsely marking affiliation is generally quite easy to do. Notably, the sartorial influence of American street gangs extends beyond the United States and serves as a "role model for street gangs throughout the world." One example of a foreign-based gang that has evolved the cholo look is the El Salvadorean gang known as MS-13. Though gangs display unique cultural characteristics, "at the core they draw much of their style from American street gangs" (Covey 2003, 55). Thus the proliferation of gang-related symbols and the reliance on codes of communication that have developed over the past hundred years are indicative of the strength and allure of dress codes to communicate group membership and of the potential for dress to inspire violence and lawlessness.

Further Reading

Andrews, E. 2013. "7 Infamous Gangs of New York." History.com, June 4. Retrieved November 21, 2016, from www.history.com.

Beshears, L. 2010. "Honorable Style in Dishonorable Times: American Gangsters of the 1920s and 1930s." *Journal of American Culture* 33 (3): 197–206.

Brotherton, D. C., and L. Barrios. 2004. *The Almighty Latin King and Queen Nation: Street Politics and the Transformation of a New York City Gang*. New York: Columbia University Press.

Covey, H. C. 2003. *Street Gangs throughout the World*. Springfield, IL: Charles C. Thomas Publisher, Ltd.

"Crime Gangs Organized as Big Business." 1926. *The New York Times,* April 4. Retrieved June 7, 2016, from www.timesmachine.nytimes.com.

Gereluk, D. 2006. "'Why Can't I Wear This?!': Banning Symbolic Clothing in Schools." *Philosophy of Education,* 106–14.

Hager, S. 2014. *Hip Hop: The Complete Archives*. Wilmington, DE: CreateSpace Independent Publishing platform.

Howell, J. C. 2015. *The History of Street Gangs in the United States*. Lanham, MD: Lexington Books.

Howell, J. C., and J. P. Moore. 2010. "History of Street Gangs in the United States." *National Gang Center Bulletin,* May (4): 1–25.

Klein, M. W. 1995. *The American Street Gang: Its Nature, Prevalence and Control*. New York: Oxford University Press.

Klein, M. W., and C. Maxson. 2006. *Street Gang Patterns and Policies*. New York: Oxford University Press.

McGuire, K., and C. Serres. 2016. "Gang Clothing Ban: Deterrent or Discrimination? Some Shoppers Say the Rule Is Leading Security Guards at Maplewood Mall to Unfairly Target Youths." *Star Tribune* (Minneapolis, MN), April 11. Retrieved June 22, 2016, from *Business Insights: Essentials*.

Moore, J. 2015. *Fashion Fads through American History: Putting Clothes into Context*. Santa Barbara, CA: ABC-CLIO.

Reinhold, R. 1988. "In the Middle of L.A.'s Gang Wars." *The New York Times,* May 2. Retrieved June 21, 2016, from www.nytimes.com.

Salisbury, H. 1958. *The Shook Up Generation*. New York: Harper & Row.

Sanders, W. B. 1994. *Gangbangs and Drive-bys: Grounded Culture and Juvenile Gang Violence*. New York: Aldine de Gruyter.

Schumach, M. 1956. "The Teen-age Gang—Who and Why." *The New York Times,* September 2. Retrieved June 7, 2016, from www.timesmachine.nytimes.com.

B-boy and B-girl (ca. 1976–ca. 1986)

The "B" in b-boy and b-girl is derived from the word "break" and is a reference to a point in recorded music created by the manipulation of two tracks by a deejay. Seminal disc jockey DJ Kool Herc (Hooch 2011, 13) coined the term "b-boy" as he observed dancers top rocking, floor rocking, popping, locking, freezing, and generally "going off" or "breaking out" at dance parties that were taking place in the South Bronx, New York City, beginning in the latter half of the 1970s. Thus a b-boy or b-girl is a dancer of the kind that has come to be referred to as a break dancer, though this term was not originally used within the scene. African American, Afro-Caribbean, and Puerto Rican young men and women largely innovated this style of dance and accompanying dress. Notably, b-boy is also frequently erroneously decoded as "Bronx boy," "bad boy," and "boogie boy" (Orejuela 2015, 29), though these mistranslations fail to acknowledge the meaning of the "b." As the popularity of b-boying (and to a lesser degree b-girling) grew and knowledge of the style spread beyond the urban nexus in which it originated, the terms "break dancing" and "break dancer" came to be routinely applied in lieu of b-boying and b-boy. B-boying was a key part of the development of what has come to be called hip-hop culture and evolved along with graffiti art (tagging), rapping (also known as emceeing), and deejaying. B-boying was originally a group activity, and b-boys and b-girls formed crews that generally wore matching or coordinated clothes. Early break dancing crews including the Rock Steady Crew, the Bronx Boys, the Zulu Kings, Rockwell Association, and the New York City Breakers were organized gangs or groups that battled each other for bragging rights and turf rights from the middle of the 1970s through the middle of the 1980s. These crews evolved from more typical street gangs that had been a persistent source of violence in impoverished inner-city neighborhoods in the earlier part of the decade. Over time, break dancing evolved into solo performances and with that change apparel styles changed and became less distinctive. Although break dancing is still performed throughout the world today, this entry is largely concerned with the iconic style that emerged and developed from the middle of the 1970s through the middle of the 1980s when this dance style was truly a phenomenon of the street. Notably, this period set the foundation for what has come to be known as hip-hop style, a term that deejay Afrika Bambaata coined in 1982 (Crazy Legs 2011, 8).

The popularity of house parties and the emergence of gang-like dance crews are two phenomena that are related to the sociocultural context of the South Bronx in the era when hip-hop culture first emerged. The Bronx, the northernmost borough of New York City, had long been populous and diverse and a stronghold for working-class families. In 1959 the fabric of the borough was literally ripped apart as the construction of the Cross Bronx Expressway, a large traffic artery that literally split neighborhoods apart, was begun. This construction project combined with the nearby race riots of the middle 1960s led to a mass exodus of middle-class and working-class residents to a new housing development north of New York City called Co-op City. Urban decay ensued. Shuttered businesses, abandoned buildings, and widespread unemployment led to gang violence, drug trafficking, and widespread vandalism, especially arson. In light of the widespread social disruption, social life and nightlife contracted inward, and deejayed parties in recreation centers, apartment complex common rooms, and "50 cent basement parties" (Sommers and Chean 2011, 47) flourished. Seminal deejays including Afrika Bambaata, DJ Kool Herc, Grandmaster Flash, and Casanova Fly (a.k.a. Grandmaster Caz) began to experiment with the creative potential of working with a dual turntable system. Additionally, deejays hired emcees to stir up the crowd; these voices calling out over the music were the progenitors of rap. It was in this context of the house party that break dancing developed. It soon trickled into the streets aided by block parties and the newfound potential of the boom box (a portable stereo system), and by the early

1980s some of the scene had moved downtown to public parks and clubs in Manhattan including The Fun House, Negril, and the Mudd Club. "Grafitti Rock," a show held in 1981 at Common Ground gallery in SoHo, New York City, is often held up as an event of great importance to the spread of early hip-hop art forms beyond their neighborhoods of origin.

The clothes that b-boys and b-girls wore were generally suited to "going off" or "burning" (Hager 2014, 51), as break dancing was originally known, and there was little difference between what was worn by males and females. Head gear such as beanies, bandanas, Kangol caps, "crusher" hats, and tucker caps were worn in part to facilitate head spins but were also stylish gear that was reasonably priced and locally available. Early images show both boys and girls wearing Lee jeans (a popular brand in the 1970s), double-knit pants, or sweatpants. Vibrantly colored nylon tracksuits, which have a slippery surface, became popular in the early 1980s. T-shirts, hooded sweatshirts, and windbreakers were common upper-body garments. Athletic shoes including Converse high-top basketball shoes, Pro Keds, and Puma low-tops were typical footwear. Sneakers and shirts generally matched, and sneakers were customized with paint and permanent markers in order to personalize and coordinate shoes in an era in which the sneaker market was far less developed than it became in the latter half of the 1980s. Many break dancers coordinated their shoelaces to match their outfits, and some break dancers went so far as to change their shoelaces in the middle of a dance party to match the change from a sweat-soaked shirt (Schloss 2009, 79). Shoelaces, an often overlooked accessory, are an example of how early break dancers made minor modifications to basic apparel to give it "flavor" (a colloquial expression for style or personality). Originally, young people, striving to make their sneakers more interesting, took basic white cotton shoelaces and stretched, starched, and ironed them to make them wider. There is also photographic evidence that shoelaces were replaced with ribbons, elastic, and strips of fabric. These inexpensive replacements for the original white, mundane shoelaces represented a way of making sneakers more interesting. Wristbands or bandanas wrapped around wrists were also common accessories, as were gloves, which facilitated floor work.

A distinctive element of the b-boy/b-girl look was crew gear, which usually took the form of a T-shirt. As a way to mark dance-crew membership, mark the importance of the wearer, and "add flavor to the gear," the largely male dancers would customize their apparel using inexpensive iron-on letters to spell out their crew or individual street names such as "Crazy Legs," "Ty Fly," "D. J. Hugo," and "Take One." Iron-on letters were most commonly applied to T-shirts, but they were also affixed to trucker caps, jackets, tote bags, athletic pants, medical scrubs, and martial-arts uniforms. Break-dancing crews ultimately developed the tradition of battling for these crew shirts, with the winner taking the apparel from the loser.

This tradition elevated the use of iron-on letters from the realm of the practical and mundane to the level of chic urban fashion and is another example of self-modification in early break-dancing apparel. As Steven Chean noted about the loss of a crew shirt, "Some losers begged to buy their shirts back, mortified at their name swinging dirty from the butt pocket of a rival" (Sommers and Chean 2011, 48). Putting the names on clothes was a way for dancers to "honor themselves" but was also done because b-boys believed others wanted to know who they were (Schloss 2009, 79).

Most of the apparel worn by early break dancers was inexpensive mass-market merchandise; however, the overall effect was distinctive. The condition and coordination of clothes was important, and while the overall look was one of ease and lack of concern, in reality outfits were carefully thought out (Schloss 2009, 78). Careful attention to color coordination, neatness, and use of accessories, along with accents of self-modification, elevated mundane ready-to-wear to a recognizable and stylish street style. Additionally, choice, quality, and condition of clothes were points of distinction among break dancers. A b-boy known as Trac 2 noted of the break-dancing scene in the 1970s, "Back then, in order for you to determine who was a good b-boy, you would look at his sneakers. If you have [a] brand-new pair of 69 Pro Keds or Chuck Taylor Converse, the canvas part would be ripped on the side from the concrete" (Schloss 2009, 162). Additionally, apparel choices could be used to discern the borough from which one came (Jenkins 2015).

B-boying lost popularity among African American boys circa 1978 (Hager 2014, 92), but crews largely comprised of Puerto Rican immigrants to New York City carried on the style of dance for several years. Break dancing was largely outmoded in the five boroughs by 1986 (Crazy Legs 2011, 8) as the musical genre that inspired the dance was increasingly becoming a recorded, lyrics-oriented rap rather than a live performance by an emcee. However, break dancing experienced a brief period of widespread popularity in the second half of the 1980s as it diffused to the mainstream, due largely to mass-media depictions of the art form.

Various forms of mass media, including print and video, facilitated the transmission of this style from a niche urban group to the masses. For example, on April 22, 1981, the *Village Voice* ran a cover story about break dancing. Documentary films such as *Style Wars* and *Wild Style* (1983), which captured images of rappers, break dancers, and graffiti artists, were also influential. Music videos for Malcolm McLaren's song "Buffalo Gals" (1982) and for "Hey You" by the break-dancing group The Rock Steady Crew (1983) broadcast images that included break dancers in action and deejays scratching records. These images were broadcast to a large young audience on the newly formed cable channel MTV (launched in August 1981). Perhaps the most widely consumed images of b-boys and b-girls were in mainstream feature films including *Beat Street, Breakin',* and *Breakin' II: The*

Electric Boogaloo, which were all released in 1984. Notably, these popular films presented a version of b-boy and b-girl style that was interpreted by costume designers and influenced by newly available commercial products, some of which were made in response to the original street style. Books such as *Breakdancing: Mr. Fresh and the Supreme Rockers Show You How to Do It* and instructional VHS cassettes also helped to spread break dancing by providing images and information to individuals across the United States and around the world. Undoubtedly, as people attempted to master the dance moves, they also interpreted and modified the dress practices.

As break dancing moved into the mainstream, contemporary fashion fads and trends were incorporated into the look. This was undoubtedly the result of mass-media imagery and the fact that a more diverse demographic of participants had greater access to a wider range of commercial products. Among the elements previously unseen in b-boy and b-girl styles were neon hues, painter caps, leg warmers, and apparel with Asian text and motifs. Additionally, manufacturers of fashionable apparel began to interpret the original street style and created new products that became associated with break dancing. For example, simple nylon track pants were transformed into parachute pants, a style of casual trousers that were typically made of ripstop nylon or polished polyester. They were characterized by shiny, slippery fabric but, most importantly, by multiple zippers (often of contrasting colors) that were both functional and decorative and that set them apart from the basic pants that inspired their design. Parachute pants were first retailed in the United States in 1983 at the trendy, upscale mall emporium Merry-Go-Round for the extraordinary price of $50 per pair (Moore 2015, 280). Coordinating waist-length jackets festooned with zippers were also made. The break-dancing scene also inspired apparel with graffiti motifs, which was commonly mass-produced using screen-printing techniques and iron-on decals, though such apparel could also be custom made (often with the use of stock patterns) at kiosks or shops that were frequently located in suburban shopping malls. Graffiti could be applied to virtually any kind of apparel; however, T-shirts and trucker caps were among the most commonly decorated items. Major retailers including Sears and Kmart sold T-shirts with printed designs that looked as if they had been spray-painted (Moore 2015, 188–90). The mass market also picked up the taste for wide, colorful shoelaces, and manufacturers such as Goodtimes Industries and CHOOZ made extensive lines of shoelaces (Moore 2015, 192).

While some aspects of the sartorial style of 1970s and 1980s break dancers has come to be associated specifically with late-20th-century dance-oriented street style and is worn today only as a retro look, other aspects of b-boy and b-girl style have developed into key components of mainstream hip-hop (alternatively referred to as urban) street style. In the 1970s and 1980s individuals who dressed in items such as hoodies, Lee jeans, Kangol caps, and Puma sneakers with wide shoelaces, and who wore these items meticulously coordinated, crisp, and "fresh" but who did not dance, were referred to as fly boys and fly girls. Fly boys and fly girls wore most of the apparel and accessories described in this entry (the notable exception is the crew gear) but accessorized with elements that were not conducive to dancing. For example, girls wore heavy "doorknocker" earrings and dress shoes, both sexes wore nameplate belt buckles, and boys favored Cazal Gazelle–style eyewear. Many of the elements worn by "fly" dressers transcended the middle of the 1980s to become part of the long-lived, constantly evolving street style that will be dealt with separately in the "Hip-Hop" entry in this text.

Break dancing continues to be performed today in both live organized competitions such as the United Kingdom B-boy Championships and the World Popping Battle and in videos that are posted to new media platforms such as You Tube and Facebook. Modern break dancers generally wear contemporary athletic apparel, and branded items are commonplace, although some 21st-century b-boys will adopt a retro look that includes apparel with iron-on letters. This is done as a form of tribute to the roots of the art form (Schloss 2009, 163). Additionally, modern b-boys and b-girls, who typically dance either singly or in pairs, may wear apparel derived from the skate scene, anachronistic ensembles that resemble zoot suits, or apparel inspired by mimes (see the photographs in Hooch 2011). Modern break dancing is done as entertainment and may be competitive, but break-dancing crews battling for turf is a thing of the past. Notably, some aspects of traditional break-dancing style pertaining to both dance and dress are retained among modern African-inspired step dancers.

The modern fashion marketplace specifically reflects break dancing to a small degree. Urban apparel manufacturer Butan presented its collection at the Cape Town fashion week in July of 2011, employing break dancers as models who used the runway as a dance floor. A handful of athletic-apparel companies also cater specifically to modern break dancers. The European website thebboyspot.eu sells apparel by brands like The Legits and Biggest and Baddest, which makes seasonal variations of a shirt with the slogan "B-boy or die."

B-boy and b-girl style is an important and distinct part of the evolution of American urban street style that is intimately linked to this unique and dynamic style of dance. Unfortunately, the exposure of the style in the mass media may have led to caricaturized recollections of the style. As Schloss has noted, "For most people 'breakdancing' belongs somewhere between parachute pants and Rubik's Cubes, a Reagan era fad that lingers only as a punch line." However, it is important to recall that break dancing was and is an important part of hip-hop culture and an innovative expression in dance that was tied to new inroads in musical performance.

As Schloss goes on to remark, "It is a profoundly spiritual discipline, as much a martial art as a dance, as much a vehicle for self-realization as a series of movements" (4). Additionally, the apparel associated with break dancing was used to express group membership, lifestyle, and personal identity both within dance crews and for later participants who danced singly. Thus b-boy and b-girl style is a noteworthy American street style that is part of the rich and diverse fabric of urban American culture.

Further Reading

Breakdancing: Mr. Fresh and the Supreme Rockers Show You How to Do It. 1984. New York: Avon Books.

Cooper, M. 2004. *The Hip-Hop Files.* New York: From Here to Fame.

Crazy Legs. 2011. "Introduction." In *B-Boy Championships: From Bronx to Brixton* by D. J. Hooch, 6–9. London: Virgin Books.

Hager, S. 2014. *Hip Hop.* Wilmington, DE: N.p.

Hooch, D. J. 2011. *B-Boy Championships: From Bronx to Brixton.* London: Virgin Books.

Jenkins, S. 2015. *Fresh Dressed.* United States of America: Distributed by Samuel Goldwyn Films.

Moore, J. 2015. *Fashion Fads through American History: Putting Clothes into Context.* Santa Barbara, CA: ABC-CLIO.

Orejuela, F. 2015. *Rap and Hip Hop Culture.* New York: Oxford University Press.

Romero, E. 2012. *Free Stylin': How Hip Hop Changed the Fashion Industry.* Santa Barbara, CA: Praeger.

Schloss, J. 2009. *Foundation: B-boys, B-girls and Hip-hop Culture in New York.* London: Oxford University Press.

Sommers, J., and S. Chean. 2011. *Hip-hop: A Cultural Odyssey.* Los Angeles: Aria Multimedia Entertainment.

Beat Generation (Late 1940s–Early 1960s)

The Beat Generation, who were also referred to as the Beats, were a loosely unified subcultural group that existed in post–World War II America. Beats varied in age from early adulthood to middle age and were racially and ethnically mixed. Late in the trajectory of the Beats, individuals associated with the subculture were also referred to as "Beatniks"; however, both commentators who were contemporary to the scene as well as academics of later generations have suggested that Beats and Beatniks were actually two separate groups—one defined by values and ideology, the other by a fashionable interpretation of the former's lifestyle. The term

"Beatnik" was a somewhat derogatory term coined by a San Francisco journalist named Herb Caen in the fall of 1957. The word "Beatnik" takes the group's self-ascribed label, "beat," and attaches a suffix associated with the Soviet Union at the time (e.g., Sputnik), thereby insinuating that Beats were Communists or in some general way un-American.

Naming this peer group or subcultural movement the Beat Generation is generally credited to the American writer Jack Kerouac, who seems to have used the terminology as early as 1948, though he did not invent the slang implications of the word "beat." In the 1940s to refer to someone or something as "beat" meant that the person or the thing was run-down, denigrated, defeated, and ultimately beaten; however, in so being, a person who was a Beat was also liberated and unfettered from the expectations of mainstream society. The Beat Generation was, in many ways, a precursor to the hippie subculture of the 1960s and early 1970s. Generally speaking, Beats were dissatisfied with post–World War II American society: its questionable morality, the slavish pursuit of commodity culture, the rush to climb the corporate ladder, the creation of the perfect nuclear family, and its attitudes toward racial segregation. Thus, Beats lived in marginal places that accepted all kinds of people (the slums of the day), experimented with drugs including marijuana and benzedrine, engaged in "free love" and same-sex relationships, and generally eschewed Western religions. An article from 1960 categorized the average Beat as follows: "He is the man who has decided to step off the treadmill of our suburban-split-level-rat-race way of life" (Barbeau 1960, 210).

Perhaps Clellon Holmes, the writer of the Beat novel *Go* (1952), summarized the Beat Generation best in an article for *The New York Times* entitled "This Is the Beat Generation." He wrote that Beats had been "adjusted" by the hardships and horrors of the Great Depression and World War II, that they had experienced humanity as so distressing and disruptive that it gave them an "ability to live at a pace that kills." Unconventional living, engagement in behavior that was considered delinquent (including premarital and interracial sex), extensive use of drugs and alcohol, artistic and literary expression, and love of bebop jazz music were common lifestyle choices among Beats, a lifestyle that is depicted in detail and with an eye for the diversity of experiences in the contemporary account of Larry Lipton entitled *Holy Barbarians* (1959). The literature of Beat writers and the ideology expressed therein is also a touchstone of the Beat Generation's outlook and ideology. Jack Kerouac's *On the Road* (1957) and *Dharma Bums* (1958) offered American readers a view of unfettered, rambling existence as both novels followed characters in their journeys around the United States, journeys that involved exploration of both the landscape and the psyche. Notably, both of these texts were based on the lives of Kerouac and his fellow writers at the nexus of Beat culture.

Allen Ginsberg's poem *Howl* (1956) also depicts a cast of characters who reflected Ginsberg's milieu—artists, poets, novelists, jazz musicians, drug addicts, and psychiatric patients. The poem, which critiques the materialism and conformism of American culture, was ultimately the object of an obscenity trial in 1957 as the poem discusses both drug use and homosexual sex in vivid detail. William Burroughs's *Naked Lunch* (1959), which also dealt extensively with drug use, utilized obscene language, and described sexual encounters between men and with minors was also the object of bans and was widely criticized. What these texts share in common is an unromanticized view of America, depictions that are candid not candied, that feature characters who have been beaten down. Although the literature of this period is held up as a unifying thread for the Beat Generation, it is important to note that some have levied the critique that even the literature fails to be bound by a unifying premise (Fleischmann 1959, 768). Ultimately, there were highly varied interests and lifestyles among the Beats.

While Beat culture is primarily associated with literary output, it was also closely linked with the bebop jazz scene of the late 1940s and 1950s; notably, the personal style of Dizzy Gillespie, who wore thick-rimmed glasses and a beret with a goatee for much of his career, became part of the stereotypical look of the Beats that was perpetuated in the mass media. *Avant garde* theater, including the theater of the absurd, was also a passion shared by many Beats. Dance, including Martha Graham's modern ballet, was admired and influential, and at least one Beat, Carolyn Cassady, trained under Graham. There are similarities between the costumes worn in Graham's ballets of the 1940s and the stereotypical Beat style of the late 1950s. Ballets such as *Hérodiade* (1944) featured simple leotard tops for women in lieu of more traditionally beaded bodices, an incredibly modern choice on the part of costume designer Edythe Gilford, which could easily be translated for the street and was a staple of Beat costume design in films made at the end of the 1950s and early 1960s.

Beat culture was centered in low-rent neighborhoods in New York City (near Columbia University in Harlem and near New York University in Greenwich Village) and in San Francisco and Berkeley, California, (near the University of California–Berkeley campus) and later near Venice Beach in Los Angeles. These locations, which already had clusters of cheap bars and coffee shops, provided the perfect habitus for aspiring writers, artists, and musicians. Some coffee shops, such as Gaslight and Epitome in New York City, attracted cultural luminaries of the day including Joan Baez and Jackson Pollock. Many Beat writers' paths can be traced to such establishments around the United States including The Place in San Francisco and Gas House in Venice Beach.

The original Beat style was truly an antistyle. It was a look born of low wages and indifference toward mainstream sartorial and social standards. Second hand clothes, military surplus, blue jeans, flannel and denim work shirts, sweatshirts, T-shirts, and indigenous dress such as huaraches and other kinds of sandals, peasant blouses, and dirndl skirts composed a style that was not a studied look. To look at photographs of early Beats is to see people who look as if they dressed to cover their bodies and did so on the cheap. Photographs are not readily dated based on the apparel of the subjects as the pieces were often not contemporary or were staple items like T-shirts that change little over time. Accessories of any kind were few and far between, and jewelry was noticeably absent. Makeup for women was generally unnoticeable or not used. Among the most notable sartorial statements made in the late 1940s through the middle of the 1950s were by women who sometimes elected to go braless and also experimented with wearing men's clothes at a time when this was generally considered to be neither appropriate nor fashionable in mainstream dress.

A highly recognizable, stereotypical Beat look emerged in the latter part of the 1950s as the Beat Generation became an increasingly visible and talked-about phenomenon. An article entitled "The Plight of the Beat" noted, "It would be well to point out that—as has happened in all such movements—the pseudos, the hangers-on, the would-be's and the deviates finding a haven under a label far outnumber the producing artists" (Barbeau 1960, 211), and these individuals gravitated toward a uniform to mark their membership. The stereotypical Beat look featured a heavy reliance on black fabrics. Black textiles were especially common for men's stovepipe pants or women's Capri-cut pants. Women also wore long- or short-sleeved dance leotards with low-scooped necklines in combination with thick black stockings. Black turtleneck sweaters were also iconic for both sexes. Black-and-white horizontal stripped T-shirts or sweaters for both men and women also became a standard dress selection, as did berets and dark sunglasses. As noted, some of these choices may be related to public figures who were associated with the Beat scene. Men often wore kerchiefs tied around their necks. Women wore exaggerated liquid eyeliner and black flats or ballet slippers. Shaggy hair and goatee beards were typical for men, whereas women's hair was kept simple and natural and was often styled in a ponytail. An article in *Time* magazine from 1961 entitled "Hipitaph" suggested that journalists had helped to turn the Beat Generation into a "movement" that had stagnated, given that it was "fueled by pot and pretension," an indication that the late stages of Beat culture lacked vision and purpose and became more of a scene for individuals who wanted to be a part of a countercultural "cool" set.

By 1957 Beat had become a commodity. Joyce Johnson (1983), who ran with the inner circle of Beat writers including Kerouac, noted, "People wanted the quick thing, language reduced to slogans, ideas flashed like advertisements, never quite sinking in before the next one came along. 'Beat Generation' sold books, sold black turtleneck sweaters, and bongos, berets, and dark glasses, sold a way of life that seemed like dangerous fun—thus to be either condemned or imitated" (198). "Weekend Beats," hangers-on to the subcultural scene, were given a variety of roadmaps via the mainstream press, including articles in publications ranging from *Mademoiselle* to *The New York Times*. Johnson noted in her memoir *Minor Characters* (the title a reference to the minor role played by female Beats) that in 1957 or 1958 Jack Kerouac observed people imitating some version of him that conveyed "bored indifference," "cultivated inertia," "laconic language," who seemed to have the "uniformity of an army" (160). The codification and commodification of Beat was also manifested in a variety of consumer products, including children's toys. For Christmas 1959 Bergdorf Goodman offered Beatnik dolls wearing bulky sweaters and skinny pants for $20 apiece. The mainstreaming of Beat was also made clear by the existence of the Rent-a-Beatnik service that was opened by a Brooklyn resident named Fred McDarrah in the late 1950s. For $25 and up, a "square" person seeking a true Beatnik experience could rent a hip person for the night (Millstein 1960).

The fashion press promoted the fashionable Beat look. A 1959 article in *Life* magazine, "Real Gone Garb for Fall, Beat but Neat," promoted a polished Beat look for collegiate back-to-school wardrobes. Memoirs from the 1950s acknowledge that the Beat look could be purchased from a vast array of boutiques, such as the Sorcerer's Apprentice in New York City. However, the strongest visual evidence of merchandise exists in the form of mail-order advertisements that ran in the last years of the 1950s and the very beginning of the 1960s. Among the products on offer to help a person achieve the Beatnik look were berets, some in plain black felt and others adorned with embroidered painters' palettes and bongo drums. Eyeglasses with thick rims, that came without prescription lenses, were also advertised as "Beatnik glasses," and false beards made of rayon were available for a few dollars. Advertisements of this kind ran in mainstream publications and appear to be unironic; however, advertisements from the early 1960s for "Beatnik kits" do seem to have been retailed as a gag.

The stereotypical beat was portrayed in films such as *Pull My Daisy* (1955), *Funny Face* (1957), *The Beat Generation* (1959), and *The Subterraneans* (1960). A stereotypical Beat was also depicted on the television show *The Many Loves of Dobie Gillis* (1959–1963). These depictions helped to further cement the stereotypical Beat look and also helped to capture Beat slang, which had developed in part from the argot of the hipster zooties who shared common musical interests. Terms such as "dig," meaning to like, and "tea," as a synonym for marijuana, are terms that are often credited to the Beats; in fact, a Beatnik Dictionary of Swingin' Syllables was published and available by mail order for a single dollar.

The stereotypical Beat look has made its way onto the 21st-century runway. A strong example of a designer's reinvention of Beat style can be found in the fall/winter 2008 collection of Marc Jacobs. Perhaps even more commonplace has been the styling of models in imitation of the Beat look: since the 1960s, models including Brigitte Bardot and Jean Seberg have been photographed in stripped sweaters, dark tights, leotards, and berets, and more recently (October 2013) Taylor Swift posed for *Glamour UK* in a carbon copy of the iconic look of the late 1950s. Retail websites such as Polyvore.com also routinely use Beat as a retailing device, bundling basic pieces of apparel into a photo array that kindles recollections of the Beat Generation.

The original Beat style, which used unstudied, unfashionable apparel as an indicator of outsider status, has enjoyed many reinterpretations over time, including the early hippies in the 1960s and grunge before it became commercialized in the 1990s. The refusal of fashion and rejection of mainstream beauty norms is a technique that will undoubtedly continue to enjoy symbolic power as long as there are standards of correctness and fashionableness in dress. The stereotypical Beat style continues to experience moments of popularity, but the ability of the style to communicate a countercultural stance has been muddied by media saturation and may be misread as a quintessentially European look (French beret, stripped shirt of a Venetian gondolier) rather than a distinctive American street style.

Further Reading

Barbeau, C. C. 1960. "The Plight of the Beat." *America* 104 (7): 210–12.

Burroughs, W. S. 1959. *Naked Lunch.* New York: Grove Press.

DiPrima, D. 1969. *Memoirs of a Beatnik.* New York: Penguin Press.

Fleishmann, W. B. 1959. "Those 'Beat' Writers." *America* 101 (26): 766–68.

Ginsberg, A. 2001. *Howl and Other Poems.* San Francisco: City Lights Publishers.

"Hipitaph." 1961. *Time* 77 (7): 50.

Holmes, C. (1952). "This Is the Beat Generation." *The New York Times,* November 16. Retrieved February 16, 2016, from www.timesmachine.com.

Johnson, J. 1983. *Minor Characters.* New York: Simon & Schuster.

Kerouac, J. 1957. *On the Road.* New York: Penguin Press.

Kerouac, J. 1958. *The Dharma Bums.* New York: Penguin Press.

Lipton, L. 1959. *The Holy Barbarians.* (Kindle version). Retrieved from Amazon.com. Originally published New York: Julian Messner.

Millstein, G. 1960. "Rent a Beatnik and Swing." *The New York Times,* April 17. Retrieved February 16, 2016, from www.timesmachine.com.

"Real Gone Garb for Fall, Beat but Neat." 1959. *Life,* August 3, 48–49.

Welters, L. 2008. "The Beat Generation: Subcultural Style." In *Twentieth Century American Fashion,* edited by L. Welters and P. Cunningham, 145–67. New York: Berg.

Black Panther Party (1966–1982)

The Black Panther Party for Self-Defense (BPP) was a paramilitary coalition of African American men and women that was formed by Huey Newton and Bobby Seale in Oakland, California, on October 16, 1966. Founding members mark the end of the BPP in 1982, coincident with the closing of the Oakland Community School; however, the end date of the party is disputed since the party was not localized. The BPP ultimately grew to include about 5,000 members spread over 28 states (Shames 2006, 138). The founders of the BPP drafted a "Ten Point Program" that outlined many of the social ills and inequalities that they felt needed to be addressed among the poor and racial minorities and created programs that provided social services including food, education, health care, and legal aid. These programs, called "survival programs," were designed to help sustain the communities they served while also preparing them for the struggle and revolution that the party envisioned. Amy Ongiri noted, "The Black Panther Party imagined liberation struggles not merely as the righting of social inequalities, but as a project that would radically reconfigure the cultural, social and political terrain of the United States and the world" (2009, 74). However, clashes with police often overshadowed the efforts of the BPP to address the vast inequalities of a capitalist and racist culture. Notably, the BPP was formed in the wake of the murder of Malcolm X (February 21, 1965) and was ascendant in the aftermath of Doctor Martin Luther King Jr.'s assassination (April 4, 1968), and a guiding notion among party members was that nonviolent protest was an insufficient form of activism. The Black Panther Party was a very visible entity; in addition to their attendance at Panther social programs and their presence performing civic policing, the Black Panthers' paramilitary style of dress, which included openly and (at first legally) carried weapons, made a profound impression on the general public in the 1960s and 1970s, spawning sartorial emulation largely among inner-city youths and evoking fear and disdain from both black and white Americans.

The sartorial style of members of the BPP, especially the style of the men, was incredibly unified and was largely derived from an ensemble that Huey Newton wore by happenstance one day in 1966 (Shames 2006, 11). Although members of the BPP wore commercially available ready-to-wear, their dress style gave the appearance of a uniform. Men wore hip-length black leather jackets with a variety of design details. Some jackets included belts, pockets varied, and a handful of garments included a fur detail on the lapel. Black dress pants were also a standard part of the look and undoubtedly varied with regard to fabric, pleats, creases, and pockets; however, the pants were worn without a turn up or cuff, in keeping with mainstream pants styles of the day. Conversely, bell-bottoms and flares seem to have generally been eschewed, though they were in fashion throughout much of the period. A flamboyant pant would have been in aesthetic opposition to the militaristic style that was otherwise being developed. A blue button-down shirt was the original choice for the uniform, intended by Newton and Seale; however, the photographic record shows that both black and white turtleneck sweaters were worn, as were white button-down shirts. Some images show men wearing, underneath the leather jacket, a gray sweatshirt printed with the party's name and an image of a panther. Footwear varied somewhat but was always black and shiny. Men wore both traditional dress shoes including loafers and lace-ups as well as both fashionable dress boots and work boots. Perhaps the most iconic aspect of the party uniform was the adoption of a wool felt beret. This feature was also developed by Newton and Seale and was inspired by a movie they had seen about the French Resistance during World War II (Shames 2006, 11). It has been suggested that the beret alone became an incredibly powerful icon and that "for many it represented an implicit association with the Panthers" (Ogbar 2004, 118). Men's hair was worn naturally, though the Afro did not seem to have been widely adopted. Again this may be because the Afro did not align with the disciplined aesthetic of this paramilitary look. Men routinely wore circular buttons on both their berets and their jackets. Pins generally related to the party and to social causes, including the release from prison of BPP members. Dark sunglasses often completed the ensemble. An iconic image of Huey Newton was widely reproduced and came to embody both the magnetic power and the alienating potential of BPP imagery. The image featured Newton seated in a large rattan chair, dressed in his Panther garb, with African shields as props, holding a spear in one hand and a gun in the other. This image was frequently used as the subject for apparel buttons.

Women's apparel was far more varied than the ensemble adopted by men. Women wore black leather jackets that were typically cut to just above the knee. Jackets were generally belted, in keeping with mainstream women's outerwear trends. Women also generally wore black skirts and dresses that varied in length from micro-mini to maxi (ankle-length), but women could also be seen in black trousers. Many images show women in turtleneck dresses that mimicked the apparel of the men, but the detailing of both bodices and skirts was as varied as the fashion marketplace. Women typically wore both knee-high dress boots or low-heeled dress shoes, always in black and in conjunction with hosiery. The iconic beret does not seem to have been regularly worn by women, though full, natural hair including the Afro was showcased in the late 1960s and early 1970s. Pins with political slogans, sunglasses, and BPP sweatshirts were also adopted by female party members. Some children of BPP members, especially those who attended BPP community schools, also dressed in uniforms that were very similar to those of their adult counterparts. Finally, especially in Oakland, California, young people who admired the Panthers adopted the uniform and were "indistinguishable" from actual BPP members (Ogbar 2004, 119).

BPP members from the very beginning realized the power of sartorial expression. Bobby Seale noted, "The uniform was an important part of our image. Huey and I understood that good visuals . . . were part of how we could successfully communicate and capture the imagination of the people" (Shames 2006, 11). The members of the party purposefully marked themselves as different from the mainstream at a time when racial markers of skin and hair and facial features were all the subjects of negative stereotypes. In keeping with larger ideas propounded by the "black is beautiful" and "black power" movements, the BPP sought to make these signifiers of race signifiers of pride and power. However, one important and visible difference between the BPP and the broader social milieu of black activism was centered on the wearing of traditional African apparel, which functioned as both an expression of black nationalist interest and black street fashion. Jeffrey Ogbar has noted that Black Panther leaders like Fred Hampton felt that "the popularity of African babas and dashikis did not reflect the radicalism the Black Panthers thought should characterize the movement against oppression" and did not see the African attire as a "real threat" to the power structure (116). Furthermore, Afrocentric imagery of this kind had been co-opted by commercial entities, thereby diffusing its meaning (Ogbar 2004, 198). Thus Black Panthers seem to have eschewed this other, popular form of black self-expression. Some have suggested that the BPP's "brand image" was ultimately detrimental to the party (Ongiri 2009, 82–83) as the paramilitary look, which communicated strength and authority, undoubtedly frightened and intimidated some people.

Positive information about the Black Panthers was spread through their newsletter *The Black Panther: Voice of the Party,* which began as a mimeographed document in the spring of 1967 but evolved into a sophisticated newspaper with caricatures by Emory Douglas. Party members sold the newspaper as part of their membership duties. Imagery and information was also routinely the subject of mainstream newspaper and magazine publications as well as televised broadcasts. The mainstream media were generally far less favorable in depictions that contributed to the negative stereotypes that came to be associated with the BPP, namely that the members were antiwhite racists. The recent documentary *The Black Panthers: Vanguard of the Revolution* (2015) was an effort to provide a more balanced history of the movement.

Perception of party members by blacks and whites alike was highly varied. For some Americans, the signing of the Civil Rights Act of 1968 by President Lyndon Baines Johnson marked the beginning of a new era of promise and equality, whereas others viewed the act as too little too late and interpreted it as a suggestion that blacks should assimilate to white standards. The social and philosophical divisions that existed among Americans with regard to civil rights in general and the BPP in particular was made clear in a study of American newspapers by Brian Thornton and William Cassidy (2008), who have suggested that the Black Panthers received little support from substantial portions of the black population. Their review of black newspaper content demonstrated that while many readers were interested in "black power" and even supported the values of the BPP, they did not support the militaristic and confrontational approach that the Panthers often utilized. Additionally, the authors deduced that Huey Newton's "fierce costume of leather, gloves, sunglasses and weaponry" alienated some people who might have liked the message but were put off by the messengers (16). Ryan Kirby (2011), however, argues, "Support for the Black Panther Party was always larger than its membership suggested" (40), and white radical organizations like the Peace and Freedom Party as well as white celebrities like Jean Seberg, Marlon Brando, and Jean Paul Sartre found lasting appeal in the BPP because of its ability to "promote the empowerment of African Americans while articulating a vision of radical political possibility and change that included refiguring of identity across a broad spectrum of political, gender, and sexual categories" (Ongiri 2009, 70).

By the middle of the 1970s some members of the BPP traded in their paramilitary garb for business apparel, realizing that the best way to overthrow their "overseers" was through political office. Other members were imprisoned, and some were dead. Infighting among group members caused irreparable divisions, and members dispersed to distant places, including Africa. The demise of the party is a subject of contentious debate. Many BPP members have suggested that the Federal Bureau of Investigation, under the leadership of J. Edgar Hoover, purposefully fomented violence and provoked dissension in the ranks, and it has been proved in many accounts that the FBI routinely placed spies within the ranks of the organization (see Shames 2006).

A New Black Panther Party for Self-Defense (NBPP) was formed in 1989 or 1990 (Mulloy 2010, 218) and adopted the paramilitary style of the original Black Panthers, using updated ready-to-wear apparel. The NBPP is best known for organizing four Million Youth Marches between 1998 and 2003; however, it is estimated that the maximum number of participants at any one of these marches was 6,000 individuals (Mulloy 2010, 224). The NBPP uses images of the original BPP on its website but has been largely disavowed by originating members of the Black Panthers including Bobby Seale and David Hilliard (Mulloy 2010, 230). The disavowal largely stems from the fact that the NBPP has been routinely accused of supporting segregation of the races and overthrow of the U.S. government, policies that were never part of the BPP platform.

The sartorial imagery of the Black Panther Party lives on. Perhaps most notably, it was interpreted in the late 1980s and early 1990s by the members of the influential rap group Public Enemy. The members of the band often wore combat boots, camouflage-patterned military pants and jackets, dark sunglasses, and berets while rapping about social injustice. The 2016 Superbowl halftime show, which took place near Oakland, California, featured Beyoncé dressed in a military-inspired black leather jacket and combat boot–inspired footwear and flanked by a team of backup dancers also dressed in black leather, with Afros and berets. This homage to the Black Panther Party was not lost on spectators and was criticized by conservative politicians and members of the media. Additionally, items emblazoned with BPP imagery and text are still available for purchase from retailers like Amazon.com. Sweatshirts, T-shirts, tote bags, and hats of this kind have recently been worn by participants in Black Lives Matter rallies.

The Black Panther Party both united and divided the races, nurtured and disrupted communities, made progress for blacks and other minorities, and curtailed civil-rights advances through their violent actions. The historical record of the BPP is one of many inconsistencies and is open to polarizing interpretations; however, one aspect of the party is clear: the visual imagery created by members of the Black Panther Party had a powerful impact that helped to situate the party as a force to be reckoned with. The physical presence of party members dressed in black leather, berets, and sunglasses incited fear, awe, and admiration; it certainly stirred people up. The Black Panther Party harnessed sartorial language in a provocative way, and that visual language helped to unite a movement and helped facilitate their revolutionary acts. The power of that visual imagery is evident in the fact that it is still employed by individuals in the 21st century.

Further Reading

Alkebulan, P. 2007. *Survival Pending Revolution: The History of the Black Panther Party.* Tuscaloosa: University of Alabama Press.

Baruch, R. M., and P. Jones. 2002. *Black Panthers 1968.* Los Angeles: Greybull Press.

Brown, E. 1992. *A Taste of Power: A Black Woman's Story.* New York: Pantheon.

Cleaver, K., and G. Katsiaficas, eds. 2001. *Liberation, Imagination, and the Black Panther Party: A New Look at the Panthers and Their Legacy.* New York: Routledge.

Foner, P. S. 1970. *The Black Panthers Speak.* Cambridge, MA: Da Capo.

Kirby, R. J. 2011. "The Revolution Will Not Be Televised: Community Activism and the Black Panther Party." *Canadian Review of American Studies* 41 (1): 25–62.

Mulloy, D. J. 2010. "New Panthers, Old Panthers and the Politics of Black Nationalism in the United States." *Patterns of Prejudice* 44 (3): 217–38.

Ogbar, J. 2004. *Black Power: Radical Politics and African American Identity.* Baltimore: The Johns Hopkins University Press.

Ongiri, A. A. 2009. "Prisoner of Love: Affiliation, Sexuality, and the Black Panther Party." *The Journal of African American History* 94 (1): 69–86.

Shakur, A. 1987. *Assata: An Autobiography*. Westport, CT: Hill.

Shames, S. 2006. *The Black Panthers*. New York: Aperture Foundation.

Thornton, S., and W. P. Cassidy. 2008. "Black Newspapers in 1968 Offer Panthers Little Support." *Newspaper Research Journal* 29 (1): 6–20.

Bobby Soxer (Mid-1940s–1950s)

Bobby soxers (also written bobby socksers both with and without a hyphen) was a name derived by American mass media to describe female teenage girls aged about 12 to 17 years. The term was in common usage from the middle of the 1940s through the end of the 1950s. Bobby soxers, named for their short (usually white) cotton socks, were not defined by their adoption of new pieces of apparel or an entirely new mode of dress; in fact, bobby socks had existed since at least the 1930s and had even been worn in that era with saddle shoes and skirts for sports and when the privations of the Great Depression made other kinds of hosiery inaccessible (Schrum 2004, 60). Rather, bobby soxers were categorized and labeled because it was perceived that they embodied a new vision of young femininity, one that was generally frowned upon in the chaotic social context of World War II and in the tradition-oriented postwar period. The press gave special scrutiny to the noteworthy behavior of bobby soxers, which included gathering in large groups, staying out late, dancing in stockinged feet, and engaging in fanatic displays of fandom (shrieking, oohing, fainting, and whimpering) for popular musicians. Bobby soxers were not a unified social group, they were a demographic with shared interests and activities; however, the press routinely used the verbiage "Bobby Socks Brigade" to refer to large groups of teenage girls. The stylistic similarities of bobby soxers are best explained by the strong tendencies toward conformity in fashion in the United States in the 1940s and 1950s, as well as group tendencies among adolescents in general, and are not indicative of a unifying ideology. However, bobby soxers do represent an important sociological shift and a visible street style that emerged from the tumult of World War II.

The war impacted the lives of women by redefining work roles and definitions of femininity. Many women, including teenagers, undertook wartime jobs that gave them greater autonomy and financial independence and in many cases required them to perform tasks previously deemed to be "men's" work. Additionally, many women who had performed traditional matriarchal roles prior to the war worked in capacities during the conflict that left children, including teenage girls, unattended and free to explore the newly emerging teen culture. Wartime definitions of femininity were notably fragmented and in a state of upheaval. The markedly masculinized woman, personified by images like Norman Rockwell's beloved icon *Rosie the Riveter* (1943), competed for the collective national imagination with voluptuous pin-up girls like Rita Hayworth, Eva Gardner, and Veronica Lake. Additionally, the sociocultural context of this period saw the rise of popular young male crooners, most importantly Frank Sinatra, and the emergence of a new kind of fandom characterized by hyperenthusiastic responses from young female fans. The convergence of sociocultural upheaval, popular culture, and the watchful eyes of largely male journalists led to the conception of the bobby soxer, a category of young American female that was both visibly present on American streets and partially constructed by observers and commentators of the period.

The dress of the bobby soxer typically consisted of a snug sweater or blouse paired with a shin-length circle skirt, which after 1949 could be a skirt that included a felt appliqué such as a poodle. Skirts were typically worn over layers of stiff petticoats. Alternatively, the sweater or shirt could be paired with jeans that were cuffed to reveal the lower half of the calf. In both instances, short cotton socks were the hosiery of choice, and they were paired with saddle shoes or loafers. These cotton socks had not previously been referred to as bobby socks, and a 1944 article noted that not even the National Association of Hosiery was sure "exactly what a bobby sock is." Tellingly, this article went on to state that an anklet "becomes a bobby sock only on the retailer's counter and then only in the presence of the purchaser, specifically a teenage 'croon-swooning' adolescent" ("What Is a Bobby Sock?" 1944). The defining feature of a bobby soxer's appearance was the pairing of a casual white sock with a leather shoe and a bare leg. According to a *Life* magazine article, colorful bobby socks had at one point been worn, but by December 1944 "no teenager dares wear anything but pure white sox" ("Teen-Age Girls" 1944, 90). This combination overthrew the accepted conventions of dress of the 1940s; ladylike dress practices of the period permitted cotton socks with trousers, concealed by the pant leg, but silk, cotton, or rayon hosiery that concealed the entire leg was most appropriate with a skirt. When wartime shortages made stockings hard to come by, many American women resorted to using leg makeup to create the illusion of hosiery. Additionally, cuffing the pant leg communicated a subtle antiestablishment sentiment. These small affronts to feminine codes of dress might have passed without controversy in other eras, but the tumult surrounding contemporary womanhood may account for why the sartorial practices of teenage girls of this period raised an alarm.

In addition to wearing cotton socks against bare legs, bobby soxers also sometimes wore men's or boy's clothes, including pajama tops, sweatshirts, plaid shirts, and neckties (Schrum 2004, 97). This crossdressing was unconventional for adolescent girls (unisex clothes existed only for small children) and broke well-established gender norms. Kelley Schrum noted, "Dressing in men's clothing and borrowing or shopping for men's clothes was exciting, a form of rebellion against the prescriptions of femininity. . . . Borrowed clothes also allowed for gender play as girls 'borrowed' or at least imagined themselves having male privileges" (48). Additionally, the wearing of men's apparel may have allowed some bobby soxers to connect with beloved male figures. The wearing of bow ties allowed girls to form a sartorial connection with Frank Sinatra, who wore the ties himself, while the wearing of articles of clothing lifted from the closets of men at war may have allowed young girls to form a bond with boyfriends, brothers, and fathers who were away in service to the military.

A *Life* magazine article (1944) entitled "High School Fashion Fads" indicated that bobby soxers also used dress as a form of nonverbal communication. For example, they wore I.D. bracelets (often in profusion) to communicate their dating histories. Additionally, hair bows were used to communicate interest (or lack thereof) in boys. A bow on the top of the head purportedly meant that the girl was "looking for a man," whereas a bow worn at the back of the head indicated disinterest (70). White ribbons were intended to indicate that a girl had a boyfriend, whereas a yellow ribbon was meant to proclaim a girl to be a "man-hater" (70). Finally, a bow worn on the right side of the face was supposed to communicate that a girl was in love, while a bow worn on the left side of the face was supposed to communicate that a girl was going steady (71). While surely these kinds of coded messages varied from place to place and shifted meaning over time, this contemporary textual evidence suggests shared ideas within a demographic bound by age and sex. Additionally, the *Life* article indicated that bobby soxers were making modifications to existing pieces of apparel. For example, girls were inclined to paint their eyeglass frames with red nail polish (90). Kelley Schrum has noted that cotton bobby socks were sometimes decorated with "gadgets and charms" and that girls "decorated saddle shoes using nail polish, shoe polish, or paint, with everything from pictures of flowers to friends names to favorite songs" (62). Thus, it is clear that bobby soxers worked with dress in the same way that many subcultural groups do.

Although the nuances of bobby soxer dress were reported in a handful of articles, it was not the sartorial innovations of these teenage girls that earned them their sobriquet and the attention of the press. Bobby soxers were conceived of as overly expressive of their emotions and sexuality, and there was widespread concern that they were promiscuous. A key moment in bobby soxer history occurred on October 12, 1944, when Frank Sinatra arrived in New York City to begin a series of performances at the Paramount Theater. An estimated 25,000 teenage girls swarmed into Times Square. Sinatra was blamed for mass truancies as well as for promoting the abandonment of proper decorum. Commissioner George Chatfield of the board of education noted, "We can't tolerate young people making a public display of their emotions" ("Sinatra Fans" 1944). Sinatra was not the only crooner of this time to attract such enthusiastic responses from young female fans. Followers of the singer Robert Mitchum were referred to as the "Bob Mitchum Droolettes" for their purported inability to control their salivation in his presence. Newspaper reports detailed that young teenage girls were also too inclined to please young servicemen on leave. Bobby soxers were thought of as delinquents who could be found in droves in juke joints, bars, and dance halls where they danced the Lindy and the jitterbug in their saddle shoes and cotton socks. In fact, there had been a huge uptick in the number of delinquency cases of young girls in the mid-1940s (Willis 1945, 223), and the police made efforts to round up the wayward teens whose bad behavior was attributed to "war conditions, working parents, neglectful parents, and distaste for school" ("Police Drive" 1944). What is notable is the close connection that was made between the actions and the apparel of these young girls. So maligned were bobby socks and all that they stood for that medical professionals took aim too, suggesting that the wearing of the short cotton socks increased incidences of colds, influenza, pneumonia, and tuberculosis ("Says Bobby Socks Invite Illness" 1945).

While the social context of the 1940s and 1950s is fundamental to the story of bobby soxers, it is also crucial to note that the bobby soxer phenomenon emerged at a time when teens were first being identified as a group with their own social spaces, ideas, and vocabulary. Dress styles, including zoot suits and bobby socks, were identified by some as markers of radicalism and indicators that other dangerous inclinations were afoot (Shaw 1945, 489). A 1944 article published in *The New York Times,* entitled "What Is a Bobby Sock?" noted that "sociologists and defenders of the home are calling meetings" to cope with the problems surrounding teenage femininity. Thus mainstream American culture was primed to exploit radical aspects of teen culture for social commentary. Within a few years, however, the teen set, which had produced so much angst amongst parents and other elders, was seen as a hotbed for commercial gain. An article in *The New York Times* in 1959 noted, "Teen-agers have store buyers and executives all shook up. They are looking at the bobby socks set with a new gleam in their eyes" (Cook 1959). *Seventeen* magazine, which published its first issue in 1949, was especially instrumental in promoting teenage girl culture and facilitating the development of a teen fashion marketplace (Massoni 2006, 40).

Films of the period immortalized bobby soxers' dress practices and the ideas associated with teenage frivolity and sexuality. The 1944 film *Meet Miss Bobby Socks* starring Louise Erickson told the story of a 15-year-old girl who started a fan club in order to win her favorite crooner fame, and of course to win his attention and affection as well. The 1947 film *The Bachelor and the Bobby-Soxer* starred Carey Grant and a young Shirley Temple, a character who was infatuated with Grant, a much-older man. The fact that dolls and other toys, including a marionette, were dressed like and marketed as bobby soxers demonstrated that the bobby soxer aesthetic had become concretized in the imagination of mid-century people ("Week's Best Promotions" 1948).

The bobby soxer phenomenon petered out in the United States by the end of the 1950s as it was replaced by new innovations in youth culture; however, the bobby soxer found new life in the post–World War II Soviet bloc in places such as the Soviet Union and Czechoslovakia. Additionally, a magazine targeting teenagers, designed to bring Western culture to the American zone in Germany and called *Der Bobby Soxer,* was printed beginning in the late 1940s, a further indication of the reach of this youth style and the ideas associated with it.

The bobby soxer aesthetic is frequently revived as a part of 1950s nostalgia. Dancers performing the jitterbug and the Lindy and participating in sock-hop recreations often adopt the look. Television shows such as *Happy Days* (1974–1984), which depicted Midwestern middle America, used the apparel as a standard way to costume teenage girls in the show. Additionally, the individual pieces that made up the bobby soxer aesthetic are routinely made and worn into the 21st century, though the composite look has not regained popularity since the end of the 1950s.

Bobby soxers are a very early example of a recognizable street style that was developed solely among young women. As Tim Snelson noted, "The bobby soxer emerged [at] a time when the conflicting pressures and social upheavals of war provided space for young women to experiment with identity formation in previously unprecedented ways" (2012, 889). Close examination of bobby soxers reveals that their dress practices included coded communications, self-modification, revolt against the gendering of clothes, and refusal of established dress practices. The sartorial practices of the bobby soxers are made all the more noteworthy given the conformist attitudes that pervaded 1950s dress culture. Bobby soxer dress is also historically important as the free-spirited rejection of norms was in essence an embodiment of the fears about teen culture that were expressed by mid-century parenthood.

Further Reading

"Combating the Victory Girl." 1944. *Newsweek,* March 6, 88, 91.

Cook. J. 1959. "Teen-age Fashions Represent a Major Business Today." *The New York Times,* July 6. Retrieved April 4, 2016, from www.timesmachine.nytimes.com.

"High School Fads: The Ever-Changing Fashions and Language of Youth Indicate a Healthy Spirit of Rebellion." 1944. *Life,* May 15, 65–71. Retrieved April 8, 2016, from www .books.google.com.

Massoni, K. 2006. "'Teena Goes to Market': Seventeen Magazine and the Early Construction of the Teen Girl (as) Shopper." *Journal of American Culture* 29 (1): 31–42.

"Police Drive on 'Bobby Socks' Girls Will Curb Teen-age Night Owls." 1944. *The New York Times,* February 15. Retrieved April 4, 2016, from www.timesmachine.nytimes.com.

"Rival for Dinah?" 1947. *Time* 50 (2): 70.

"Says Bobby Socks Invite Illness." 1945. *The New York Times,* February 3. Retrieved April 4, 2016, from www.timesmachine.nytimes.com.

Schrum, K. 2004. *Some Wore Bobby Sox: The Emergence of Teenage Girls' Culture 1920–1945.* New York: Palgrave Macmillan.

Shaw, G. H. 1945. "Let's Do Less for Youth." *America* 73 (25): 489–90.

"Sinatra Fans Pose Two Police Problems and Not the Less Truancy." 1944. *The New York Times,* October 13. Retrieved April 4, 2016, from www.timesmachine.nytimes.com.

Snelson, T. 2012. "From Juke Box Boys to Bobby Sox Brigade." *Cultural Studies* 26 (6): 872–94.

"Teen-age Girls: They Live in a Wonderful World of Their Own." 1944. *Life,* December 11, 91–99. Retrieved April 8, 2016, from www.books.google.com.

"That Old Sweet Song." 1943. *Time* 42 (1): 78.

"Week's Best Promotions." 1948. *The New York Times,* March 21. Retrieved April 4, 2016, from www.timesmachine.nytimes.com.

"What Is a Bobby Sock?" 1944. *The New York Times,* March 5. Retrieved April 4, 2016, from www.timesmachine.nytimes.com.

Willis, R. 1945. "Among the New Words." *American Speech* 20 (3): 223.

Bodybuilder (1940s–Present)

The entry that follows is substantially different from all the other entries in this text in that what makes the dress practices of the bodybuilding subculture unique has markedly less to do with apparel and accessories and infinitely more to do with the modification of the physical body itself. Thus, before embarking on this exploration, it is important to remind the reader that *dressing* is a practice in which we do two separate but equally important things. First, dressing is a process in which we add to the body elements such as shoes and socks, bracelets and watches, pants and shirts. Dressing is also a process in which we make changes to the body. We tattoo skin, paint eyebrows, lacquer nails, tease hair, tan the body, shrink waistlines through diet, and tone muscles through exercise. Bodybuilders have created an art, science, and subculture out of the practice of extreme body modification, and while weightlifting and body training did not develop as forms of bodily discipline exclusively in the United States, a uniquely American bodybuilding subculture and body aesthetic have developed here, while an apparel industry has also emerged as the number of devotees to this pursuit has grown, especially in the last 50 years or so.

Men who lifted heavy weights and performed extreme feats of physical strength were a visible phenomenon and form of entertainment in ancient times and were more recently found in venues like carnival sideshows from the latter half of the 19th century onward. However, these monumental strong men differed from modern bodybuilders with regard to both their *raisons d'être* and their physical appearances. Men who performed feats of strength impressed spectators with their weightlifting abilities, and while large muscle masses were required to do so, these muscles were generally veiled by a natural layer of body fat. Modern bodybuilders, by contrast, do not make a performance of lifting weights (that is a separate discipline with its own athletic goals and rules of competition); rather, the athletic performances of bodybuilders are confined to the acts of posing and flexing. Additionally, modern bodybuilders follow strict regimens of diet and exercise in order to create extreme definition or muscular striation, commonly referred to as "cuts." The marked definition between muscles is then judged in competitions that consider the symmetry of the physique, muscle size, and overall conditioning.

The modern bodybuilding subculture began to develop in the United States around the turn of the 20th century. Early bodybuilders including Al Treloar and Charles Atlas participated in competitions and were captured in photographs and on early films by Thomas Edison. These images show scantily dressed men with broad shoulders, narrow waists, and rippling muscular definition. Into the 1940s bodybuilding was a small, un-unified subculture that had neither a geographical nexus nor shared modes of communication. Before the development of bodybuilding magazines, advertisements promoting bodybuilding products including exercise equipment were typically run in the comic books where impressionable young readers could not miss the connection between the chiseled and broad shouldered superheroes and the promises attached to commercial products. Advertisements encouraged youths to "Stop Being a Dwarf" and queried readers, "Hey Skinny! Are They Laughing at You?" (Merritt 2013). One such reader of these comic books, Joe Weider, impassioned by the pursuit of physical perfection, became an instrumental figure in unifying and shaping bodybuilding culture in the United States.

Weider, known as "The Trainer of Champions," began to reshape American bodybuilding in 1940 when he first published a newsletter called *Your Physique,* using a mimeograph machine. By 1942 he had begun selling weight sets and other exercise equipment. A series of magazines followed throughout the 1950s, 1960s, 1970s, and 1980s. Later publications included *Muscle Power, Muscle Builder, Muscle and Fitness, Flex,* and *Shape,* each of which promoted the notion of happiness and satisfaction through physical fitness. In addition to publishing these influential serials, Weider founded the International Federation of Bodybuilding and Fitness (IFBB) in 1946. This organization has a long track record of promoting physical fitness and hosting competitive bodybuilding events. Notably, it was the launching of the "Mr. Olympia" competition through the IFBB in 1965 that many regard as the advent of the modern bodybuilding era (Merritt 2013) because the IFBB brought organization, communication, and a body ideal together in an event that has grown to have international significance. Weider has also been influential in developing bodybuilding among women. As early as 1979 his muscle magazines printed columns of specific interest to females. Additionally, the "Ms. Olympia" competitions began in 1980, and it was in this decade that *Life* magazine declared bodybuilding the sport of the 1980s.

Weider's many and varied commercial enterprises were undoubtedly influential in spreading bodybuilding culture. In addition to publishing magazines and staging competitions, he also authored numerous books including *Bodybuilding: The Weider Approach* (1981) and *The Weider System of Bodybuilding* (1983), texts that enjoyed mainstream success. Weider also began selling a wide range of commodities with broad appeal. Among the products that came to bear his name were nutritional supplements and meal replacements, exercise apparel, exercise equipment, and videos; "Joe Wieder Antiques" (synthetic bronze sculptures of muscled bodies) rounded out the empire.

The primary method that a bodybuilder uses to build body mass and muscle striation is weightlifting. For decades books and videos have been made to teach the philosophy and technique of renowned bodybuilders. Gyms that cater to bodybuilders also serve as an incubator for techniques and a forum for sharing knowledge. While bodybuilders largely work alone, they may cooperate with one another, encourage one another, and share tips and secrets within the world of the bodybuilding gym. Alan Klein's (1993) years-long survey of bodybuilding gyms in California revealed that, despite the severe health risks, anabolic and androgenic steroids are routinely used to build muscle mass, especially in the world of professional bodybuilders. Additionally, some bodybuilders use synthol, an injectable liquid that is described as a "site enhancement oil."

Apparel for bodybuilders includes workout clothes, posing suits for competitions, and street apparel. Workout gear for bodybuilders has changed modestly over the decades, responding to both fashion and technical advances in athletic-apparel fabrics. In the 1970s athletic apparel was not as fashion forward nor as diversified by sport as it came to be in the 1980s and beyond. Workout clothes in the 1970s were largely made of cotton jersey or lightweight nylon. Pants were loose, shorts were short, and logos were small. In the 1980s, in response to an exercise craze that impacted a wide variety of sports from distance running to cycling and mountain climbing, athletic-apparel makers responded to the unprecedented number of participants in sports by creating colorful, oftentimes sport-specific garb. Bodybuilding apparel of the 1980s typically included spandex shorts resembling cycling shorts (but without the padded seat, and made in bright colors and bold patterns) for both men and women who paired them with low-cut tank tops (and sports bras for women), thick, ruched socks, and high-top sneakers. Women also wore body suits over their spandex shorts. These pieces of workout apparel were still in use in the 1990s, but low-cut unitards with slender straps became common for men and women, and women began to wear thongs over the spandex shorts that composed the lower half. These unitards were not widely worn for other sports. These workout-apparel staples continue to be used into the 21st century, with color, pattern, and logo sizes responding to fashion trends. Fingerless gloves, headbands, wristbands, and leather or nylon support belts complete the ensembles for working out.

Posing suits, which are worn in bodybuilding competitions, have also changed little over time. The outfits generally consist of string-bikini bottoms for both men and women, which are cut high and narrow on the hip. Women's posing suits include a string-bikini top. Colors and fabrics are the elements of posing suits that are most susceptible to change over time. Wet-look fabric and neon colors are among some of the trends that came and went in posing suits. Posing suits are made by specialty companies including Titan and Andreas Cahling and were originally available predominantly through mail order.

Leisure clothes for bodybuilders generally follow fashion trends; however, many male bodybuilders rely on "big and tall" companies for tailored apparel like dress shirts and trousers. Some male bodybuilders also rely on custom order or custom modification of clothing, as pleats and darts are sometimes required to make tailored clothes fit the bodybuilder's enormous proportions. Leisurewear for men has routinely included loose-fitting pants and tight T-shirts that reveal the sculpted physique. Leisurewear for women, at least since the 1990s, is far less problematic with regard to fit given the large percentage of women's apparel made of stretch fabrics.

The mass appeal of bodybuilding that developed through the 1970s had created a substantial marketplace for apparel by the 1980s. Among the types of clothes on offer were inspiration T-shirts with slogans like "If It Hurts It Works" and "Steel Worker" as well as T-shirts adorned with innuendo-laced slogans like "Bodybuilders Pump Harder" and "Female Bodybuilders Like Being Pumped." Shirts of this kind were generally available through mail order. T-shirts, sweatshirts, sweatpants, socks, gym bags, and baseball caps for men and women adorned with the name and logo of famous gyms like Gold's Gym and World Gym were also heavily promoted beginning in the 1980s, and copycat products from lesser-known outfits including Powerhouse Gym, Zinn's Gym, and Manion's Gym appeared in the marketplace soon thereafter. Apparel branded with the name and likeness of a celebrity bodybuilder was also a phenomenon in the 1980s. Arnold Schwarzenegger, Lou Ferrigno, and Boyer Cole were among the professional bodybuilders who had a footprint in the apparel industry. A boom in the production of branded bodybuilding apparel was in evidence in muscle magazines published in the 1990s. Companies including California Crazee Wear, World Class Muscle, and Perfetto offered workout gear, while NPC (National Physique Committee) Active Wear offered branded street clothes. Perhaps the most broadly influential and widely adopted form of bodybuilding apparel is a style of pants known as Zubaz. First offered in 1988, Zubaz are loose-fitting pants made of gaudily printed polyester/cotton fabric. These pants, which were designed by two bodybuilders, were widely worn both within and outside the bodybuilding community in the early 1990s. Specialty shoes including the Otomic bodybuilding shoe, which was marketed as the first of its kind to offer a full range of motion during weightlifting, was advertised in *Muscle and Fitness* in the 1990s.

The dress of the modern bodybuilder also relates to grooming. Tanning is important to many bodybuilders and is a standard in the competition circuit. Tanning beds, ingestible tanning supplements made of a substance called Canthaxinthin, and instant competition tans (also known as contest coloring) have all been used by bodybuilders. Instant tans have evolved most dramatically over time from self-applied products with brand names like Dyoderm and Tan Now! to professionally applied spray tans. Waxing and electrolysis are also important to bodybuilders who usually oil their skin for competitions. Many bodybuilders also dye their hair; bleached blond has long been a widespread choice within the subculture. Bodybuilding magazines also show the efforts of cosmetic and fragrance manufacturers to market directly to this group. Advertisements for fragrances promising instant seduction were commonplace throughout the 1980s and 1990s, including scents called Physique for Men and Potent 8.

The bodybuilding subculture has been promoted to the mainstream through ticketed competitions including Mr. Universe, Mr. America, and small, regional IFBB competitions. Films have also been influential in promoting bodybuilding. Early films include *Pumping Iron* (1977) and *Pumping Iron II: The Women* (1985). *Conan the Barbarian* (1982) starring Arnold Schwarzenegger and the television show *The Incredible Hulk* (1978–1982) starring Lou Ferrigno featured world-class bodybuilders as the stars and thereby also helped promote the sport. Notably, the high point in the popularity of bodybuilding overlapped with the immense popularity of the World Wrestling Federation (WWF) in the late 1980s and early 1990s. Many of the performers in the WWF are not truly wrestlers and manifest a body type that is similar to the ideal represented in the sport of bodybuilding.

For some people the allure of bodybuilding is strong. Bodybuilding offers individuals the promise of transformation, a vehicle to develop self-reliance, and a community through which one can ascend the hierarchy by increasing one's body proportions. Success can be physically measured and can be attained through a fixed set of practices. Additionally, the training, dietary discipline, and culture of secrecy surrounding steroid use work together to create subcultural bonds despite the fact that the sport itself is almost entirely individualized. Bodybuilders suffer greatly for what they deem to be physical perfection. Anthropologist Alan M. Klein has offered a critical read of the inner workings of the bodybuilding subculture. Klein has described the subculture (he was particularly focused on the epicenter of the bodybuilding world in Venice and Santa Monica, California) as "arrogant" and "insular" and has noted that the appearance of health is important but that the use of steroids, starvation, and dehydration belies any commitment to real physical health (1987, 119, 128). Klein has further suggested that male bodybuilders devote themselves to creating "the appearance of hegemonic masculinity with nothing behind it" (1993, 18). By this Klein suggests that male bodybuilders obsessively strive to create a body with masculine features that are regarded as indicators of male power and dominance the world over (1993, 16), yet Klein suggests that bodybuilders have little to back up the claim to hypermasculinity. Rather, he suggests that many bodybuilders are really just self-indulgent followers of a practice designed to help American men manage their inferiority complexes (1993, 38). Klein's interpretation of women's bodybuilding subculture is somewhat more favorable. Klein has pointed out that the emergence of women's bodybuilding coincided with the wider impact of feminism and "exploded myths of female inferiority" (1985, 69). However, Klein asserts that many bodybuilders suffer from poor body image and "neurotic conflict" between their real and ideal selves (1985, 71).

Participation in the bodybuilding subculture, like participation in any subculture, exists along a spectrum, and Klein's interpretation of the meanings and motivations inherent among bodybuilders were based on core or die-hard practitioners of the sport. Certainly among American bodybuilders a great deal of variety exists in terms of practices, physical appearance, motivations, and goals. In the early 21st century the world of bodybuilding continues to flourish but is less visible and influential than it was in the 1980s and 1990s. However, given the cyclical nature of fashions and the propensity in modern American culture to sample from historical and subcultural styles, it is perhaps only a matter of time before bodybuilding once again takes hold in the mainstream and finds expression in American popular culture, sport, and dress practices.

Further Reading

Klein, A. 1985. "Pumping Iron." *Society,* September/October, 68–75.
Klein, A. 1987. "Fear and Loathing in Southern California: Narcissism and Fascism in Bodybuilding Subculture." *The Journal of Psychoanalytical Anthropology* 10 (2): 117–37.

Klein, A. 1993. *Little Big Men: Bodybuilding Subculture and Gender Construction.* Albany: State University of New York Press.

Merritt, G. 2013. "The Life of Joe Weider—The Man Who Transformed Bodybuilding and Fitness." *Joe Weider's Muscle and Fitness,* April, 108–25.

Burning Man (1994–Present)

Burning Man is the name of a weeklong annual event that takes place in the desolate and arid Black Rock Desert in Nevada, about three hours north of Reno. The event has evolved dramatically over time. It began in 1986 as a rather spontaneous and intimate gathering of about 20 people who came together to ritually burn a wooden man on a summer evening on Baker Beach in San Francisco. The allure of the ritual burning of the man was such that by 1990 police curtailed the celebration, and organizers made the decision to relocate the event to Nevada where the crowd of revelers and the burning effigy would not draw the attention of local law enforcement. Early Burning Man festivals were far less organized and elaborate than the current incarnation. It was not until 1994 that the tradition of dressing in a site-specific manner began. In the second decade of the 21st century Burning Man manifests itself as a weeklong pilgrimage, devoid of corporate sponsorship, branding, and almost all cash exchange. Burning Man is now an event that includes art installations, performances, theme camps, mutant cars, drumming, dancing, self-mutilation in the tradition of modern primitives, and myriad forms of cultural exchange. The roughly 70,000 "burners" who attend the clothing-optional event often adopt pseudonyms (called "playanyms") and typically dress in wildly diverse ensembles that generally play with conventions of propriety, modesty, and gender, a gesture that indicates they have left the "default world" (the regular world that most people live in) and its sartorial codes behind.

What began as a simple act of catharsis, the burning of a wooden effigy of a man, has evolved into a subcultural phenomenon, a belief system, and a temporary society. Every year participants in the Burning Man festival erect a temporary city, known as Black Rock City. Streets are planned in concentric circles and named according to the annual theme, public places are set aside, a massive wooden man decorated with neon lights is constructed, and legions of participants arrive with the supplies they will need to survive their stay in the otherwise uninhabitable desert. Geographers Kerry Rohrmeier and Paul Starrs have noted that Black Rock City is designed with utopian principles that can be linked to Hygeia, the legendary city of Atlantis, and Ebenezer Howard's garden-city concept. Interestingly though, this utopia is constructed "where there are eddies of the alien or echoes of an apocalypse" in the natural landscape (Rohrmeier and Starrs 2014, 160). Residents of Black Rock City are expected to abide by the 10 principles of the event, which include abstention from traditional market culture by participating in a society that works communally and exchanges assets like food and drink through gifting. Burning Man participants are encouraged to actively engage with the community of burners, behave inclusively and responsibly, and "leave no trace" on the landscape. Perhaps most important to the dress practices of Burning Man is the principle of "radical self-expression," which manifests itself in the unconventional, unique, and imaginative assemblages that attendees create and wear.

As noted, the outrageous dress practices did not exist during the first few seasons of Burning Man. Dr. Lizard, one of the original participants in the burning ritual, recalled that in the early days people showed up at the event in camping clothes and occasionally took the opportunity to be nude or to wear something that they would not have worn in their regular workaday lives. Dr. Lizard further noted that individuals dressed in black tie for the preburn cocktail party. It was in 1993 that the catalyst for dressing outrageously occurred. He noted, "From one side of the circle, arm-in-arm, a troupe of fully decked-out and frocked-up drag queens from San Francisco came sauntering up to the party. . . . They had pulled out all the stops. Velvet corsets, fishnets, enough make-up to embarrass Mary Kay herself." Dr. Lizard went on to describe vibrant colors and textures, gaudy combinations, and fabulous apparel. He recalled, "In the glow of the sun-streaked sky their outfits were positively stunning. . . . This purely gratuitous display of ostentation became the modus operandi of the entire community" (Dr. Lizard 2003). By the following season, most Burning Man participants came to the revel dressed in costumes.

Dress at Burning Man has become part of a transformative experience that is shaped by a variety of factors: geographical, cultural, and personal. The desert landscape, referred to by burners as "the playa," is inhospitable. Temperatures soar past 100 degrees, and winds exceed 60 miles per hour. This inhospitable climate necessitates certain kinds of sartorial adaptations. Protective eyewear including sunglasses and goggles are a necessity adopted in countless forms and variations including eyeglass frames in vibrant hues or with bedazzled three-dimensional features and goggles derived from adventure sports or reflecting steampunk tastes for retrofuturistic, postapocalyptic flourishes. Burners protect themselves from the sun with headwear that ranges from typical baseball caps and broad-brimmed hats to anachronistic children's winter hats shaped like animals, to rubber masks gleaned from masquerade costumes, to fully fashioned headdresses crafted from materials like feathers and faux fur. Bandanas and scarves of all kinds are wrapped around the head and over nose and mouth in a variety of ways that are both practical and creative.

The hot climate also inspires many burners to dress minimally. While full nudity is seen, it is perhaps more common to find a burner half-dressed. Some men may wear a T-shirt and shoes but no pants or underwear, a choice that reverses the custom of appropriate beach attire. Leather chaps and tutus are worn without the requisite pants or panties underneath, leaving bare buttocks exposed. Bikini bathing suits are common among women, but bikini tops may be paired with pants, skirts, or shorts, and the top is often discarded. Lingerie is also worn as outerwear, and it is common for men to wear lacy foundations that were clearly designed for women. Bare skin is often decorated with body paint, and minimally dressed individuals may wear colorful wigs, beads, wings, or jester hats. The ways in which Burning Man apparel may be combined is as diverse as the participants in the festival.

Much of the clothing worn at Burning Man is typical mainstream ready-to-wear, but the ways in which the pieces are worn create visual impact. Items are frequently sourced from thrift stores, and dated, anachronistic apparel is assembled into curious juxtapositions. Clothes made with distinctive ethnic textiles (or fabrics that have the appearance of traditional fabrics) are also a common element and are similarly worn in unexpected combinations. Camping clothes, Tevas or other sports shoes, and functional carryalls like fanny packs are worn because of their practicality and durability but are typically combined in clashing, jarring, or traditionally unfashionable ways, such as pairing Tevas with black socks.

Handmade clothes that break in some way with conventional modes of dress—such as using fabrics like faux fur in an unconventional way or using multiple neon hues or psychedelic patterns in a single garment—are frequently seen. Pieces of masquerade costumes, including tails, ears, feet, and masks, are worn in combination with many of the aforementioned pieces of typical apparel. LED lights and electroluminescent wires are also often incorporated into clothes, many of which are handmade. Many aspects of Burning Man attire overlap in aesthetics and intentions with the sartorial practices of rave club culture.

Breaking with sartorial convention is perhaps most vividly expressed at Burning Man through choices that play with gender. While women largely challenge the notions of propriety by revealing the body in a way that flaunts taboos, men, as revealed in a scholarly study, "use their appearance . . . to draw attention to the absurdity of masculine norms and their underpinnings" (Kaiser and Green 2011, 9). Within the special confines of Burning Man, men can "visibly question hegemonic masculinity" (7). Wearing women's lingerie, makeup, and wigs are examples of the kind of gender bending that is common, and it has been argued that this is not crossdressing because the men largely utilize exaggerated or clichéd feminine tropes (12). Challenging norms, radically expressing oneself, and breaking conventions of all kinds through dress practices are fundamental to the Burning Man experience and are an accepted part of the culture.

In addition to the individual sartorial choices made by Burning Man participants, dress is also informed by a handful of theme camps. Theme camps, which are residential sections of Black Rock City that are organized around an idea, constitute more than a third of the camping site. Some of these camps are devoted to providing costumes and other apparel. Kostume Kult (a fixture since 2008) gives away hundreds of pounds of costumes that have been donated by New York City costume rental shops. The Black Rock Boutique, a theme camp with Portland roots, provides free clothes of all kinds, whereas the Panty Camp, which includes a tent made out of underpants, gives away hundreds of pairs of panties over the course of the festival. The presence of these theme camps is further evidence of the importance of radical dress practices at Burning Man as well as evidence of the spirit of communality that is fundamental to the festival experience.

Outside of the boundaries of Black Rock City a vibrant commercial landscape exists to prepare burners for their week of self-sufficiency. Although many participants meticulously source wardrobes from secondhand stores or carefully craft their apparel by hand, complete costumes can also be purchased from specialty stores like Screaming Mimi's in New York City or Piedmont Boutique and Praxis in San Francisco. In specialty boutiques of this kind, "high-roller" customers have been tracked spending thousands of dollars for Burning Man apparel dating back to at least 2008 (Williams 2013; Schreiber 2013). Retailers like Screaming Mimi's, recognizing this specific consumer trend, have made a point of stocking inventory based on the upcoming Burning Man theme and have paid attention to Burning Man restrictions on materials like glitter, sequins, and feathers, items that had at one point been determined to be M.O.O.P. (matter out of place) and therefore forbidden (Schreiber 2013). As a side note, feathers and certain kinds of glitter fabrics were later determined to be an acceptable element in dress and are now widely used. Much like cosplay culture, Burning Man benefits a wide variety of apparel-related industries. Online retailers like Etsy feature products tagged for Burning Man, and ecommerce websites like PlayaCracks.com cater to burners. Notably, all these cash exchanges take place outside of the actual event, and the purchase of custom-made products or fully executed costumes is a point of contention among some burners who view the purchase of prefabricated Burning Man outfits as a departure from the "radically self-reliant" dictate that is integral to the festival.

For self-proclaimed burners, Burning Man is more than just a week of camping in the desert and wearing unusual apparel. Stuart Mangrum, writing for the *Burning Man Newsletter* in 1994, noted, "Burning Man is one of the last places on Earth where people from all walks of life, all social strata, and all points of the compass can come together and share a common and primal experience, surviving as a group in a challenging environment, creating a temporary culture of their own design and sharing one of the most elemental experiences of our species, the awesome mystery of fire" (Timeline). For many participants, Black Rock City is like a "gated utopia," and the trip to the temporary city is a "secular pilgrimage from everyday life" (Rohrmeier and Bassett 2014). In fact, some individuals find Burning Man to be a transformative experience on par with those transcendent experiences sought within organized religions (Feldman 2013). Some have gone so far as to say that Burning Man "provides a religious or spiritual function as a substitute for mainstream religious institutions" (Morehead 2009, 20), and there is evidence that followers of mainstream religions use Burning Man as a way to proselytize and reach individuals who are deemed to be at an optimal point for awakening while they are at the festival (Wyman 2012).

Conceiving of Burning Man as a locus of spiritual revelation attributes a great deal of power to this temporary city in a Nevada desert. Consumer scientist Robert Kozinets (2002) has applied an understanding of marketplace logic to explain the transformative power of Burning Man. He argues that the rise of industrialization and the development of a postindustrial social milieu have created "self-interested logics" in the market that "have filtered into communal relations" and have undermined "the realization of the caring, sharing, communal ideal" (22). Thus if the capitalist, commodity-oriented consumer society robs individuals of these nurturing influences, then Burning Man, which suppresses the effects of the marketplace, is therefore positioned as a special kind of marketplace in which consumption is "expressive, voluntary, genuine, and creative" (25). Kozinets argues that the temporary emancipation from modern consumer society creates a "personally enriching youtopia—a good place for me to be myself and you to be yourself together" (36). Regardless of the theory or logic that is applied to the powerful allure of Burning Man, there is clear evidence, provided in part by dress practices, that Burning Man is, for many people, a deeply meaningful and potentially transformative experience.

The Burning Man festival is also criticized by some people who have watched its growth and development over the past three decades. The presence of rich European socialites (Norwich 2006, 392) who fly in for a day or two of debauchery and of Silicon Valley businesspeople who use the event as a networking party led a *New York Times* reporter to comment that "lately it [Burning Man] feels like a dusty alternative to Davos" (Williams 2013), a reference to a city in Switzerland known for high-stakes business transactions. The packaging of the Burning Man festival experience by tour groups, many of which provide all the food and gourmet chefs to prepare it, electrical generators (which may power air-conditioning units), wildly decorated bicycles, and wardrobes filled with costumes, as well as the development of closed camps and a "Billionaire's Row," have led some to question whether the core values of Burning Man are still intact (Gillette 2015, 60). Notably, one of the values, "radical self reliance," is compromised when individuals spend $16,500 per person to stay in a camp that provides an experience "like staying in a pop-up W Hotel" (Gillette 2015, 60). Arguably, selecting one's Burning Man apparel from a curated closet also calls into question whether the act of donning those clothes is truly an act of radical self-expression.

For those who lack the time, money, or daring to attend the Burning Man festival, a wide array of documentary movies can help to recreate some of the experience. Documentary titles include *Burning Man: Beyond Blackrock* (2005), *Dust & Illusions* (2009), *Spark: A Burning Man Story* (2013), and *Taking My Parents to Burning Man* (2014). The festival has also been documented in numerous lavishly illustrated books including *Burning Book: A Visual History of Burning Man* (2007), *Desert to Dream: A Dozen Years of Burning Man Photography* (2011), and *Burning Man: Art on Fire* (2014). Burning Man culture also has a visible presence on the Internet. The blog burners.me is a conduit for sharing and debating burner culture. The official Burning Man website also hosts ePLAYA, a discussion board through which burners can share ideas. Additionally, individual theme camps maintain an Internet presence. Among the camps that do so is the apparel-related camp previously discussed, kostumecult.com, while the Black Rock Boutique and the Panty Camp maintain social-media presences.

Over the years the Burning Man festival has evolved to become more than just a week-long event. It is now a year-round culture that is celebrated through social media and at regional "burns," smaller versions of Burning Man that take place throughout the world. Additionally, it has been suggested that Burning Man "transcends the event to travel with its desert denizens out into the real world" (Rodriguez 2014) by shaping their values and worldview and even making them more comfortable expressing themselves (Nir 2015). Burners unite around their shared interest in Burning Man and socialize, fundraise, and do community-service projects. Burners make art and films outside of the confines of the festival and use their Burning Man identity as a public-relations technique and as a way to grow a commercial enterprise. Research by Kaiser and Green has found that there is a carryover of Burning Man dress practices into the "default world" (2011, 18). They noted of the male participants whom they studied, "They ultimately began to push individual and collective understandings of 'normal' masculine style to new frontiers" (20). These observations, derived from doing on-site analysis and follow-up visits with Burning Man participants, point to the notion that burners may have evolved into a subculture and as such may ultimately have the ability to impact the dress practices of a wider populace.

Further Reading

Dr. Lizard. 2003. "Why People Dress Funny at Burning Man." October 17. Retrieved June 9, 2016, from www.burningman.com.

Feldman, R. H. 2013. "Sleeping in the Dust at Burning Man." *Tikkun* 28 (3): 17–20.

Gass, L. 2008. "Radical Self-Expression: The Costumes of Burning Man." *Fiberarts* 34 (4): 34–39.

Gillette, F. 2015. "Occupy Burning Man." *Bloomberg Businessweek* (4414): 60–63.

Johnson, F. 2012. "Burning Man, Desire, and the Culture of Empire." *Tikkun* 27 (3): 20–63.

Kaiser, S., and D. Green. 2011. "From Ephemeral to Everyday: Costuming Negotiations of Masculine Identities at the Burning Man Project." *Dress* 37: 1–22.

Kozinets, R. V. 2002. "Can Consumers Escape the Market? Emancipatory Illuminations from Burning Man." *Journal of Consumer Research* 29 (1): 20–38.

Marks, J. 1997. "Burning Man Meets Capitalism." *U.S. News & World Report* 123: 46–47.

Morehead, J. W. 2009. "Burning Man Festival an Alternative Interpretive Analysis. *Sacred Tribes Journal* 4 (1): 19–41.

Nir, S. M. 2015. "Burning Man's Fashion Is Wild, but There Are Rules." *The New York Times,* August 21. Retrieved June 12, 2016, from www.nytimes.com.

Norwich, W. 2006. "Features: Euroflash!" *Vogue* 196 (December 1): 390–97, 423, 424. Retrieved May 25, 2016, from http://search.proquest.com/docview/879325741?accountid=130772.

Rodriguez, M. G. 2014. "'Long Gone Hippies in the Desert': Counterculture and 'Radical Self-Reliance' at Burning Man." *M/C Journal* 17 (6): 1.

Rohrmeier, K., and S. Bassett. 2014. "Planning Burning Man: The Black Rock City Mirage." *California Geographer* 54: 23–46.

Rohrmeier, K., and P. F. Starrs. 2014. "The Paradoxical Black Rock City: All Cities Are Mad." *Geographical Review* 104 (2): 153–73.

Schreiber, A. 2013. "Wall Street Guys Are Dropping $1500 for Burning Man Costumes at Screaming Mimis." *Paper Magazine,* August 27. Retrieved June 12, 2016, from www.papermag.com.

"Timeline." Retrieved June 9, 2017, from www.burningman.com.

Williams, A. 2013. "Running on Fumes." *The New York Times,* September 6. Retrieved June 12, 2016, from www.nytimes.com.

Wyman, P. 2012. "Finding Jesus at Burning Man." *Christianity Today* 56 (7): 52–56.

Cholo (1950s–Present)

The word "cholo" is a centuries-old term that referred originally to Latin American Indians who had become partially acculturated to Hispanic customs in the colonial and postcolonial periods (Vigil 1988, 3). Over time the term came to refer specifically to marginalized Latino populations, especially immigrants from Mexico who came to reside in regions of the United States, especially southern California. In contemporary parlance cholo refers generally to a street style that is adopted pre-dominantly by young Mexican American men and women, who are referred to as cholos and cholas, respectively. The label, which can refer to speech, dress, and other customs or habits, is now frequently adopted with pride (Vigil 1990, 117). Some Mexican immigrants, who have historically been marginalized both socially and economically, and who have been relegated to what J. D. Vigil calls a "persis-tent underclass" (1988, 5), have adopted this style as a means of sociocultural bonding among peers, and in that context cholo style is strictly a culturally based street style. Additionally, some people who identify as cholos and cholas are mem-bers of organized street gangs; thus cholo style is also sometimes a gang style. Among cholos who are gang members, the adoption of specific colored pieces of apparel such as a bandana and the acquisition of tattoos are often part of initiation into the gang (Sanders 1994, 49). A discernible cholo style emerged in the wake of World War II, "around the same time that the group [Mexican Americans] was recognized as a problem source" (Vigil 1988, 110), and has remained fairly consis-tent over the decades. Socioculturally, cholos are related to the Hispanic zoot suit-ers (Pachucos) of the 1930s and 1940s, although their dress styles do not share a visual correlation.

Cholo style is largely unisex and is composed of elements of basic, inexpen-sive, durable, and interchangeable pieces of ready-to-wear apparel. Oversized work pants or khakis made by companies such as Ben Davis (the "Gorilla Cut" is preferred), Dyse, and Dickies ("Double Knee" line) are standard, and a preference for them is likely derived from the regulation apparel worn by servicemen return-ing from World War II and Korea. Baggy jeans, sometimes referred to as "county jeans," derive their aesthetics and nomenclature from prison culture (Vigil 1988, 32). Since the 1990s trousers may be worn sagging to reveal the waistband of underwear, an aesthetic that is linked to both skate and hip-hop dress practices. Cross-pollination with the California skate scene and gangster rap are perceptible in cholo style as these subcultural groups move through many of the same social spaces. Pants are often worn long in the leg so that the cuff covers the heel of the shoe. Three-quarter-length pants of the same oversized proportions, makers, and fabric types were popularized beginning in the 1990s. These kinds of pants are typically paired with a white undershirt or tank top and an oversized work shirt, short-sleeved plaid shirt, or Pendleton wool shirt. It is important to note that these basic apparel components are maintained in fine condition with a crisp crease usu-ally set in the pants and white clothes kept pristine. Shirts, while worn untucked, are typically buttoned high, collars are buttoned down, and the body of the shirt is creased with three lines in the back and one on each side of the front of the shirt (Reynolds 2014, 140). Alternatively, the shirt may be worn so that only the top but-ton is fastened and the remainder of the shirt falls open to reveal the white undergarment beneath it. Baseball, football, and basketball jerseys (especially from the Los Angeles Dodgers and Oakland Raiders) are also worn. White knee socks are typically worn with work boots, Hush Puppies, deck shoes ("winos"), or colorful sneakers from a popular brand like Air Jordan, but black dress shoes with tapered toes such as Imperials, Florsheim French toes, or Stacy Adams shoes are worn for special occasions (Reynolds 2014, 140). A bandana, which might indicate gang affiliation by its color, is characteristically worn folded flat across the front of the head. Alternatively, a beanie or watch cap may be worn as a standard head covering. Fine line tattoos are common, and they often feature a nickname, gang name, or neighborhood name executed in a Gothic script, a stylistic feature that recalls the lettering used for official proclamations in colonial Mexico (Dery 2005, 90). The phrase "*la vida loca*" (the crazy life) is also a common subject for a tattoo and is sometimes represented on the hand as a triangle with three dots, one dot representing each word (Covey 2003, 49). Spider webs, religious icons, teardrops, and laughing or crying clowns are also common subject matter for tattoos. From the 1980s onward, men generally have worn their hair short or shaved, but some men opt for a retro look that includes slicked-back hair, and they may elect to wear a hair net over it. This stylistic choice may again be a reference to prison culture or menial labor.

Women who identify as cholas generally wear the same pants, shirts, shoes, and accessories as their male counterparts. A main difference in their apparel is that cholas may wear a tight white tank top or crop top with suspenders stretched snugly over the breasts in lieu of or underneath a baggy, figure-concealing work shirt. The grooming techniques of cholas also set them dramatically apart from their male counterparts as well as from women who do not identify as cholas. Cholas generally wear dramatic makeup that includes plucking the eyebrows and then drawing semicircular arcs in their place. White eye shadow, black mascara, liquid eyeliner, and false eyelashes are used to complete the pronounced eye makeup, and a dark lipstick color worn with an even darker lip liner is generally favored. Long synthetic fingernails are also popular. Hair is generally worn long and loose but may be teased into a high poof or slicked at the top with heavy hair pomade, preferably the Tres Flores brand. Small wisps or curls of hair, often referred to as baby hair, may also be adhered to the forehead and cheeks with the pomade. All of the aforementioned stylistic features are iconic and typical and are adopted to varying degrees according to personal tastes and influences derived from mainstream fashion as well as other street styles.

It is notable that the basic features of cholo style have changed very little since the visual language coalesced in the wake of World War II. The fact that the look is based on pieces of functional apparel that themselves change very little in response to the whims of fashion is a factor that has contributed to the concretization of the style. Additionally, the adoption of the style by individuals who are members of a marginalized sociocultural group, and whose ancestors were also part of the same marginalized group, help to build a strong affinity for the visual language of the dress practices. Cholo dress represents a stylish and contemporary street-style option for young Latinos, but it is not fashion in the true sense of the word, which implies fleeting change. Cholo sartorial style is subcultural, is used to declare ethnic and sociocultural identity, and is entrenched in cultural norms and traditions.

Cholo style is used as a subtle affront to mainstream dress and cultural practices, and its adopters use it as part of a "front" or public face regardless of whether or not the person who wears it is affiliated with gang activity. Vigil notes, "Police officials have often viewed such creative cultural forms as representative of deviance. The media, especially newspapers, have followed a similar course in making such dress styles a badge of dishonor. The facts belie the image, however, as most cholos and pachucos, even though street-raised and undergoing culture conflict, are nonparticipants in deviant, anti-social patterns" (1988, 40). For most people, the adoption of the cholo or chola public front is part of creating a social identity, the personal meaning of which is highly varied. The wearer of cholo dress expresses through sartorial choices a disinterest in, disdain for, or alienation from mainstream values. Ditching school and eschewing a career course in favor of hanging out, drinking, getting high, cruising in a lowrider, and tagging are some of the lifestyle choices associated with cholos (Sanders 1994, 130) that sociologists have documented, but certainly the actions and ideals of individuals who dress in this manner are nuanced and varied. As Herbert Covey has noted, "Many of the studies on Hispanic gangs have concluded that Hispanic youths are marginalized to the mainstream society and must find status though gang membership" (2003, 45). Gangs provide a sense of family and help young Chicanos to identify with their neighborhood and with other young people in similar social circumstances. As gang activities are as varied as the gangs themselves, and as members participate in any organization in varying degrees, the signifying properties of cholo style also exist on a spectrum, and stereotypes should be engaged with caution. Cholo style is viewed from varied perspectives within the Chicano community. William Sanders has noted, "In the larger Chicano community, the *cholo* is variously viewed as anything from a transitory youthful style to a 'low life'" (1994, 129). Additionally, the fact that Hopi, Sioux, and Apache gang members have adopted the baggy clothes, colors, and tattoos of Los Angeles street gangs highlights the allure of cholo style (Hazelhurst and Hazelhurst 1998, 22).

Cholo street culture and dress practices have been captured in a broad variety of media. The films *Boulevard Nights* (1979), *Walk Proud* (1979), *Mi Vida Loca* (1993), and *La Mission* (2009) are all narrative movies that depict the neighborhoods, argot, dress, and culture (including iconic lowrider cars) that surround Hispanic American street culture. A variety of popular performers have also mimicked, interpreted, and stereotyped cholo street style in popular culture. Gwen Stefani, who used the classic Gothic lettering for her L.A.M.B fashion line, represented the street style in her music videos for *Luxurious* (2005) and *Hollaback Girl* (2006). Fergie featured cholo-styled backup dancers in her music videos for *London Bridge* (2006) and *Glamorous* (2007). Popular musicians Pink, Christina Aguillera, and Ricky Martin have also interpreted the style in their music videos and live acts. In a few instances famous women have come under fire for appropriating chola style as a cultural stereotype. Sandra Bullock received a "chola makeover" on the *George Lopez Show* in 2009 and proceeded to "front" as a chola in a manner that caused offense to some viewers and became the subject of social commentary. Selena Gomez also adopted stereotypical chola style for the 2011 *MTV Music Awards,* while Rihanna posted a "zombie chola" ensemble for Halloween 2013 on Instagram, a social-media misstep that created a backlash among some fans. The song "Lean Like a Cholo" (2007) by Down AKA Kilo includes lyrics that present a rather stereo-typical depiction of cholo style and behavior. Popular musicians have also helped to spread elements of cholo style by embodying it outside of performances. The Los Angeles tattoo artist Mr. Cartoon (Marc Machado) has popularized cholo tattoo styles by creating artwork for artists such as Justin Timberlake, Beyoncé, and Eminem.

Cholo style and culture is also visible in *Lowrider* magazine, a publication that is devoted to lowrider car culture but that does also regularly feature fashion arti-cles, many of which are geared toward urban styles including cholo. Companies such as Firme Clothing, Joker Brand, and Industries Illegales have commoditized and commercially produced cholo style. Additionally, Mr. Cartoon collaborated with Nike in 2005 to produce sneakers featuring spider webs, skulls, and Gothic script inspired by cholo tattoos. The popular video game *Grand Theft Auto: San Andreas* also references cholo street culture and includes a feature with which one can customize a tattoo for one's avatar. Notably, Mr. Cartoon created all the design features that are available for the player to customize. High-fashion runways have also offered interpretations of cholo street style. The spring/summer 2014 collec-tions by Nasir Mazhar and Rodarte both included strong visual references to cholas that were achieved through both the apparel and the styling of the models. The Givenchy fall/winter 2015 presentation featured apparel that was strongly influ-enced by Victoriana but included wisps of baby hair plastered to the mostly white models' faces. Mention of the chola influence for this styling choice earned the design team, led by Ricardo Tisci, a modicum of negative backlash.

Cholo street style utilizes traditional or staple articles of mainstream American dress but creates a unique sartorial gesture through interpretation, modification, and improvisation. Thus the street style plays with mainstream dress practices and produces an effect that is somewhere in between establishment and antiestablishment, cultural and countercultural, or appropriate and inappropriate. The use of dress to obfuscate social and cultural boundaries speaks to the liminal space to which many Chicanos feel they have been marginalized—no longer exclusively Mexican and not entirely accepted as American. The use of cholo street style may also be empowering for its wearers. The oversized garments take basic pieces of apparel and give the wearer street swagger in part by making the person look physically larger than he or she really is. The similarity in dress that is observable across adopters of this style also implies group identity and empowerment through affiliation. Thus for as long as there are young Mexican Americans who feel marginalized by mainstream American society or who are seeking a way to stake a unique identity within the panoply of identities that are part of the fabric of the United States of America, cholo street style will likely continue to find new adopters who will undoubtedly continue to evolve the style with subtle modifications. This unique American street style, which is a reflection of the problematic racial, ethnic, and social boundaries that persist in this country, is very much a part of the fabric of Mexican American culture, and it remains to be seen precisely how the style will develop in response to the evolution of attitudes and opportunities in American society.

Further Reading

Covey, H. C. 2003. *Street Gangs throughout the World.* Springfield, IL: Charles C. Thomas Publisher, Ltd.

Dery, M. 2005. "Brown Power." *Print,* September/October, 94–101.

Hazelhurst, K., and C. Hazelhurst. 1998. *Gangs and Youth Subcultures.* New Brunswick, NJ: Transaction Publishers.

Karen, T. 2003. "Cholo Is Bursting out of the Barrio." *USA Today,* October 9. Retrieved April 19, 2016, from Canadian Reference Center.

Reynolds, J. 2014. *Blood in the Fields: Ten Years inside California's Nuestra Familia Gang.* Chicago: Chicago Review Press.

Sanders, W. B. 1994. *Gangbangs and Drive-bys: Grounded Culture and Juvenile Gang Violence.* New York: Aldine de Gruyter.

Vigil, J. D. 1988. *Barrio Gangs: Street Life and Identity in Southern California.* Austin: University of Texas Press.

Vigil, J. D. 1990. "Cholos and Gangs: Culture Change and Street Youth in Los Angeles." In *Gangs in America,* edited by C. R. Huff, 116–28. Newbury Park, NJ: Sage Publications.

Vigil, J. D., and J. M. Long. 1990. "Emic and Etic Perspectives on Gang Culture: The Chicano Case." In *Gangs in America,* edited by C. R. Huff, 55–68. Newbury Park, NJ: Sage Publications.

Coachella (1999–Present)

The Coachella Valley Music and Arts Festival is a multigenre music festival that takes place each year at the Empire Polo Club in Indio, California, a locale in the Colorado Desert that is situated about 125 miles east of Los Angeles. The event, which began as a single-day festival in 1999, has mushroomed in popularity, was extended first to become a two-day event, and ultimately expanded in 2012 to span two full weekends. The event, which was originally conceived by concert promoter Paul Tollet as a venue for alternative and emerging artists, has changed substantially over the past decade. As the popularity of the festival has grown, the star power of the artists who perform has also increased, and the activities have diversified to include art installations, performance art, and pop-up stores that sell items like limited-edition posters as well as special Coachella fashion collections. While the mixed musical fare, which includes heavy metal, hip-hop, country, electronica, and alternative artists, is still a draw for crowds of spectators, Coachella has also developed into an important fashion incubator from at least the latter part of the aughts onward. Coachella festival style shares aesthetic features with the street style of other festivals, but the heightened media coverage, vast brand integration, and celebrity presence at this festival support the notion that Coachella participants are making sartorial choices that set and shape the dress style adopted at many other venues.

Coachella is one of many music festivals that take place the world around, but unlike Bonnaroo, Glastonbury, or Lollapalooza, Coachella is uniquely positioned both geographically and annually. The festival takes place in April, at a point in time when most of North America and Europe are still shaking off the last vestiges of cool and wet wintry weather. However, the desert climate of Indio, California, virtually guarantees blue skies, bright sunshine, and warm temperatures—factors that encourage festival attendees to experiment with new ideas for the coming spring and summer seasons. The proximity of the Coachella festival to the greater Los Angeles region is also geographically important as it ensures that legions of young, fabulous, famous, and attractive individuals are likely to attend at least one weekend of the event and are equally likely to post images of themselves and their friends to social-media platforms like Facebook, Twitter, Instagram, and Snapchat. Omnipresent paparazzi and street-style bloggers as well as the mainstream fashion press (*Vogue, WGSN, Women's Wear Daily*) are similarly important conduits for documenting the event and its attendees. Location, weather, famous guests, and mass-media conduits have converged to shape Coachella into an important street-style phenomenon with an impact that influences the fashion marketplace and consumers around the world in an exceptional way.

This music festival is not just an event—it is a destination. As such it is not just a music-infused experience, it is a temporary escape from mainstream life, a bohemian escapade into which revelers immerse themselves. Festival attendees dress the part for this departure from workaday life, and thus Coachella festival style draws from a variety of historical and sociocultural influences that evoke bohemian connections. These sources of inspiration can be divided into manageable and meaningful categories, though notably some of the categories overlap conceptually and aesthetically.

The first and most obvious point of reference that is visible in Coachella festival dress is elements of 1960s countercultural dress and grooming as it is imagined by 21st-century women (and men to a far lesser degree). The hippies of the 1960s were known to eschew commodity culture and to make and modify their own apparel and accessories. This essential impulse is translated in Coachella festival style in items such as crocheted halter tops and bikinis, ethereal knits fashioned into shawls, scarves, and dresses, and embroidered details that are applied to shorts, shirts, jackets, and bags. The hippies of the 1960s were often referred to as flower children, and images from Woodstock, perhaps the most famous music festival of all time, reveal members of the crowd wearing flower crowns, a feature that was a mainstay of Coachella style until 2016 when it was deemed "out" by members of the in-crowd including pop singer Taylor Swift. Floral frocks and peasant blouses provide an alternative means of interpreting the flower-child aesthetic. The hippies of the 1960s also relied heavily on denim as a staple of their apparel; thus denim overalls (which are often shorts length) and denim cut-off shorts, cut high enough that the pocket bags are exposed, are standard festival attire worn by both sexes.

Coachella attendees also explore hippie dress aesthetics through the adoption of psychedelic elements, which are related both to 1960s counterculture as well as to 1990s rave culture. Tie-dyed apparel is ubiquitous and often executed in neon-hued dyes. Densely patterned skirts, shirts for men and women, and dresses in brilliant hues and "trippy" patterns including amoeba-like paisleys and Emilio Pucci–inspired prints potentially serve to connect the wearer to the decadent era in which psychedelic drugs were freely (and often legally) used. Headbands and scarves wrapped across the forehead often feature patterns of this kind and frame hair that is styled in messy waves or loosely braided. Large, round sunglasses with rose-colored lenses may also be grouped within the hippie- and psychedelic-inspired festival styles. Wildly embellished sunglasses featuring three-dimensional adornments are also a popular choice. Sunglasses of this kind are manufactured by some major labels like Miu Miu but are also readily available through small artisans who retail on websites like Etsy (a site that advertises Coachella merchandise in the months preceding the festival) and can be crafted through do-it-yourself techniques.

Elements of ethnic dress are also a mainstay of Coachella, and the source of inspiration for this connection may once again be made to the counterculture of the

1960s, the members of which experimented with Asian, North African, and Native American dress. Festival-goers at Coachella seem to be omnivorous when it comes to consuming apparel and accessories garnered from foreign cultures. Native American elements are visible in the form of traditional patterns derived from ancient rugs and pottery and printed onto or woven into apparel ranging from bikini tops and T-shirts to leggings, shorts, and loose-fitting trousers. The wearing of feathers is ubiquitous in earrings, necklaces, hair ornaments, trim applied to apparel, and even (though they are considered incredibly controversial) headdresses inspired by Native American chieftains. Fringed elements, inspired by apparel like traditional deerskin shirts, are also commonplace and can be found attached to shirt and jacket sleeves, pants, boots, and handbags. Sterling silver and turquoise jewelry and belts are also typical. In addition to Native American influences, Coachella festival style also borrows heavily from South Asia, especially India. Diadems, ear clips, nose rings that link to ears, and bracelets with chains attached to rings are all worn, but perhaps the most eye-catching and controversial Asian accessory is the bindi, an ornament worn between the eyes as part of Hindu and Jain beliefs and symbolic of the "third eye." This symbol, appropriated and popularized by celebrities like Selena Gomez, has been the target of both widespread emulation and condemnation by individuals unnerved by this kind of cultural imperialism. South Asian textiles, or textiles thereby inspired, are used to make all manner of women's apparel, and men's to a lesser degree. Caftans and tunics, staples of dress traditions ranging across North Africa to the Middle East and Asia, are also festival favorites.

It only stands to reason that a festival featuring many rock groups would also bring attendees with a rocker aesthetic. This genre of festival style is largely unisex with cut, fit, and detailing marking the differences between men's and women's apparel. Men and women regularly wear classic rock T-shirts from bands like the Ramones, the Who, Guns N' Roses, and Pink Floyd in classic, ladies', and cropped cuts. Many examples are artfully faded, frayed, and fringed. Motorcycle jackets, despite the hot daytime climate, can also be seen in conjunction with motorcycle boots, ripped jeans, and studded accessories. Aviator sunglasses and straw, distressed cowboy-style hats or black broad-brimmed hats, including fedoras, often complete the look. Visible tattoos, which are common across demographics in the first decades of the 21st century, enhance the rocker aesthetic; however, stick-on metallic tattoos are also routinely worn at Coachella.

The hot climate of the Colorado Desert also inspires the appropriation of beach and other revealing apparel. Bikini tops, hot pants, or high-waist pin-up-style shorts, midriff tops, and transparent garments are made with hippie, psychedelic, and rocker influences. Floppy beach hats and sandals of all kinds are also frequently worn. Coachella festival fashion does also reflect broader fashion trends.

For example, the 2016 festival featured many guests in see-through maxi dresses that revealed high-waist panties and bra tops underneath, a trend also seen in high-style evening wear in the preceding fashion seasons. Designer-branded apparel, "it bags," and faddish items can also be found in the wardrobes of Coachella attendees; however, the aforementioned categories and items are iconic and widely copied.

Conceiving of Coachella fashion as hippie-, psychedelic-, rocker-, and ethnic-inspired is a convenient way of outlining the key sartorial features of festival style; however, the mixing of categories is fundamental to festival fashion and is reflected in the observations of the fashion press. Expressions like "hippie rocker," "hippie hipster," and "Navajo cowboy" are bandied about by reporters from a wide variety of publications seeking to capture the essential characteristics represented at the festival. Artfully combining historical references (flower crowns), on-trend items (choker collars in 2016), and pieces of apparel that relate to a specific type or character (such as rock T-shirts and motorcycle boots) can prove to be a challenge. Elisabeth von Thurn und Taxis, writing for *Vogue,* noted, "You definitely see a bit of trying too hard" (Flash: TNT 2014).

The importance of fashion and personal appearance at Coachella is heightened by the pervasive presence of social-media use at the festival. Interest in making a fashion statement is demonstrated largely through clothing and accessories but is augmented in part by strict fitness and diet regimens. The existence of a "Coachella diet," crash dieting based on consuming juices, which has been shared with numerous variations through social media, is testimony to the interest in making skimpy festival fashions look just right. The 30-day workout promoted by Well + Good called "Cut by Coachella" prepares festival goers for wearing barely there cut-off shorts and midriff-baring tops and is just one additional example of how personal appearance shapes both the Coachella experience and people's perception of it. The increasing focus on fitness provoked one *Elle* writer to ask, "Um, isn't the festival supposed to be about music?" (Hoff 2014).

Social media is also incredibly important to the promotion and retailing of Coachella festival style. In 2016 Snapchat offered a Coachella filter that featured a flower crown, a playful way to promote a festival fashion concept. Kelsi Smith, founder of Stylesmith.com, noted, "Since Coachella's inception in 1999, style has almost become as synonymous to the festival as music. Much of this is directly related to the fashion blogger and the way in which the Internet has changed the way we access fashion and how it is covered" (#Blogchella 2015). Street-style bloggers have been instrumental in perpetuating the idea of Coachella style, and more recently their tactics have been used to promote concepts through retailing. For example, in 2012 the makers of a smartphone application called Kaleidoscope partnered with *Details* magazine to facilitate browsing and buying from street-style photographs taken at Coachella, thereby allowing consumers to "crowd-source their fashion cues" from fresh, new, relatable, and accessible images (Adam 2012). Additionally, brands have invested in celebrities who attend the festival. Kate Bosworth, a celebrity actress who can count on being photographed on the street, has been the official brand ambassador for Topshop since 2013. Her attendance at the festival is now predicated on the display of a Topshop wardrobe, making her every move around the polo grounds as influential as a strut down the runway.

In recent years many music critics and commentators have roundly criticized Coachella. The music commentators for *The New York Times* recently noted that the music at large festivals around the world offers an "unrelenting sameness" and described Coachella in particular as a "codified, consensual, safe, and purchasable bohemia" (Pareles, Ratliff, & Caramanica 2016). A writer at the dailybeast.com critically noted of Coachella, "What was initially intended to be a celebration of music has degenerated into a weird marriage of fashion and commerce," and he went on to decry the "wacky, barely there duds" and the "ubiquity" of Paris Hilton "clad in a variety of neon bikinis and floral headdresses" (Stern 2014). Fashion and popular music have long fit together like a hand in a glove, but the emphasis on fashion at Coachella has become so pronounced that this kind of critical commentary has become increasingly common.

Amidst this kind of incisive analysis, the fashion industry is thriving at Coachella and is clearly shaping festival style. One unnamed stylist noted to the *Hollywood Reporter*, "It's getting harder to dress girls for Coachella because now they're demanding money. One actress asked for 50 grand to wear one item" (Ginsberg 2014, 31). This stylist's complaint is a reflection of how important the festival is as a marketing tool and trend incubator. The high dollar value placed on a celebrity street-style appearance reflects the wide and diverse audience that views Coachella festival pictures. Further evidence of the importance of celebrity style at Coachella is reflected in the gifting of fashion merchandise by a wide cross section of brands. In advance of the festival, "style lounges" are established in Los Angeles as a means to connect celebrities with brands and their products so that they can be photographed as indicators of contemporary festival style (Sandy 2015). Some brands are also using the Coachella name as a way to market apparel that has been designed and produced in advance of the festival. In 2015 the Swedish retailer H&M, a longtime sponsor of the festival, launched its official Coachella collection called "H&M Loves Coachella," which featured ripped jeans and psychedelic patterns. These festival-inspired fashions were available in 350 stores throughout North America (A First Look 2015). In 2016 the women's fashion label Alice & Olivia launched a see-now, buy-now collection at the Coachella festival. Many fashion brands including Diesel, Swatch, Forever 21, Edun, and BCBG Max Azria routinely have been a presence at the festival, sponsoring pool parties, fashion shows, deejayed after-parties, and free pampering sessions for celebrities who require pedicures or massages after a long day at the festival. These kinds of promotions help to link brands with popular youth culture. A fashion reporter for *The Canadian Press* recently observed, "Brands are seizing the opportunity to be part of the Coachella conversation and see the festival as a place to connect directly with young consumers" (Sandy 2015). Furthermore, established fashion designers including Jeremy Scott, Hedi Slimane, and Alexander Wang are regularly in attendance at Coachella and have discussed using the event as an incubator for new ideas. Notably, they also use their widely photographed presence at the festival as a way to prop up their images and credibility in popular culture. *Vogue* Style Editor Emma Elwick-Bates recently described Coachella as "a very corporate culture" (Laura 2013), a statement that is supported by the wide range of marketing and retailing endeavors that are part of the festival.

Coachella festival style is constantly evolving and responds to both trends in the marketplace as well as innovations made by celebrity attendees who channel their inner hippie, hipster, or rocker persona while bathed in the warm California sunshine. Coachella has, for more than a decade, incubated a specific festival style that has been copied at other festivals and has become the source of inspiration for a substantial portion of the fashion marketplace. The impact of the intense commercial focus that has been accorded Coachella remains to be seen. As with all street and subcultural styles that are commoditized, commodification has the capacity to alter aesthetics and meaning and the potential to stunt or reroute development. At present Coachella continues to draw large crowds and inspire legions of fashion-conscious young festival attendees, designers, and retailers, while at least marginally retaining the semiotics of bohemian abandon. However, in this age in which consumers seek authenticity, novelty, and nostalgia all at once, it remains to be seen how long Coachella festival style can continue to evolve as it has been evolving.

Further Reading

Adam, T. 2012. "It's Not Just about the Music, Retailers Are Cashing In on Coachella's Fashion Parade." *The Hamilton Spectator,* April 20. Retrieved June 2, 2016, from http://search.ebscohost.com/login.aspx?direct=true&db=rch&an+q4k053964205012&scope=site.

"#Blogchella: Introducing Fashion's Newest Website, blogchella.fashion at Coachella." 2015. *PR Newswire US,* April 9. Retrieved June 2, 2016, from http://search.ebscohost.com/login.aspx?direct=true&db+bwh&AN=201504090800pr.news.uspr.enuk201504094028&scope=site.

Blumenthal, E. 2016. "Festival Fashion without Fringe or Feathers." *The New York Times,* April 13. Retrieved May 30, 2016 from www.nytimes.com.

"A First Look: H&M Coachella." 2015. *Women's Wear Daily* 209 (32). Retrieved June 3, 2015, from www.wwd.com.

"Flash: TNT." 2014. *Vogue* 204 (June 01): 94. Retrieved May 26, 2016, from http://search .proquest.com/docview/1540295053?accountid=130772.

Ginsberg, M. 2014. "The New Dirt Carpet." *Hollywood Reporter* 420 (14): 30–31. Retrieved June 2, 2016, from http://search.ebscohost.com/login.aspx?direct=true&db+ bth&AN=95584225&scope=site.

Hoff, V. D. 2014. "'The Coachella Diet' Is Now a Thing." *Elle,* April 2. Retrieved June 8, 2015, from www.elle.com.

Holgate, M. 2010. "View: All Dressed Up: When Did Chic Get So Cool?" *Vogue* 200 (July 1): 60, 62. Retrieved May 26, 2016, from http://search.proquest.com/docview/879 327447?accountid=130772.

Laura, C. 2013. "Why You'll Be Wearing What They're Wearing." *The Times,* April 17. Retrieved June 2, 2016, from http://search.ebscohost.com/login.aspx?direct=true&db =nfh&an=7eh71445663&scope=site.

Pareles, J., B. Ratliff, and J. Caramanica. 2016. "Why We're Not Making Plans for Coachella and Bonaroo." *The New York Times,* March 18. Retrieved June 3, 2016, from www.nytimes.com.

Sandy, C. 2015. "With Runway Shows and Pop-up Shops, Fashion Aims to Share Spotlight with Music at Coachella." *The Canadian Press,* September 4. Retrieved June 3, 2016, from http://search.ebscohost.com/login.aspx?direct=true&db+rch&an=myo020707085 515&scope=site.

Singer, S. 2010. "Fashion & Features: Second Acts: Bird of Britain." *Vogue* 200 (August 1): 196–99. Retrieved May 26, 2016, from http://search.proquest.com/docview /879326040?accountid=130772.

Stern, M. 2014. "Coachella, Oasis for Douchebags and Trustfund Babies Should Be Avoided at All Costs." *The Daily Beast,* April 11. Retrieved June 2, 2016, from www .thedailybeast.com.

Walpita, S. 2016. "Coachella 2016: Young Men's Apparel." *WGSN,* April 25. Retrieved May 30, 2015, from www.wgsn.com.

Cosplay (1980s–Present)

Cosplayers have existed in the United States since the 1930s or 1940s, emerging during the first major wave of science-fiction writing, but came to prominence roughly 50 years later in the 1980s at a time when computer graphics and video gaming were rapidly developing. The term "cosplay" is a portmanteau of the words "costume" and "play." Cosplayers are individuals who dress like and perform the character traits of figures from both American and Japanese comic books and cartoons, as well as Hollywood movies, television shows, and video games. Cosplayers regularly select characters from the genres of science fiction, fantasy, and superhero action stories; however, there is a great deal of variety and freedom for selecting and interpreting characters. Some cosplayers dress to accurately represent a specific recognizable character, while others dress to represent an archetype, such as a robot or generic superhero. Cosplayers may fuse an existing character with attributes from a subcultural style such as steampunk or may alter the character with either retro or futuristic attributes. Additionally, cosplayers may modify the gender of an existing character through "crossplay" (crossdressing cosplay). Finally, some cosplayers develop new characters, complete with a complex backstory and fully developed visual language.

Dressing to hide one's identity or dressing in a costume for the purpose of entertainment, ritual, or masquerade has a long and varied history that ranges across cultures and centuries. For example, masquerade balls and other Mardi Gras celebrations involving costuming date to at least the 15th century in Europe. Halloween, a celebration that was originally devoted to honoring saints (hallows) and that is celebrated in several dozen countries around the world, and *Día de los Muertos* (Day of the Dead), a Mexican festival in celebration of the deceased, both involve elaborate costuming and seem to have their roots in customs originating more than 1,000 years ago. Cosplaying, however, is different from masquerades of these kinds in that it involves performing the attributes of a specific character as a way of personally identifying with the character's traits and story arc. The roots of this custom seem to have evolved out of early science-fiction conventions that took place in the United States beginning in the 1930s. Fans of the literary genre developed the practice of creating costumes that were described in texts or depicted on book covers and wore them to gatherings of like-minded fans. This practice embodied a way of connecting with the texts and experiencing the fantasies they described. This practice of embodying a character, performing a text, and participating in a subculture of science-fiction fandom is exemplified in the history of the propeller beanie, which has been recounted by its inventor Radell "Ray" Faraday Nelson, who developed the hat when he and his friends were enacting an image from a book. The hat was later worn to a fan convention and went on to be a fashion fad in the 1950s (Moore 2015). Interest in fan conventions grew in the United States in the 1980s, and the growth seems to be at least partially attributable to increased interest in Japanese anime and manga and the fan-conventions scene that was developing in Japan (Tysk 2013, 5–6).

Conventions, referred to among cosplayers as "cons," are a key part of the cosplaying scene as cosplayers attend the cons and their satellite events in costume. Throughout the duration of a convention, cosplayers may be seen virtually anywhere about town in full regalia. The conventions themselves generally include the attractions of a traditional trade show such as vendors and information booths;

however, panel discussions on issues such as diversity, disability, and pop-culture influences on cosplay are also key features. Screenings of films and autograph sessions with actors who portray characters frequently emulated by cosplayers are often main attractions at the conventions, as are costume competitions. In addition to the conventions, a wide variety of satellite events are often part of the multiday fan meet-ups. Among the commonly occurring events are costume and trivia contests, speed dating sessions for both gay and straight cosplayers, after-parties, and interest-specific gatherings at bars and cafés for fans of specific movies or video games.

The styles and aesthetics embodied by cosplayers are incredibly varied. Characters are derived from sources such as Marvel Comics, *Game of Thrones,* anime and manga, *Star Wars,* and popular or classic video games. Some costumes are such elaborate constructions that the wearer's natural movements are restricted, whereas many characters, both male and female, wear costumes that showcase the body in sensual and provocative ways. Costumes may be purchased or handmade. Purchased versions may consist of mass-produced, packaged outfits in standard sizes, but there are also garment makers who cater to the cosplay community and custom make cosplay ensembles to a client's proportions and specifications. Many cosplayers consider handcrafting their own costumes to be a point of pride and personal development, and also integral to connecting with and embodying a character. Many cosplayers devote months of time and hundreds of dollars to the process of creating a single character, teaching themselves the arts and crafts of patternmaking, sewing, beading, painting, and embroidering in the process. Cosplayers who engage in highly sophisticated costume design and construction often cite online tutorials as sources of assistance; thus the development of this kind of Internet content has also helped cosplaying culture to grow. In addition to the apparel that is used to construct a character, cosplayers often utilize wigs, elaborate makeup, and props. Weapons are a featured accessory of many superhero, fantasy, and science-fiction characters, but most conventions have strict rules regarding the types of prop weapons that may be carried.

Cosplayers generally choose a character with whom they identify in some way, particularly with the character's narrative. For many cosplayers, creating an accurate reproduction of an existing character is of paramount importance. For example, Amon has noted that Disney cosplayers tend to be particularly devoted to adhering to the "canon" and do not "enjoy freedom of play" (2014, 2). For some people within the cosplay scene, the accuracy of an enactment is a point of controversy. Individuals who play with issues of race, gender, and disability by enacting characters who do not match their body type, skin color, or physical ability transform and animate characters in ways that some consider antithetical to the art of cosplay. Matthew Hale has noted that this kind of transformative cosplay "reduces fidelity, promotes critical ironic distance, and creates a point of contrast between the imitated and the imitative text" (2014, 19). He goes on to note, "Where there is contrast there is the possibility to generate commentary through parody, pastiche, satire, burlesque, and caricature" (20). For some cosplayers this type of embodiment and performance is meant to provoke introspection and dialogue. Cosplay can serve as commentary. But for other cosplayers, embodiments that detract from the original characterization are seen in a negative light.

The diversity that exists in the interpretations of characters points to the larger issue of why individuals cosplay. The reasons are incredibly varied; however, there are recurring themes. Ger Tysk's (2013) book *Breaking All the Rules: Cosplay and the Art of Self-Expression* consists of an impressive collection of photographs of cosplayers, showing the broad range of characters and interpretations thereof that exist. Additionally, a narrative from the person depicted accompanies each image. Many cosplayers told Tysk that cosplay is a social endeavor. Going to cons means entering a space filled with people of similar interests; cons are equated with communities and also with carnivals, places where one can be free of the norms of regular culture and unfettered from one's regular body (see Lamerichs, 2014 for a theoretical discussion of this). Furthermore, many cosplayers remarked to Tysk that the regular world is fraught with social pitfalls, and many cosplayers, who are self-proclaimed "geeks," struggle with the social politics of school or work but thrive and find lasting friendships among fellow cosplayers. Some cosplayers also noted that they have developed creative and technical skills through cosplay that have utility and even profitability in the "outside world." While cosplaying is escapist and a form of masquerade, it can also function as a mechanism for self-expression and personal growth.

In the 21st century a variety of media have disseminated cosplay culture to the general public. Numerous books filled with full-color portraits of cosplayers have been published, including the aforementioned exceptional text by Ger Tysk. Digital publications are also an important vehicle for communicating cosplay culture and clothing. *Cosmode,* a publication from Japan, offers an English-language digital edition, while two American digital magazines have published since 2015: *Cosplay Culture* and *Cosplay Zine.* Independent films, both shorts and features, have also been made in substantial numbers in the first two decades of the new millennium. Among the films that document the American cosplay scene are *Animania: The Documentary* (2007), *Cosplayers: The Movie* (2009), and *Comic-Con Episode IV: A Fan's Hope* (2011). Many films that document cosplay can be viewed on the Internet, whereas a television series from the SyFy channel called *Heroes of Cosplay* could be viewed on broadcast television, though it ran for only a single 12-episode season from 2013 to 2014. An exhibition presented by the Costume Institute at the Metropolitan Museum of Art in New York City in 2008 entitled

Superheroes: Fashion and Fantasy is also testament to the increasing interest in the embodiment of fantasy through dress as the exhibit explored both the development of superhero characters through their dress and the interpretation of these powerful aesthetics by fashion designers.

As interest in cosplaying has grown, so too have commercial entities that cater to the scene. First and foremost, the number of cons has dramatically expanded in the 21st century. Comic-Con in San Francisco and ComiCon (omitting the hyphen is a trademark issue) in New York City are the largest and most popular events in the United States. Other examples of conventions that draw large crowds of cosplayers are Dragon Con (Atlanta) and Awesome Con (Washington, D.C.). Cons are also held throughout Europe and Asia. In addition to entrance fees and fees for special events within the conventions, these meet-ups are places for cosplayers to purchase an endless array of merchandise with licensed imagery to suit virtually every taste and interest. For example, Her Universe is an apparel company founded in 2009 to address the "fangirl" (female fantasy, science-fiction, and gaming) market. The company produces fitted T-shirts, tank tops, dresses, and hoodies with licensed imagery from fan favorites like *Star Wars, Star Trek, The Walking Dead,* and Marvel Comics.

The reason why these fan conventions have grown so dramatically since the 1980s is open to interpretation. However, the abundance of fantasy, superhero, and animated media, produced both in the United States and internationally, is clearly a contributing factor. New narratives and characters are constantly in development in this new golden age of mass media that includes streaming services, webisodes (episodic series distributed through the World Wide Web), and interactive online gaming. Additionally, reboots and sequels of long-lived characters are mainstays of large Hollywood studios, thereby keeping classic characters like Superman and Spiderman in the public eye. Furthermore, the profusion of Internet sites related to science fiction, fantasy, gaming, and other animation fosters virtual communities that in turn seek out periodic interaction in real time and space.

The culture of cosplaying shows no signs of waning in the second decade of the 21st century. In fact, the inclination toward engaging in fantasy enactment seems to be developing in other arenas. Massive multiplayer online role-playing games (M.M.O.R.P.G.) such as *World of Warcraft, Second Life,* and *Mindcraft* immerse players in a story that is enacted with animated characters and, therefore, don't require costumes but demonstrate the inclination to enact fantasy. Live action role-playing games (L.A.R.P.) that involve multiple players meeting to enact a story are increasingly commonplace. Individuals who "larp" typically do so in full costume, and science fiction and fantasy are genres that are preferred. *Harry Potter* stories have been a common source of inspiration for this kind of role play. Historical re-enactments, taking the forms of Civil War battles and Renaissance fairs, which have been popular for decades, continue to thrive as venues for the embodiment of characters and the development of elaborate costumes to facilitate the enactment.

The impact of the worlds of fantasy, science fiction, and superheroes often reaches beyond the realm of cosplay to the larger realm of fashionable dress. Strong interpretations of superhero imagery can be found in John Galliano's haute couture collection for the house of Dior, wherein he utilized sartorial references from Wonder Woman (Spring/Summer 2001). Additionally, the Fall/Winter 2006 collection by Moschino referenced both Clark Kent and Superman. In sampling from this iconography, both designers created designs that channeled the power of these iconic characters. Dress that is strongly inspired by fantasy can also be found in the haute couture collections of Thierry Mugler (1997, 1998) and in the work of Alexander McQueen (Fall/Winter 2007). These collections presented sensual, otherworldly women whose strange beauty was visually arresting and indisputably powerful. These connections between fantastic fictional characters and fashionable dress are testimony to the power and allure of these visual references and provide yet another path to understand the ways in which cosplayers bond with their characters and thereby express themselves.

Further Reading

Amon, M. P. 2014. "Performance of Innocence and Deviance in Disney Cosplaying." *Transformative Works and Cultures* 171. Retrieved March 3, 2016, from http://dx.doi .org/10.3983/twc.2014.0565.

Bolton, A. 2008. *Superheroes: Fashion and Fantasy.* New Haven: Yale University Press.

Gn, J. 2011. "Queer Simulation: The Practice, Performance and Pleasure of Cosplay." *Continuum: Journal of Media & Cultural Studies* 25 (4): 583–93.

Hale, M. 2014. "Cosplay: Intertextuality, Public Texts, and the Body Fantastic." *Western Folklore* 73 (1): 5–37.

Jones, B. 2015. "Fannish Tattooing and Sacred Identity." *Transformative Works and Cultures* 181. Retrieved March 3, 2016. from http://dx.doi.org/10.3983/twc.2014.0626.

Lamerichs, N. 2014. "Costuming as Subculture: The Multiple Bodies of Cosplay." *Scene* 2 (1&2): 113–25.

Moore, J. 2015. "Propeller Beanies." In *Fashion Fads through American History: Putting Clothes into Context* by J. Moore, 136–38. Santa Barbara, CA: ABC-CLIO.

Savage, S., and E. Marlow. 2011. *Focused Fandom: Cosplay, Costuming and Careers.* Seattle: Create Space Independent Publishing Platform.

Schmidt, G. 2016. "Narrowing a Gap in the Sci-Fi Universe: One Fangirl Giving Voice to Others." *The New York Times,* January 17. Retrieved March 3, 2016, from www .nytimes.com.

Tysk, G. 2013. *Breaking All the Rules: Cosplay and the Art of Self-Expression.* Berkeley, CA: Edition One Books.

Dead Head (Mid-1980s–Present)

Dead Heads are followers of the American rock band the Grateful Dead. The Grateful Dead (also commonly referred to as simply "The Dead") formed in Palo Alto, California, in 1966, and released its first of 13 studio albums in 1967. The band was originally composed of five members: Jerry Garcia, Phil Lesh, Bob Weir, Bill Kreutzman, and Ron "Pigpen" McKernan. However, over the course of the band's 50-year trajectory, many members came and went. The music of the Grateful Dead was an amalgam of classic rock, folk, country, bluegrass, and blues, performed in a freestyle, "jam session" manner that facilitated long meandering songs that could easily last for 20 minutes each. The Grateful Dead were constantly on tour during the course of their existence and distinguished themselves from other touring groups by the fact that they did not perform the same set list night after night. This tendency encouraged fans of the music to follow the band from town to town, camping in parks and parking lots, setting up encampments that included various items for sale or trade, and thus creating a veritable community of Dead Heads that ultimately developed a variety of cultural characteristics.

The Grateful Dead, named for a type of folktale character, formed in the heyday of the hippie subculture and played and resided at the epicenter of the scene, the Haight-Ashbury neighborhood of San Francisco. The Grateful Dead was part of the intricate fabric of 1960s popular and countercultures. They were linked early on to the psychedelic movement and Ken Kesey's Acid Tests (group LSD trips that took place between 1965 and 1966), they were involved in environmental and civic activism including a concert to aid an imprisoned Black Panther, and they performed for free at various love-ins and be-ins including events held in Golden Gate Park. The Grateful Dead performed more than 2,200 concerts in their long-lived trajectory and created a community of fans that, from the middle of the 1980s onward, developed a distinctive sartorial style.

The dress styles of the members of the Grateful Dead and the dress styles of Dead Heads were essentially the same in the first 20 years of the band's existence, and both groups largely reflected widespread tendencies in 1960s and 1970s dress practices. Photographs from concerts reveal that musicians and spectators alike consistently wore basic, staple pieces of apparel: jeans, T-shirts, bandanas, flannel shirts, sneakers, and sandals. Army-surplus apparel, handmade items like crocheted vests, and articles of dress from foreign cultures (Mexican peasant blouses, caftans, huaraches) were also visible but were interspersed with a very large proportion of more basic clothes and accessories. Both men and women generally wore their hair long; full beards and moustaches were also common for men. At venues where spectators listened to the music from a lawn, bare feet were commonplace. Essentially, a natural, unstudied look prevailed, though some images do show contemporary fashionable or trend items in the mix: stovepipe pants, paisley and psychedelic prints, crushed velvet, love beads, peace signs, and tie-dye. A staff writer at *Time* described Grateful Dead audience members in 1967 as "hippies and teenyboppers, wearing everything from Arab caftans and top hats to frock coats and turbans . . . casually daub[ing] the floors and each other with fluorescent paint" ("Open Up" 1967). While this kind of iconic 1960s dress was part of the early scene, it seems that the writer focused on the most outlandish attributes of the sartorial scene while ignoring the widespread adoption of understated dress. Generally speaking, the sartorial style surrounding the Grateful Dead and their fans between 1966 and approximately 1986 is rather unremarkable and most importantly not distinctly emblematic of the Grateful Dead.

Beginning in the middle of the 1980s there emerged a distinctive Dead Head style. While members of the band continued to dress in basics and maintained their unstudied, casual, mode of dress and lackadaisical attitude toward grooming, many Dead Heads began to adopt a dress style that might be characterized as a bohemian, heightened hippie-revival style. Perhaps the most visible and prevalent component of the new Dead Head style was the heavy use of tie-dye, which was generally executed in vibrant colors including neon hues. Tie-dyed T-shirts were the most ubiquitous kind of apparel, but skirts, scarves, shorts, floppy hats, and loose drawstring pants were also worn in tie-dyed fabric. Many tie-dyed T-shirts also included one of the seven distinctive logos the Grateful Dead had developed for album covers or liner art. The logos included a skull with roses (1966), the "steal your face" logo (skull with a lightning bolt across the cranium) (1969), a 13-point lightning bolt (1969), a jester (1972), dancing bears (1973), Terrapin turtles (1977), and the Uncle Sam skeleton (1977). Apparel with band logos was made both legally under license and in violation of the band's intellectual property rights, an issue that the band did not litigate until the middle of the 1990s. In addition to tie-dye, the new distinctive Dead Head style often included pieces of mass-produced, imported ethnic dress, especially machine-woven textiles imported from places like Mexico, Peru, and Guatemala. Textiles of this kind were routinely fashioned into loose pants, skirts, satchels, and hooded pullovers of basic, undiversified design. A homogeneous mix of apparel decorated with beads, fringe, and embroidery were also commonly featured. Accessorizing the look was generally accomplished with long strings of colorful beads that were reminiscent of the "love beads" exchanged among hippies in the 1960s. Beads were sometimes adorned with a pendant in the form of a peace sign, ankh, Dead symbol, or marijuana plant. Sunglasses, especially "granny styled" with tinted lenses, also became commonplace and recalled the rose-colored glasses of the 1960s. Feathers were a popular feature that could be fashioned into earrings or attached to a roach clip, which could either adorn one's hair or facilitate the smoking of a joint.

The presence of a recognizable Dead Head style is not an implication that *all* followers of the Grateful Dead began to dress alike but, rather, indicates that a *large number* of fans began to dress alike; and this in turn points to the easy availability of consumer goods to achieve the look. In the latter part of the 1980s, following the commercial success of the song "Touch of Grey," the Grateful Dead began to play increasingly large arenas. Devoted fans, who had for decades set up shop on "Shakedown Street," the improvised parking-lot bazaar, saw the opportunities inherent in a new, young, affluent demographic that had largely learned about the Dead from the pop charts and was enamored with the lifestyle the band and its followers represented: a free-flowing community that did not cast aspersions on users of marijuana, LSD, peyote, and other hallucinogenic drugs. The influx of "Touchheads" (Dead Heads who "got on the bus" after "Touch of Grey") led to the development of "truly mammoth bazaars" (Jackson 2003, 263) that sold knick knacks and trinkets from the Orient and South America including incense burners, drums, tapestries, hand blown glass, custom-strung beads, hand-knit sweaters, silver jewelry, woolen hats, hemp shirts from Nepal, and figurines of Ganesh, Buddha, and Quetzacoatl— all the things a "bourgeois hipster trying to cultivate a look of third-worldy sophistication" might need (Carr 2012, 167). Notably, many aspects of Dead Head style recall cultural and sartorial elements from the 1960s, especially from the hippie subculture, and it seems that this specific Dead Head style emerged only as new, young followers of the scene began to make an effort to tap the ethos of the era by dressing the part. Of course, it would be far too broad of a statement to suggest that none of the older, seasoned followers of the band bought the newly available merchandise. Rather, the evidence supports the notion that a unique Dead Head style was directly related to the influx of a large number of new, generally young followers.

The late-career flourishing of the Grateful Dead cannot be understated. The band was the number one touring group from 1985 to 1995 (Lisanti 2014, 36). As *Rolling Stone* noted in 1990, "Their frequent concerts were a place where the spirit of the counterculture lived on. . . . The members of the Dead gave themselves to their fans, and many of their fans responded by structuring their lives around the Dead" (Goodman and Whiteside 1990, 21). In the last decades of the group's existence, fans young and old continued to camp at venues, follow the band, and seek out the Grateful Dead experience, which "the band members themselves have always insisted . . . had as much to do with the sort of person you were (or were evolving into) as it did with the sort of music you listened to" (Kolker 2012, 12). For many, the Dead shows were a place for self-discovery, personal exploration, spiritual journeying, and community—freeing themselves from mainstream constraints, at least for the duration of a show.

The historical evidence suggests that the aging band became aware of the commercial potential and spending power inherent in their fan base, which also contributed to the development of a specific visual language. In 1993 the band brought all of their merchandising in house (Brokaw 1994, 90), ended licensing agreements, and cracked down on the unauthorized use of their intellectual property. What ensued was a wild spate of unbridled selling of their countercultural cachet. In fact, Brokaw noted, it was "remarkable" that the Grateful Dead had "managed to retain any of their countercultural image"; surprisingly, the band seemed to have remained countercultural "in spite of its growing network of businesses" (90). In light of this new commercial control, the Dead began to produce a document called *The Grateful Dead Almanac,* which combined a band newsletter with a mail-order catalog that sold more than 150 items including T-shirts, mouse pads, and golf balls. In addition, in 1992 Jerry Garcia–designed neckties (an accessory that is most certainly not associated with the Dead) began to retail in upscale department stores like Marshall Fields. In the summer of 1997, less than two years after the death of Garcia, the Dead partnered with VH1 to broadcast a home-shopping program called "Goods from the Dead." It aired 12 times and captured a new, even younger audience.

The Grateful Dead lifestyle and sartorial style continued to develop in the new millennium. In 2006 the band turned their merchandising effort over to Rhino Entertainment. Among the products that were developed in the wake of this business move were a Grateful Dead Monopoly game, a video game in which the player could hang out on Shakedown Street, skateboard decks, and lunch boxes— products designed to meet the desires of a market aged 15–24 (Browne 2012, 16). Under the leadership of Rhino, the Grateful Dead licensed its name and imagery to the San Francisco Giants, the Dogfish Head brewery (which brewed a beer with granola), Burton snowboards, street-wear brand The Hundreds, and Converse. A Sirius XM station was also launched (Lisanti 2014). What all of these moves show beyond the effort to earn revenue is a desire to keep Dead Head culture alive by bringing new fans to the music. It is important to note there are still individuals who identify as Dead Heads, though the band no longer performs. In the summer of 2015 the remaining members of the Grateful Dead played a series of five shows in the United States billed as the *Fare Thee Well* tour that was advertised as the final performances of the band. Some of the original musicians continue to play with other bands, however, including Ratdog, Phil and Friends, and Further, thereby allowing Dead Head culture to persevere. Many fans of these spin-off groups largely conform to the sartorial types described earlier in this entry.

In addition to studio albums spreading the Dead ethos, the group released 140 official live albums, and fans produced countless thousands of additional recordings with the blessing of the band. All of this music helped to spread the culture of the Dead. Visual imagery of the Grateful Dead, including dress practices, was communicated through *The Grateful Dead Movie* (1977), "Dead Head

TV" (a monthly show that ran in the late 1980s), as well as concert footage and music videos. Countless books including *Skeleton Key: A Dictionary for Deadheads* (1994), *A Long Strange Trip* (2001), and *Grateful Dead: The Illustrated Trip* (2003) document the music, the culture, and the clothing associated with the Grateful Dead. A 2010 exhibition at the New-York Historical Society entitled "Grateful Dead Now Playing at the NYHS" is another example of the myriad ways in which Dead culture has been communicated to the masses in recent years. Finally, a "jam-band" magazine called *Dead Relix,* which began as a publication devoted to Dead show tapers, now deals with the scene that the Grateful Dead essentially founded and includes images and information about Dead spin-off bands.

All bands have fans, but not all bands form communities. All bands have a culture and a history, but not all bands make cultural history. The Grateful Dead were and are a cultural force of no small merit. Blair Jackson aptly remarked, "By the early 1990s the Dead had become both the countercultural establishment and the established counterculture" (2003, 414). The fact that late-20th-century fans of the Dead chose to adopt aspects of 1960s counterculture as a way to express their affiliation with the band is, therefore, no surprise. For many fans, the Grateful Dead and their music represented freedom from constraint and workaday boredom, rebellion from the mainstream, a context for the ecstatic exploration of the self, and the opportunity to simply commune with fellow fans. Adopting the aesthetic elements of the hippies, an idealistic counterculture made more perfect and more idealistic by the passage of time, makes sense as a form of self-expression. While some dyed-in-the-wool Dead Heads who have followed the band since its early days in California may take issue with this quasicommercial style, which is largely the expression of latecomers to the scene, the desire among younger followers to express their affiliation with the band is no more or less sincere than the passion expressed by fans who simply come as they are. The devotion of Dead Heads is often quite remarkable and was summed up quite succinctly by Jerry Garcia in conversation with Geraldo Rivera. He noted, "Our audience is like people who like licorice. Not everybody likes licorice, but people who like licorice really like licorice" (Grushkin 1983, 18). Similarly, not everyone likes street style that is in large part a reboot of street style from the 1960s, but those who do like it really like it because it helps them to connect to the greater narrative that is part of the culture of the Grateful Dead.

Further Reading

Brokaw, L. 1994. "The Dead Have Customers, Too." *Inc* 16 (9): 90.
Browne, D. 2012. "Business Booming for the Dead." *Rolling Stone* 1149: 15–18.

Carr, J. R. 2012. "Shakedown Street: A Benjamin Approach to the Grateful Dead." In *Reading the Grateful Dead: A Critical Survey*, edited by N. Meriwether, 163–80). Toronto, ON: The Scarecrow Press, Inc.

Cohen, N. 2000. "Introduction." In *The Grateful Dead: The History of a Folk Story* by G. H. Geroule. Chicago: University of Illinois Press.

Goodman, F., and T. Whiteside. 1990. "The End of the Road?" *Rolling Stone* (585): 21.

Grushkin, P. 1983. *Grateful Dead: The Official Book of the Dead Heads.* New York: William Morrow & Company, Inc.

Jackson, B. 2003. *Grateful Dead: The Illustrated Trip.* London: DK Publishing, Inc.

Kolker, A. 2012. "What Are Dead Heads? An Informal Survey." In *Reading the Grateful Dead: A Critical Survey*, edited by N. Meriwether, 181–92). Toronto, ON: The Scarecrow Press, Inc.

Lacayo, R. 2008. "A Piece of Our Time." *Time* 171 (14): 64.

Lisanti, T. 2014. "Jam-on." *License Global* 17 (6): 35–42.

"Open Up, Tune In, Turn On." 1967. *Time* 89 (25): 61.

Scott, D. M., and B. Halligan. 2010. *Marketing Lessons from the Grateful Dead: What Every Business Can Learn from the Most Iconic Band in History.* Hoboken, NJ: John Wiley & Sons.

Emo (Late 1990s–ca. 2014)

The term "emo" is an abbreviation of the word "emocore" (emotional hardcore) and is applied to a category of music of the 1980s and the street style of individuals who identify with the music derived from that genre. The term seems to have first been applied in 1985 to describe new currents in the Washington, D.C., hardcore punk scene (Greenwald 2003, 14) in which a handful of bands began to integrate emotional and introspective lyrics into the fast, loud, angry hard-rock sound that typified punk rock in that era. Over time, most emo music has evolved into melodic pop rock (sometimes called pop punk), with only the subtlest vestiges of driving punk guitar riffs and raucous drumbeats remaining audible in subtle undercurrents and select instrumentation. Originally, followers of emocore generally dressed as any other punks of the 1980s might have, and a sartorial style distinct, though derived, from punk did not develop until more than a decade later. Interestingly, the emo label, much like the hipster label, is generally refused and denied by the musicians to whom it is applied. Writing about the emo scene, Andy Greenwald noted in 2003, "There is not now, nor has there ever been, a single major band that admits to being emo. Not one" (1–2). Furthering this point with literary humor, Peter Hoare (2014), writing for MTV.com, noted that the emo label "is the equivalent of Hester Prynne being branded with the scarlet A." Notably, though, youths who follow the scene, which has a strong Internet presence, have been far more likely to accept the moniker and use it to describe both themselves and their interests. As much as emo is a music scene and a look, it is also an attitudinal stance that highlights emotions including depression, indifference, empathy, angst, and insecurity, and it is because of these points of focus that the scene is centered in a youthful demographic.

A variety of commentators (some writing from within the scene and others from a scholarly perspective) have suggested that emo is not really a specific genre of music nor a sociocultural movement but is rather an emotional response to the normative, angry, aggressive, heterosexual masculinities that are part of American culture at large and that were central to punk's countercultural stance (Carrillo-Vincent 2013, 36). Alternatively, emo has been defined quite simply as "a particular relationship between a fan and a band" (Greenwald 2003, 4), in particular one in which the band facilitates the expression of emotional content and energy. Others have argued that emo is a kind of music, in particular a "tuneful strain of punk rock"; but more importantly, emo is thought to be a "state of mind" and "a place where people who don't fit in—but who long to fit in with *other* people who don't fit in—come to find solace" (Simon and Kelly 2007, 1). All of these theoretical angles point to the idea that emo is a somewhat unified approach that allows young people to embody, affect, and express a raw, emotional lived experience and worldview. The lyrics of bands that are categorized as emo reflect personal angst and social struggle. They are frequently confessional, often melodramatic, and routinely introspective. Among the bands that are generally considered emo (though there are perpetual debates) are the 1980s punk band Rites of Spring and contemporary bands including Jimmy Eat World, Saves the Day, Sunny Day Real Estate, Dashboard Confessional, and Good Charlotte. Acting as a conduit and unifying force within the emo subsection of youth culture, these bands have also been highly influential with regard to establishing and communicating a unique emo street style.

The sartorial language of punk is clearly perceptible in a modified, modernized way that melds elements of Goth, skater, and hipster street-style characteristics into a look that is largely adopted by adolescent boys and girls. It seems that this unique emo look developed only at the very end of the 1990s, in the wake of grunge's demise, and this evolution occurred in large part because record companies were looking for a way to market some of the bands that filled their rosters (Carrillo-Vincent 2013, 46). In particular Rich Egan of Vagrant Records seems to have been the key innovator who marketed emo as a cohesive whole with bands like Jimmy Eat World and Dashboard Confessional (Greenwald 2003, 70) at the forefront of this effort. A primary characteristic of emo sartorial style relates to bending and testing the boundaries of traditional gender norms (a characteristic also found in hipster street style). While both male and female emos wear much the same apparel (much of which is unisex), some emo sartorial choices specifically feminize the male body, making it a potential site of controversy, and in turn neutralize the standard, culturally mandated sexual appeal of the female body. The close cut and slim fit of basic pieces of apparel become a site for redefinition when they dress the young, ideally slender male body. Tight, typically black, clothes including skinny jeans, snug band T-shirts, shrunken cardigans or V-neck sweaters, diminutive hooded sweatshirts, and slim-fitting polo-style shirts worn with the collar popped or buttoned all the way up are among the defining pieces of apparel that are worn by both sexes but make the greatest challenges to mainstream sartorial practices when they are worn by males. An homage to Goth is made via heavy black makeup including thick eyeliner, mascara, and dark-colored nail polish. These cosmetics are worn by both sexes but more overtly challenge sartorial conventions when applied to the male body. Iconic emo hairstyles draw from the punk vocabulary but are far less varied. Hair is typically dyed. A jet-black hue is most common; however, streaks of brightly colored hair in hues like hot pink or electric blue have been common in the first decades of the new millennium, when colored hair dye has generally been on trend. Hair is typically worn short and messy or spiky on top with the sides cut short and jagged and brushed forward. Long, greasy bangs that shield the eyes complete the look and are iconic for both male and female emos. Notably, both sexes often augment the style with decorative barrettes. Both sexes also favor piercings worn in the ears, nose, eyebrows, tongue, cheeks, and lips. Studded belts, buckled at the side, leather wrist cuffs, and horn-rimmed or thick-rimmed glasses are all popular accessories. Tattoos, including emo song lyrics of special importance to the wearer, are also common in the emo scene. Preferred footwear styles include heavy black shoes like Doc Martens or low-top Converse All Stars.

The emo look, which borrows heavily from the long-established punk-rock and Goth sartorial vocabularies and the more modern and widespread iterations of skater and hipster, while also reconfiguring very common and basic pieces of apparel, has been the target of school dress bans, widespread parental concern, and unprovoked physical attacks (Riggs 2008). School administrators and parents alike, from locales spanning the globe, have been influenced by media reports that link the emo scene to teen suicides and other forms of self-harm including self-cutting and anorexia. Dress bans in schools have been one tactic that has been used to try to limit the influence of emo and presumably address its attending social problems. Both the popular press and social media confirm that there is a relationship between emo and self-harm and emo and a beauty standard that emphasizes extreme slenderness; however, the notion that emo is indelibly linked to either of these cultural currents is unfounded and dispelled by the photographs posted on social media that show smiling young people of highly varied body types identifying with emo. However, the term "emorexia" was coined to refer to the superslim ideal perpetuated by individuals like Pete Wentz of Fall Out Boy who purportedly wore a size 26 girls pant in the first decade of the new millennium, at the height of emo's popularity (Ringen 2006, 84). The link between emo music, dress, and various forms of self-harm largely seems to be a leap of logic perpetuated by ratings-driven popular media including televised news magazines. The emo look has also been the target of physical violence against its adopters in locations around the world including the United States, Central America, the Middle East, and Russia. Social media is frequently used to facilitate "emo-bashing" at designated times and places. The emo scene itself is not generally linked to street brawls, and the violence largely seems to be "provoked" by the dress practices of emo males. Writing for the journal *Social Text,* Matthew Vincent-Carrillo interpreted such violent outbursts against emos as examples of "conservative policing of rigid gender norms" that attack "emo's fey ambiguities and feminine style" because it is perceived as "a threat to normative logics of privilege, threats serious enough to merit violent responses, both physical and otherwise" (2013, 39). In some circles the emo refusal of traditional masculine norms is read as a powerful gesture that undermines important and meaningful social norms, an indication of the subtle but pervasive power inherent in dress practices. While individuals in some circles attack emos based on their undermining of heteronormativity, emo has also been critiqued as a cultural entity that reinforces heteronormative cultural hegemony. It has been pointed out that misogynistic tendencies run rampant through song lyrics and pervade chat-room discussions (Ryalls 2013, 84). It has also been noted that emo style is "reflective of traditional assumptions of gay aestheticism associated with femininity and androgyny" (Ryalls 2013, 88). This criticism, aimed at male emos, asserts that they capitalize on allusions to femininity and weakness as a way of consolidating social power.

While the musicians associated with the emo music scene eschew the label, teenagers who identify with the bands have used the label quite frequently in social-media spaces like MakeoutClub, MySpace, and Facebook and blogspots like LiveJournal and EmoPuddle. Websites dedicated to emo culture like fourfa.com have also been created to disseminate emo style, tastes, and interests. Reliance on the World Wide Web has shaped the emo scene in a few important ways that differentiate it from other, earlier music-based social milieus. First, the Internet has made emo a national (Greenwald 2003, 58) and ultimately international subculture. Unlike the punk scene of the late 1970s and early 1980s, which slowly incubated regional differences and which relied on media sent through the mail or retailed at local specialty shops, emo is easily accessible to a universe of youths who have Internet access. The importance of the virtual community of emo has been aptly noted.

Social-media spaces serve as places for "kids who feel otherwise exiled out in the suburbs—a place to hang out . . . for people who generally don't have a place to hang out" (Simon and Kelly 2007, 73). The fact that many emos "hang out" in virtual spaces means that the cultural production is less varied and robust than the cultural product created by groups like Goths or skateboarders, who routinely interact in real space and create cultural products including printed publications and films.

The consumption of music is integral to emo identity formation, and emo kids are consumers of a wide variety of products promoted by leaders and followers of the scene. Emos use social media to share information about favorite bands, brands, and products, including mainstream apparel companies such as American Apparel and Converse All Stars. Brands like Heartcore Clothing and Bleeding Star Clothing have special appeal among emos (their graphics include images with strong emotional content like bleeding hearts torn in two pieces) and rely heavily on social media for their promotion and for retailing. The intersection between emo music, celebrities, and apparel is an interesting aspect of this 21st-century sartorial scene. Members of many emo bands have created celebrity-owned or -designed clothing lines. For example, the members of Blink 182 have started two separate labels. One line is called Macbeth (by Tom DeLonge), and a second line is labeled Atticus (by Mark Hoppas and Tom DeLonge). Brothers Benji and Joel Madden of the band Good Charlotte also founded two clothing labels: DCMA Collection and Made. Additionally, Pete Wentz, the front man of Fall Out Boy, founded the label Clandestine Industries. The apparel offerings in these lines consist largely of T-shirts, hoodies, hats, and sneakers, and the aesthetics rely heavily on screened graphic designs that have been created to appeal to emo tastes and sensibilities. As emo gained in popularity toward the middle of the aughts, retailers like Hot Topic have also become an important conduit for selling emo style. Product offerings geared to the emo scene are not restricted to apparel. For example, in 2005 Emo Kid Gum was launched and marketed as "specially formulated for those with sensitive souls."

At the time of writing this entry the term emo has been "all but retired" (Hoare 2014). Many bands that were routinely labeled emo in the aughts have attained and held mainstream acceptance and widespread popularity for close to a decade. For example, Panic! At the Disco and Fall Out Boy have both performed on daytime talk show *Ellen* in 2016 as a way of promoting their top-ten records to an increasingly diverse demographic. Notably, the dress practices of the leaders of the emo scene have also largely been mainstreamed, with few of the defining emo dress characteristics prominently visible in the current dress practices of emo celebrities. While vestiges of the iconic emo look can still be found, the peak of emo street style was reached circa 2008 and seems to have disappeared in the first decades of the 20-teens, though vestiges of the look are still found internationally, especially within the tween demographic.

From the late 1990s through the first decade of the new millennium emo offered an expressive outlet for teens who wanted to stand apart from the mainstream through their musical and sartorial choices. Drawing on the subcultural stances of punk, Goth, and skaters, as well as the ultratrendy aesthetics of the hipster, the emo devotee created a sartorial impact that was antimainstream without being radical or truly countercultural. The emo stylistic amalgam was an excellent sartorial vehicle for expressing teenage angst until it became mainstreamed. The rather quick decline in popularity of the emo aesthetic is undoubtedly due to its widespread adoption that was facilitated through various outlets of the Internet. Rapid dissemination and adoption of dress ideas are part of culture in the age of the Internet, but what is also a clear and widespread facet of modern fashion is the quick return to sartorial ideas that have only recently been outmoded. Thus, as bands considered emo retain their popularity in the second decade of the new millennium, it is entirely possible that the emo dress practices outlined in this article will return to popularity in the years to come.

Further Reading

Carrillo-Vincent, M. 2013. "Wallflower Masculinities and the Peripheral Politics of Emo." *Social Text* 31(3): 35–55.

Greenwald, A. 2003. *Nothing Feels Good: Punk Rock, Teenagers, and Emo.* New York: St. Martin's Griffin.

Hoare, P. 2014. "The Rise and Fall of Emo: Why You Shouldn't Be Ashamed for Liking Emo Music." www.mtv.com, May 24. Retrieved August 16, 2016, from www.mtv.com.

Riggs, M. 2008. "Emo Rescue." *Reason* 40 (6): 72.

Ringen, J. 2006. "Emorexia." *Rolling Stone* (October 19): 84.

Ryalls, E. 2013. "Emo Angst, Masochism, and Masculinity in Crisis." *Text and Performance Quarterly* 33 (2): 83–97.

Simon, L., and T. Kelly. 2007. *Everybody Hurts: An Essential Guide to Emo Culture.* New York: Harper Entertainment.

Williams, S. 2007. "A Walking Open Wound: Emo Rock and the 'Crisis' of Masculinity in America." In *Oh Boy! Masculinity and Popular Music,* edited by Freya Jarman-Ivens, 145–60. New York: Routledge.

Gay Pride (1970–Present)

The sartorial style of LGBTQ (lesbian, gay, bisexual, transgender, queer) people is a constantly evolving phenomenon that, over time, has responded to the sociocultural contexts in which LGBTQ individuals have lived. Thus LGBTQ dress practices are diverse, complex, and always in flux. A comprehensive, historically contextualized discussion of all LGBTQ sartorial practices would require a thorough investigation of mainstream fashions over time, the societal attitudes toward diversity pertaining to sexuality and gender identity, and whether or not LGBTQ individuals felt compelled to reveal or conceal their sexual orientations from the populace at large. Such a discussion would require hundreds of pages to survey these topics in sufficient detail. However, in the latter part of the 20th century annual celebrations of LGBTQ identity have evolved. These events are generally referred to as "gay pride" celebrations, and these parades and street parties provide a special context in which gender and sexual identity are performed and thereby provide a microcosm in which the multitude of LGBTQ sartorial styles can be considered in brief. The sartorial performance of sexual and gender identity is incredibly personal and subject to endless nuances; therefore, this entry seeks only to document major trends and trajectories that have been visible in the LGBTG community for the past 40 years or so.

The first gay pride parade (known originally as the Christopher Street Liberation Day Parade) was held in New York City in 1970 and was in part a reflection of the cohesion of the gay rights movement that was in evidence in the wake of the Stonewall riots that had taken place in New York City in June 1969 (these riots were a response to repeated police raids of gay and lesbian social spots, including the Stonewall Inn). The first gay pride parade represented an opportunity to be "out" and to make a demonstration for civil rights. By 1971 gay pride events were held in cities around the United States including San Francisco, Boston, Dallas, and Milwaukee, and internationally in cites including London, Paris, Stockholm, and West Berlin. These parades and celebrations provided an opportunity for like-minded individuals to come together, declare their identities in a safe space, and vocalize issues of concern to their communities. Over time the celebrations have evolved to include religious leaders, politicians, and parents of LGBTQ people, and both independent marchers and organized groups such as (in New York City) the Gay Officers Action League, an organization of LGBTQ police officers and firefighters, and activist group the Radical Faeries.

It is important to note that in the 1970s, at the advent of gay pride gatherings, closeting of sexual identity was widespread, and the law often provided for discrimination against LGBTQ individuals. Thus gay pride events gave LGBTQ people the opportunity to proclaim and display their sexual and gender identities in a manner that was strengthened by their numbers. Gay pride has always been an unbridled performance space and an incubator for ideas related to declaring personal identity. Amy Waldman writing for *The New York Times* in 1999 aptly referred to the New York City gay pride parade as an international "coming out" and a "rite of passage," a place where individuals can openly convey an authentic personal identity. Eric Lipton, writing for the same newspaper one year later, noted that the march is a "rowdy event, sort of half Mardi Gras, half political rally" for LGBTQ people, an indication that gay pride gatherings often utilize heightened, ostentatious displays of sexual and gender identity as a tool for communication. Gay pride celebrations have become sites where one can see the manifold declarations of sexual and gender identities, and thus exploring gay pride as a category of street style facilitates an introduction to the topic of the manifold LGBTQ street styles in the United States.

Prior to the Stonewall riots the communicative power of the sartorial style of LGBTQ men and women often relied on symbols that were recognizable within the subculture but were not wholly legible to outsiders, though individuals beyond the LGBTQ community may have perceived certain indefinable qualities that were out of synch with mainstream dress practices. Additionally, prior to the gay civil rights movement, gay and lesbian signifiers were largely locale specific, with sartorial choices like red ties and bleached hair functioning in New York City and Liberty ties and suede shoes functioning in London (Steele 2013, 29) as signifiers of gay men. A book called *Gay Semiotics* (1977) by Hal Fischer provided specific documentation of how apparel and accessories could be coded among gay men (a theme that is covered in some detail in the entry on leathermen). Gay and lesbian street-style aesthetics have changed dramatically over time, ranging from overt femininity to hypermasculinity, and attitudes conveyed by influential organizations like the Mattachine Society and Daughters of Bilitis have also fluctuated with the times, advocating conformity as a political strategy in the 1970s (Cole 2013, 139; Katz 2013, 222) and visibility in later decades. Thus LGBTQ style has been about both visibility and invisibility (Cole 139). In the following paragraphs the dominant (and sometimes overlapping) themes that have been developed as expressions of LGBTQ identity will be explored in specific, though not necessarily exhaustive, detail.

One way in which LGBTQ people express identity is through bending the boundaries of gendered clothes. Since the 19th century lesbian women have adopted aspects of dress that were designed for men. Among the components that were worn were button-down shirts, neckties, various kinds of suit jackets, and most importantly, trousers. It is important to note that this sartorial move, made prior to the women's rights movement, made lesbians "defiantly visible" (Wilson 2013, 185) in eras in which there were legal and social prohibitions against women wearing pants. From the middle of the 20th century onward, some lesbians have adopted a "butch" manner of dress that utilizes the tropes of working-class men to create a sartorial statement that confronts cultural standards of femininity. Among the elements that have commonly been employed are loose-fitting blue jeans, boxy T-shirts, flannel work shirts, work boots, and short haircuts, whereas makeup has generally been eschewed. Gay men have long tested the boundaries of gendered clothes by wearing vibrant colors and decorative patterns that were deemed feminine in the wake of the Great Masculine Renunciation of the 18th century (a sociocultural offshoot of the Enlightenment in which men renounced things considered decorative and ostentatious and, therefore, feminine). Grooming practices that were widely considered feminine (including applying makeup, waxing, getting facials, and moisturizing) were until quite recently dalliances beyond the boundaries of a rigid masculine-feminine binary and were long considered hallmarks of gay manhood. Crossdressing is ostensibly distinct from experimenting with and sampling from gendered dress practices. The term "crossdressing" implies a more holistic approach to transgressing the boundaries of gendered dress and, in a sense, performing the gender not typically associated with one's sex. Crossdressing is commonly adopted as a means of self-actualization for transgender individuals, but it is also done as a means of social and political commentary by some drag kings and drag queens.

The adoption of dress practices that employ hyperbolic (exaggerated) gendering is also a widespread theme across LGBTQ dress practices. Hyperbolic gendering involves adopting iconic, exaggerated, or extreme iterations of masculine or feminine dress. Hyperbolic gendering may involve embodying a heightened interpretation of one's own sex and commonly ascribed gender, or as has already been discussed with regard to the "butch" aesthetic, it may involve transgressing the boundaries that are commonly accepted. The "clone" look is one example of hyperbolic gendering. Gay men adopted this post-Stonewall street style, which utilized the tropes of stereotypical working-class masculinity including tight T-shirts, blue jeans, motorcycle boots, and aviator sunglasses. The "bear" look is also a style adopted by gay men that employs a vision of hyperbolic masculinity. Typical tropes of this aesthetic include the wearing of beards and moustaches, and adoption of articles of clothing that kindle notions of lumberjacks, hunters, and rustic outdoorsmen. Flannel shirts and jackets in Buffalo plaid, Henley undershirts, and work boots are worn to conjure images of ardently masculine men.

Drag performance is also an important part of LGBTQ culture and a visible component of gay pride celebrations. Drag queens and drag kings are males and females, respectively, who dress in over-the-top, often complex ensembles to perform a stereotypical vision of a gender. Outside of gay pride celebrations, drag is not generally a street style, as it is a style adopted for performance and entertainment, but within the context of gay pride parades and parties, drag kings and queens move to the streets to perform and influence conceptions about the gender binary and accepted norms for dress, decorum, and enactment of gender. Elizabeth Wilson has noted that drag king performance is about "decentering and deconstructing dominant paradigms of masculinity" while also expressing aspects of personal identity (2013, 206). Some drag kings and queens may also use their sartorial presentation as a form of activism, using their appearances to "challenge notions of identity and truthfulness" and refute "natural categories" (Katz 2013, 227).

Gay pride celebrations present an opportunity for some participants to bring overt sexuality to the streets. Parade participants may strut the streets wearing scanty or see-through apparel like bikini bathing suits and hot pants paired with platform shoes. Such highly revealing apparel is often styled in an eccentric manner. In 2000 one reporter noted a marcher dressed in a silver cape and jock strap who was also wearing roller skates and a tiara (Lipton 2000). Such presentations of the body seem designed to allow the wearer to unabashedly publicly present the sexual self while employing a species of shock tactics upon spectators. Individuals who identify with leather sexuality, BDSM, or dominance and submission also bring aspects of their (typically) private sexual proclivities to the public sphere during gay pride as a way to openly declare their orientations.

While heightened presentations of gender and sexuality are visually arresting forms of identity performance that are widely employed in gay pride celebrations, there are also revelers who employ an androgynous self-presentation to express their identity. Individuals who dress in an androgynous manner wear apparel and accessories that hide sexual characteristics and style hair and use makeup in a way that makes the sex of the person ambiguous. It has been suggested that the androgynous aesthetic first gained widespread appeal among gay and lesbian men and women in the 1980s with the rise of new wave music (Wilson 2013, 199). By considering a wide crosssection of cultural products—including advertising campaigns, popular musicians, and Hollywood movie characters—it is clear that employing an ambiguous presentation of gender has gained widespread appeal across youthful demographics in the new millennium. The desire to circumvent the gender binary reflects the desire to remain uncategorized and ideally escape judgment. For LGBTQ people searching for identity in a culture that thrives on categories, androgyny may represent a strategy of refusal.

Gay pride celebrations are also an opportunity for activist groups to convey their messages *en masse*. Groups like the Lavender Menace have used slogan T-shirts since the 1960s, but they have increased in visibility since the 1980s in response to the vitriol expressed by the religious right and have become standard since the 1990s as a "new politics of visibility then took hold" (Katz 2013, 224–25). Activist groups seeking attention for the AIDS epidemic, gay marriage, anti-discrimination, and antiviolence issues have used apparel as a canvas for communicating an activist agenda. Among the most prominent activist groups in the United States are ACT UP (AIDS Coalition to Unleash Power), GLAD (Gay and Lesbian Advocates & Defenders), and Lambda Legal, an association of LGBTQ lawyers.

Rainbow apparel is another way in which LGBTQ individuals express aspects of identity through dress. The rainbow flag, which was created by Gilbert Baker in 1978 at the behest of gay rights activist Harvey Milk (Baker 2007), was first conceived as an expression of diversity. The rainbow flag was first flown in the Castro District of San Francisco but has since been transformed into all manner of apparel including T-shirts and tank tops, socks, suspenders, sunglasses, bow ties, hair extensions, tutus, leg warmers, capes, and wings. While the rainbow motif is especially visible during gay pride celebrations, it is also visible throughout the year, and online specialty retailers including Rainbow Depot and Pride Shack specialize in the multicolored apparel and accessories, while mainstream brick-and-mortar retailers like Target include LGBTQ-centric apparel in the summer when most pride events occur in the United States. The rainbow can also be used for political or activist purposes. In 2014 members of the Boy Scouts of America marched in their khaki scouting uniforms accented with rainbow neckerchiefs (Yee 2014). In addition to the wearing of the rainbow, some members of the LGBTQ community also wear specific graphic symbols that communicate aspects of identity. Among the symbols that are utilized are both the pink and black triangles that were used in Nazi concentration camps to mark gays and "a-socials," respectively. The Greek lambda symbol (λ), which was declared the international symbol for gay and lesbian rights by the International Gay Rights Congress in 1974, is also a commonly used motif.

Of course, gay pride celebrations are also populated with countless people who dress in a manner that does not fit tidily or specifically into an LGBTQ street-style category. For some people, gay pride and identity are simply personal identity—a unique, unstudied, creative, constantly shifting concoction of apparel, accessories, and symbols that expand and evolve as the person moves through life. Countless participants in gay pride events simply come as they are to celebrate in an event that is personally meaningful. Additionally, the presence of uniformed personnel, including police officers and firefighters who come attired in their dress uniforms, demonstrates how gay pride may be performed by showing one's professional identity.

LGBTQ culture, long a wholly marginalized subculture, has a rich history of underground systems of communication. Independent serial publications, with international, national, and regional scope, include titles like *Lesbian Tide, The Gay and Lesbian Review Worldwide, Lesbian Connection,* and *The Advocate.* Publications of this kind have long communicated both images and text of interest to their readership as well as advertisements for specialty products including apparel. Since the middle of the 1990s LGBTQ culture and identity have become increasingly mainstreamed in the United States. Among the examples of national programming that have brought versions of LGBTQ identity into American homes were the situation comedies *Ellen* (1994–1998), starring Ellen DeGeneres, and *Will and Grace* (1998–2006), and the dramas *The L Word* (2004–2009) and *Transparent* (2014–present). *RuPaul's Drag Race* (2009–present), a reality-show competition featuring sparring drag queens, has also served as a vehicle for communicating aspects of LGBTQ culture and identity. In the last several decades American celebrities have become increasingly open about sexuality and gender identity that does not conform to the traditional binary. The long-running *The Ellen DeGeneres Show* (2003–present), an hour-long talk and variety show, is a notable example of mainstream programming that has found a broad audience and is hosted by a woman who identifies as lesbian and often dresses in an androgynous or masculine-inspired manner.

It is important to note that expressing LGBTQ identity openly and freely has been a long-lived struggle. American public policy has consistently been written to exclude individuals who did not conform to the established gender binary and heterosexual behavior (for example, the McCarran–Walter Act of 1952 was written and implemented to exclude homosexual foreign visitors—a policy that was enforced through visual identification into the late 1970s). Furthermore, the politics of sexuality in the United States in the 20th century made many homosexual acts illegal, and people (especially men) could be arrested based on how they walked, talked, or dressed or with whom they socialized. Merle Killer's articles for *The New York Times,* written in the early 1970s, describe being blacklisted and threatened in the wake of coming out as a gay man. Notably, it was only in 1973 that the American Psychiatric Association determined that homosexuality was "not a mental disorder," though crossdressing (what is labeled in the APA's *Diagnostic and Statistical Manual of Mental Disorders* as "Transvestic Disorder") remains a diagnosable psychological defect at the time of writing. Studies finding that sexual preferences are inherent rather than preferential or socially conditioned were not published until the 1980s (see the Kinsey Institute for Sex Research, *Sexual Preference: Its Development in Men and Women*). This small sample of data points to the fact that visible, legible declarations of sexual and gender identity on the part of LGBTQ people were for a long time made in the face of hostility and under threat of punishment or reprisal.

Asserting a blanket statement about the meaning or importance of LGBTQ street and subcultural styles in general seems misguided, as gender and sexual identity are so profoundly personal. Yet a concluding and summative remark may be made about the techniques that are employed by the many versions of LGBTQ style described in the preceding paragraphs. Many forms of LGBTQ street and subcultural style exploit the rigid gendering of apparel, accessories, and grooming that are embedded in contemporary Western dress practices. By bending and reshaping meaning through juxtapositions and by exercising hyperbolic manifestations of gendered dress, LGBTQ people are able to make personal statements about their own identities while also pushing at the boundaries of other people's conceptions of gendered dress.

The impact of LGBTQ style on mainstream fashion has been profound. Not only have LGBTQ individuals influenced the mainstream by working as fashion designers (see Steele 2013), but the specific dress aesthetics of leathermen, bears, clones, and drag queens (to name but a few archetypes) have influenced countless collections (see Versace Autumn/Winter 1992), both by literal sampling and by serving as a more general source of inspiration. More broadly, as we move through the second decade of the 21st century radical change is percolating through both high-style fashion and street styles. Some long-lived prohibitions regarding what men can and should wear seem to be breaking down (at least in some social circles), and widespread experimentation is evident. Although the motivating factors for these shifts are numerous and diverse, the sartorial contributions and revolutionary practices of LGBTQ individuals are undoubtedly among the relevant factors.

Further Reading

Baker, G. 2007. "Pride-Flyin' Flag: Rainbow Flag Founder Marks 30 Year Anniversary." *Metro Weekly,* October 17. Retrieved September 8, 2016, from www.metroweekly.com.

Cole, S. 2013. "Queerly Visible: Gay Men, Dress, and Style." In *A Queer History of Fashion: From the Closet to the Catwalk,* edited by V. Steele, 135–65. New York: Fashion Institute of Technology.

Katz, J. D. 2013. "Queer Activist Fashion." In *A Queer History of Fashion: From the Closet to the Catwalk,* edited by V. Steele, 219–32. New York: Fashion Institute of Technology.

Killer, M. 1971. "What It Means to Be a Homosexual (continued)." *The New York Times,* October 10. Retrieved September 10, 2016, from www.nytimes.com.

Lipton, E. 2000. "Politicians March in a Racy Celebration of Gay Progress." *The New York Times,* June 26. Retrieved September 10, 2016, from www.nytimes.com.

Steele, V. 2013. "A Queer History of Fashion: From the Closet to the Catwalk." In *A Queer History of Fashion: From the Closet to the Catwalk,* edited by V. Steele, 7–75). New York: Fashion Institute of Technology.

Waldman, A. 1999. "30 Years after Stonewall, Diversity Is Shown in Gay Pride Parade." *The New York Times,* June 28. Retrieved September 10, 2016, from www.nytimes.com.

Wilson, E. 2013. "What Does a Lesbian Look Like?" In *A Queer History of Fashion: From the Closet to the Catwalk,* edited by V. Steele, 167–91. New York: Fashion Institute of Technology.

Yee, V. 2014. "With Rainbow Neckerchiefs, Celebrating Pride and Progress at Parade: Boy Scouts Make Provocative Statement at Gay Pride Parade." *The New York Times,* June 29. Retrieved September 10, 2016, from www.nytimes.com.

Goth (Early 1980s–Present)

Goth or Gothic style first emerged in the United Kingdom in the late 1970s and was a visible aesthetic movement in the United States by the early 1980s. The label, which is essentially a pejorative term that references a barbarian clan and a style of art that flourished between the Classical Period and the Renaissance, is also used to refer to a postpunk genre of music as well as its accompanying sartorial style. Additionally, the term is used by many to refer to a larger, more complex Goth identity. Individuals who identify with Gothic culture or as a Goth may identify with a music scene but may also identify with the occult or horror literature (especially from the Victorian era) and may be enamored with the beauty and sublimity of death. However, as with all subcultural styles, affiliation with a look and with any accompanying ideology always exists on a spectrum, and those who dress in an identifiable Gothic style may not personally identify as Goth. Goth music, style, and identity emerged from the social and musical milieu of punk music, amidst all of the angst and anger it expressed, and individuals developed a new mode of expressing disaffection, alienation, and otherness that was more contemplative, introspective, and romantic than punk. The lyrics of early Goth musicians as well as their personal style seem to have been the catalyst for what ultimately became a unique, identifiable offshoot of the punk scene.

Siouxsie Sioux (born Susan Janet Ballion), the lead singer of the British Goth band Siouxsie and the Banshees, is often cited as the prototype for both Goth music and style. Ballion was a follower of the early punk-music scene in London and was a member of a group of young, stylish fans who were referred to as the Bromley Contingent by journalist Caroline Coon. Members of the Bromley Contingent dressed the part of the punk-rock fan, sporting plenty of black clothes, leather, chains, safety pins, and spiked hair. Ballion, who was not trained as a musician, was inspired by the raw, free-form, highly improvised music of early punk and formed a band in 1976 that was supported by Malcolm McLaren, the manager of the seminal punk band the Sex Pistols. Siouxsie Sioux's arresting appearance and command of the stage led to quick success on the pop-music charts. The evocative, introspective lyrics that dealt with themes of alienation, fear, and perversity as well as the eerie, atonal musical strains that echoed musicality from horror soundtracks marked a stylistic point of departure from punk as it had been. Notably, female front women were a minority in the punk scene. Siouxsie Sioux's personal appearance blended hard-rock masculinity and beguiling feminine traits into a unique form of androgyny and thereby set the stage for new sensibilities for the enactment of gender. Other early postpunk acts with similar attributes were soon perceptible within the British music scene. Among them were The Cure and Bauhaus, while

Joy Division was a band that developed similar musical interests but was generally understated with regard to sartorial style.

As the Goth music scene developed a legion of followers, the subculture connected to the music flourished, and new veins of interest developed that aligned with the musical themes. Some followers of Goth explored horror literature such as *The Castle of Otranto* by Horace Walpole (1764), *Frankenstein* by Mary Shelley (1818), *Dracula* by Bram Stoker (1897), the works of Edgar Allen Poe (1809–1849) and the more modern *Interview with the Vampire* (1976) by Anne Rice. Early horror movies were also a source of interest and inspiration, including Robert Wiene's *Cabinet of Doctor Caligari* (1920) and F. W. Murnau's *Nosferatu* (1923). Romantic paintings, most famously Henry Fuseli's *The Nightmare* (1781), were also a wellspring that lent themselves to interpretations. The images and ideas present in and related to these works are linked to developments in Goth sartorial style, especially the inclusion of apparel inspired by the Victorian era and accessories and affectations related to vampirism. As Catherine Spooner noted in "Undead Fashion: Nineties Style and the Perennial Return of Goth," "Gothic literary and cinematic tradition provide a ready-made lexicon of otherness and difference through which the disaffected are able to articulate alienation" (2007, 153). By tapping into these sources of inspiration, Goths of the 1980s distanced themselves both sartorially and subculturally from their punk roots.

Goth sartorial style from the late 1970s through the 1980s was typically derived from a combination of influences from punk rock, fetish dressing, and 19th-century sources. Black was the dominant color for apparel, hair, and makeup, but accents of red, white, green, and purple were sometimes used. Notably, black is the color that is used to symbolize mourning across many cultures worldwide. In 19th- and early-20th-century Europe and North America, both purple and white were used to designate later stages of mourning, while green may be associated with putrefaction and decay. The use of red as an accent color may be related to its symbolic reference to blood. The apparel worn by Goth men and women varied greatly according to preference. Women often wore skirts and dresses; however, some women wore long, billowing garments whereas others opted for shorter, tighter ensembles that could have dominatrix and S/M (sadomasochistic) overtones. Similarly, some men opted for pants that were cut narrow and tight and paired them with tailored upper-body garments, whereas pants with legs cut very wide were also commonplace. Apart from the proportions of the apparel, certain aesthetic themes were common in this period. The use of straps with silver buckles on shirtsleeves, pant legs, and boots was a popular aesthetic device that referenced bondage and confinement in straightjackets, a device that was also popular among punks beginning in the 1970s. Lacings were also seen in both men's and women's apparel. Corset tops, which traditionally are laced up the back, laced up both the back and the front. Lacings could also be built into dresses, shirts, and pants. Doc Marten boots were standard footwear, as were platform-soled and pointed-toe boots or shoes. Materials associated with fetishes and S/M, such as leather, vinyl, and rubber, could also be found in Goth apparel and were often juxtaposed with a more-traditional fabric such as satin, velvet, or lace. Religious and occult symbols including crosses, crucifixes, skulls, and pentagrams were worn, often along with a tangle of silver chains and charms. Jewelry made of bones was also iconic in Goth aesthetics. Many accessories and pieces of apparel associated with Goth in this period included items sampled from historical dress such as mitts (fingerless gloves), capes, corsets, and frock coats. Many of the aesthetics that were popular in the 1980s and 1990s are still popular today.

In the 1990s Goth style changed in two ways. First, the style evolved because of a crossover between Gothic rock and the hard-rock industrial-music scene. Rock bands like Ministry and Nine Inch Nails interpreted Gothic-rock themes of transgression but set them to an experimental hard-rock sound. Furthermore, the sartorial style of the musicians reflected the merger of the two tastes. Thus, military- and industrial-inspired apparel entered Goth dress, as did highly technological influences including the use of LED lights. The latter iteration of Goth style is considered by some to be a unique style group referred to as cybergoth. In addition to influences from the industrial-music scene, mimicry and portrayals of the undead evolved and in some cases became far more heightened. Beginning in the 1990s some Goths began wearing prosthetic teeth resembling vampire fangs or the fangs of a werewolf. Additionally, colored contact lenses in hues such as white, purple, or yellow were worn by Goths wishing to capture the aesthetics of the undead. Goth hair styles had been characterized by spiky and disheveled shapes and the use of deep black hair dye since the late 1970s, but in the 1990s new ways to augment visually arresting coiffures were explored. Among the options newly arrived to the Goth scene were hair extensions in vibrant colors, the wearing of both real and artificial dreads, and greater reliance on the use of vibrant hair-dye colors.

The Goth look could be created in a variety of ways. Besides do-it-yourself clothing, thrift stores and vintage-clothing dealers were options for acquiring unusual pieces of apparel and accessories. Specialty designers and boutiques also existed around the world, offering things like corsetry and vinyl apparel. In addition, specialty mail-order companies like Bogey's from London (now defunct) provided a means for acquiring apparel with skulls, straps, and cobweb features. In the late 1990s a chain store called Hot Topic opened in the United States, offering alternative and rocker apparel to the masses. Hot Topic continues to retail in the 21st century.

Goth has always been a style that pushed at the boundaries of gender. Male Goths wear apparel with fetish influences, utilize dramatic cosmetics, and construct high-maintenance coiffures. Goth males often wear ostentatious clothes that do not conform to sartorial norms and generally confront mainstream ideas of masculinity by indulging in a romantic outlook, albeit one that may be colored by an interest in death. As Catherine Spooner noted in "Goth Boys in the Media: Femininity and Violence," "Describing Goth as 'feminine' underestimates the way in which Goth style constantly puts gender into play through performance" (2008, 147). Goth dress for males and females alike does not always conform to the neat binary of gendered clothing that is an imperative in most fashionable dress. The reasons why and the degree to which both male and female Goths play with gender constructions is highly varied in terms of both aesthetic choices and the reasons for making those choices and should not be narrowly interpreted or assumed to be a specific statement about any one thing.

Gothic subculture finds expression not just in music and dress but also in written publications. Magazines and e-zines such as *Propaganda* (discontinued in 2002), *Meltdown, Gothic Beauty, Grave Concerns,* and *Sideline* are vehicles for disseminating a wide range of Goth interests including music, dress, books, nightclubs, and social events. Websites including Gothic.net, DarkSideoftheNet.com, WaningMoon.com, and AsylumEclectica.com are also portals for a wide range of information of likely interest to individuals who identify with Goth. Goth cultural production even includes a few games for at-home entertainment: *Gother Than Thou* and *Vampire: The Masquerade.*

Goth style always has been largely communicated through musical performers including music videos. In the 1980s and early 1990s, images that accompanied vinyl albums were also common ways in which Goth style was communicated to followers of the music. Another way in which Goth style was shared was through the social scene. Many clubs in the 1980s and 1990s had Goth nights where like-minded and similarly dressed individuals could meet. Additionally, some Goths also joined vampire societies such as The Society of Nocturnus of Gotham, the Court of Lazarus, and the Court of the Iron Garden, which provided a venue for the development of ideas. Mainstream fan magazines like *Bop* and *Tiger Beat* were also important vehicles for spreading Goth style to a larger audience from the late 1980s onward. Some mainstream movies have included characters who represented as Goth. The director Tim Burton frequently makes stylistic choices that evoke Goth; however, one character in particular, Lydia Deetz (Winona Ryder) from *Beetlejuice* (1988), is often held up as an iconic example. Elvira (Cassandra Peterson) is a mainstream, campy, kitschy, "valley girl" Goth. Originally the host of a California television station's Friday night horror movies, she went on to become the star of a 1988 film entitled *Elvira, Mistress of the Dark* and has used her likeness for the promotion of a wide array of commercial products. Goth music, clothing, and attitudes were also parodied on *Saturday Night Live* in a skit called

"Goth Talk" (1997–1999). In the skit Circe Nightshade (Molly Shannon) and Azrael Abyss (Chris Kattan) hosted a talk show that featured stereotypical Goth characters and poked fun at their rarefied sensibilities. Goth fashion is so archetypal in the 21st century that even the comedic cartoon series *South Park* has an elementary school–aged Goth girl named Henrietta, a testament to the fact that a concretized, stereotyped version of Goth style exists in the mainstream imagination despite the evolution of the style in the street.

Fashion designers have regularly interpreted Goth from the 1990s onward. *Dark Glamour,* a show curated by Valerie Steele for the Gallery at F.I.T. (Fashion Institute of Technology) that ran from 2008 to 2009, presented a fine array of fashionable apparel that was inspired by Goth, and much of that exhibition is documented in her 2008 text of the same name. Among the exceptional designer collections represented in the show and text were the Fall/Winter 2006 collections of Alexander McQueen, Jean Paul Gaultier, and Gareth Pugh. However, the high-style interpretations of Goth are many, varied, and continuously in development.

Goth dress and experience are creative and individualized experiences. As the Goth author Voltaire has noted, "Goth can entail many things. For some it represents a life-encompassing philosophy that permeates every corner of existence. For others it is far more superficial" (2004, 16). Not only do people express their interest in Goth on a broad sartorial spectrum, but they also identify with the community or subculture to highly varying degrees. Creativity and individuality are as important to Goths as to any other subcultural group; however, as Ionela Iacob has argued, Goths do find unity in their opposition to homogeneity and the "limited freedom of thought" found in the mainstream (2010, 17). Goths embrace the past, the occult, the macabre, and the obscure, and in so doing they create a world that is potentially more interesting and fulfilling than the one enjoyed by the mainstream. Sharon Miklas has observed that tapping the Gothic past allows the Goth to create a "purposeful separation from everyday experience" and that identifying with Gothic history and imagery is a way of connecting to the "extraordinary," which can be concretely constructed through dress and other objects (1999, 567–68). Thus Goth is alluring for those who find the workaday world to be unsatisfying. It is a style that is a form of resistance to and escape from the mainstream.

Further Reading

Goodland, L., and M. Bibby, eds. 2007. *Goth: Undead Subculture.* Durham, NC: Duke University Press.

Iacob, I. F. 2010. "Rethinking Goth Identity as Style." *The Scientific Journal of Humanistic Studies* 2 (2): 13–25.

Kilpatrick, N. 2004. *The Goth Bible.* New York: St. Martin's Press.

Miklas, S. 1999. "The Extraordinary Self: Gothic Culture and the Construction of Self." *Journal of Marketing Management* 15: 563–76.

Spooner, C. 2007. "Undead Fashion: Nineties Style and Perennial Return of Goth." In *Goth: Undead Subculture,* edited by L. Goodland and M. Bibby, 143–54. Durham, NC: Duke University Press.

Spooner, C. 2008. "Goth Boys in the Media: Femininity and Violence." In *Men's Fashion Reader,* edited by A. Reilly and S. Cosbey, 145–59. New York: Fairchild.

Steele, V., and J. Park. 2008. *Gothic: Dark Glamour.* New Haven: Yale University Press.

Voltaire. 2004. *What Is Goth?* York Beach, ME: Weiser Books.

Whittaker, J. 2007. "Dark Webs: Goth Subcultures in Cyberspace." *Gothic Studies* 9 (1): 35–45.

Greaser (1950s–Early 1960s)

Greaser is a name given to an American youth street style that was predominantly visible in the 1950s and early 1960s, although it is possible that the style was present in the late 1940s, as the greaser look is aesthetically related to the style of dress adopted by the early motorcycle clubs and gangs of the postwar period. The problem with dating the greaser aesthetic relates in part to the fact that the term "greaser" seems not to have been applied to this look in writing until the middle of the 1960s (see the *Oxford English Dictionary* for key dates of use), well after the street style had peaked in popularity and begun to fade from use and morph into a new aesthetic. Thus, ascertaining when the look emerged is contingent upon locating dated photographs, an effort that presents challenges for the researcher. While a specific date for the advent of the style may be elusive, a well-documented history of the polysemous label is informative. The word "greaser" has been applied since the 19th century as a pejorative term for underclass laborers, especially those of Mexican origin (Bender 2003, xiii). The term has also long been used to indicate a profession: that of a machine "greaser." The greasers discussed in this entry were generally male, often but not exclusively working class, typically white, and often involved in (or associated themselves with) American hotrod or motorcycle culture. Greasers could be gang members, but dressing like a greaser did not definitively mark gang status; rather, the look was affected to communicate an antimainstream or subcultural stance, which many middle-class youths may have been attracted to. Notably, both the pejorative connotation of the ethnic slur and the interest in mechanical work are evoked in the application of this label to this specific street style. Additionally, in the context of the greaser street style, the term was also in part a description of the heavily greased hairstyles that were adopted by youths who seem to have been largely disenfranchised from the mainstream, either because of their low socioeconomic status amidst post–World War II prosperity or because of the widespread impulses toward homogeneity that pervaded American culture in this period.

Photographic evidence shows that what has come to be known as greaser style was an authentic street style in the 1950s. However, greaser style, like rockabilly style, must be considered with caution as ample documentation (especially what is found on the Internet) blurs the line between the true greaser of the postwar period and the nostalgic archetype that took root from the late 1960s onward. The 1967 publication of S. E. Hinton's *The Outsiders* used the label (which the author knew from her youth in the 1950s) in conjunction with detailed descriptions of characters, their interests, their behaviors, and their dress. Additional works of mass media, which will be discussed toward the end of this entry, were also influential in terms of codifying these subcultural dress practices in retrospect. Thus, this entry seeks to describe a very well-known American street style of the 1950s and strives to carefully separate the true nature and scope of the look in its original context from the associations and generalizations made about greasers years after their prominence.

The predominant hallmark of a greaser was a greased hairstyle. Using pomade, styling cream like Brylcream, or even Vaseline, young men slicked and sculpted their hair (which was grown long on the top and cut shorter on the sides) into elaborate styles that were known by names like the Folsom, the Pompadour, the Elephant's Trunk, and the D.A. ("duck ass"). Part of the inspiration for such coifs could have been found among performers of early rock 'n' roll or rockabilly music like Elvis Presley. Given the properties of the styling products that were commonly used (i.e., they were not sticky and did not dry), these elaborate up-swept hairstyles had to routinely be reshaped by combing, and thus the image of the greaser fixing his hair in the reflection of a window or a car's rearview mirror (a visual marker of greasers as presented in the popular mass media of later decades) undoubtedly reflects real behaviors of the 1950s. In addition to the greased hairstyle, greasers commonly wore dark blue Levis jeans (a staple of 1950s youth culture in general). Photographic evidence shows that jeans were commonly worn cuffed over black leather harness-style motorcycle boots as well as any number of other kinds of ankle-height leather boots in black or brown. Converse high-top sneakers were also commonly worn, and the various kinds of footwear could also be coupled with loose cotton-twill work pants. Black, white, or two-hued ringer T-shirts (T-shirts with contrasting neck and arm bands) were also commonplace, and rolling the armbands seems to have been a common modification designed to add swagger to the look. Some men who adopted the greaser look also wore tank tops (which would have been retailed as underwear). Greaser outerwear typically consisted of either a leather jacket or a jean jacket. The leather jacket could be a black leather motorcycle-style (Perfecto) jacket; however, any notion that this particular sartorial choice was iconic seems to be the product of later mass-media images.

The combined look of the greaser had substantial overlap with the sartorial aesthetics of motorcyclists in the 1950s. However, it is important to note that greasers were not necessarily members of street or motorcycle gangs. Although greasers were marginalized youths (or youths who affected a marginalized stance) who may have participated in street crime, and some gang members in the 1950s dressed like greasers (Salisbury 1958, 197), individuals who adopted the greaser look do not appear to have been organized into cohesive subcultural groups. Rather, the similarity in dress seems more likely to be related to a widespread understanding (perpetuated through mass media) of the communicative power of working-class clothes. Writing about American gangs in the 1950s, journalist Harrison Salisbury noted that youths across the nation listened to the same records, read the same comics, and watched the same television shows and movies. As a result, he argued, "They are subject to the same propaganda and advertising to influence their selection of dress" (1958, 204). The homogeneity in teen dress practices was also documented in a 1958 article in *The New York Times* that described young rock 'n' roll fans all dressed in the same manner. The writer of the article observed that many of the boys were wearing leather jackets and jeans (Samuels 1958), an assertion that suggests that an average fan of early rock music might have dressed in a manner resembling the greaser archetype in order to impart a rocker aesthetic rather than to assert a substantive countercultural stance.

Female greasers seem to have existed to a far lesser degree than their male counterparts. For young women who interpreted this aesthetic, the look included leather jackets and subtly sexually provocative clothes including the widely popular tight and cropped pants (especially Capri pants or pedal pushers) and off-the-shoulder tops. Teased or back-combed hairstyles and pronounced makeup were also typically part of the look for young women who associated with the greaser image and adopted its aesthetic.

Mass-media representations of rebellious youths made both in the 1950s and later have undoubtedly influenced the adoption and execution of this street style both at mid-century and in later incarnations. *Rebel without a Cause* (1955) and *West Side Story* (1961) both show a variety of interpretations of a rebellious and youthful street style that may fairly be labeled as greaser. The creators of these works of fiction were living in a period when the style was still flourishing, and in the case of *West Side Story* the writers were inspired by actual events including a 1955 article in the *Los Angeles Times* that detailed a gang fight that had taken place in San Bernardino ("Telling the Story" 2012). However, works of mass media that came later seem to have shaped the iconography of the greaser most profoundly. Perhaps most important among such works was the film adaptation of the musical *Grease* (1979) and the cinematic version of S. E. Hinton's book *The Outsiders* (1983). Hinton's 1967 book, which was based on her teenage experiences in the 1950s in Tulsa, Oklahoma, provides both the greaser sobriquet and key descriptions. From the very first page Hinton refers to her antiheroes as "greasers," describes the sartorial language of her characters including their long, greasy hair (1), blue jeans, T-shirts, leather jackets, and tennis shoes or boots (3). She further codifies the essential character of the greaser by ascribing universalizing character traits. Her narrator noted, "Greasers are almost like hoods; we steal things and drive old souped-up cars and hold up gas stations and have a gang fight once in a while" (3). Hinton's book may well have influenced and inspired creators of other works of popular culture, which presented an increasingly homogenized version of the greaser. For example, the situation comedy television series *Happy Days* (1974–1984) and the doo-wop variety show *Sha Na Na* (1977–1981) routinely depicted a synthesized, iconic representation of the greaser look that was far more formulaic that the 1950s original.

The widespread appeal of the greaser look is evident from the international interpretations of the aesthetic that developed from the 1950s onward. Among the groups who interpreted the aesthetic were the Raggare in Sweden, the Bosozoku in Japan, the Blousons Noirs in France, the Schwarze Jakken in Germany, and the Bodgies and Wedgies in both Australia and New Zealand. American popular culture as it was presented in mass media largely influenced the proliferation of this American street style in the late 20th century, rather than images of authentic street style, for which there was not the kind of user-driven, up-to-the-minute social-media outlets that are utilized in the 21st century.

The greaser street style does not seem to have relied on specific connections to the apparel industry (i.e., no retailers catered specifically to individuals who dressed in this manner, nor do there seem to have been individuals who dressed as greasers who became active participants in the fashion industry in order to promote this aesthetic). Rather, it would seem that individuals who dressed as greasers utilized purveyors of apparel basics like jeans and T-shirts and possibly specialty dealers who sold items like motorcycle jackets and boots. Given that the greaser look relied largely on working-class clothes, access to the components required to style the look would have been quite easy in most parts of the United States. Unlike individuals who identified with some aspect of motorcycle culture (through clubs or gangs), greasers did not have interest-specific organizations, publications, or other forms of cultural output; thus there does not seem to be evidence of marketing or advertising specifically to individuals who adopted this sartorial style.

A nostalgia for the youth fashions of the 1950s routinely bubbles to the surface of contemporary fashion design; thus there are countless examples of collections that loosely reference the greaser look. Runway presentations frequently reboot the upswept Pompadour and Duck Ass hairstyles, motorcycle jackets are ubiquitous, and periodically the tendency to turn up the cuffs of dark blue jeans becomes stylish. Fashion publications including *Vogue, GQ, Seventeen,* and *Lucky* routinely include editorials that group contemporary pieces of apparel together thematically, and 1950s revivals in general, as well as *Grease*-inspired photo arrays in particular, are commonplace. Contemporary references to the greaser aesthetic typically have a stronger connection to the cinematic interpretations of the look than the authentic street style of the middle of the 20th century.

Although the iconic greaser aesthetic seems to have faded from use in the late 1960s, it may be fair to say that the social and sartorial impulses did not die, but rather they changed as the culture and dress practices changed. For example, by the late 1960s short greased hair was utterly passé, while long, unkempt hair gained prominence as a marker of subcultural inclinations. Dark blue, cuffed jeans were outmoded as a marker of a rebellious sensibility and were replaced in subcultural circles by faded, ripped, patched, and flared or bell-bottom jeans. Leather jackets and jean jackets continued to enjoy their place in the rocker-rebel wardrobe, but pairings of the latter half of the 20th century gave the pieces of apparel a fresh look, and new subcultural scenes gave the look new names. Thus the greaser look is a street style that is both specific to the 1950s and 1960s and also one that enjoys endless permutations as youthful street and subcultural styles evolve.

Further Reading

Bender, S. 2003. *Greasers and Gringos: Latinos, Law, and the American Imagination.* New York: New York University Press.

Hinton, S. E. 1967. *The Outsiders.* New York: The Penguin Group.

Neumaier, J. 1998. "Happy Days: Greasers, Sock Hops, Poodle Skirts—Those Were the Days." *Entertainment Weekly* 132. Retrieved June 11, 2016, from http://search.ebscohost.com/login.aspx?direct=true&db=rch&AN=54516217&scope=site.

Salisbury, H. E. 1958. *The Shook-Up Generation.* New York: Harper & Row.

Samuels, G. 1958. "Why They Rock 'n' roll—and Should They?" *The New York Times,* January 12. Retrieved September 30, 2016, from timesmachine.nytimes.com.

Smith, D. 2005. "An Outsider, Out of the Shadows." *The New York Times,* September 7. Retrieved October 1, 2016, from www.nytimes.com.

"Telling the Story behind the Story behind *West Side Story.*" 2012. *The Los Angeles Times,* February 27. Retrieved October 1, 2015, from latimesblogs.latimes.com.

Grunge (Early to Mid-1990s)

The grunge music scene, also referred to as the "Seattle sound," began as a fairly isolated movement in the late 1980s in the Pacific Northwest of the United States and was originally centered in cities in Washington State, with the epicenter of the new look and sound emanating from Seattle. The term "grunge" seems to have been first put in print by executives at the Seattle record label Sub Pop, who were seeking a way to categorize new rock bands on their roster, including Nirvana, Mudhoney, and Soundgarden. Both the look and sound of grunge were stripped down and raw. Song lyrics reflected the pain and anxiety of youth, disillusionment, apathy, angst, and social alienation. The music, which drew on punk and hard-rock traditions, was characterized by a fast, rock beat and was filled with distortion. The visual style of grunge marked a rejection of mainstream sartorial values by communicating a strong indifference. Through the wearing of basic and utilitarian clothes that often showed signs of abuse and disrepair, followers of this scene marked themselves as outside of the mainstream. Grunge was a street style that was, at its essence, antifashion and thus shares a lineage with the original Beats, hippies, and punks. Furthermore, as an antifashion street style, grunge facilitated individual creative expression. Originally, the style was produced in response to the social, economic, and geographical context of the Pacific Northwest and did not indicate a specific membership in a group or subculture. Grunge was originally a regional style that was packaged into a "movement" by various arms of the mass media.

In addition to the aforementioned bands signed to Sub Pop, Pearl Jam, headed by Eddie Vedder, and Hole, fronted by Courtney Love, were stylistically influential. In the late 1980s and the first year or two of the 1990s, acts like these played at venues such as Crocodile Café, the Moore Theater, and the Off Ramp Café. Grunge bands were largely covered by the independent ("indie") music press, including a Seattle music magazine called *The Rocket* and a fanzine entitled *Desperate Times.* Scene insiders made heroes and celebrities of the local musicians and copied elements of their personal style that weren't already part of the naturally occurring street style of disaffected youth at the end of the 20th century. It cannot be overemphasized that what came to be known as "grunge" was really a very organic sartorial response by Generation X (people born from the early 1960s to the early 1980s) to a social context bound by economic recession, a widespread perception of bleak social opportunity, the rampant spread of the HIV/AIDS epidemic, and increased social alienation in an age of social fragmentation. As Jonathan Poneman eloquently relayed to Rick Marin (1992) of *The New York Times,* "It wasn't like somebody said, 'Let's all dress like lumberjacks and start Seattle chic!' This stuff [the apparel] is cheap, it's durable, and it's kind of timeless. It runs against the grain of the whole flashy esthetic that existed in the '80s." The aesthetic that developed into a contrived fashion statement was born of a generation that was adrift: a generation that evolved a style of indifference that conveyed a downtrodden spirit.

The look that came to be known as grunge was composed of basics: jeans and T-shirts (especially old and tattered band or concert shirts), flannel or lumberjack shirts, chunky knit sweaters, thick hiking socks, woolen caps, Doc Marten combat-style boots, logger boots by Georgia or Timberland, Converse Chuck Taylor high or low tops, leather or leatherette (faux leather) accessories, and long johns or thermal long-sleeved undershirts. Clothes purchased at thrift shops were also important to the original grunge look. For men, the secondhand clothing aspect of grunge did not have a strong aesthetic component, as men typically purchased flannels and jeans secondhand (see Lewman 1993), but for women thrift stores provided vintage dresses and skirts from the 1960s and 1970s and thereby lent a bohemian flair to the female follower of the grunge scene. These basic pieces of apparel were layered in a somewhat haphazard way, and this tendency undoubtedly relates to the climate in which grunge originated: wet, damp, and subject to fairly dramatic variations in temperature. Clothes were also worn tattered, frayed, and stained—an aesthetic that emerged naturally but was later augmented and exaggerated as part of the style. Hair was typically worn undone, disheveled, and greasy—a look that was first developed through lax hygiene regimens. Charles Cross, the editor of *The Rocket,* once noted, "Kurt Cobain was just too lazy to wash his hair" (Marin 1992). Hair locked into dreads was also popular. Body piercing, including of the nose, eyebrow, lip, and nipple, was newly integrated into youth culture by followers of this scene, as were tattoos. An androgynous aspect and the wearing of unisex apparel were also features of early grunge style. Brands and labels were unimportant, except for the fact that some brands indicated higher quality and a better guarantee of durability.

The grunge aesthetic was one that could be easily copied by using products that were readily available in the marketplace, and some brands were promoted through celebrity endorsements as viable options for evoking grunge. For example, members of both the Red Hot Chili Peppers and Sonic Youth were depicted in Gap advertisements in 1993. Apparel brands that had always retailed the kinds of basic and durable pieces that were part of the grunge look, including L. L. Bean, Land's End, and Timberland, also benefitted from the fashion craze that was a spin-off of the grunge scene as consumers sought out plaid flannel shirts and work boots from these marketplace mainstays, though it does not seem that any of these brands specifically modified their brand image or advertising to address the style. Retailers also sought to position existing merchandise to appeal to people interested in grunge. A writer for *Entertainment Weekly* noted that both Bloomingdales and Macy's had opened "grunge departments" in their stores and commented that by

1993 "grunge has devolved into a high-gloss sales tool" (Kobel 1993). Interestingly, the grunge look was also adapted and adopted by other style tribes of this period, including snowboarders and skateboarders, the latter of which has had a well-documented connection to the punk-rock scene. Barbara Lloyd (1996), reporting on the second X Games in 1996, noted that the competitors looked grungy in their oversized clothes, and she remarked on their unusual piercings.

The grunge look quickly spread beyond the music scene and youth fashion and was promoted as high fashion in collections that were shown in the autumn of 1992. Marc Jacobs infamously did a grunge collection for Perry Ellis that season (the company closed the women's fashion line soon thereafter). The collection included cashmere sweaters and woolen caps as well as sand-washed silk "flannels." Oribe styled the models' "greasy" hair. Ana Sui and Christian Francis Ross also presented grunge-inspired collections for the spring of 1993 that included combat boots, knit caps, plaid, and somewhat disheveled layers of clothes. Other high-fashion and middle-market brands like DKNY offered key pieces of apparel that could be used to create the look, though there is evidence that some consumers balked at $100 price tags on thermals and flannel. *Vogue* promoted the grunge aesthetic in a multipage editorial with text by Jonathan Poneman in December 1992. The images by fashion editor Grace Coddington featured clothes by Ralph Lauren, Chloe, and Marc Jacobs alongside mass-market items such as a Nirvana T-shirt and combat and work boots. The stylized and composed images of grunge are markedly different from the authentic street style and have a much stronger neo-hippie, bohemian flair than what was generally worn on the street. Additionally, *Vogue*'s view of grunge included diaphanous fabrics for women and Scottish kilts for men.

The Calvin Klein runway that took place in the fall of 1992 is also considered an influential moment in the spread of grunge-inspired style to high fashion. The presentation, which included Kate Moss, a slender, waifish model, featured disheveled styling of hair and makeup and thereby marked a departure from the high glamour of 1980s fashion. The look of the runway and the high-style fashion photography that followed came to be referred to as "heroin chic," an aesthetic that glamorized the downtrodden, hopeless youth and communicated a naked vulnerability that had not previously been a focus of fashion imagery, but which was directly related to the dominant themes found in grunge. Writing about heroin chic, fashion theorist and historian Rebecca Arnold noted, "[Heroin chic] encapsulates contemporary anxieties and desires: the myriad of identities that have developed in this fragmented period, a nihilistic aesthetic that finds escape by retreating from conventional reality and conventional beauty" (1990, 280–81). Efforts to package rawness, indolence, and authenticity can be seen in a wide variety of fashion advertising campaigns of the early 1990s including a series of CK One fragrance advertisements that featured Kate Moss and an advertisement for the apparel brand

Sisley that featured two gaunt women in disheveled evening apparel, with smudged makeup and the appearance of sweaty or greasy skin, seemingly caught in the act of snorting cocaine (which on closer inspection is a white women's strappy tank top).

It has been suggested that the spread of grunge was due in part to a concerted effort on the part of the music industry to make "alternative" music mainstream. Big labels, like A&M and Geffen, seeking to tap the desire within American youth culture to express uniqueness and individuality promoted acts that conveyed raw sensibilities (Neely 1992). Grunge music was also spread in part through the college radio scene in Washington State and beyond, which collectively worked as an early promoter of the sound, but perhaps most important was the influence of the cable network MTV. Beginning late in 1991, bands that were part of the Seattle sound became part of the regular rotation of music videos, and the network even hired a "grunge" VJ (video jockey). Music videos for songs like Nirvana's "Smells Like Teen Spirit" (1991) and Pearl Jam's "Alive" (1991) were uniquely able to spread both the new musical sound and the Seattle sartorial aesthetics at once. In addition to music videos, the narrative film *Singles* (1992), which told the story of an aspiring musician (played by Matt Dillon) who fronts a Seattle band called Citizen Dick, helped to develop the allure of the grunge scene. The film showcased the streets of Seattle and included cameo performances by members of Pearl Jam, making the scene (or the illusion thereof) accessible far beyond the Seattle city limits. The documentary film *Hype* (1996) was released after the peak of grunge's commercial popularity but represents yet another vehicle for communicating grunge style.

In addition to moving images, the grunge look was proliferated through photographs. Charles Petersen, who photographed the Seattle music scene and took pictures for a 1988 Sub Pop three-box set called "Sub Pop 200," is often credited with promoting the disheveled, greasy, slept-under-a-bridge aesthetic. Publications such as *The Face, I.D., Details,* and *Paper* also promoted elements of the look in photo essays. The British photographer Corinne Day developed an influential visual style independently of the American grunge scene but within a similar cultural context of despair and dissolution.

By 1993 some commentators were already declaring grunge to be dead from overuse and overexposure. Amy Spindler (1993b), writing for *The New York Times,* offered a different explanation for the demise of high-fashion grunge. She noted that consumers did not identify with the look and that it did not sell products. As a result, advertising had diminished in publications like *Vogue,* so a market correction was sought by presenting a more glamorous, high-fashion look, beginning in late 1993. According to Spindler, the desire to exorcise grunge from high fashion motivated "magazine editors, certain designers, and retailers [to] join forces like characters in an Agatha Christie novel" to change the tone and stimulate sales. Fashion advertising from 1994 onward proves that the concerted effort to expunge grunge from the high-style fashion marketplace was successful. Both fashion-trend followers and more specifically followers of the music scene began to lose interest in grunge as the decade progressed. The deaths of prominent musicians from heroin overdose impacted popular grunge bands, and the suicide of Nirvana front man Kurt Cobain in 1994 was also a powerful blow to the development of the music and social scene. By 1995 some music producers were already predicting the future of popular rock. That year the label Elemental 12 released a compilation album of "post-grunge" music called *Northwest Post-Grunge*. The record featured artists such as Dirt Fishermen and Floater, bands that failed to attain the international allure of earlier grunge acts.

Interpretations of grunge style continue to find their way to both the street and the runway. Hipsters of the early 21st century have repackaged many aspects of grunge dress, including the reliance on chunky knits, flannels, and piercings, though the complete impact of hipster style is notably different from grunge. High-fashion designers who were in their formative years when grunge first impacted music and dress also continue to revisit some aspects of the style. Recently, Hedi Slimane for Saint Laurent (Fall/Winter 2013) reworked and upgraded the aesthetics, as did Philip Lim for the same season. Alexander Wang routinely reworks staples of grunge but gives them a more polished and upgraded appeal by working in monochromatic palettes with fine fabrics. Modern variations on the grunge look continue to allow people young and old to express rebelliousness, creativity, and individuality.

The movement of grunge from street style to mass fashion was incredibly rapid. As Rick Marin (1992) noted, "From subculture to mass culture, the trend line gets shorter and faster all the time." The widespread popularity of grunge and the morphing of the style into a conformist uniform made available through the fashion marketplace were undoubtedly part of the demise of the style in the 1990s; however, elements of the look continue to find traction in youth culture, as sloppy, disheveled, and tattered clothes continue to communicate disaffection with mainstream ideals and, therefore, serve countercultural and "indie" scenes effectively.

Further Reading

Arnold, R. 1999. "Heroin Chic." *Fashion Theory: The Journal of Dress, Body & Culture* 3 (3): 279–95.

"Back to Twiggy." 1993. *Newsweek* 121 (5): 64.

Cerio, G., and P. Rogers. 1993. "Goodbye, G Word." *Newsweek* 121 (20): 8.

Dalbow, T. A. 2015. "Grunge Is Good." *Footwear Plus Magazine,* April/May, 44–45.

DiMartino, D., and C. Greyshock. 1990. "A Seattle Slew." *Rolling Stone* (587): 23.

"For Gamines' Gams, It's Grunge Gear." 1993. *Newsweek* 121: 65.

Grimes, W. 1992. "1992: The Year in Style." *The New York Times,* December 27. Retrieved October 15, 2015, from www.nytimes.com.

Kobel, P. 1993. "Smells Like Big Bucks." *Entertainment Weekly,* April 2. Retrieved February 22, 2016, from www.ew.com.

Lewman, M. 1993. "Grunge Shopper Mike Watt." *Entertainment Weekly,* March 26. Retrieved February 22, 2016, from www.ew.com.

Lloyd, B. 1996. "Extreme Sports; In Newport, a Grunge Grand Prix." *The New York Times,* June 29. Retrieved October 15, 2015, from www.nytimes.com.

Marin, R. 1992. "Grunge: A Success Story." *The New York Times,* November 15. Retrieved October 15, 2015, from www.nytimes.com.

Menkes, S. 1993. "Vogue's Point of View: What's Modern Now?" *Vogue* 183 (January 1): 91–101. Retrieved February 22, 2016, from http://search.proquest.com/docview/87929 5463?accountid=130772.

Neely, K. 1992. "Alternative Music." *Rolling Stone* (645/646): 43.

Poneman, J. 1992. "Features: Grunge & Glory." *Vogue* 182 (December 1): 254–63, 313. Retrieved February 22, 2016, from http://search.proquest.com/docview/879295203?acc ountid=130772.

Seliger, M. 1993. "Normal Weirdness in Seattle." *Rolling Stone* (652): 34.

Spindler, A. 1993a. "Patterns." *The New York Times,* September 7. Retrieved October 15, 2015, from www.nytimes.com.

Spindler, A. 1993b. "How Fashion Killed the Unloved Waif." *The New York Times,* September 27. Retrieved October 15, 2015, from www.nytimes.com.

Heavy Metal Rocker (Late 1960s–Present)

Followers of the heavy metal scene, individuals referred to as heshers, metal heads, headbangers, and just plain rockers, represent a distinct though varied corpus of American street style that is related to an equally varied popular music scene. With its musical roots in 1950s rock music and rhythm and blues, heavy metal music emerged in the late 1960s and expanded upon those musical foundations with hard-driving electric-guitar riffs, wailing electric-guitar solos, and incessant, amplified percussion. This form of rock and roll music continues the tradition of music for and by young people and as such is often expressive of rebelliousness, teenage angst and alienation, lust, sex, drugs, partying, and the hypocrisy of adults. Additionally, some heavy metal music explores themes related to Satanism, a fact that has routinely raised adult ire, fueled by the urban legend that records played backward revealed satanic messages (see Aranza 1983). Censorship groups like the PMRC (Parents Music Resource Center) were especially concerned about the ill-effects of heavy metal music on American youth in the 1980s, which notably evolved into a period of immense mainstream popularity for the genre.

Heavy metal rock and roll has developed into a broad genre of music that has diversified to include several subgenres of appearance and sound including glam metal (largely a reference to gaudy visual aesthetics), thrash metal (characterized by a rapid, thrashing beat), death metal (differentiated by morbid, gruesome lyrics and growling vocals), black metal (characterized by anti-Christian sentiments), industrial metal (typified by a distorted and cacophonous sound), metalcore (metal plus punk hardcore), and pop metal (mainstream pop rock with a electric guitar as a defining feature). These genre categories are merely organizational guidelines. Writing for *Billboard* magazine in the early 1990s, Paul Henderson noted that categorizing heavy metal created "seemingly insurmountable problems" and suggested that, "attempts at a comprehensive and contemporary definition of the multi-colored, multi-limbed beast that it has evolved into seem futile"(1993). As the music has diversified, largely since the middle of the 1980s, and since the advent of MTV in 1981, the dress practices of heavy metal rockers and the sartorial aesthetics of the followers of the scene have diversified and in some cases have become quite exaggerated. Nevertheless, while there is diversity over time and across subgenres of heavy metal, there are also basic dress practices that are constantly reworked and reimagined across the span of the more than five decades that the scene has existed.

Heavy metal music developed both in the United States and the United Kingdom in the late 1960s, and while countless heavy metal acts began as garage bands from towns big and small, by the end of the 1970s there were nightclubs in urban settings like Philadelphia, New York City (namely CBGB, where the punk sounds had also incubated), and Los Angeles (a series of clubs that dotted the Sunset Strip). In the 1980s, many considered the Sunset Strip to be "the most rock 'n' roll place on the planet" (Klosterman 2002, 70). This assertion relates to the caliber of music being played but also references the scene at large—drug- and alcohol-fueled and populated by a coterie of vampy would-be groupies. Heavy metal music performances and the fan culture at large are male dominated in several ways. The vast majority of heavy metal acts are exclusively male, and song lyrics frequently veer toward misogynistic themes in which women are construed as objects for pleasure and sources of trouble and pain.

The basic components of heavy metal dress practices were established in the late 1960s, in an age before music videos. The tendencies described here were largely innovated by men in the public eye but were generally copied by men and women alike. The early heavy metal look was undeniably unstudied and easily achieved. Bands like Led Zeppelin, Deep Purple, Black Sabbath, Blue Oyster Cult, Aerosmith, and later Van Halen originally appeared in ensembles that relied heavily on tight blue jeans or leather pants, jackets or vests made of denim or leather, and T-shirts with the name of their own band or a brand related to the music industry like Fender (guitars) or Pearl (drums). From very early in the evolution of the heavy metal scene, male performers and concert goers alike embraced the option of going shirtless, and a necklace or two might be worn to accentuate the bare skin. Additionally, from very early on, the wearing of elaborately printed, billowing blouses, unbuttoned to reveal hairless chests, was a common feature of the look that tested the bounds of gendered clothing and was in all likelihood a tendency derived from the hippies and peacocks of the 1960s. Traditional heavy metal footwear included cowboy boots and Converse or other sneakers. Perhaps the most defining feature of heavy metal style over time has been hair. Originally, men and women alike wore long, often seemingly unkempt hair. Especially in the late 1960s and early 1970s, the heavy metal hair aesthetic had a grown-out, shaggy appearance that was not obviously impacted by the use of styling products.

Beginning in the early 1970s the outrageous costuming of the glam (short for glamorous) music scene sartorially influenced some heavy metal bands. Heavy metal bands including Kiss and Twisted Sister wore their long hair teased into voluminous manes taking the rebelliousness of long hair in a new, dramatic direction. Glam metal bands wore Lycra spandex pants (which became a staple of the scene going forward), platform shoes, and heavy makeup. The dress practices of glam metal bands may largely be categorized as costume—designed exclusively for the stage; beyond the presence of the occasional "super fan," who dressed like a band member (particularly at a concert), the glam aesthetic does not seem to have fully translated to the street, though arguably the glam rock bands generally influenced the wearing of color, spandex, and increasingly styled manes of hair. It is also important to note that heavy metal bands that were "glam" in the 1970s and early 1980s did not remain glam if they continued to perform in the latter decades of the 20th century.

The punk scene of the middle 1970s also seems to have impacted heavy metal music and its sartorial style. This is evidenced by the thrash and metalcore bands that evolved from the 1970s into the 1980s, and the industrial metal bands that developed from the 1980s into the 1990s. Beginning in the middle of the 1970s bands such as Motörhead, Metallica, Megadeath, Anthrax, and Corrosion of Conformity and later industrial metal bands like Nine Inch Nails, Ministry, and Skinny Puppy made hard-driving music with punk-inspired riffs. The sartorial style of these groups also borrowed from the more austere aesthetic of American punk rock. Band members wore ripped jeans, motorcycle jackets, combat boots, leather caps, and metal-studded belts and cuffs. Hair was often, but not always, worn long and was generally less voluminous and precisely coiffed than the hairstyles worn by rockers in other subgenres. Black eyeliner and black nail polish were accepted as part of the look. The thrash/metalcore/industrial look was not entirely new. Many of the sartorial elements and the ways in which they were combined evoked the rebellious dress practices of both punk rockers and motorcyclists or leathermen. As the thrash metal scene evolved, some bands also evolved dress practices that overlapped with the skateboard scene of the 1990s, a scene in which thrash music was enjoyed; the soundtracks of many skateboarding videos of that era attest to this influence. The intersection of heavy metal thrash music and skating provides a context for understanding the adoption of baggy flannel shirts, loose knee-length board shorts, and sneakers from brands like Vans by some headbangers. This skate-influenced style was embodied for a time by the members of Anthrax and demonstrates how street and subcultural dress styles can inform one another and mix as followers of a given social milieu may elect to hop-skip from one scene to the next over time or may pick and choose elements from a variety of social groups at once. Such was the nature of street and subcultural style at the end of the 20th century. It was used to describe identity and taste but did not necessarily assert a singular, unified, unchanging point of view.

The heavy metal aesthetic was most profoundly modified beginning in the early 1980s when heavy metal performers from so-called "hair bands" took the standard aesthetics of the heavy metal rocker to new heights. Rock bands including Bon Jovi, Poison, Ratt, Skid Row, Cinderella, and the Christian heavy metal band Stryper wore tight, colorful clothes, stacks of bracelets, rings on multiple fingers, chests full of necklaces, dangling earrings, and flowing, diaphanous scarves. Hairstyles remained long but dramatically increased in volume thanks to bottles of mousse and Aqua Net hairspray and energetic use of the teasing comb. Many artists sported processed platinum-blond dye jobs, and frosted accents were commonplace. Perhaps the most striking development, however, was the heavy use of colorful cosmetics. Pink and red lipsticks and wet-look lip gloss were used to highlight pouty lips. Colorful eyeliner and eye shadow were worn in conjunction with bold slashes of blush along the ridges of the cheekbones. Eyebrows were plucked into perfect arches and carefully penciled to dramatic effect. The unbridled use of makeup was largely in line with tendencies displayed by fashionable women in the 1980s but was a notable departure from the restricted use of products like black eyeliner in previous decades and had a decidedly different impact than the theatrical effects worn by glam rockers.

Both the hair and makeup of the 1980s "hair bands" were in line with broader trends in gender-flouting tendencies that had existed since the earliest years of the scene. Notably, a great many new wave acts were exploring similar dress practices at the same time, and these were, in turn, being interpreted by legions of youthful followers of that scene. However, like the glam rock aesthetic, the "hair band" aesthetic did not translate in its entirety to the street and was interpreted with at least a modicum of subtlety, including more limited use of color, jewelry, and cosmetics. Restraint in the realm of street style may be related in part to media commentary and the fact that some reporters in the 1980s described the look as including a "blatantly feminine wardrobe" (Hogan 1987, 13). The visually arresting style played well on MTV, but the fan magazines of the day offered contradictory interpretations of the look. Posters and color foldouts reinforced the notion of these heavy metal stars as sex symbols, while ample evidence of derogatory labels like "guitar totin' near-Misses" (Halbersberg 1987, 10) aligned the flamboyant style with musical shortcomings. The fact that hairdressers and makeup artists were frequently cited in the liner notes of late 1980s heavy metal acts gave some observers of the heavy metal scene cause for dismay (Dr. Rock 1987, 30), and only a handful of bands like Mötley Crüe could manage the tension between lip gloss and musical credibility. Many artists grew out of the look. For a time Jon Bon Jovi, whose mane was often equated with a poodle, was referred to as the "Duran Duran of metal" (Simmons 1987, 40), a negative reference to the popular new wave band. However, 1990s sartorial tastes, which favored a toned-down, more traditionally masculine aesthetic, coupled with a substantial recording history seem to have worked together to free Bon Jovi of the snide sobriquet.

This discussion of heavy metal rocker style as it was evolved by musical acts has largely ignored the matter of dress for women. Male performers dominate the heavy metal music scene. Consequently, the number of female performers who have set dress practices for female rockers is few. Thus the sartorial code for female followers of heavy metal seems to be set primarily in two ways. First, some female rockers interpret sartorial practices set by men. Tight, ripped, or faded jeans worn with rock and roll T-shirts, layers of jewelry, and long hair is commonplace dress; however, it is also commonplace to see a female heavy metal rocker amp up the sexuality of these rocker basics. For example, a T-shirt or tank top might be worn tight with an exposed bra, and high-heeled shoes might replace boots or sneakers. Some heavy metal rocker girls also take their cues from the highly sexualized images that appear on album covers, in lyrical descriptions, and in music videos. Female followers of this music scene have interpreted the heavy metal vamp ideal by wearing apparel like short, tight dresses and skirts made of spandex or leather in conjunction with stiletto high heels and lace or fishnet tights. Plunging necklines, and exposed lingerie are also typical sartorial choices, especially in nightclubs and at concerts. Long hair, dyed platinum blonde, is also a preferred sartorial choice.

Charting the development of heavy metal music provides a sort of shorthand for tracking the street style of followers of the heavy metal music scene. However, it is crucial to note that the broad dress trends demonstrated by popular musical acts were worn by young men and women in incredibly varied combinations and with an eye to street wear as opposed to apparel for performance. Notably, the population at large has not adopted some of the sartorial oddities that have been incubated by performers (like Angus Young, the lead guitarist of AC/DC, who dressed in a schoolboy uniform or Slash, from Guns and Roses, who wore a top hat). Furthermore, the discrete categories described above did not exist quite so distinctly on the street. Two nuances should be clarified. First, even in the height of the popularity of glam bands like Kiss in the 1970s or hair bands like Poison and Cinderella in the 1980s, it was uncommon to find young men wearing heavy, colorful makeup, though it is possible that women in the 1980s took makeup cues from some of the men in these bands. Second, while musical acts may conform to a single genre over an extended period, followers of the heavy metal rock scene may be interested in more than one genre at a time, thereby exposing themselves to varied dress aesthetics, which are then interpreted as individual street style. Therefore, the true street style embodied by followers of the heavy metal music scene is far more complex than the categories outlined according to music genre. True rockers may be liberated enough to mix animal-print spandex pants with a Harley Davidson T-shirt and motorcycle jacket while wearing fringed fingerless gloves, feathers in his or her hair, and a pentagram tattoo. The heavy metal rocker style fluidly mixes elements of 1960s hippies, leathersexual and motorcycle culture, glam, punk, and gender-fluid dress practices into a varied yet immediately identifiable aesthetic.

Sourcing apparel to create the heavy metal rocker look could be done in a variety of ways. Basics such as T-shirts, jeans, and sneakers could be purchased at mainstream retailers, whereas leather jackets and pants were more likely to be acquired from outfitters to the motorcycle or leathermen subcultures. Aspects of the heavy metal look could also be purchased through mail order from the 1970s onward. Advertisements at the back of fan magazines like *Creem* and *Heavy Metal Thunder* from companies like Metal Express Clothing offered spandex pants for men and women in tiger and leopard prints. Specialized grooming products, including Spike Spray, were also available through mail order and promised hair like Jon Bon Jovi's in the late 1980s. Purveyors of current and classic band T-shirts, embroidered back patches, necklaces featuring band logos, fan buttons, Velcro wallets with band names and logos, and even boxer shorts that carried the name of a famous rocker were also available through mail order from companies like Musicade. Similar items as well as color posters and fanzines could also be obtained in record shops, which were especially important conduits for sharing heavy metal interests in the 1970s and 1980s.

In the 1970s and 1980s the heavy metal scene used many of the same techniques that the punks had used to communicate aspects of the hard-rock scene. Photocopied fanzines and flyers were important ways to share largely local information about up-and-coming bands, scheduled performances, products, and, of course, photographs that represented the most current iteration of heavy metal dress practices. Printed publications including professionally produced magazines and tabloids such as *Creem, Heavy Metal Thunder, Revolver,* and *L.A. Rocks* (often referred to as the "metal bible") also provided important information to fans of heavy metal music. Documentary movies including *Heavy Metal Parking Lot* (1986), *The Decline of Western Civilization Part II: The Metal Years* (1988), and *Metal: A Headbanger's Journey* (2005) as well as documentaries about Motörhead, Metallica, and Pantera have also functioned as important vehicles for communicating the heavy metal look and sound, while MTV was indisputably a critical conduit, especially in the 1980s and 1990s before the widespread availability of Internet portals like metalunderground.com.

In all likelihood MTV in the 1980s was also influential with regard to shaping the sartorial aesthetics of up-and-coming musical acts. The new visual medium put the personal appearances of performers on par with the actual musical performances and undoubtedly incubated dress practices that were novel and visually arresting. Writing about Poison and Mötley Crüe in the early 1980s, music journalist Elianne Halbersberg noted, "No rock and roll band worth its hairspray would ever DREAM of releasing product without a few glossy, glitzy, and ever-so-happening videos"(1987, 10), an indication that the power of this new visual medium could facilitate the sales of records or "product." The importance of image seems to have impacted live performances, which were routinely filmed and broadcast in the 1980s as well. Writing in 1987, *Creem* columnist Richard Hogan reported that the lead singer of Cinderella went through multiple wardrobe changes in a set. He recorded, "He dons and doffs assorted hats, jackets, guitars and sunglasses like a girl stepping out of her mom's walk-in closet" (1987, 13). This kind of performance, which reinforced the importance of dress aesthetics may not have engendered mimicry of the artist in question, though the emphasis on sartorial splendor in general makes a statement about heavy metal culture at large—one can still be rock and roll and at the same time care about coordinating one's ensemble.

Heavy metal music and heavy metal dress practices have the ability to voice rebellion, discharge aggression, and mark a loose affiliation with others who similarly find pleasure and release in the hard-driving music and themes of fast and wild living. Lawrence Grossberg, a cultural studies scholar, noted that rock and roll music is more than just sound, it is a "corporeal and invasive" experience (Grossberg 1986, 52) that can infiltrate the mind and body and help to create a rupture with the mundane. The music and the dress associated with the sound "energize new possibilities within everyday life," a life that may seem meaningless or fruitless to a disenchanted young person (56). Heavy metal music, like other forms of popular music, can galvanize the spirit, relate stories that are inspiring, and simply cause adrenaline to flow. Notably, the galvanizing techniques in some subgenres of heavy metal have included the use of symbols like the pentagram, the inverted cross (popularized by Ozzy Osbourne), and the wearing of the numbers 666, which is the "number of the beast" according to the book of Revelation 13:18 (popularized by Iron Maiden). The use of these kinds of symbols, both visually and lyrically, has a long history of engendering negative attention toward the heavy metal scene and those who participate in it, though this may be part of their allure. Sociologist Ross Haenfler has noted of the use of Satanic imagery, "Satan is a metaphor for everything society rejects" (2013, 67) and thus is a tool that is used to alienate others. "Just as punks who wore swastikas were not necessarily Nazis, metal heads who sport inverted crosses or pentagrams are likely not actually Satanists. Satan is a symbol of rebellion and open disdain for mainstream society" (68). This facet of heavy metal dress is often misunderstood, and parental fear about the ill effects of heavy metal has periodically reached fever pitch. For example, in the late 1980s "de-metaling" organizations including Back in Control of Orange County, California, strove to rid youths of the metal mania by confiscating heavy metal apparel, posters, magazines, and music.

Heavy metal music and the dress practices associated with it will undoubtedly continue to evolve as the music evolves. The dress of the heavy metal rocker may respond to mainstream fashions and trends in the music, but the core of the look will always draw upon the history of American rebelliousness, echoing hippies, punks, motorcycle riders, and individuals who refused to conform to cultural expectations about gender. With a longevity of more than four decades, the heavy metal rocker scene has provided generations of people—young and not so young—with an outlet for self-expression and thus is a rich expression of American street style.

Further Reading

Aranza, J. 1983. *Backward Masking Unmasked: Backward Satanic Messages of Rock and Roll Exposed.* Shreveport, LA: Huntington House.

Berelian, E. 2005. *The Rough Guide to Heavy Metal.* London: Rough Guides.

Dr. Rock. 1987. "Silent Night, Troglodyte (or Corporate Metal, Yo Mama)." *Creem,* December, 30–31.

Grossberg, L. 1986. "Is There Rock after Punk?" *Critical Studies in Mass Communication* 3: 50–74.

Haenfler, R. 2013. "Heavy Metal—Moral Panics, Satanic Scares, and Moral Entrepreneurs." In *Goths, Gamers, & Grrrls: Deviance and Youth Subculture* 2nd ed. by R. Haenfler, 61–75. New York: Oxford University Press.

Halbersberg, E. 1987. "Black and Decker Meets Miss Clairol: Poison vs. Mötley Crüe." *Creem,* December, 4–11.

Henderson, P. 1993. "With the U.S. New Wave Ascendant, Is It Over for U.K.'s Old Guard and Poodle-Head Bands?" HM4, May 22.

Hogan, R. 1987. "Cinderella Be A'happenin'." *Creem,* December, 12–15.

Klosterman, C. 2002. "Paradise City." *Spin,* September, 70–78.

Simmons, S. 1987. "Bon Jovi: Can They Bake a Kidney Pie?" *Creem,* December, 40–43.

Trunk, E. 2011. *Eddie Trunk's Essential Hard Rock and Heavy Metal.* New York: Abrams Image.

Hip-Hop (Mid-1980s–Early 2000s)

This entry documents the urban American subcultural style, fashion-industry category, and street style that emerged out of the b-boy look. B-boy style, which had developed in connection with break dancing beginning in the late 1970s, is dealt with in a separate entry. The editorial decision to separate b-boy style from the rest of hip-hop style was made in part because the b-boy style itself remained fairly homogenous and unvaried over time; additionally, the cultural context surrounding early hip-hop culture in general and the b-boy street style in particular was far more localized and focused. Dance, music, sociocultural context, and clothes were all intimately connected in the advent of hip-hop. Most importantly, b-boy style is the foundation of fly boy style, which in turn is the backbone of hip-hip sartorial practices. Thus it deserves detailed scrutiny in a chapter of its own. In addition, the evolution of hip-hop style from the middle of the 1980s onward has included several evolutions, myriad inspirations, the layering of influences, and the development of an entire industry sector of professional urban-apparel producers, marketers, and stylists. Thus, this entry is notably longer than the text devoted to other street and subcultural style groups that are reviewed in this book. Hip-hop street style is a recognizable aesthetic entity, but it is also a sartorial phenomenon that has evolved considerably over time in response to cultural and commercial influences. Among the variations that will be explored in this section are fly boys, new jack swing, African nationalist and paramilitary influences, "gangsta" style, and the ghetto fabulous look. Each of these subcategories, it will be shown, was both unique and recognizable at one point but has become incorporated into the larger realm of hip-hop street style over time. This entry will also consider the realm of commercial hip-hop fashion that individuals use to construct a personal street-style aesthetic influenced by hip-hop but perhaps not actually situated in a hip-hop cultural identity. While street styles and subcultural styles typically have links to commercial producers and retailers, hip-hop street style is noteworthy in that it has spawned a multibillion dollar sector within the fashion industry.

The expression "hip-hop" is derived from the playful lyrics of one of the earliest recorded rap songs, "Rapper's Delight" (1979) by the Sugarhill Gang. However, according to the seminal break dancer Crazy Legs, the term "hip-hop" was first used as a descriptor in 1982 by the stylistically influential deejay Afrika Bambaata. Bambaata used the term to refer to the multifaceted, expressive urban culture that was developing in New York City at that time (2011, 8). The urban landscape of the late 1970s and early 1980s was a hotbed for the development of rap, graffiti art, new deejaying techniques, and an athletic form of dance that became known as break dancing. Throughout the later part of the 1980s and beyond, the influence of these four categories of hip-hop culture reached past urban centers, and each of these art forms became increasingly subject to interpretation and commodification. Music videos, feature films, network and cable television shows, and glossy music magazines facilitated the spread of hip-hop culture, which led to diversity within cultural production and interpretation of hip-hop identity across racial and social demographics. Thus hip-hop and its sartorial style were quickly transformed from subcultural expression to a unique American street style, and ultimately to an international phenomenon within a short period of time.

Fly Boy Style

Fly boy style is the street style that is most closely related to the look adopted by b-boys in the late 1970s and early 1980s and was worn by contemporary young men who did not dance but were part of the hip-hop subculture. This statement is not meant to imply that one group or the other originated this style, nor that the aesthetics of the fly boy disappeared by the close of the 1980s. Early hip-hop style seems to have developed organically out of the multifaceted social milieu of urban culture, using the apparel and accessories that were locally available. As noted, fly boy style is the foundation of hip-hop street style. The basic components of the look include jeans, T-shirts, hoodies, baseball caps, and tracksuits, which were adopted by dancers and nondancers alike. Fly boys did not generally adopt components that were integral to break dancing (nylon pants and jackets and T-shirts with iron-on letters, bandanas worn over the hair). Accessories that were not conducive to floor rocking such as Kangol caps, black "godfather hats," three-finger rings, name belts, and dookie chains (thick gold necklaces) completed the look for fly boys. Fly boys and b-boys alike wore sneaker brands including Adidas, Converse, and Puma, and while both style groups made color coordination a priority, fly boys were better positioned to keep their sneakers fresh since they did not subject their sneakers to the wear and tear incurred through dancing. Low-top Adidas shell-toe sneakers were often worn without the laces or could be worn with extra-wide shoelaces run through the eyelets of the shoes to form horizontal bands. Air Jordans, first introduced in 1984, and other athlete-endorsed sneakers became important status symbols and staples of the fly boy look in the latter half of the 1980s. Fly boy style was entirely crafted from basic pieces of ready-to-wear that were available in the marketplace, some of which were subjected to modification by the wearer (i.e., worn oversized, askew, or backward). The garment selection, coordination, layering, and the *way* in which a piece of apparel was worn created the distinctiveness of the look.

The street style of the fly boy is well documented in the snapshots captured in Jamel Shabaz's book *Back in the Days* (2001) and in Martha Cooper's *Hip-Hop Files* (2004). Additionally, the noteworthy rap group Run DMC, distinguished in part by the members' direct lineage to the streets of New York City's early hip-hop scene and by their early mass-market and mass-media success, portrayed an iconic and influential embodiment of fly boy style. Marcus Reeves, commenting on an image of Run DMC that was taken in 1983, captured some of the nuances of what made their basic pieces of ready-to-wear special. He noted, "Standing their signature b-boy stance staring defiantly at the camera, Run and D . . . were the hardest and the coolest and the realest Negroes in music" (2008, 41). His comment highlights that the *attitude* inherent in early images of rap artists was palpable and inspirational—worthy of emulation. Additionally, the proliferation of images of these fly boys that were printed in teen magazines and that were streamed in music videos that aired regularly on MTV in the 1980s was profoundly influential to individuals far beyond the nexus of the scene. Reeves went on to point out, "their look was bare bones and forceful" as it was the hip-hop uniform "straight from the street corner" (41). This second point is noteworthy. While the many iterations of hip-hop style that evolved later all share links with celebrities and musicians, the fly boy style was most directly linked to an unmediated, shared street culture. Notably, the photographs of this period reveal a distinctive street style only for young men, while there are few defining sartorial features exhibited among young women in this social milieu—basic pieces of ready-to-wear were worn in conventional combinations and were not generally modified.

The quick movement of hip-hop style from a localized street style to mass cultural phenomenon occurred early in the history of the subculture. Music scholar Greg Dimitriades noted, "Hip hop's musical discourse was at one point integrated in the context of live social interaction and dance" (1996, 183). Music, dance, and fly boy clothes were all part of a lived experience. Recording rap music, institutionalizing cultural production, and commoditizing hip-hop style altered the context of cultural production and ultimately what was produced. He further points out that the mass dissemination of music and other forms of culture envisions an "imagined community" (187) with a visual language that is engineered. Thus, while later forms of hip-hop style maintain a link with authentic street style and culture, it is important to consider that they were also heavily mediated by commercial forces.

New Jack Swing

The terminology "new jack swing" is traditionally applied to a genre of music that is characterized by the blending of African American styles such as rhythm and blues, funk, and rap. This musical style emerged in the middle of the 1980s when artists such as Janet Jackson, Bel Biv Devoe, Bobby Brown, and MC Hammer created popular songs that incorporated the emerging urban influences and attained mainstream appeal. The television show *The Fresh Prince of Bel Air* (1990–1996) is perhaps the neatest encapsulation of this subgenre of hip-hop sartorial style. Oversized athletic apparel including hoodies and T-shirts were staples of the look, as were long color-coordinated button-up collared shirts, baseball caps, and high-top sneakers. These staples of hip-hop style were given a new flair through the use of trendy neon and candy colors, sparkly accents, bold graphic patterns, and meticulous color and pattern coordination. Some pieces of standard hip-hop attire were also modified in terms of silhouette. Sweaters and jackets were often created with broadly padded shoulders, and loose pants were tapered at the ankle and sometimes given a drop crotch. Hairstyles for men in this category were noteworthy. The high-top or flat top, which consists of natural hair clipped into a cubic or angled crown with close-shorn sides, was iconic and was popularized by the actor Will Smith and the rap duo Kid 'n Play. Coordination of apparel and accessories and meticulous grooming gave the look a decidedly polished, commercial, and accessible feel.

The style associated with new jack swing is closely related to the apparel that was initially offered by the first commercial hip-hop fashion brands, and it is notable that this layer of hip-hop street style was impacted by trained fashion designers and was mass produced in this time period. Among the seminal brands that retailed hip-hop style at the height of the new jack swing phenomenon were Cross Colours (founded 1989), Karl Kani (founded 1989), and FUBU (founded 1992), which stands for For Us By Us. Loosely cut sportswear and athletic apparel, often designed in bright, arresting hues, was branded to connect the purchaser to the swagger of the urban streets. For example, the tags on Cross Colours clothes indicated they were apparel for a "Post Hip-Hop Nation" and utilized the slang "Ya Dig, Ya Dig, Ya Dig!" Promotion of the Cross Colours label by the all-female musical group TLC (who wore men's Cross Colours apparel ahead of the launch of a women's line) helped to connect the clothes to authentic hip-hop cultural production and helped give the apparel street credibility. Notably, these seminal brands modified their aesthetics and their brand identities as hip-hop culture evolved. For example, while the Karl Kani brand emerged at the height of new jack swing and mirrored its aesthetics, advertising campaigns of the early 1990s kept with hip-hop trends and featured photographs of gangsta rapper Tupac Shakur and the ghetto fabulous Sean "Puffy" Combs. Advertisements for these new urban brands had new media outlets in this period. *The Source* (first published in 1988) and *Vibe* (first published in 1993) largely reported on the hip-hop music scene but ran advertisements for all kinds of commercial products targeted toward followers of African American culture. *Yo! MTV Raps,* a show devoted to rap music videos, debuted in 1988 and ran until 1995 and was also influential in spreading hip-hop culture, including music, dance, and sartorial style.

Militant and African Nationalist

In the late 1980s and early 1990s two interrelated aesthetic themes were layered onto the foundational elements of hip-hop style that were developed by fly boys. A new generation of black pride and black power imagery, not widely seen since the end of the 1960s, became perceptible in hip-hop culture. Popular musicians including Queen Latifah, X Clan, Two Kings in a Cipher, ISIS, and A Tribe Called Quest promoted a new wave of African pride. Music videos and album artwork for groups like these included elements such as elaborately patterned kente cloth, dashikis, kufis, medallions in the shape of the African continent, beaded jewelry, red, gold, and green colors (related to the Ethiopian flag and Rastafarian culture), and shirts with Afrocentric slogans such as "Black by Popular Demand." These elements were incorporated to varying degrees into looks that also included staple items such as jeans, hoodies, bomber jackets, and athletic shoes. Differing in aesthetics, but with similar black pride and black power associations, was the incorporation of paramilitary aesthetics that referenced the subcultural style of the Black Panthers. The wearing of camouflage patterns, tactical vests, T-shirts, cargo pants, and bomber jackets in black or military green and the adoption of black leather combat boots combined to create a very specific aesthetic that was most clearly embodied by the members of N.W.A. This cohesive militant look was short-lived, and both of these currents in hip-hop dress were largely outmoded by the gangsta aesthetic by 1993.

Gangsta Style

In the early 1990s the original fly boy style was influenced by the style associated with gangsta rap. Gangsta rap, a subgenre of rap music that was first audible and visible in Los Angeles by 1991, became the most influential and controversial force in hip-hop culture in the early 1990s. Rappers, including Tupac Shakur, Ice-T,

Public Enemy, N.W.A., and Ice Cube, rapped tales of hardscrabble neighborhoods and police aggression as well as gang and prison life. Profanity, misogyny, and violence characterized the lyrics of hard-rocking music that was often the target of censors, while the dress style associated with these rappers evoked sartorial stereotypes of gang and prison apparel. Baggy jeans were worn low on the hips and without a belt as an allusion to ill-fitting prison uniforms and the confiscation of belts by corrections officers. Dickies, the pant of choice among cholos (a Mexican American street style associated with Southern California gangs), were also worn in this manner. Sagging pants revealed the waistband and sometimes several inches of the wearer's underpants. Displaying designer-branded underpants by companies such as Tommy Hilfiger and Ralph Lauren became popular in the latter half of the 1990s. Oversized T-shirts and "wife beater" tank tops that revealed toned muscular bodies and tattoos were popular. Professional baseball, football, and basketball sports jerseys, starter jackets, and hoodies were worn oversized and in layers, and some rappers who had real gang affiliations promoted the idea of selecting team jerseys based on their color and the relationship of that color to a specific gang. Baseball caps with professional sports team logos were frequently worn, styled with the brim to the side or the back, and beanies were also popular. Do-rags (nylon head coverings with attached ties worn tightly over the skull) and typical paisley bandanas were sometimes worn beneath the baseball caps. Bandanas, especially colored blue or red (code for Crips and Bloods, respectively), were worn folded over the head or tucked into pockets. Work boots, a type of footwear associated with prison apparel, were popularized, and the Timberland brand was especially favored, causing sales of the traditional work boot to spike in 1993. Tattoos, gold teeth, and custom-made grills (dental jewelry that covers numerous teeth) completed the look.

Both existing urban-apparel brands and mainstream fashion brands quickly and widely commodified the gangsta look. Designer brands such as Marithe & Francois Girbaud and Polo Ralph Lauren produced oversized pants, referred to as saggin' or slackin' pants. Levis offered their "baggy fit" silver tab for men and 560 loose fit for women. Jeans that were manufactured with an exposed underwear waistband attached were sold briefly in 1993. Makers of team jerseys and caps responded to the newfound identity associated with the wearing of team gear and diversified their offerings. Especially popular were retro or throwback jerseys that were first retailed under license by the Philadelphia boutique Mitchell & Ness. By the end of the decade apparel with the names of urban centers of importance to hip-hop including Compton, Hollis, and the Bronx were available and popular, as were T-shirts with mug shots. Grills and gold teeth could be purchased across price points, though inexpensive dental jewelry made of various alloys were notorious for causing both gum and tooth ailments. A 1996 marketing report noted, "By spring 1993 80 percent of teens favored the style" (Spiegler 1996, 19). Furthermore, whites composed at least half of hip-hop consumers by 1993 (Miller 1993, 10), a further indication that hip-hop culture had moved well beyond its roots in urban centers.

Gangsta rap and its style were widely criticized, which may have contributed to its widespread popularity. In February of 1994 Representative Cardiss Collins and Senator Carol Mosley-Braun initiated congressional hearings on gangsta rap and the impact of lyrics that were deemed violent and demeaning. Apparel associated with gangsta rap was widely restricted in schools, and local governments across the United States imposed fines on individuals who sagged their pants (such laws still exist in the second decade of the new millennium). Gangsta rap and its style have also been critiqued as representing inauthentic, purely commercial expressions of black American culture. David Samuels of *The New Republic* argued that "white demand" determines the direction of rap music and hip-hop culture and that "crude stereotypes" of "blackness" shape that demand (1991, 26, 28). Journalist and political analyst Bakari Kitwana shares this view, pointing out that the music reinforces negative stereotypes to increase sales (1994, 3, 4).

Ghetto Fabulous

By about 1995 the straightforward gangsta style that was achieved largely through basic pieces of mass-produced ready-to-wear was influenced by stylistic attributes that are typically referred to as "ghetto fabulous." Ghetto fabulous street style incorporates designer luxury brands and flamboyant gold and diamond-encrusted watches and other jewelry into the preexisting hip-hop aesthetic. The aesthetic shift seems to have been related to a shift in the content of rap music. According to sociologist Geoff Harkness, artists such as Dr Dre, Snoop Dog, and Notorious B.I.G. changed the conversation in rap music by shifting the focus from the violence of gangbanging to images of pimps, "playas" (players), hustlers, and prostitutes. "These artists represented a significant development for gangsta rap because they removed much of the subgenre's sense of systemic injustice and replaced it with an emphasis on wealth and materialism" (2014, 101). By shifting the lyrical emphasis and commenting on specific luxury items including cars, vintage wines and liquors, and European luxury apparel brands, these rappers created widespread interest in an array of existing products that were not at that point widely sought after among followers of hip-hop.

Among the brands that were especially prized were the European luxury brands Gucci, Fendi, Louis Vuitton, and MCM. The logos of these designer brands were flaunted across pieces of apparel, accessories, and jewelry. In the early part of the 1990s when the tastes of rap stars and the offerings of designer labels failed to converge, the design houses created custom-made pieces through special order, though more commonly customized apparel was produced through the illegal use of brand trademarks. The original purveyor of ghetto fabulous was Dapper Dan (Daniel Day) whose boutique on East 125th Street in Harlem predated widespread adoption of the look (the boutique was in business from 1987 until 1992, when it was shut down due to copyright violations). Dapper Dan's 24-hour custom clothier was known for cutting up authentic designer merchandise and restyling it and more commonly for hand-screening logos from companies such as Gucci, Fendi, Louis Vuitton, and MCM onto leather in order to make such staples of the hip-hop look as coats and bomber jackets, baseball caps, tracksuits, and even customized automobile interiors. Customers such as LL Cool J, Fat Joe, Eric B. & Rakim, and Big Daddy Kane custom-ordered garments that could include logos from more than one brand in a single article of apparel. Dapper Dan's designs were available with bulletproof Kevlar linings, an indication of the crossover between true gangster lifestyle and the ghetto fabulous posture. Ultimately, by the middle of the 1990s luxury companies like Gucci and Louis Vuitton, which had recently ceded creative control to young American designers like Tom Ford and Marc Jacobs, responded to the tastes represented across the hip-hop scene by including heavily logoed sneakers, ball caps, and jewelry in seasonal collections.

In addition to luxury branded items, the ghetto fabulous look included luxury materials such as cashmere, leather, and silk. Sweat suits—long an iconic feature of hip-hop street style—were made of velour or suede material, Kangol caps were paired with cashmere sweaters and leather jackets, and oversized zoot suit–inspired men's suits were worn. Women were routinely featured in rap music videos associated with this genre and were instrumental in establishing a ghetto fabulous style for women. In addition to flashy branded items, the female version of this look included revealing clothes such as slip dresses, cropped halter tops, hot pants (booty shorts), and precipitously high-heeled shoes that often included a platform.

Perhaps the most ostentatious aspect of ghetto fabulous style was the wearing of diamond-encrusted jewelry that was colloquially referred to as "bling" or "bling-bling." Rap superstars including Slick Rick (who wore a diamond-encrusted eye patch), Biz Markie (who sported a custom-made, black- and white-diamond–encrusted headphones pendant), and Lil Jon (whose "Crunk Ain't Dead" pendant was adorned with more than 3,700 stones and weighed more than five pounds) set a standard that was widely emulated by hip-hop fans through the use of inexpensive diamond chips set in low-carat gold alloys and cubic zirconia stones set in nonprecious metals. Notably, the quality and, in some cases, the verity of stones worn by hip-hoppers in the public eye became a matter of controversy and debate that played out in the media as rap stars used their jewelry as a way to proclaim personal success and status.

The ghetto fabulous aesthetic gained widespread recognition and adoption with the rise in popularity of artists like Puff Daddy and Big Daddy Kane, and the aesthetic has changed as the tastes of preeminent and affluent artists have changed. While conspicuous consumption (buying and wearing overtly expensive items) remains an important part of hip-hop culture, the ways in which fabulousness and affluence are expressed have changed in response to larger fashion trends, and in the 21st century it is notable that the standards set by prominent rappers are often shaped more by the tastes of Parisian couturiers than by the aspirations of the American ghetto.

Co-option, Crossover, Branding, and Commodification

Hip-hop style from the latter half of the 1990s onward has embodied a multitude of irreverent approaches to dressing such as the use of components of varied apparel categories (preppy, blue-collar), involving the crossover of existing brands from one demographic to another, the development of specific hip-hop labels with diverse aesthetics, and the commercial sale of hip-hop style. Co-option of apparel from apparel makers that are notably not urban is a curious phenomenon that has already been touched on with the examples of both Timberland boots and athletic jerseys entering the hip-hop wardrobe when gangsta rap was dominant. The preppie look is also an example of hip-hop style co-opting a look and reinterpreting it. Artists such as Biggie Smalls and producer Russell Simmons, through his Phat Farm brand, promoted the preppie-inspired look, which included oversized polo and rugby shirts, argyle-patterned apparel, and golfing clothes. Established brands including Nautica, Polo Sport, Polo by Ralph Lauren, and Tommy Hilfiger were worn in iconoclastic ways that mixed inner-city swagger and elite, traditionally conservative sartorial metaphors. A 1996 article that ran in *Esquire* referred to the oversized preppy look as a "walking oxymoron" that was "baffling" in its appearance with its "blend of inner city angst and private school *sang froid*," which read as a "combination of the renunciation of the principles of classic men's dress (tailoring, fit, elegance) with a few touches of clean-cut classics" (Hochswender 1996, 131–32). The hip-hop scene also co-opted blue-collar and "redneck" clothes in the middle of the 1990s. Flannel shirts, quilted vests, Carhartt work jackets and T-shirts, and Eddie Bauer hunting and fishing apparel were worn oversized and mixed with other elements of hip-hop style to give the traditional apparel a fresh new look. A 1994 *Advertising Age* report referred to this kind of co-option as an "urban outback" look (Davis 1994, 12), an expression that seems to recognize the disconnect between the intended purpose of the clothes for agricultural work and outdoor sporting and their actual use in urban settings for fashionable display. The co-option and crossover of brands like Nautica and Carhartt and the use of these apparel basics as hip street style harkens back to the beginnings of hip-hop style and the fly boys of the late 1970s. Far from being oxymoronic, the adoption of these traditional apparel styles and brands was a testament to the creativity and power of urban street style to bring flavor and attitude to the most mundane articles of clothing.

It is important to note that some co-option and crossover occurred because of purposeful promotion on the part of designers and brands, a phenomenon that is not fully documented. Perhaps the most notable example of this relationship can be attributed to Tommy Hilfiger. The Hilfiger brand, which was launched in 1984, had for years been accused of being a Ralph Lauren copycat, a second runner-up in the domain of prep. Hilfiger, an avid music fan and fashion professional who had long realized the importance of the connection between popular music and fashion (he began his career selling hippie-inspired apparel) made his clothes available free of charge to up-and-coming rap artists and struck gold in 1994 when Snoop Dogg wore a Hilfiger-branded rugby shirt on *Saturday Night Live.* Not only did that particular shirt sell out, but it repositioned the Tommy Hilfiger brand in the domain of hip-hop street style. "In exchange for giving artists free wardrobes, Hilfiger found his name mentioned in both the rhyming verses of rap songs and their 'shout out' lyrics" (Spiegler 1996, 22). Artists like LL Cool J and Jay-Z did promotions for mainstream companies like the Gap and Reebok before the 1990s had come to a close, which may be read as an effort to help those brands cross over. Thus, while co-option and crossover of brands into hip-hop style is at its heart a creative endeavor with deep roots in the street style, by the 1990s there were also commercial implications.

Perhaps the most profound impact on hip-hop style has been the branding and commodification of the continuously evolving look, both by insiders to the scene and by large multinational corporations and fashion conglomerates. As noted, many early hip-hop labels depicted celebrities in their advertising campaigns, and the importance of celebrity endorsements to hip-hop fashion labels may have contributed to the entrance of a great many hip-hop celebrities to the apparel marketplace, including filmmaker Spike Lee (Spike's Joint), the Wu Tang Clan (Wu-Wear), Jay-Z and Damon Dash (Rocawear), Sean Combs (Sean John), as well as efforts by Kid 'n Play, Naughty by Nature, Outkast, Eminem, and Jennifer Lopez, to name just a small sample. Initially referred to as "black fashion," "gang style," "urban wear," and "street wear," the fashions associated with hip-hop were originally viewed negatively by industry professionals; however, the collective buying power of hip-hop followers meant that the retailing of these apparel lines quickly moved from small urban-specialty stores like Mr. Rags, Jimmy Jazz, and Uncle Ralph's Urban Gear to national chains such as JCPenney, Spiegel, Macy's, and Dayton Hudson. By the late 1990s some hip-hop brands like Sean John and Wu-Wear were successful enough to create stand-alone stores for their labels. In 1993 *Marketing News* journalist Cyndee Miller noted, "While hip-hop started out as a 'black thing,' marketers are realizing they can use the culture to mo' better target youth of any culture" (1993, 10). Thus, by the early 1990s, hip-hop style was both a street style and a mass-market fashion phenomenon with the line between authentic and corporate becoming increasingly blurred. For example, Tommy Boy, an urban-apparel brand that was retailed through specialty shops and mail order, was owned by Time Warner (Miller 1993, 10), and many brands that bore the names of hip-hop celebrities were owned and run by major fashion conglomerates.

The type of clothing that hip-hop brands have made has changed substantially since the 1990s. As hip-hop fashion has increasingly become big business, brands have diversified their offerings and aesthetics in order to stay relevant and fashionable; thus, with the arrival of commercial or commodified hip-hop fashion, the connection to a unique *street* culture has changed. In a 1999 article that appeared in *Rolling Stone,* Ryan Cross, the marketing and advertising director of hip-hop brand Mecca, noted, "The term urban wear is kind of tired. . . . We just consider ourselves a men's collection (Dunn 1999, 54). In the same article, Jeff Tweedy of Sean John noted that that collection was inspired by Prada, Gucci, and Versace. Thus the inspiration for the commodified version of this urban "street style" was not necessarily coming from the street, from an urban center, or even from the United States.

In the 21st century affluent tastemakers who have strong connections to the formal fashion industry are increasingly shaping hip-hop fashion. Artists including Kanye West and Pharrell Williams have partnered with Louis Vuitton to design shoes and bags, Jay-Z co-designed watches for luxury watchmaker Audemars Piguet, and Sean Combs won the CFDA menswear award in 2004, a sign that the fashion establishment had embraced urban menswear. A 2002 *Black Enterprise* article observed that Combs had "just introduced Saville Row to the hip-hop world" (McKinney 2002, 98), a further indication of the change in tone and aesthetics that can be found in portions of the hip-hop marketplace. Many hip-hop artists move in the same circles as famous fashion designers and are dressed by them for red-carpet events and for concert tours. For example, Kanye West worked with Marc Jacobs for the wardrobe associated with his 2007 *Graduation* album. Hip-hop stars are routinely front-row fixtures at fashion shows, and many contemporary artists continue to develop their own clothing lines, which take influences from their current lives, not from inner-city streets. Thus, "urban-apparel" brands often reflect the imaginations of millionaires, not kids on the corner. For example, Russell Simmons noted of KLS (Kimora Lee Simmons) that "KLS is Kimora's closet," a closet undoubtedly filled with expensive designer apparel given her long-lived ties to the fashion industry (Greenberg 2007, 11). The name of Pharrell Williams's apparel line, Billionaire Boys Club, says much about its source of inspiration. If the changes in hip-hop style can be attributed to hip-hop celebrities and hip-hop brands, it is important to note that consumers of hip-hop fashion and wearers of hip-hop street style have evolved too. Damon Dash, cofounder of Rocawear, noted, "The consumer that used to buy urban has evolved. . . . They want real fashion by real fashion designers" (Greenberg 2007, 11). With this statement Dash is implying that urban wear is not actually urban but is the product of Seventh Avenue designers.

Concluding Thoughts

The influence of hip-hop culture on both fashion and street style is vast. In addition to marking aspects of identity, it has spawned a sector of the fashion industry and has influenced countless high-style collections including both Chanel and Isaac Mizrahi, both in the fall of 1991. Hip-hop artists have also strutted the catwalk for major labels, including Method Man of Wu-Tang Clan and Treach from Naughty by Nature, who worked the runway for Tommy Hilfiger for his Fall 1996 collection. In fact, noting specific instances of hip-hop in high style belies the sweeping influence of the aesthetic as hip-hop has had so much influence on commercial fashion that one may wonder if it is still a specific and unique street style. Hip-hop–inspired fashion has enjoyed such a broad reach in terms of the demographics of the people who adopt it that one may wonder if the wearing of this kind of apparel indicates anything beyond a stylistic preference. In fact, Jameel Spencer, chief marketing officer of Rocawear, observed in 2007, "You used to be able to tell who was a fan of hip-hop and who wasn't just by looking at them. Today the read is much more diverse, and you can no longer tell who is and who isn't a fan of hip-hop—the music has hit the mainstream and so have the clothes" (Greenberg 2007, 11). While Spencer's take on the situation is open to debate, the fact remains that the urban-apparel sector is worth more than $50 billion per year (McKinney 2002, 99); this kind of marketplace dominance is achieved by creating broad appeal, and big businesses have taken notice. By 2003 many hip-hop labels had been sold to major conglomerates. For example, Liz Claiborne bought Enyce, Kellwood bought Phat Fashions, and in 2007 Iconix purchased Rocawear.

So what is hip-hop style in the second decade of the 21st century? Is it a recognizable entity? Is it an identity? The answers to these questions are undeniably open to debate. However, a few points can be made with some certainty. First, there is a large prosperous portion of the fashion marketplace that is influenced by hip-hop tastemakers, many of whom have roots in urban America but who now move in elite, international social circles. Additionally, there are individuals from all walks of life who use that apparel in interesting and creative ways to create a unique street style. Furthermore, sociological research has indicated that some African American teens use hip-hop dress, knowledge of music, dance, gestures, and argot as a way to gain cultural capital, as a way to gain inclusion status and legitimacy in a group (Clay 2003, 1346). However, generalizing findings of this kind to the wider population is undoubtedly too broad of a gesture.

A second point that is clear is that the foundational aspects of hip-hop style, those that were developed by b-boys and fly boys in the late 1970s, are still fundamental to creating a sartorial statement. The ubiquity of the kinds of clothes cited in the early part of this entry in contemporary urban-apparel lines demonstrates the strong link between fly boy style and contemporary dress practices. For many individuals, traditional hip-hop clothing remains an important marker of identity. However, bans of hip-hop apparel by local governments, schools, and the NBA are an indication that outsiders to the cultural traditions of hip-hop make unwarranted, blanketing stereotypes surrounding the adoption of this apparel. Negative identity implications are an important aspect of hip-hop apparel in the 21st century. For example, the wearing of a hoodie was part of the justification offered by neighborhood watchman George Zimmerman for the brutal murder of young Trayvon Martin, and the wearing of hoodies was used as a symbol of protest by individuals who responded to the lax attitude of law-enforcement officials to Martin's slaying. Undoubtedly, the historical connections between hip-hop apparel and the rough-and-tumble urban streets that spawned this culture is part of the appeal of some of the staples of this kind of apparel, but it is also worth noting that hip-hop style (or whatever label one wishes to apply to this constantly evolving fashion category and street style) is comfortable and versatile, laid back and casual. The pieces that constitute the look are open to improvisation, conveying attitude, swagger, and feeling good, which are ultimately the most important cornerstones of looking good.

Further Reading

Clay, A. 2003. "Keepin' It Real: Black Youth, Hip-hop Culture, and Black Identity." *American Behavioral Scientist* 46 (10): 1346–55.

Cooper, M. 2004. *Hip-hop Files.* Cologne, Germany: From Here to Fame.

Crazy Legs. 2011. "Introduction." In *B-Boy Championships: From Bronx to Brixton* by D. J. Hooch, 6–9. London: Virgin Books.

Davis, R. A. 1994. "Urban Outback Puts Hip-hop on a Hanger." *Advertising Age,* March 21, 12.

Dimitriades, G. 1996. "Hip Hop: From Live Performance to Mediated Narrative." *Popular Music* 15 (2): 179–94.

Dunn, J. 1999. "How Hip-hop Style Bum-Rushed the Mall." *Rolling Stone,* 808: 54.

Greenberg, J. 2007. "Hip-hops Fashion Evolution." *WWD,* April 5, 11. Retrieved April 30, 2016, from www.condenast.com.

Harkness, G. 2014. *Chicago Hustle and Flow: Gangs, Gangsta Rap, and Social Class.* Minneapolis, MN: University of Minnesota Press.

"Hip-hop Fashion." 1992. *Essence* 23 (November 7): 26.

Hochswender, W. 1996. "Prep Urban." *Esquire* 125, 131–32.

Kitwana, B. 1994. *The Rap on Gangsta Rap.* Chicago: Third World Press.

McKinney, J. 2002. "Rags to Riches." *Black Enterprise* 33 (2): 98–104.

Miller, C. 1993. "Marketers Tap into Rap as Hip-hop Becomes 'Safe.'" *Marketing News,* 10, 15.

"New Trends in Urban Style." 1999. *Ebony* 54 (6): 48.

Reeves, M. 2008. *Somebody Scream: Rap Music's Rise to Prominence in the Aftershock of Black Power.* New York: Faber & Faber.

Royal, L. E. 2000. "Hip Hop on Top: Urban Fashion Designers Rule." *Black Enterprise* 30 (12): 91–94.

Samuels, D. 1991. "The Rap on Rap." *The New Republic,* November 11, 24–29.

Sanneh, K. 2013. "Harlem Chic." *The New Yorker* 89 (March 25; 6), 52.

Shabaz, J. 2001. *Back in the Days.* New York: Power House Books.

Spiegler, M. 1996. "Marketing Street Culture: Bringing Hip-hop Style to the Mainstream." *American Demographics* 18: 28–34.

Hippie (Mid-1960s–Early 1970s)

The term "hippie" (or "hippy") is used to refer to the incredibly heterogeneous countercultural movement that emerged in the early 1960s and that was a strong visible presence into the early 1970s. The label "hippie" seems to have first been applied to this particular youth culture in September of 1965 by a journalist named Michael Fallon who was discussing the youth scene in San Francisco. Notably, the hippie label had also been applied to the Beats during the 1950s and coevally in the 1960s to the British Mods. Derived from the term "hip," meaning to live on the edge, the label has endured with this specific subcultural group despite the fact that insiders to the movement referred to themselves as "freaks," "heads" (from "acid heads"), and "longhairs."

Hippies share a subcultural lineage with both the Beat Generation and the surfer lifestyle that had both gained major traction in the 1950s. All three of these subcultural groups may simply be labeled as "dropout" groups that were disenchanted with the mainstream American values of the post–World War II period. Commodity culture, traditional domesticity, conformity, bureaucracy, and the military-industrial complex that was being propped up by the Vietnam War were all deemed anathema to a life well lived, and hippies responded to these cultural variables in a variety of ways. Protests, especially of the Vietnam War, were regular events that disrupted mainstream life, commerce, and traffic by overtaking public spaces and thoroughfares. Many protests were fleeting disruptions that have largely been relegated to historical footnotes, though protests that culminated with violent responses by the police and military, such as the student protests at Kent State University in Ohio in 1970, have become emblematic of the convulsions that hippies caused within the mainstream. Sit-ins, be-ins, and love-ins, gatherings in which hippies overtook public spaces to sing, dance, smoke, and *be,* were also regular occurrences that permeated the visual and cultural landscape of the United States in this period.

Various forms of mass media contributed to the diffusion of the hippie counterculture, including its sartorial innovations. Music that expressed the sentiments of the counterculture was perhaps the most widely received expression of hippie ideology and can be found in songs such as Bob Dylan's "The Times They Are a Changin'" (1964), The Beatles's "All You Need Is Love" (1967), Cream's "Sunshine of Your Love" (1967), and Stephen Stills's "If You Can't Be With the One You Love, Love the One You're With" (1970). The poignancy and allure of much of this music came to a crest at the famous Woodstock Music Festival, which took place in 1969 in the town of Bethel, New York. Album covers, concert posters, and press photographs conveyed the dress aesthetics of many influential musicians to the masses, and many became models for imitation. Movies such as *The Trip* (1967), *The Love-Ins* (1967), *Head* (1968), and *The Monterey Pop Festival* (1968) also provided the general public with a view into aspects of the subculture and its style, as did the profoundly influential musical *Hair,* which ran on Broadway for almost 2,000 performances beginning in 1968. Books such as *We Are the People Our Parents Warned Us Against* (1968) by Nicholas Von Hoffman and *The Politics of Ecstasy* (1968) by Timothy Leary also expressed key sentiments of the counterculture and influenced both insiders and members of the cultural mainstream.

The hippie counterculture was not monolithic in its ideologies or the way in which ideas were expressed. Arguably, no two hippies thought alike or looked alike. The street style of the hippie counterculture manifested itself in an endless stream of permutations and has links to clothes that both surfers and Beats wore (jeans, sweatshirts, secondhand clothes); however, two discernible, novel aesthetic veins, which were not always distinctly separate, can be identified. The two branches consisted of a lifestyle grounded in a "return to nature" and a lifestyle guided by the therapeutic powers of psychedelic and psychotropic drugs. These two subgenres of hippie style will be analyzed separately, and their interrelationship will be examined toward the end of this discussion.

The Back-to-Nature Movement

For some members of this counterculture, a return to nature, accomplished by living in commune with others and living off the land, was the primary solution to their dissatisfaction with post–World War II America. Communes big and small developed throughout the United States, including The Hog Farm (originally Tujunga, California), Mystic Arts (Sunny Valley, Oregon), Black Bear Ranch (Forks of Salmon, California), and The Farm (Summertown, Tennessee). In addition to these relatively large, organized, and intentional communes, there were also countless small, relatively unknown communes, such as the one created in North Carolina by Robert Roskind and documented in his book *Memoirs of an Ex-Hippie: Seven Years in the Counterculture.*

The manner of dress adopted by hippies living in communes tended largely toward simplicity and functionality. Clothes that could withstand laborious agricultural work (denim, flannel, and cotton canvas, including military-surplus gear) were favored based on their utilitarian features, as many commune members were involved in agricultural work that enabled members to live off the land and thereby abstain from commodity culture. Handmade or homespun knits and textiles were made on site and also purchased from nonindustrialized parts of the world such as Haiti, Morocco, Mexico, and Swaziland. The wearing of natural fibers and textiles with a handmade lineage evoked a return to simpler, preindustrial times. Do-it-yourself modifications were also an important part of the style. Embroidery, patchwork, and tie-dye were ways to channel the desire to be self-sufficient and to mask the aura of mass production and commodity culture. The modification of ready-made clothes through decorative techniques was also a way to personalize apparel, make a statement about oneself, or gift a sentiment to a friend by decorating his or her clothes with hearts, flowers, peace signs, or slogans. Regular bootcut jeans could be transformed into bell-bottoms by inserting a triangular panel in the inseam (peace protesters infamously used panels of American flags). Jeans were also bound and dipped in bleach to create a spotted pattern and were sometimes referred to as "pinto pants." Shoes were oftentimes omitted from the ensemble of a back-to-nature hippie if weather permitted, but simple sandals and un-lasted moccasins were often adopted because they were simple, connected to preindustrial cultures, and, in the case of moccasins, could be manufactured without the need for specialized equipment. An affinity for dress derived from non-Western cultures was also incorporated into the dress of some hippies because of its symbolic value. Native American beadwork and deerskin shirts with fringe, Central or South American serapes, caftans, tunics, and textiles from North Africa, the Middle East, and Central Asia were all incorporated to varying degrees, in part as a subtle statement about the beauty of traditional dress practices and decorative techniques. The adoption of these forms of dress may also be read as a form of rejection of mainstream American cultural ideals. Grooming practices for back-to-nature hippies were minimalist in their efforts. Early followers of the back-to-nature movement advocated abstention from bathing; however, skin ailments were a common malady resulting from this neglect, and bathing with natural oils and soaps was advised in lieu of hygiene products with chemical components. Makeup was generally avoided as its use essentially creates the inverse of a natural look, though body paint was sometimes worn, especially as part of a public spectacle such as a concert or protest. Both sexes allowed their hair to grow long, and tresses were generally left untamed or were braided and plaited in simple styles that referenced the grooming practices of native peoples. Women often wore flowers in their hair, and both sexes wore jewelry made of seeds strung as beads, which could be gifted as tokens of affection.

Over time, as the cultural cachet of the back-to-nature movement grew and knowledge of the movement became more widespread through publications such as the *Whole Earth Catalog* (published 1968–1971, 1974), commodities reflecting the ideas espoused by these hippies came to the mass market. Boutiques in cities great and small imported apparel from artisans throughout the world. Magazines such as *Vogue* promoted elements of the look as high fashion, and branded and designer products that tapped into either the aesthetics or the sentiments of the back-to-nature movement entered the market. Earth Shoes, a type of shoe characterized by a wedge-shaped sole that is the reverse of a standard wedge design (it is wide and high at the toe and about one-quarter of an inch lower and narrower at the heel), are a poignant example of the commodification of the natural movement. Designed in 1957, the shoes were originally sold in Copenhagen, Denmark, under the name Anne Kalso Minus Heel and were marketed as a way to walk more healthfully (to improve gait and posture). In 1969 Kalso licensed the shoes to Eleanor and Raymond Jacobs who, seeing the throngs of hippies passing by their store on the first Earth Day (April 22, 1970), were inspired to put a sign in the window of the shop that advertised "Earth Shoes." This apt rebranding proved profoundly successful, and the popularity of these shoes took off, with sales peaking over $14 million in 1974. Simple strands of beads, which were worn by hippies, also became commodified and ultimately were rebranded as "love beads." Originally, the back-to-nature hippies favored beads that were made of natural elements or derived from nonindustrial or "tribal" cultures; however, the term "love beads" seems to have come into use in 1967, and the wearing of these necklaces became a fashion statement. By 1968 *The New York Times* was reporting strong sales of the beads as a women's fashion accessory. The beads could be purchased at mainstream apparel retailers and also at emporiums that catered to the hippie subcultural scene. Tie-dye was also elevated from the realm of do-it-yourself, anticommodity culture to the realm of fashion. High-fashion designers, including Halston, embraced the aesthetic for their pricey designer apparel, thus creating the market for professionally made tie-dye. Tie-dye cooperatives such as Smooth Tooth Enterprises, located on Great Jones Street in lower Manhattan, were among the places where designers could source the fabric for their work. So great was the demand for tie-dye that an entrepreneur named Hy Langer developed a tie-dye machine that could complete the tie-dye process in one-sixteenth of the time it took to do it by hand, and in 1970 a company called Soptra developed a roller-printing process that mimicked the appearance of the technique, a further indication of the demand for the textile and an indication of the movement of hippie street style from the commune to the mainstream.

Psychedelic Life and Psychedelic Drugs

Probing consciousness, subconsciousness, the nature and meaning of existence, and human relations (among other things) through the use of mind-altering substances such as LSD, peyote, mescaline, and hallucinogenic mushrooms was a passion and pursuit for many members of the hippie subculture; and the use of psychotropic substances of this kind were certainly commonplace among commune members and adherents of the back-to-nature movement. Psychedelic fashions inspired by the culture surrounding these drugs are distinctive in their aesthetics. The term "psychedelic" bears some explanation. Originally, the implication of psychedelic art, music, design, or experience was that it made concrete or manifest the inner workings of the mind or the psyche. Thus psychedelic designs found in two-dimensional works on paper or cloth were universally ornate and incredibly complex, featuring densely worked patterns. Serpentine lines, amorphous shapes, and high-key colors, including hues that verged on neon, reflected the energy, complexity, and surreality of the mind's inner workings. Psychedelic experience was also augmented through musical performance that was accompanied by psychedelic light shows featuring complex pulsations of strobe lights in brilliant colors. The multisensory experience created in this context, and augmented with psychotropic substances, was designed to transport the concert- or club-goer to a heightened and enlightened realm. However, over time, as the mainstream came to appropriate and commoditize hippie subculture, the psychedelic experience was frequently undertaken for purely recreational purposes, and the meaning of the term "psychedelic" was increasingly interpreted to mean wild, trippy, or "psycho."

Psychedelic fashions featured richly saturated colors that were often used in combinations that produced glaring contrasts (neon yellow against acid green or shocking pink paired with safety orange). The patterns were typically very complex, ornate, and dense and featured distorted, amoeba-like shapes that had the potential to shape-shift before the viewer's eyes. Psychedelic textile patterns were inspired by poster art, album covers, and the psychedelic light shows that accompanied the musical performances of bands such as The Grateful Dead and Jefferson Airplane. Psychedelic patterns were applied to a wide range of apparel for both men and women. Shirts and blouses, tunics, caftans, dresses, and wide-legged palazzo pants or bell-bottom trousers were frequently made with this kind of pattern, and the textile of choice was typically polyester, a fabric constructed of fibers that are especially capable of bonding highly saturated colors. Psychedelic patterns can be found in apparel ranging from French haute couture (see Yves Saint Laurent's 1970 collection) to mass-market fashions retailed in the Sears catalog. The psychedelic look was not typically achieved through the head-to-toe use of the aforementioned ornate patterns. Among the other key elements were velvet textiles, enjoyed for their rich colors, reflectivity, and sensuous tactile qualities. Sunglasses, especially those with round lenses, were popular for the ability to tint the world via colored lenses while protecting eyes dilated from drug use.

In addition to these two aesthetic categories of dress, there is also a category for hippie fashion commodities. *Fashion commodities* may be defined as products that were designed and manufactured to reflect hippy values (to varying degrees) but that were primarily made for their commercial value. Psychedelic textiles, which were mass-produced, may be included within this general category, as they do not seem to have developed organically from within the subculture. Mass-produced objects, emblazoned with peace signs, were also widespread commodities. Companies such as Underground Uplift Unlimited and New World's Eve Group produced slogan pins, sweatshirts, and T-shirts (as well as bumper stickers and posters) with expressions such as "Love Is a Many Gendered Thing," "Burn Pot Not People," and "Make Love Not War." Items of this kind were sold through mail-order advertisements that were featured in subcultural publications such as *The Berkeley Barb* and *The East Village Other.* Shops also sprang up that sold paraphernalia that catered to the hippie set and its hangers-on. In New York City, such shops included the Psychedelicatessen, The Tribal Connection, and The Electric Lotus, whereas in the Haight-Ashbury, San Francisco, the Psychedelic Shop and Wild Colors were retailers of this kind of merchandise. Hippie-inspired fashions could also be purchased in London in shops such as Granny Takes a Trip and Lord Kitchener's Valet. An article that appeared in *The New Republic* in 1966, entitled "The Hippie Business," noted the shift that was under way in the hippie subculture whereby things that had been "*outré*" were being "cleaned up" and appropriated by the mass market. Members of the hippie subculture living in the Haight-Ashbury responded to this widespread commodification, which they saw as part of the death of their community. In October 1967 a funeral processed down Haight Street, and members of the counterculture tossed their beads and other artifacts into a coffin.

Fashion designers of the late 1960s and early 1970s continued to interpret the hippie aesthetic despite disenfranchisement from subcultural insiders. Designers co-opted simple elements of authentic hippie dress practices and exploded their visual impacts. Ossie Cark, Thea Porter, Zhandra Rhodes, and Jean Muir elevated elements such as patchwork, beadwork, and fringe and worked them in intricate patterns, in copious quantities, in luxurious fabrics, and in trendy colors. Designs of this kind explored the visual aesthetics of the period but essentially created a new visual language as the use and meaning of these high-style clothes were far removed from the original context. Designers of the late 20th and early 21st centuries continue to explore elements of hippie street style. Strong references can be found in the Dolce and Gabbana Spring/Summer 1993 collection and in the Tommy Hilfiger Spring/Summer 2015 line, though countless other examples exist, a clear testimony to the lasting allure of this late-20th-century style. For many people in the 21st century hippie-inspired aesthetics continue to have allure, as the ghost of the counterculture seems to live on in tie-dye, beadwork, and crochet, and wearing these kinds of clothes seems to facilitate a connection with a bohemian ethos. In addition to seasonal fashions that rework the aesthetics described in this entry, echoes of hippie street style can be seen among followers of the jam-band scene as well as attendees at the Coachella festival.

Further Reading

"The Hippies." 1967. *Time* 90 (1): 22.

Miller, T. S. 2012. *The Hippies and American Values.* Knoxville: University of Tennessee Press.

Morris, B. 1970. "Java's Gift to Seventh Avenue—Fabrics with a Tie-Dyed Look." *The New York Times,* February 16. Retrieved January 17, 2016, from timesmachine.nytimes.com.

Newfield, J. 1967. "One Cheer for the Hippies." *Nation* 204 (26): 809–10.

"The Psychedelicatessen." 1967. *Time* (February 2): 96.

Roskind, R. 2001. *Memoirs of an Ex-hippie: Seven Years in the Counterculture.* Blowing Rock, NC: One Love Press.

Sanford, D. 1967. "The Hippie Business." *New Republic* 156 (23): 7–8.

"Squirrels, Beads, and the Hippie-Bead Fad Give Navajos a Lift." 1968. *The New York Times,* September 7. Retrieved March 27, 2015, from timesmachine.nytimes.com.

Taylor, A. 1974. "Shoes That Make You Waddle Like a Duck—and They Sell." *The New York Times,* February 25. Retrieved January 17, 2016, from http://timesmachine .nytimes.com/timesmachine.

"Where Have All the Flowers Gone?" 1967. *Time* 90 (15): 40.

"Wilting Flowers." 1968. *Time* 91 (19): 37.

Hipster (1999–Present)

The term "hipster" is perhaps the longest-lived, most frequently utilized term that is applied to American street style. However, it is also possibly the least specific and is undoubtedly currently the most contentious. The term "hipster" essentially means one who is "hip," "cool," or in the know about the most contemporary hip and cool things. The term "hipster" or "hepster" has been used to refer to a person with knowledge of cutting-edge contemporary culture since at least the 1930s and was initially applied to bebop jazz musicians and the zoot-suited youth who jived to their music. Cab Calloway, the famous jazz artist and bandleader, codified the term in the *Hepster's Dictionary: Language of Jive,* which was first published in 1939. Beyond the meaning of the term, however, there is a great deal of debate. At the most fundamental level, individuals debate whether or not *the* hipster is a discernible and specific category. Acclaimed sociologist and street-style expert Ted Polhemus noted in 1994 that to be a hipster is to have a state of mind that rejects the "straight" lifestyle, therefore making the Beats and bikers hipsters based predominantly on their attitudes rather than on a specific set of stylistic characteristics (1994, 29). However, beginning in the late 1990s a specific sociocultural milieu emerged and coalesced that has since been regularly labeled with the hipster moniker. Whether the late-20th-century hipster is a subcultural group, a series of overlapping fashion trends, or a consumer phenomenon is open to debate, and notably, those to whom the designation is applied soundly reject the label. It is this amorphous group of young, urban, often Caucasian adults, which emerged from the alternative and indie (independent) scenes of the middle 1990s, that is the target of this entry.

What specifically is a hipster (person)? Where is hipsterdom (place)? What are the key hipsterisms (beliefs and ideas)? It has been suggested, quite critically, that the sum total of all these is the "dead end of western civilization" and a "self-absorbed aesthetic vacuum" (Haddow 2012, 74). In essence, such statements undermine the notion that contemporary hipsters are anything of note. More specifically, it has been suggested that "hipsterism is a nebulous moniker for a subculture of young urbanites fond of artisanal pickles and ironic t-shirts" (Silva Laughlin 2015). It has been suggested that hipsters are not a subculture but rather a "consumer group" (Haddow 2012, 77) of a certain age that gravitate to obscure or unwieldy products such as fixed-gear bikes, outmoded designs and technologies including vintage apparel and Polaroid cameras, and low-brow consumer products like Pabst Blue Ribbon beer. The notion that being a hipster is related to connoisseurship and the accumulation of what Pierre Bourdieu referred to as cultural capital (social merit attained through knowledge) are ideas that are regularly circulated regarding hipsters. Journalist Marc Grief, who has written extensively about this social group, noted, "All hipsters play at being the inventors or first adopters of novelties: pride comes from knowing and deciding what's cool in advance of the rest of the world" (Grief 2010b). It is also widely argued that the hipster designation is generally considered a "pejorative label for anyone who presents their cultural tastes or their considered aesthetics as indicators of independence and creativity but are [*sic*] seemingly unaware of their superficiality, or of the normative impulse that might be underpinning their chosen aesthetics"

(Hill 2015, 47). Douglas Haddow noted, "It is rare, if not impossible to find an individual who will proclaim themselves a proud hipster" (2012, 76). Hipsters are reviled for acting as though they are in the know by individuals who believe *they* know better, a fact that further convolutes the task of identifying the true hipster.

Unlike many subcultures that incubated on the fringes of society (see the history of punks and hippies), hipsterdom first emerged in upwardly mobile areas that ultimately became gentrified by young, often college-educated middle- and upper-class youths. Neighborhoods including Williamsburg, Brooklyn; Wicker Park, Chicago; Silver Lake, Los Angeles; Inner Mission, San Francisco; and Capitol Hill, Seattle, were working-class neighborhoods in the late 1990s, which have since evolved to become destinations for the young and fabulous. In the late 1990s and early 2000s, in each of these neighborhoods, young men and women were drawn to inexpensive real estate in proximity to an established urban scene. Over the course of the last two decades these neighborhoods have changed from urban backwaters to epicenters of cool, incubating sartorial and culinary tastes and sociocultural trends that have evolved as widespread adoption has depleted the cachet of coolness associated with being in the forefront of adoption. Thus hipster culture is a moving target linked not to a singular message or standpoint but to the mission of finding the next novelty.

Hipster sartorial style has evolved over time, but a few important hallmarks are clearly decipherable over the past two decades. First and foremost in terms of visibility and importance is the gender-fluid approach to dress, which made menswear staples like flannel shirts and knit watch caps fashionable for women and fitted tops and skinny jeans fashionable for men. The second tendency that has had widespread influence is the exploitation of an aesthetic that may coyly be labeled "the questionable taste look." Mining and mixing elements that are widely considered ugly, tacky, unflattering, or outdated have long been a hallmark of the hipster approach to street style. A subset of this tendency is a reliance on vintage apparel. Dress elements that span a wide variety of time periods, contexts of use, and places of origin are playfully juxtaposed to create eclectic mixes. Additionally, an emphasis on the unusual, genuine, homemade, locally sourced, and vintage has meant that a great deal of variety has existed, and it has been suggested that hipsterism has "less to do with a specific aesthetic style and more to do with the attempt to foster a counter-mainstream sensibility" (Hill 2015, 45). That debate aside, there are several phases of hipster style that have been clearly visible.

The earliest iteration of the style was an evocation of stereotypical white, working-class dress aesthetics. Among the most iconic (and presumably ironic) elements of this look were foam front, snap-back trucker hats and T-shirts from brands such as John Deere, Von Dutch, and Miller Beer. Aviator sunglasses often accompanied the caps, and iconic elements of 1970s dress including knee-high tube socks with colorful horizontal bands and quilted nylon vests were key accessories that were widely adopted. By the early 2000s many of these features had become mainstreamed and were dropped by fashion innovators and replaced by a look that married elements of grunge with stereotypical "nerd" features. Woolen knit beanies, flannel shirts, Henley shirts, ribbed long johns, Vans, and Converse recalled the Seattle scene but were paired with V-neck undershirts, leggings, skinny jeans, very short cut-off jean shorts, overalls, hoodies, and high-end, over-ear headphones. Eyeglasses with thick frames (with or without lenses) and trilby hats completed this dress aesthetic. Once these dress choices were mainstreamed, new tendencies emerged. By the end of the decade the hippie-hipster was visible. This iteration of hipster-chic embraced sustainability, organic fabrics, and used and vintage clothes that embodied a neo-hippie sensibility, and affected an aesthetic that was decidedly more bohemian than that of its predecessors. As this look reached critical mass it was replaced in the first years of the twenty-teens by a decidedly retro look that was especially evident among males. Waxed moustaches, long and bushy beards, lumberjack shirts, suspenders, collarless button-up shirts, and scuffed work boots evoked a decidedly 19th-century aesthetic. The retro look for women has been less cohesive, but 1950s-inspired housedresses, high-waist pants, and acid-wash denim were all widespread revivals in this period. Notably, at the time of writing, this iteration of hipster chic seems to be waning in popularity among the hip as elements of the style have been mainstreamed. The aforementioned hipster sartorial statements are among the most visible and iconic; however, it has been suggested that there are many more variations on this theme including 1980s retro hipster, preppy hipster, proletariat hipster, Hollywood hipster, geezer-style hipster, and high-fashion hipster (Kurutz 2013).

Efforts by some writers, commentators, and in-the-know insiders (who might incidentally be labeled hipsters) to defuse the term and deny the existence of hipsterism are belied by countless articles that have been written on the subject and by the many consumer products that have been developed to reflect the cultural and aesthetic trend. A number of books, both expository and satirical, have been published, including *A Field Guide to the Urban Hipster* (2003), *The Hipster Handbook* (2003), and *Stuff Hipsters Hate* (2010). A number of magazines are also closely related to hipster interests and aesthetics. Among them are *Vice, Paper,* and *Another Magazine.* Celebrities have also been instrumental in terms of setting and conveying hipster style. Ashton Kutcher, especially during his first years as the host of the television show *Punk'd* (first aired in 2003), was a trendsetter for men, while Kristen Stewart often embodies the hipster aesthetic and is regularly photographed by street-style photographers. The heavy reliance of millennials (a demographic cohort born between about 1982 and 2004) on social media has meant that social-media sites like Facebook and Pinterest have been instrumental in conveying hipster sartorial style and have undoubtedly led to the quick commodification of looks that were incubated in places like Williamsburg, Brooklyn.

While hipster sartorial style has its roots in apparel basics and vintage clothing, many brands have been adopted consistently by individuals striving to attain the look and are closely associated with hipsterism since the advertising campaigns of the brands reflect hallmark characteristics. Favorite hipster brands include apparel retailers American Apparel, Top Shop, and Urban Outfitters and classic shoe brands Converse, Vans, and Keds. Classic American brands like Levis and Pendleton have benefited from hipster patronage, and eyeglass sales have soared in the first decades of the 21st century (Silva Laughlin 2015). Some brands favored by hipsters, including L.L. Bean and Lands' End, have tailored their lines to meet hipster tastes and have started selling products like skinny jeans and tailored flannels in an effort to monetize the popularity of the aesthetic. There is also some evidence that the hipster label is used as a marketing tool. For example, in 2010 Nine West offered the "Hipster Sandal." Hipsterdom in general has been monetized. Cool-hunters, marketers, and promoters of all kinds have tapped into this cultural milieu, and commodification occurs so quickly that it is sometimes difficult to tell if a sartorial gesture emerged on the streets of Los Angeles or on Seventh Avenue. Douglas Haddow, in his scathingly critical essay on hipsters, noted, "In the end, hipsters are sold what they think they invented and are spoon-fed their pre-packaged cultural livelihood" (2012, 77). While Haddow's statement seems to be too universalizing, it is clear that 21st-century street style can be quickly replicated by fast fashion and that social media quickly disseminate ideas, so that being in the know is always a short-lived experience. Oversaturation is quickly achieved in the age of Snapchat, Instagram, and other social-media sources, and these outlets quickly turn the novel and unusual into the normal and the handcrafted into the mass-produced. In the blink of an eye, what began as dissent becomes *de rigueur*.

The future of *the hipster,* this current incarnation of hipness, and whether or not hipsters will have any lasting impact remain to be seen. The critique levied at hipsterdom is that it does not really stand for anything and that everything is façade. Posturing about being working class or poor, refusing to be labeled, and reveling in knowledge of the useless and obscure are attributes that seem to lack lasting sociocultural importance. Perhaps hipster style is just a mash-up of other subcultures amalgamated to strike contemporary sensibilities as different, just for the sake of being different. If the hipster cultural milieu is just about change and difference it would, therefore, be perfectly poised to influence fashionable dress, which is similarly defined by unceasing cycles of change. Some critics of hipsters see this particular intersection of youth culture and commodity culture as particularly egregious. Mark Grief, writing for *New York Magazine,* has argued that hipsterdom, which aligns with both the rebel and dominant cultures, "thus opens up a poisonous conduit between the two" (2010a, 34). In essence, if the hipster is the contemporary *avant-garde,* then there is no *avant-garde,* for in the moment that the new frontier is identified it is mainstreamed. Grief went on to note, "The hipster is a savant at picking up the tiny changes of rapidly cycling consumer distinction" (2010a, 36). It is this focus of concern that puts the hipster in remarkable contrast to the many rebellious subcultures that were focused on social and cultural upheaval as well as aesthetic change. Critiques of this kind position hipsterdom in a very different league from the radical and revolutionary subcultures of the latter half of the 20th century.

There are critics of hipsterdom who go beyond the assertion that hipsters are simply devoid of positive impact. Some feminist theorists have noted that hipsters often adopt a posture of delighting in irony while actually using that posture as a disguise to protect themselves from critique for bad behaviors (Murphy 2013, 17). Sexist actions and attitudes, "soft porn" Instagram postings, and racist-themed parties are among the gestures that capitalize on stereotypes, mocking, and appropriation (Murphy 2013). Alternatively, the hipster cultural milieu may point to some of the shortcomings of youth culture in the 21st century. This author's conversations with fashion-design students, held over the course of several years, suggest that bricolage and nostalgia may be symptomatic of the emotional toll taken by the rapid speed of life in the 21st century and that interest in the obscure and arcane may be a response to information overload and the difficulty individuals face in differentiating themselves in a world where there is incessant and immediate access to ideas, stylistic and otherwise.

Dov Charney, the former CEO of American Apparel, announced in August 2010 that "hipster is over" (Grief 2010a, 34). However, it is not clear that his assertion is true. While it may be true that some elements of hipster style such as craft and retro have "reached critical mass," it is likely that some new aesthetic is on the horizon for the perpetually cool and in the know (Laura 2013). Critics, commentators, and trend forecasters around the world are still discussing hipster, noting its arrival in Europe (Mataillet 2015) and predicting its evolution (Ferrier 2014). Some aspects of hipster style seem now to be just a part of contemporary fashion and potentially also part of long-lived dress practices. In particular, it has been suggested that aspects of hipster street style including tailored menswear for women, androgynous dressing, V-neck undershirts, flannels, and bandanas have been adopted as a uniform of sorts by substantial numbers of women who are lesbian, and it has been predicted that the look will persist as a lasting style within that social demographic (Casino 2010). This last thought provides room to end on a definitive and positive note about a street style that is widely maligned and almost universally disavowed, at least in name. Whatever this 21st-century youth style may be, whether it has deep meaning or not, there is strong evidence to suggest that contemporary dress practices continue to be shaped by consumer-driven practices in the new millennium, and this is evidence of the continuing importance of dress practices shaped by the American streetscape.

Further Reading

Casino, K. 2010. "Why Lesbians Hang On to the Hipster." *The Gay and Lesbian Review,* September/October, 25–27.

Ferrier, M. 2014. "The End of the Hipster: How Flat Caps and Beards Stopped Being So Cool." *The Guardian,* June 21. Retrieved June 21, 2016, from www.theguardian.com.

Grief, M. 2010a. "What Was the Hipster?" *New York Magazine* 43 (November 1; 35): 32–37.

Grief, M. 2010b. "The Hipster in the Mirror." *The New York Times,* November 12. Retrieved June 21, 2016, from www.nytimes.com.

Haddow, D. 2012. "Hipster: The Dead End of Civilization." In *The Meanings of Dress* 3rd ed., edited by K. Miller-Spillman, A Reilly, and P. Hunt Hurts, 74–77. New York: Fairchild Books.

Hill, W. 2015. "A Hipster History: Towards a Post-critical Aesthetic." *Critical Studies in Fashion and Beauty* 6 (1): 45–60.

Kurutz, S. 2013. "Caught in the Hipster Trap." *The New York Times,* September 14. Retrieved June 21, 2016, from www.nytimes.com.

Laura, A. 2013. "How Hipster Lost Its Cool." *Sunday Telegraph Magazine,* 16.

Mataillet, D. 2015. "From Zazous to Hipsters." (A. Uff, Trans.). *France-Amérique,* November, 76.

Murphy, M. 2013. "The Rise of Hipster Sexism." *Herizons* 27 (1): 16–19.

Polhemus, T. 1994. *Streetstyle: From Sidewalk to Catwalk.* London: Thames and Hudson.

Silva Laughlin, L. 2015. "The Hipster Trend Going Flat?" *Fortune,* January, 12.

Leathermen (1950s–Present)

Leathermen is a label that is used to categorize a subset of men (and to a far lesser degree transgender and transsexual individuals who identify as male) within the gay community who communicate their sexual orientation and interests through the wearing of leather apparel and accessories. While there are men and women of varied sexual orientations who utilize leather apparel as part of their sexuality and are involved in leather culture, their dress is incredibly varied and is generally not a street style. This entry deals with the dress of a specific group of gay males, who innovated this particular style of dress and who make up the majority of individuals who dress in this manner. Leathermen and leather culture emerged in the United

States in the wake of World War II and are derived directly from the motorcycle-club scene that was developing at that time. Motorcycle clubs in general translated the structured social and cultural traditions of military life into a civilian context that nurtured fraternity and camaraderie among men. The leather scene emerged out of motorcycle clubs comprised of gay members, including the Satyrs of Los Angeles, the first gay motorcycle club, which was founded in 1954. Some of the dress practices and ideologies of leathermen also share a lineage with the Modern Primitive subculture that was also in its nascent state in the postwar period.

Myriad factors provided the social context for the development of leather culture in the United States in the 1950s. First, homosexuality in the United States at this time was generally marginalized, and homosexual acts were illegal throughout the United States until 1962 (first decriminalized in Illinois); thus individuals who identified as gay typically tried to pass as straight during their workaday lives. Dressing in leather was a release from these social and cultural strictures for some gay men, who originally wore the countercultural apparel to bars and clubs on the outskirts of towns, near loading docks and fishing wharves. Additionally, the prevailing cultural construct of gay masculinity in the postwar period construed a gay man as silly, effeminate, and weak. Leathermen adopted a hypermasculine appearance and attitude as a way to confront and upend that stereotype. The camaraderie of the motorcycle club and its connection to military culture have already been mentioned, but another layer of attraction to leather culture for some men may also be ascribed to military service. While serving in World War II many men bonded in life-or-death situations, trusting one another and surviving profound stressors. The sexual practices that are linked to leather culture, which often include sado-masochism (S/M) and bondage, create a similar context of adrenaline-fueled stress, and those who participate in these kinds of acts place their personal well-being and full trust in the hands of a fellow man. Thus leathersexuality allowed some men to emotionally and psychologically return to a state of personal fulfillment that was otherwise lost in the postwar social context. Finally, the social structure of postwar America had reverted to traditional and conservative mores that emphasized the nuclear family and established gender roles. Leather culture and its dress practices provided a release from the strictures of traditional mainstream culture.

The standard dress of leathermen is characterized by the wearing of thick, black leather, which may be considered a "second skin" and a point of reconciliation between the human and the animal (Mains 1984, 34, 35). The material itself is thus chosen not only for its visual, olfactory, and tactile characteristics but also for its symbolic potential. Leather motorcycle jackets are generally paired with blue jeans or leather pants that are worn with or without black leather chaps. Black leather vests worn with or without a shirt underneath are also typical, as are heavy, black leather motorcycle boots, knee-high patrolman's boots, or combat boots.

Black leather Muir caps, black leather gloves, and harnesses that crisscross the chest or groin are also worn. Belts are often worn with large metal buckles. Chrome accents, especially chains, are common, as are military-inspired insignia, which historically has included some Nazi paraphernalia. Military insignia as well as motorcycle-club pins are typically affixed to hats and jackets. Leather shirts, neckties, and leather with fringe are also worn but are not archetypal. Some modern leathermen adopt similar kinds of leather apparel colored red, green, or blue or made of latex. The wearing of latex indicates a crossover between leather culture and the larger world of fetish dressing.

The iconic dress of a leatherman extends beyond apparel and accessories to grooming and body modification. Men who participate in leather culture generally favor close-cropped hairstyles that recall the strict grooming practices of the military or police. Full beards and moustaches are also commonly adopted and meticulously groomed. Such grooming practices allude to both virile masculinity and strict discipline (Mains 1984, 36). Fragrance is generally eschewed, as the scent of leather, skin, and sweat is widely considered desirable within the subculture (Bean 1994, 19). Accessories including handcuffs, collars, and colored handkerchiefs have traditionally been worn to indicate specific attributes of sexual orientation and desire (Bean 1994, 21–22). The piercing of ears, nipples, and genitals has long been a part of the culture and is done both to facilitate the display of jewelry and as a part of a pain ritual whereby a piercing is allowed to heal so that it may be re-pierced. Finally, leathermen often have tattooed skin. These last two dress customs parallel practices in heterosexual motorcycle clubs and practices of Modern Primitives.

The communicative ability of clothing is powerful but is always in flux. While contemporary leathermen clearly use the aforementioned apparel and accessories as a system of sartorial symbols to express sexual identity, historically there were very specific codes and communications embedded in dress practices, though the codes embedded in clothes were never universal. They varied from coast to coast and from locale to locale, and some of the codes have been abandoned or modified as the culture has changed. However, a few of the coded dress practices merit consideration and are discussed with the understanding that their grammar is neither universal nor eternal. The wearing of colorful bandanas has been a long-lived practice that indicated specific sexual proclivities. Up to 16 different colors have been used to indicate varied desires, and the wearing of the bandana on the left side versus the right side of the body indicated whether the wearer wanted to give or receive the act indicated by the color (Cole 2000, 114). Similarly, the wearing of collars around the neck or looped through the epaulet of a jacket and under the arm and the wearing of chest or groin harnesses initially indicated specific sexual interests and whether or not a man was available or already committed to another partner. Joseph Bean, writing in the middle of the 1990s, indicated, however, that the use and meaning of these items were changing and were leading to confusion within the community as new, young participants in the scene adopted specific items for their look rather than their meaning (1994, 21–22). Additionally, leathermen have worn motorcycle-club uniforms, pins, patches, insignia, and heraldry over the decades, and items of this kind are subject to modification or abandonment as tastes change and organizations evolve.

Leathermen, like every subcultural group, are not a monolithic entity. As Geoff Mains noted, "Some men may dress in leather; these and others may play with it. But leather is no affectation; it is an expression of the soul" (1984, 27). Mains's writings clearly demonstrate that he was deeply and fully committed to the leather scene; certainly, not all individuals who engage in these dress practices or this social scene are as deeply immersed as Mains was. While beliefs and commitment to leathersexuality, S/M, and bondage are as varied as the men who dress in the aforementioned manner, it is clear that leathermen do form a community of sorts in that they exist outside of the gay mainstream and are often not accepted by or integrated with the larger gay culture. Mosher, Levitt, and Manley interviewed modern leathermen and determined that dressing in this manner is not only a way of communicating sexual preferences but is also a way of marking marginality, freedom from convention, and community in which men can "find interpersonal validation, and develop a sense of acceptance" (2006, 106–7). Mosher et al. went on to suggest that the wearing of leather creates a sort of brotherhood and functions as a "signifier of belongingness" (2006, 109), while Tyburczy characterized leathermen as "a tribe of sexual warriors and societal outcasts" whose expression "leather is thicker than blood" encapsulates their ethos (2014, 281). Kantrowitz suggested, "Many gays, feeling shut out of the mainstream by its institutionalized homophobia, turn their backs on polite society (at least after working hours) and see the [Hells] Angels and other cyclists as Romantic antiheroes, rebellious individualists whose toughness bears imitating" (2001, 194). Regardless of the precise relationship that an individual man has to these dress practices and the culture of leather, it is clear that identifying with leathersexuality is something that many individuals can do only in a specified time and place given mainstream aversions that exist into the 21st century. Additionally, it is notable that using leather as a vehicle for role playing is an important facet of leathersexuality that is heightened by the fact that the apparel is not typically worn all the time.

The community of leathermen is visible in leather organizations including the National Leather Association and in countless motorcycle clubs, which Ridinger (1998) has noted select their names from sources such as religion, mythology, and the military to signify the independence and marginality of their members. These clubs, such as the Leather Knights, the Sons of Apollo, and the Sabres of Artemis, participate in runs (meets) that are social events. BDSM (bondage and discipline/domination and submission/sadism and masochism) clubs such as the Chicago Hellfire Club and Society of Janus are also locales in which leather culture flourishes, as are nightclubs and bars. Annual events including competitions at International Mr. Leather (first held in 1979), the more inclusive Pantheon of Leather (begun in 1988), and the National Leather Association "Living in Leather" conference are also places where leather culture thrives and evolves. Printed publications targeted at the leather scene are also an important vehicle for communication within the subculture and began to be published in the early 1970s. Early titles include *Drummer* and *Scene and Machine,* and in the late 1980s *The Leather Journal.* In the age of the Internet there are increased opportunities to share images and ideas about leather culture. One notable blog is entitled *Letherati,* which addresses the broad spectrum of people who are interested in leathersexuality.

The clothes that leathermen wear were originally purchased from shops that catered to motorcycle enthusiasts, which were the primary retailers for specialized riding clothes in the middle of the 20th century. Over time, however, specialty stores that catered to people interested in leathersexuality were opened, such as the Leather Man in New York City and The Trading Post in San Francisco. In addition to brick-and-mortar establishments, many Internet retailers cater to leathermen in the 21st century. The appearance and quality of leather items are linked to where they were purchased and the purpose for which they were made. Bean noted, "National chains offer leather vests that are handsome enough in their way, but they stand out like Easter bonnets in a crowd of leathermen" (1994, 23). Heavy, durable leatherwear continues to prevail as the standard among leathermen even though many fashion brands make lightweight motorcycle jackets and leather pants that are in keeping with the leathermen aesthetic.

Leather culture and dress practices began to gain visibility beyond gay culture beginning in the late 1970s. Some punk rockers, who aimed to make a particularly provocative sartorial statement, wore leather motorcycle jackets as well as choke collars and harnesses as antifashion in the late 1970s, thereby helping to bring these items more clearly into public view. Additionally, the controversial and provocative black-and-white photographs of Robert Mapplethorpe's *Portfolio X* from the late 1970s documented both the dress practices and some of the sex acts (though they were staged in Mapplethorpe's studio) of leathermen as well. Their display and viewing by *avant-garde* artists, gallery directors, and other cultural luminaries paved the way for more popular acceptance of this kind of visual culture. A mainstream personification of a leatherman was probably first seen in Glenn Hughes's portrayal for the pop band Village People (formed in 1977), whose members personified archetypes of masculinity and sang provocative and campy lyrics that became disco anthems. Ideas about leather culture and images of leathermen have also been diffused through cinema, including Kenneth Anger's art-house film *Scorpio Rising* (1963). The Hollywood movie *Cruising* (1980) starring Al Pacino depicted dress and other aspects of the gay leather scene, and the more recent documentary *Kink Crusaders* (2010) provides a source of information and visual language for modern viewers. The leathermen ideal has also been documented and disseminated through fine art including the drawings of Tom of Finland and the paintings of Etienne (Dom Orejudos). Since the late 1980s the apparel associated with leathersexuality has become far more visible in the mainstream. Pop-music artists including George Michael, who wore leather apparel in his video for "Faith" (1987), helped to mainstream the aesthetic. Fashionable interpretations of leathermen by high-style designers and stylists were plainly visible in the early 1990s and was seen in the work of Thierry Mugler (Fall/Winter 1991) and in the fashion photography of Peter Lindberg in a *Vogue* editorial styled by Grace Coddington entitled "The Wild Ones."

The sartorial style of leathermen functions as a declaration of subcultural membership and interest in certain kinds of sexual practices. Leathermen use the visual language of dress to draw a marginalized group together and to facilitate communication. Although the semiotics of dress are subject to corruption that results in confusion as wearers modify dress practices and make personal choices, the dress within this particular subculture has largely maintained its integrity over the course of more than 50 years, which may be read as a testament to the strength of the symbols as well as the overall insularity of the group of men that employs them.

Further Reading

Bean, J. W. 1994. *Leathersex: A Guide for the Curious Outsider and the Serious Player.* Los Angeles: Daedalus Publishing Company.

Cole, S. 2000. *Don We Now Our Gay Apparel.* New York: Berg.

Kantrowitz, A. 2001. "Swastika Toys." In *Leatherfolk: Radical Sex, People, Politics, and Practice,* edited by M. Thompson, 193–209. Los Angeles: Alyson Books.

Mains, G. 1984. *Urban Aboriginals: A Celebration of Leathersexuality.* Los Angeles: Daedalus Publishing Company.

Mosher, C., H. Levitt, and E. Manley. 2006. "Layers of Leather: The Identity Formation of Leathermen as a Process of Transforming Meanings of Masculinity." *Journal of Homosexuality* 51 (3): 93–123.

Ridinger, R. 1998. "Children of the Satyrs: Naming Patterns of Leather and Levi Clubs." *Names* 46 (2): 97–111.

Ridinger, R. 2002. "Things Visible and Invisible: The Leather Archives and Museum." *Journal of Homosexuality* 43 (1): 1–9.

Tyburczy, J. 2014. "Leather Anatomy: Cripping Homonormativity at International Mr. Leather." *Journal of Literary and Cultural Disabilities Studies* 8 (3): 275–93.

"Wild at Heart." 1991. *Vogue* 181 (September 1): 484–99. Retrieved March 28, 2016, from http://search.proquest.com/docview/879297547?accountid=130772.

Modern Primitive (Late 1970s–Present)

Modern primitives are a loosely affiliated subcultural group that emerged in the United States in the late 1970s. Modern primitives, also referred to as neoprimitives and neotribals, are citizens of the "modern" industrialized world (primarily North America and Europe) who are dissatisfied with and unfulfilled by modern social conditions and mores such as monogamy and contemporary notions of marriage, modern monotheistic religions, and capitalism and, therefore, resort to "primitive" practices, especially body modifications, as a way to attain personal fulfillment. Modern primitives adopt and adapt tattooing, piercing, gauging, branding, stretching, and scarification practices that permanently mark the body as well as rituals of physical endurance that involve piercing, compressing or constricting, sensory deprivation, weight bearing, and suspending the body from hooks. The use of the term "primitive" necessitates some consideration as it could potentially be interpreted as a pejorative term that implicates a "post-colonial legacy" (Kleese 2000, 19). Primitive in this context does refer to preindustrial tribal cultures and their practices. Modern primitives strive to pay homage to Native American, South American, African, Melanesian, Aztec, Mayan, Micronesian, and Polynesian tribal groups and their long-lived communal practices, which are deemed by members of this subcultural group to be superior to the practices of modern communities. The use of the term "primitive" is a convenient catch all that refers to this panoply of tribal cultures and is not meant to be derogatory, though outsiders commenting on the subculture have levied critiques on the use of the all-encompassing terminology as well as the co-opting of tribal practices by modern primitives who are largely white, middle-class, and educated. Additionally, Fakir Musafar (born Roland Loomis), the man who coined the term "modern primitive" in the late 1970s, has noted that his selection of the word "primitive" was intended to have a double meaning: primitive as tribal and primitive as primal or primary, meaning that the subcultural practices address basic human needs (Winge 2004, 128–29).

The visual identification of a modern primitive is complex. Some of the body modifications that modern primitives embrace are also embraced by other subcultural and street styles. For example, modern primitives may have pierced ears, brows, lips, noses, cheeks, tongues, and genitals. Punks, Goths, people who participate in leather culture, S/M (sadomasochism) followers, and members of motorcycle gangs also favor many of these types of piercings. Thus the visual language of modern primitive is not of itself enough to identify an adherent. Modern primitivism is a visible sub-cultural style, but those who identify with the label are differentiated from other groups that are visually similar by a range of intentions that underpin the body modifications they undergo. A basic tenet of modern primitivism is that body modification can change one's outlook on life. Despite this unifying concept, modern primitives are varied in their outlooks and affiliations and, therefore, may also identify as queer, bisexual, straight, transgender, androgynous, radical, freak, or some combination thereof (Pitts 2003, 133–34). Some scholars have argued that, in fact, modern primitivism is not actually a subcultural group, that its concepts are ill-defined and its spirituality "wooly" (Lodder 2011, 100). If, however, we accept that modern primitivism has sufficient cohesion to be considered a cultural entity, a few shared tenets may be outlined. Modern primitives embrace body modifications as a form of self-expression, and many openly discuss the importance of the aesthetics of extreme body modifications. These aesthetics (blackwork tattoos, a pierced septum, stretched earlobes) mark them as outside of the mainstream while also marking them as members of a community of sorts (see Meyers 1992; Shilling 1993). Modern primitives also engage in body modification and ritual mutilation of the body as a path to spiritual exploration, a rite of passage, or a way of healing or reclaiming the body after trauma experienced from a failed relationship or some kind of physical or sexual violence. The practices that modern primitives explore allow them to take control over their bodies, thereby giving themselves a sense of control in their lives at large (Vale and Juno 1989, 5).

There is evidence that practices associated with modern primitivism emerged in secret in post–World War II America. Fakir Musafar, an outspoken proponent of modern primitive practices, discussed with Vale and Juno the self-piercing and other physical tests of endurance that he performed as a young man in the 1950s. Musafar explained that he had felt like an "alien" from a young age and perceived, "Whatever was natural, rational, and sensible to me, was unnatural and repulsive to other people" (6). However, it was not until the late 1970s that Musafar "came out" to the public at a California tattoo convention. In the wake of the appearance, Musafar met and formed partnerships with a variety of people with shared interests including Jim Ward, who is generally regarded as the founder of the modern piercing movement. Ultimately, Musafar assisted Ward with the establishment of a piercing studio called Gauntlet where Ward developed both piercing techniques and innovative jewelry designs that facilitated nontraditional piercing practices.

Simply listing the types of body modifications that modern primitives utilize is the first of several steps in understanding the changes that these individuals are enacting on their bodies and the overall aesthetic impact of this subcultural style. Tattoos are commonplace among modern primitives. Blackwork "tribal" tattoos are widely adopted, though designs are not generally taken from stock images.

Modern primitives will spend substantial time in researching and creating designs that have personal or spiritual significance; thus the tattoo design may or may not be faithful to an authentic tribal pattern. Tattoos are often applied using modern electrified equipment that injects ink through multiple needles, but some modern primitives have tattoos applied using traditional techniques involving bones or quills, and mallets, that are far more laborious, time-consuming, and painful. The piercing of ears and other parts of the face such as the tongue, eyebrow, and septum, and of nipples, belly button, and genitals is often done in profusion and may be done by a professional piercer using modern equipment or may be executed by a modern primitive on himself or herself. In the latter case the process is often slow and painful, and the difficulty of the modification is valued as part of the experience. The stretching of flesh such as the earlobes and nipples is also undertaken. This process, which can be achieved only over an extended period of time, is viewed as a part of a journey that refashions both the body and the spirit. Scarification (cutting the skin) and branding (burning the skin) are also ways of marking the body that some modern primitives explore. Some modern primitives also used three-dimensional Teflon implants to create patterns and symbols on the surface of the skin. The markings that are chosen may be aesthetically pleasing and complementary to the body but are also generally chosen for their symbolic or spiritual value. Furthermore, the pain involved in these processes is viewed as inherently positive and valuable. Modern primitives, seeking to explore the primal parts of human existence, embrace all sensations that can be experienced by the human body and seek to break down the positive/negative, pleasure/pain dichotomies. Notably, many tattoo parlors and piercing studios function as social spaces for meetings and classes—places for like-minded people to congregate. Professional tattoo artists and piercers do also execute piercings in other event spaces and social gatherings outside of their workspaces. Some individuals undergoing a particularly painful marking of the body embrace communality and support from a group or audience.

In addition to permanent body modifications that are generally visible markers of this subcultural street style, some modern primitives undergo ritual body play that leaves only a temporary mark. Ritual cutting (often of designs) generally heals, leaving no permanent mark. Cupping—a technique whereby cups filled with heated air are placed on the skin, thereby creating a vacuum—leaves temporary welts and bruises. Some modern primitives will have their bodies pierced, but no jewelry will be left in the opening, allowing the modern primitive to repeat the process at will. Among the more extreme practices undertaken by some modern primitives are ritual hook hangings derived from the Plains Native American traditions. Large, deep incisions are made in the back or legs, and surgical steel hooks are inserted; the person is then suspended several feet above the ground. The pain of this temporary body modification is experienced as part of a quest for a transcendent experience. Some modern primitives also interpret the Native American Sun Dance, which traditionally involves attaching rawhide thongs to large wooden pegs that are inserted into the chest at one end and attached to a pole at the other. Modern primitives have also performed the Hindu ball dance, whereby a multitude of weights suspended on hooks are attached to the skin prior to a ritual dance. Fakir Musafar once performed the ritual with 48 half-pound weights affixed to his torso. Western modern primitives have also adapted and performed the Hindu Kavandi-bearing ritual, wherein a multitude of tiny spears of Shiva pierce the upper body. In each of these rituals the endurance of pain is embraced as a path toward spiritual transcendence. Notably, these rituals are generally done publicly, and the communality of the experience is a further indication that modern primitivism is a subcultural group rather than simply a societal trend found only in individual practices of body modification. Some of the venues/events that routinely host such events are Torture Garden, London; the Fetish Ball, Boston, Massachusetts; and the Organ Grinder's Ball, Cleveland, Ohio.

Modern primitive people and rituals can be seen in films including *Dances Sacred and Profane* (1985), *Modern Tribalism* (2001), *The Social History of Piercing* (2004), and *Body of God* (2013) as well as videos such as *Initiation* (2007) that have been posted on the Internet on YouTube and Vimeo. Both Ward and Musafar have also sold educational videos that teach techniques for specific modern primitive body modifications and rituals. Printed publications have also been instrumental in terms of communicating modern primitive body modifications and ideology. Perhaps the most important text was Vale and Juno's 1989 publication of interviews with people who identified as modern primitives. The text, entitled *Modern Primitives: An Investigation of Contemporary Adornment and Ritual,* demonstrates through both firsthand accounts and photographs the diversity of both practice and ideology that exists among modern primitives. Serial publications including *Piercing Fans International Quarterly* and *Body Play and Modern Primitives* (both of which are no longer published) also documented the subculture and its style, as does the more recent book by Fakir Musafar, *Spirit & Flesh* (2002).

In addition to the aforementioned media specifically dedicated to communicating modern primitive subculture, a great many mainstream forms of mass media have developed in the new millennium to communicate the fashionableness of piercing, tattooing, and gauging the skin. In 2000 the American Museum of Natural History presented an exhibition entitled "Body Art: Marks of Identity," which showcased the historical trajectory of body modifications in an educational context. Shows for broadcast on television and streaming over the Internet include *Bad Ink, Inked, Tattoos after Dark, New York Ink, LA Ink,* and *Pangea Piercing.* Programs of this kind feature attractive, young, urban people who are typically heavily invested in personal transformation through the routine acquisition of body modifications. In addition to programs dedicated to the art and craft of body modification, the mainstream media has also depicted characters such as Lisbeth Salander (Rooney Mara), the titular character from *The Girl with the Dragon Tattoo* (2011), adorned with a variety of body modifications. This type of programming does not generally delve into the spiritual or transformative properties of body modification, nor are the virtues of pain routinely extolled. Rather, these programs help to make the visual language of the modern primitives mainstream, thereby impacting the communicative power of piercings, tattoos, gauges, branding marks, and keloid scars.

Permanent body modifications of the kind described in this article are no longer necessarily a marker of affiliation with modern primitive ideals. They are no longer able to mark group affiliation. Furthermore, in some demographics, modifications of this kind have become so commonplace that they do not really mark dissent from mainstream values, but rather they mark adherence with a current in contemporary fashion. There is a body of gradually accumulating evidence that points to the fashion industry and high-style fashion's increasing acceptance of extreme body modifications. Menswear runways routinely feature male models with full sleeves of tattoos in conjunction with artwork on their chests, legs, and backs. Diminutive anklet and bracelet tattoos have been visible on female fashion models since the 1990s, but lately models such as Cara Delvigne (small facial tattoos) and Kendall Jenner (nipple piercing) have been pushing the boundaries of what is acceptable mainstream beauty. Runway shows have also made a point of highlighting body modifications. Tommy Hilfiger (Spring/Summer 2015) covered many of the models in an array of temporary tattoos, while in 2011 French designer Thierry Mugler featured Rick Genest as a model (his entire body is tattooed to give him the appearance of a zombie). Jean-Paul Gaultier's Spring/Summer 2012 haute-couture collection featured models with large, colorful tattoos (both permanent and temporary), gauged ears, and facial piercings (both real and simulated). The presence of this kind of body art on the runway implies that attitudes about extraordinary body modifications have evolved in the 40 years since the term "modern primitive" was coined.

The ease with which modern primitive style can be acquired has also improved in the new millennium. Tattoo parlors are commonplace throughout the Western world, and many call themselves "modern primitive" tattoo parlors, including locations in Milwaukee, Wisconsin; Utica, New York; Dublin, Ireland; and Bologna, Italy. Jewelry for the myriad piercings embraced by modern primitives, once so hard to find, is now retailed at mainstream franchises such as Hot Topic, Claire's, and Piercing Pagoda, as well as by countless retailers online. The spread of the visual language of the modern primitives is certainly not an indication of widespread acceptance of the beliefs and extreme pain rituals that are also important aspects of modern primitive subculture, but rather the diffusion of stylistic traits once deemed shocking and countercultural is indicative that in the new millennium, consumers freely sample from the vast rage of possibilities that exist in the globalized marketplace.

Further Reading

Atkinson, M., and K. Young 2001. "Flesh Journeys: Neo Primitives and the Contemporary Rediscovery of Radical Body Modification." *Deviant Behavior: An Interdisciplinary Journal* 22: 117–46.

DeMello, M. 1995. "Not Just for Bikers Anymore: Popular Representations of American Tattooing." *Journal of Popular Culture* 29 (3): 37–52.

Kleese, C. 2000. "'Modern primitivism': Non-mainstream Body Modification and Racialized Representation." *Body Modification,* edited by M. Featherstone, 15–38. London: Sage Publications.

Lodder, M. 2011. "The Myths of Modern Primitivism." *European Journal of American Culture* 30 (2): 99–111.

Mercury, M. 2000. *Pagan Fleshworks: The Alchemy of Body Modification.* Rochester, VT: Park Street Press, 2000.

Musafar, F. 1996. "Body Play: State of Grace or Sickness?" In *Bodies under Siege: Self-Mutilation and Body Modification in Culture and Psychiatry,* edited by A. R. Favazza, 325–34. Baltimore: Johns Hopkins University Press.

Musafar, F. 2002. *Spirit and Flesh.* Santa Fe, NM: Arena Editions.

Musafar, F. 2015. Fakir.org. Retrieved February 12, 2016, from www.fakir.org.

Myers, J. 1992. "Nonmainstream Body Modification: Genital Piercing, Branding, Burning, and Cutting." *Journal of Contemporary Ethnography* 21 (3): 276–306.

Pitts, V. 2003. *In the Flesh: The Cultural Politics of Body Modifications.* New York: Palgrave McMillan.

Rosenblatt, D. 1997. "The Antisocial Skin: Structure, Resistance, and 'Modern Primitive' Adornment in the United States." *Cultural Anthropology* 12 (3): 287–334. Retrieved November 11, 2015, from www.jstor.org/stable/656555.

Shilling, C. 1993. *The Body and Social Theory.* London: Sage Publications.

Vale, V., and A. Juno 1989. *Modern Primitives: An Investigation of Contemporary Adornment and Ritual.* San Francisco: Re/Search Publications.

Ward, J. 2013. *Running the Gauntlet.* San Francisco: Re:Ward, Inc.

Winge, T. M. 2003. "Constructing 'Neo-tribal' Identities through Dress: Modern Primitives Body Modifications." In *The Post-Subcultures Reader,* edited by D. Muggleton and R. Weinzierl, 119–32. Oxford: Berg.

Winge, T. M. 2004. "A Survey of 'Modern Primitive': Body Modification Rituals: Meanings of Pain." In *The Meanings of Dress* 2nd ed., edited by M. L. Damhorst, K. A. Miller-Spillman, and S. O. Michelman, 127–32. New York: Fairchild.

Motorcyclist (Late 1950s–Present)

The first self-propelled cycles, precursors to the modern motorcycle, were developed in the last decades of the 19th century, and the design and reliability of the vehicles improved over the course of the first decades of the 20th century. Early enthusiasts, who were predominantly men, rode alone and in small groups, rode for pleasure, used motorcycles as a source of transportation, and competed in speed and agility competitions. Large group rides seem to have emerged during the Great Depression (1929–1939) as migrant males crisscrossed the Southwest in search of work (Wood 2003, 340); however, a unique social and recreational culture and a distinctive style of dress surrounding motorcycling was not perceptible until after World War II. In the wake of the war, returning veterans, some of whom had utilized motorcycles as soldiers, sought excitement in their newfound peaceful existence, liberty from the mundane workaday lifestyle of postwar America, and the camaraderie of other men. This pursuit was especially prescient given that postwar American culture manifested itself in ways that are best described as conservative and traditional. Mainstream postwar American culture contracted in response to the tumultuous, unsettling war years, which had seen family values and gender roles upended. Traditional dress practices, traditional roles for men and women, and an emphasis on success in the workplace were key markers of the postwar value system. Many men found a remedy for all these potentially repressive forces by riding a motorcycle. Writing in 1965, William Murray noted that the Harley Davidson motorcycle allowed riders to "smash through the sad square world that hems [them] in, leaving no past behind . . . expecting nothing of the future" (1965, 37). Notably, in the latter part of the 20th century, motorcycle design and use splintered into two distinct categories: large, heavy motorcycles for road riding and lighter, more agile motorcycles for use off-road or in motorcross events. This article is concerned with the style associated with the former category of bikes and their riders.

The earliest motorcyclists (both men and women) wore apparel of a design that was generally in keeping with the mainstream dress styles of their respective eras. Most apparel was not unique in cut nor was it used exclusively to ride a motorcycle, but it was executed in leather as opposed to a woven textile to better suit the conditions and risks of motorcycle riding. For example, jodhpurs and boots derived from horseback riding and jackets with a cut consistent with hunting and other kinds of sports were adapted to the new pursuit. Additionally, early aviating apparel, which was made out of leather to protect pilots from the chill of unheated cockpits and splattering motor oil, was logically useful for motorcycle riding, which involved perils similar to those of aviation. Into the early 1950s motorcycle riders could be seen wearing various kinds of pants, shirts, and leather jackets, including the classic Perfecto motorcycle jacket, which was designed by the Schott company in 1928. Notably, although makers like Schott had designed apparel specifically for motorcyclists, many riders selected other kinds of apparel. A codified or iconic style, however, was not in widespread evidence until sometime in 1954, following the release of the American film *The Wild One* in December 1953. In that film Johnny and his fellow members of the Black Rebels Motorcycle Gang wore Perfecto leather jackets, T-shirts, and blue jeans cuffed over black leather boots. While the story arc of the movie is largely about the rivalry between two motorcycle gangs, the greater metaphor of the film valorized a rebellious spirit and outsider status—themes that appealed to postwar men and youths. Thus this style became the source of widespread emulation amongst rebellious young males in the 1950s and soon thereafter was adopted and modified by a diverse population of motorcyclists. Outlaw motorcycle gangs (gangs involved in criminal enterprises), namely the all-male Hells Angels Motorcycle Club (who are sometimes referred to as the "mafia on wheels"), which had been founded in 1948, also strongly impacted the development of a unique motorcyclist style.

The basic components of motorcyclist dress worn from the middle of the 1950s onward include blue jeans worn with or without black leather chaps or, alternatively, black leather pants. Denim or black leather vests (referred to as "cuts" in the subculture), worn over plain or logoed T-shirts, may be styled with or without an accompanying black leather jacket. Heavy-soled black leather boots (often designed with a steel toe) are also standard and are favored for both their aesthetics and their utility. Early in the evolution of motorcyclist style a billed cap, often made of leather, completed the ensemble, but helmet laws instituted in the United States in the late 20th century impacted that sartorial choice. Tattoos, which have long been markers of fraternity in the military, of rebellion, and of subcultural affiliation also became commonplace among motorcyclists, as did piercings, which have long been considered a marker of outsider status for men. Male motorcycle riders commonly wear full, bushy facial hair, which has been the target of derision in much of the late 20th century and has regularly been associated with countercultures including the Beats and the hippies. Notably, full facial hair also protects the skin from windburn and sunburn, ailments that commonly bedevil riders. Of course, variations on these basic components exist depending on the motivations, affiliations, and interests of the rider, but a typical mode of dress is very discernible. Women, who have long been a minority in the world of motorcycling, began to interpret these male-driven aesthetics in a variety of ways beginning in the late 1960s. Some women have adopted these basic components with little interpretation and may appear quite androgynous as a result. Other women have interpreted the look by amplifying their sexuality. For example, a woman might wear very tight pants, a plunging T-shirt or tank top, or even a bikini top underneath a vest or leather jacket. However, motorcyclist street style is a male-driven style based in pieces of menswear.

It is important to the story of motorcyclist sartorial style to note that sociologists and criminologists have divided the world of motorcycle riders in many different and complex ways (see Barker 2011; Shields 2012); however, for the purposes of discussing sartorial tendencies, two major group affiliations need to be distinguished: motorcyclists who belong to social associations that may also be characterized as riding clubs, and motorcyclists who belong to outlaw motorcycle gangs (OMG, a term used by the FBI, Europol, and Interpol) that regularly engage in criminality and brutality, including murder, rape, extortion, and drug dealing. The apparel discussed in the preceding paragraph may identify both groups; however, important, highly legible aesthetic variations also exist. Interestingly, the latter of these two groups is clearly the style leader among motorcyclists of incredibly varied interests, and the aesthetic contributions of hardened criminal gangs have infiltrated both mainstream riding clubs and high-style fashionable dress.

The primary sartorial element that separates motorcycle enthusiasts from members of outlaw motorcycle gangs is the wearing of "colors." Colors are composed of a combination of patches that are usually worn on the back of a leather or denim vest. Colors for gang members generally consist of two "rockers," U-shaped patches that identify the gang name and the local chapter or location that the gang controls; these portions of the colors are usually located, respectively, at the top and bottom of the back panel of the garment. Some members of the gang who have special roles, including the road captain, also wear a third rocker at the bottom of a jacket to identify that role. In the center of the back panel of the garment, a large embroidered patch of the gang insignia is affixed. The most renowned American motorcycle gang is the Hells Angels Motorcycle Club, whose insignia is a skull with wings derived from World War II fighter-pilot tradition (referred to as Death's Head). Another gang, The Outlaws, represents itself with a skull and two crossed pistons. The skull icon is typically referred to as "Charlie," and it is believed that the image and name are derived from the jacket worn by Marlon Brando in *The Wild One.* The Bandidos Motorcycle Club (a predominantly Mexican American gang) has adopted a symbol that is a caricature of a Mexican (possibly derived from the Frito Bandito) wearing a sombrero and serape and holding a gun and sword. Some motorcycle gangs use historical references in their colors, including the Mongols Nation Motorcycle Club, which utilizes an image of the Asian medieval Mongol leader Genghis Khan, and the Pagans, who use an image of the Norse god Surt, a fire giant who is mythologized as a fighter who leads his kin into a battle to destroy the cosmos. Colors worn by criminal motorcycle clubs also often use the initials M.C. (motorcycle club) and a patch shaped like a diamond embroidered with the number "1%," a reference to the notion that only 1 percent of motorcyclists engage in criminal behavior. The calculation that only 1 percent of motorcyclists are troublemakers was first proffered by the American Motorcycle Association (AMA) in 1947 in the wake of a riot in Hollister, California, that followed a motorcycle rally (and may have inspired the script for *The Wild One*). Though the comment was meant to be a compliment to AMA members and a critique of outsiders, Hells Angels and other outlaw motorcycle gangs have adopted the comment as a badge of honor. Finally, gang colors may also include the gang's slogan or the initials that imply it. For example, the Outlaws' slogan, which is directed at Hells Angels members, is "Angels Die in Outlaw States" (ADIOS). The Bandidos use the phrase "God Forgives, Bandidos Don't," and the Mongols' motto is "Respect Few, Fear None." Notably, getting "patched" or "patched-in" is an important rite of passage earned by individuals aspiring to be members, and once earned, patches are guarded as a prized possession. Tom Barker, writing for the *American Journal of Criminal Justice,* noted, "The patch or gang symbol worn on their cut—vest— facilitates criminal activities . . . members join for the 'power of the patch' which gives them protection when they engage in criminal activities" (2011, 208).

Riders who belong to other kinds of associations have also adopted the wearing of apparel decorated to mimic the aesthetics of gang colors. In 1989 Harley Davidson formed its Motor Clothes division, and since then it has become commonplace for riders of Harley Davidson motorcycles to wear vests and jackets that are emblazoned with large embroidered Harley Davidson logos, the bald eagle, depicted with wings extended, and sometimes the brand name shaped into a rocker. Apparel of this kind is worn by individuals who simply own a Harley and by riders who ride with groups like the Harley Owners Group. Christian biker groups have also adopted these aesthetics. Groups including the Unchained Gang, Bikers for Jesus, and Christ's Cruisers (some of whom were once members of outlaw motorcycle gangs) wear their own versions of colors that include large embroidered crosses centered on the back panel of the vest, an M.C. patch that is virtually identical to the ones worn by outlaw motorcycle gangs, and a patch that reads "100% for Jesus," which often takes the place of the "1%" patch. Christian motorcycle groups exist across the United States, and countless variations exist in terms of imagery and text; however, the correspondence with gang colors is unmistakable. A variety of other kinds of motorcyclist groups exist. Some are formed around ownership of a certain kind of bike, others around interests such as abstaining from alcohol or drugs, and even some referred to as "mom and pop" groups that are social clubs for older riders. Regardless of the specific affiliation of the riding group, interpretations of colors are commonplace.

Some aspects of outlaw-motorcycle-gang dress is unique to motorcyclists with an inclination for criminal activity. Use of the Nazi swastika or Luftwaffe insignia and the wearing of a ball-peen hammer or four-cell MAG flashlight from a belt loop (these are used as weapons but do not require a permit) are consistent elements of OMG dress. In the 1960s, the number 13, indicative of the 13th letter in the alphabet (M), was a code for marijuana that was worn by members of OMGs, though in the 21st century the more relaxed attitudes to this drug make that kind of veiled declaration less poignant. The wearing of socially disruptive insignia was and is, of course, purposeful. A Hells Angels member interviewed by *The Saturday Evening Post* writer William Murray, noted in 1965, "When you walk into a place where people can see you, you want to look as repulsive as possible" (1965, 32). It is clear that pushing the boundaries of rebellious, countercultural imagery is an important aspect of dress for many motorcyclists.

Group meetings have been important to the spread of a unified motorcyclist style. Associations of motorcyclists, created to promote a shared interest and to organize riding competitions, have existed since the very beginning of the 20th century, including the AMA, the largest association in the United States, which was formed in 1924. Perhaps even more important than associations are rallys and meets that take place across the United States each year. Without a doubt the rally in Sturgis, South Dakota, is the largest and best known, and the attendance figure attests to the increasing popularity of motorcycling. About 800 people made the journey to Sturgis in 1960, whereas close to half a million were in attendance 50 years later (Dragseth 2012, 89). Biketoberfest and the Daytona Bike Week (both held in Daytona, Florida) also attract a tremendous number of riders each year who meet to ride, socialize, and shop. The majority of riders in the 21st century tend to be white men in their 40s and 50s who have disposable income. One reporter noted of Sturgis participants, "They look like walking billboards for the Harley Davidson brand, and buying the fantasy of the subculture doesn't come cheap" (Dragseth 2012, 88).

Popular culture has been very influential in spreading both the narrative of the motorcyclist as a rebellious outsider and the visual culture of motorcycle sartorial style. Pop songs that valorized motorcycling include "Black Denim Trousers and Motorcycle Boots" (1955), "Leader of the Pack" (1964), "He's a Rebel" (1965), and "Born to Be Wild" (1968). Movies including the aforementioned *The Wild One* (1953), as well as *The Wild Angels* (1966), *Devil's Angels* (1967), *Cycle Savages* (1969), and *Easy Rider* (1969) presented images of bikers as individualists and nonconformists riding away from oppressive bourgeois society. Although the "bad guys" in the surfer films of the 1960s were often motorcycle gang members, they were always innately cool as well. The motorcyclist gang member as lovable rebel outsider was a popular image until the Hells Angels were hired to manage security at a free Rolling Stones concert at the Altamont Speedway near San Francisco. The event, which was fueled by drugs and alcohol, spiraled out of control, and spasms of violence left several attendees dead. The Hells Angels were pinpointed as cata-lysts for the violence, and as John Wood noted in "Hell's [*sic*] Angels and the Illusion of the Counterculture," the events of December 6, 1969, forever changed mainstream America's view of the Hells Angels from countercultural heroes to criminals. The policing of mainstream motorcycle rallys and bars is testimony to the notion that the motorcyclist–violent criminal linkage is alive and well in the American imagination.

Documentary films such as *Wild Ride of Outlaw Bikers* (1996) and *Mongol Nation* (2008) as well as the web presence of motorcycle gangs on sites like hells-angels.com and mongolsmc.com can provide insight into motorcycle culture, and in the 21st century virtually any person can buy into the motorcycle style. In addition to the aforementioned Harley Davidson apparel, one can purchase apparel that includes insignia from motorcycle gangs. For example, the Hells Angels logo was copyrighted in 1972 (Wood 2003, 344) and has since been applied to a wide variety of commercially available apparel and other merchandise. Additionally, special-interest motorcycle affiliations make their own versions of motorcycle style available for sale. For example, Christian Bikers Supply Store, an Internet retailer whose slogan is "Glorifying God While You Ride," offers a wide range of apparel including T-shirts with slogans like "Driven by the Spirit" that marry motorcycling and religious sentiments.

Motorcycling apparel has impacted fashion countless times. Motorcycle jack-ets and boots in particular have been interpreted over and over again since the 1950s. They have been executed by designer brands and in luxury materials, and they have been tapered, tailored, and bedazzled for both men and women and pro-duced by entities ranging from haute couture to fast fashion. The allure of the motorcycle aesthetic is clearly far-reaching.

Motorcycle style continues to evolve. Modern synthetics such as polyamide and Gore-Tex are better suited for protection from abrasions than leather and have impacted the appearance of some modern motorcycle apparel. However, a tremen-dous amount of uniformity exists on the streets despite the fact that many different kinds of clothes could be used to adequately protect a rider. Apparel is important to motorcycle riders who are notably on display as they ride their bikes. The bike and the biker's dress work in unison to convey a stylistic message. The message in the 21st century is still focused on a symbolic rejection of bourgeois values and main-stream ideals, and there are clear overlaps between motorcyclist style and the style of hippies, punks, and metal heads, to name just three examples. As Quinn and Forsyth have noted, "The subculture is more thoroughly grounded in Anglo-American culture and its symbols than many would like to admit" (2009, 262). Undoubtedly, many motorcyclists adopt some aspects of their dress because it con-veys a strong antiestablishment message and perpetuates a recognizable image of the American outlaw. Although the percentage of riders who truly conduct themselves as outlaws is incredibly small, large numbers of riders clearly respond to the symbolism, undoubtedly taking pleasure in the unmistakably rebellious aesthetics.

Further Reading

Allford, S., and S. Ferriss. 2007. *Motorcycle.* London: Reaktion Books.

Barger, R., and K. Zimmerman. 2002. *The Life and Times of Sonny Barger and the Hell's Angels' Motorcycle Club.* New York: William Morrow.

Barker, T. 2011. "American Based Biker Gangs: International Organized Crime." *American Journal of Criminal Justice* 36: 207–15.

Cooke, C. 2012. "Right Turn on the Open Road." *National Review,* April 30, 36–38.

Dragseth, D. 2012. "The Rally Ritual." *South Dakota Magazine,* June/July, 84–90.

Langton, J. 2009. *Fallen Angel: The Unlikely Rise of Walter Stadnick and the Canadian Hell's Angels.* Ontario, CA: John Wiley & Sons Canada, Ltd.

Lavigne, Y. 1996. *Hells Angels: Into the Abyss.* New York: Harper Collins.

Murray, W. 1965. "Hell's Angels." *The Saturday Evening Post* 238 (23): 32–39.

Queen, W. 2007. *Under and Alone: The True Story of an Undercover Agent Who Infiltrated America's Most Violent Outlaw Motorcycle Gang.* New York: Balantine Books.

Quinn, J. F., and C. J. Forsyth. 2009. "Leather and Rolexes: The Symbolism and Values of the Motorcycle Club." *Deviant Behavior* 30: 235–65.

Remsberg, R. 2000. *Riders for God: The Story of a Christian Motorcycle Gang.* Chicago: University of Illinois Press.

Reynolds, T. 2000. *Wild Ride: How Outlaw Motorcycle Myth Conquered America.* New York: TV Books.

Rothman, L. 2015. "Motorcycle Culture's Long History of Image Problems." *Time.com.* Retrieved March 13, 2015, from www.time.com.

Serwer, A. E., E. Schonfeld, and W. Woods. 1992. "The Hells Angels' Devilish Business." *Fortune* 126 (12): 118–22.

Shields, D. 2012. "The Infamous 'One Percenters': A Review of the Criminality, Subculture, and Structure of Modern Biker Gangs." *Justice Policy Journal* 9 (1): 4–33.

Thompson, H. S. 1967. *Hell's Angels: A Strange and Terrible Saga.* New York: Ballantine Books.

Wood, J. 2003. "Hell's Angels and the Illusion of the Counterculture." *Journal of Popular Culture* 37 (2): 336–50.

New Wave (Late 1970s–Late 1980s)

The sartorial style that was part of the postpunk new wave scene emerged in the late 1970s, was especially visible at mid-decade, and generally fell out of use by the end of the 1980s. The term "new wave" requires some explanation, as it has been used in more than one context. Francois Giroud, the editor of the French cultural magazine *L'Express,* first used the terminology in 1957 to describe the groundbreaking work in the realm of French cinema that directors like Jean-Luc Goddard and François Truffaut were creating. The expression *nouvelle vague* implies a sea change in general and has thus been used time and again to refer to a new movement in a certain realm of cultural production. The term "new wave" was originally applied to punk rock but came to be consistently applied to a diverse group of musicians who emerged from the ashes of punk's brief florescence in the latter half of the 1970s. British pop bands largely set the new wave style, though important acts that set interesting dress trends also emerged from other parts of Europe, Australia, and the United States. These diverse and international sartorial aesthetics were easily transmitted to the United States, due in large part to the launch of MTV and the proliferation of many teen magazines. Notably, the new wave of the 1980s was far more unified in terms of visual aesthetics than it was in terms of musical style, and thus there are perennial debates about which bands counted as new wave. Additionally, some would argue that the term is too vague. That said, this author remembers this street style well (and has amusing class pictures to prove many of its characteristics) and feels confident in the application of the terminology. Putting controversy about music largely to the side, the focus here is primarily on the dress aesthetics that emerged out of this popular music scene, which were copied and interpreted by people who enjoyed some portion of the incredibly diverse music that was being created.

New wave music developed at the crossroads of punk, disco, and glam and sometimes drew musical inspiration from reggae, ska, rap, hardcore, art rock, and rockabilly. Additionally, the music evolved in a period when electronic instruments were becoming affordable, which streamlined the process of making and recording music and allowed a few musicians to create a full sound with relative ease. Lyrically, most new wave music avoided politics, rhetoric, and controversy; lyrics were often inconsequential and were frequently indecipherable. Unfettered experimentation was a fundamental part of new wave music, and as the sounds developed so too did alternative radio stations, which generally spun the records without receiving promotional considerations. Thus, while the genre of new wave was diverse and the sartorial inclinations varied, there was a discernible scene that existed outside of the mainstream. Music historian Theo Cateforis has suggested that "new wave's main unifying theme was its modern freshness and daring and its separations from rock's conventions" (2011, 6). Thus both new wave musicians and fans alike joyfully embraced a multitude of markings of outsider status. However, unlike the punk scene, which had claimed the periphery with brash and sometimes violent declarations and sartorial emblems designed to shock and offend, new wave embodied quirkiness, playfulness, theatricality, and the unbridled creativity of an art-school milieu.

New wave icon Nick Rhodes of the British band Duran Duran summed up the new wave style when he noted, "It was a culture where the predilection was for standing out from the crowd rather than fitting in" (2014, 9). Many avenues for establishing sartorial distinctions were explored, and while the impulses may be categorized, they most certainly were not discrete or independent sets of ideas but, rather, were integrated and overlapping. One source of stylistic characteristics was the punk scene. Many new wavers happily adopted iconic aspects of punk including combat boots, graphic T-shirts, ripped clothes, chains, and studs. However, while a punk rocker was likely to style himself or herself as disheveled, the new waver affected a studied composition of elements. New wave hairstyles, among the most distinguishing characteristics of the scene, also paid homage to punk. Punks had innovated spiked, uneven, brutally cropped coiffures and had reimagined the Mohawk as a towering mass of gelled daggers in the late 1970s and early 1980s. New wavers took the predilection for styling gel and hairspray in new directions, and big, back-combed, spiky, tangled, curled, upswept, and generally complicated hairstyles became a hallmark of the scene. Whereas punk coiffures often had a slapdash, disaffected presentation, the new wave style was carefully conceived and subject to seemingly infinite variations.

Some new wave acts and the fans that followed them explored art-school modes of expression. Thus the wearing of ironically outdated secondhand apparel including 1950s party dresses and mid-century costume jewelry was *de rigueur*. Some iconic new wave elements for men including skinny ties, colorful blazers, and shiny, baggy trousers were reboots of apparel that were worn by early rockabilly artists in the 1950s. It was often the case that vintage clothing was worn in eclectic combinations with more modern pieces, creating an anachronistic bricolage of sartorial elements. For example, a 1950s-era dress complete with tulle petticoats could be worn in conjunction with combat boots and a motorcycle jacket. Strange juxtapositions of this kind marked the postmodern breakdown of the "rules" of dress and were emblematic of a period in which camp (parody) and kitsch (trash) were embraced for their expressive possibilities. The new wave band that perhaps best expressed these inclinations was the Athens, Georgia, band the B-52s.

The new wave look also borrowed from stylistic trends that had been developed in the glam rock scene in which artists like David Bowie had purposefully blurred the established boundaries of gendered dress by wearing apparel, hairstyles, and makeup that created an androgynous impact. The tendency to confound gender boundaries was particularly evident in new wave hairstyles, which were not specifically gendered and tended to be quite theatrical. The use of colorful cosmetics by men was specifically evident among popular new wave artists like Duran Duran and Culture Club and transferred to the street style of young men in the 1980s, though often in a less ostentatious application. Crossing the boundaries of gendered dress is generally less obvious among women given the widespread, mainstream transgressions of these limits that had previously taken place, especially in the 1960s when designers like Yves Saint Laurent put women in pantsuits and ensembles inspired by men's hunting apparel. That noted, new wave fashions included unisex apparel, and artists like Annie Lennox affected an androgynous look for part of the 1980s. Additionally, the rock and roll ethos borrowed from punk conceptually, though not necessarily musically, also informed a look that was often less traditionally feminine.

New wave dress practices were markedly different from the street and subcultural styles from which they borrowed in that new wave affected an aura of newness and hypermodernity that was not perceptible in the American street styles that predated it (though notably there are conceptual links to the "mod" look of the 1960s, which was largely a European phenomenon). Many articles of new wave apparel and accessories had a markedly slick, modern, even futuristic aesthetic. Glossy, oversized, colorful plastic jewelry was worn in profusion. Sunglasses that had slats like Venetian blinds instead of lenses, had frames that were markedly asymmetrical, or were fashioned to make one look like a robot or Cyclops were iconic accessories of this street style. Textile choices included bold animal prints juxtaposed with neon hues, metallic textiles, neoprene, and shiny ripstop nylon. Makeup was also a point of distinction and included vibrantly colored lipstick and blush and atypical eye makeup colors like yellow and red eye shadow or blue and green mascara. Temporary hair color that was brushed into spiky locks with a bristled wand was also a new wave fad. Brightly colored, metallic streaks gave spiky, asymmetrical hairstyles even more visual impact.

Taken as a whole, the new wave aesthetic was eclectic and incredibly creative. The bigger the hair, the brighter the makeup, the more peculiar and iconoclastic the juxtapositions of apparel, the better. The new wave of the 1980s was neither political nor subcultural, it was simply a popular youth scene that was about being different from the norm, and expressing difference in taste and attitude was a point of distinction. While this general impulse certainly is a mainstay of youth culture, by 1988 the vast majority of new wave music had disappeared from the popular music charts (Cateforis 2011, 64) and was replaced by "alternative" or "indie" (independent) acts like R.E.M. and the Cranberries and later the Seattle sound of Pearl Jam and Nirvana that affected a simple, grungy style of worn-out T-shirts, jeans, and flannel shirts (see the entry on Grunge). Although the new wave style lived on in youth culture for a few years past the popularity of the music, the new wave aesthetic was largely over by the dawn of the 1990s.

The vast majority of apparel and accessories that were utilized to create the new wave look could be obtained from the mainstream mass market, and many of the iconic pieces like Venetian-blind sunglasses and neon-hued apparel were related to short-lived fashion fads that enjoyed popularity outside of the new wave (see Moore 2015). In addition, the secondhand- and vintage-apparel marketplace provided a surfeit of 1950s and 1960s apparel. Notably, the term "new wave" was used to promote items via mail order. For example, a sunglasses advertisement from 1980 that ran in a popular music magazine featured "Incognitos," which were promoted as "crazy new styles from Italy" and "new shades for the new age." Additionally, an advertisement that ran in *Creem* magazine in March 1983 promoted a catalog that could be acquired from Diana's boutique in New York City for one dollar. The advertisement described Diana's as "a complete new wave shop in your living room" and promoted clothing, "shades," jewelry, and wristbands among its offerings.

Ideas for combining on-trend and vintage items were largely communicated through the music press including the American publications *Trouser Press* and *New York Rocker* and the British fan magazine *Smash Hits,* which was inexpensive and easy to acquire in the United States. Additionally, the launch of MTV in August 1981 was profoundly influential with regard to broadcasting new wave music and depicting the style of the musicians. The music videos of these new, often European, often one-hit-wonder acts ran regularly on the music channel, which early in its history did not keep apace with commercial popular-music radio stations. The writers of *Mad World: An Oral History of New Wave Artists and Songs That Defined the 1980s* asserted that when MTV launched there simply were not enough music videos by mainstream artists like Journey, Rod Stewart, and Loverboy to fill programming; thus there was no choice but to play the videos from British new wave bands (Majewski and Bernstein 2014, 12). Music historian Theo Cateforis (2011, 54) backs this assertion and points to the fact that new wave was a youth phenomenon that was perpetuated by the young demographic that consumed MTV. He also points to the fact that new wave thrived in opposition to mainstream currents in popular music that were promoted by major labels who lavished big budgets and highly engineered production values on acts that filled huge arenas. Writing in 1979, music critic Jim Miller noted that the recording industry was saturated with overproduced "platinum bands" like Elton John and Fleetwood Mac, which conveyed an "unsatisfying aura of canned charisma." New wave artists, he went on to observe, were trying to stake claims of authenticity in the wake of punk's demise (1979, 25, 28). Many new wave records were produced with very low production costs and were created in a context in which "anyone with a skinny tie could get a [recording] contract" (Cateforis 2011, 38). New wave music and style were also promoted in films that were targeted to a young demographic. Among the notable titles were *Valley Girl* (1983) and a number of John Hughes's movies including *Sixteen*

Candles (1984) and *Pretty in Pink* (1986). These movies featured young, creative, outsider characters who made being different a point of positive distinction.

There is some evidence that new wave performers established direct relationships with fashion. For example, in 1980 Debbie Harry of Blondie was a spokesperson for the then enormously trendy Gloria Vanderbilt jeans. However, promotion of branded products ran counter to the new wave *avant-garde* outsider position. And "selling out" was a risk that performers ran if they engaged in this kind of commercial activity. A dismayed fan letter from Em J. Zee that ran in *Creem* in 1980 chastised Blondie for her promotional role and quipped that perhaps all rockers should have designer clothes lines, noting that punk rockers from the Clash could sell "heavy duty riveted jeans with a small embroidered gun" and new wave act Devo could sell pants made of "sturdy plastic" in "industrial hues" ("Mail" 1980, 8). The fact that commercial links to popular music were so anathema to this fan in particular, and to new wavers in general, is a distinctive feature of this scene, and it is worth noting that other music scenes of this era (hip-hop in particular) were on the verge of making major forays into commoditizing street style.

Although new wave acts had only fallen off the popular music charts in the last years of the 1980s, a revival of new wave music was already evident by the early 1990s as nostalgia for the decade just passed prompted record companies to release compilation albums and publish previously unreleased recordings on the newly popular compact disc format (Rosen 1994, 14). New wave acts continued to play live shows and record new work, and a 1998 revival tour call the "Big Rewind," which featured Howard Jones, Human League, and Culture Club, allowed new wave fans to reunite *en masse*. Although much of the new wave look was iconic to the 1980s, nostalgia for the time and the scene has meant that certain aspects of new wave have continuously been revived over the years. For example, Kanye West popularized Venetian-blind sunglasses in 2007 when he wore a pair that had been custom designed for him by Alain Mikli (Moore 2015, 297). West's enormous popularity and fashion influence may have contributed to the launch of a brand called Shutter Shades, which promoted this new wave idea with updated high-tech features. Additionally, the general aesthetic of 1980s new wave is periodically interpreted and reworked by designers for the runway. A very obvious interpretation of 1980s new wave was visible in Jeremy Scott's Spring/Summer 2014 collection.

Writing in the "Introduction" of *The New Trouser Press Guide to New Wave Records,* a book that runs for several hundred pages and lists almost 1,000 bands, the editor noted, "New wave is admittedly a pretty meaningless term" (Robbins 1983, xiii). Yet artists like the Cars, the Talking Heads, Animotion, and Howard Jones embraced the new wave label, as did scores of teenagers throughout the 1980s. To be a new wave act was to be in marked contrast to "old wave dinosaurs" like Journey, Styx, and Foreigner (Goldberg 1983, 24), and for fans and followers who liked new wave music and dressed the part, their sartorial gestures marked them in opposition to the people who liked that kind of old wave music. The new wave made the unbridled expression of individuality, quirkiness, and playful opposition to the mainstream a state of mind and a lifestyle as well as a visually arresting and memorable street style.

Further Reading

Advertisement for Diana's. 1983. *Creem,* March, 24.

Advertisement for Incognitos. 1980. *Creem,* October, 9.

Buckley, D. 2001. "New wave (ii)." *Grove Music Online. Oxford Music Online.* Oxford University Press, accessed October 13, 2016, from http://www.oxfordmusiconline.com .ez-proxy.brooklyn.cuny.edu:2048/subscriber/article/grove/music/49689.

Cateforis, T. 2011. *Are We Not New Wave?: Modern Pop at the Turn of the 1980s.* Ann Arbor: The University of Michigan Press.

Goldberg, M. 1983. "Ric Ocasek: Worms on a String." *Creem,* March, 24–25.

Graves, S. 2013. "New Wave Music." In *St. James Encyclopedia of Popular Culture* 2nd ed., vol. 3, edited by T. Riggs, 748–50. Detroit: St. James Press.

Himes, G. 2014. "What New Wave Brought to Rock 'n' roll." *Smithsonian* 45 (5): 1.

"Mail: Letter from Em J. Zee." 1980. *Creem,* October, 6, 8.

Majewski, L., and J. Bernstein. 2014. *Mad World: An Oral History of New Wave Artists and Songs That Defined the 1980s.* New York: Abrams.

Miller, J. 1979. "Jim Miller on Pop Music: Some Future." *The New Republic,* March 24, 25–28.

Moore, J. 2015. *Fashion Fads through American History: Putting Clothes into Context.* Santa Barbara, CA: ABC-CLIO.

"The Punk Rock and New Wave Movements." 2001. In *American Decades* vol. 8, edited by J. S. Baughman, V. Bondi, R. Layman, T. McConnell, and V. Tompkins. Detroit: Gale. Retrieved from http://go.galegroup.com.ez-proxy.brooklyn.cuny.edu:2048/ps/i.do?p =GVRL&sw=w&u=cuny_broo39667&v=2.1&it=r&id=GALE%7CCX3468302577&s id=exlibris&asid=c95d7019efef50d2a9b133bc11067515.

Rhodes, N. 2014. "Foreword." In *Mad World: An Oral History of New Wave Artists and the Songs That Defined the 1980s,* edited by L. Majewski and J. Berstein. New York: Abrams.

Robbins, I. A. 1983. *The Trouser Press Guide to New Wave Records.* New York: Charles Scribner's Sons.

Rosen, C. 1994. "Labels Raid New Wave Vaults as 'Valley Girl' Makes Charts." *Billboard* 106 (13): 14.

Punk (Mid-1970s–Late 1980s)

A punk by definition is a worthless individual. The punk movement drew upon the notion of worthlessness and channeled that nihilism into a groundbreaking subcultural style. The beginnings of punk-rock music, dress, and other forms of cultural production, including graphic design and dance styles, began to emerge in New York City around the year 1972, and punk was a visible subcultural movement in the United States by 1974. A vibrant punk scene had emerged in the United Kingdom by mid-decade. This scene displayed some of the same sartorial tendencies as its American counterpart—in part arriving at the same choices independently and in part adapting and adopting American trends that had been made visible through album covers and other printed materials. British punk quickly expanded upon ideas first seen in the United States and through commercial production created new forms while also exaggerating, refining, and reproducing extant stylistic tropes. British commercial production in turn influenced American punk style. Thus this discussion of American street style is intertwined with certain key happenings that took place in and around London in the mid-to-late 1970s.

Punk in the United States was a youth movement that responded to the social context of the early 1970s, a context characterized by the seemingly pointless violence and destruction created by the Vietnam War, the perceived failure of the hippie quest for a peaceful utopian society, political corruption, warnings that human agency was causing the slow death of the Earth, economic turmoil, and an overall perception that the promises of happiness and prosperity that were made to earlier generations would not be renewed for youths of the late 20th century. Punk culture and style sought a break from the mainstream and its morass of failed social projects; thus the basic tenets of punk were denial or destruction of mainstream ideals. Punk's primary expression was through music that was fast, loud, raucous, and primal. Both performers and audience members sometimes explored violent expressions such as smashing glasses, furniture, instruments, or people. Self-mutilation such as cutting or burning the skin was part of the scene. Spitting (gobbing) at bands was also an accepted behavior. Bands including Richard Hell and the Voidoids, the Heartbreakers, the Ramones, and later, from Britain, the Sex Pistols, the Clash, and the Damned formulated the punk-rock sound in small clubs and bars including CBGB in New York City and The Roxy in London. Song lyrics of early punk music were often bleak, nihilistic, or provocative (politically and sexually) and inspired raucous dancing such as the pogo, which essentially consisted of jumping straight up and down, and slam dancing or moshing, which largely consisted of slamming into other people. Punk performance and the subculture that formed around it were initially very raw and may be viewed as at least partially a response to the larger music scene of the 1970s that featured professional, polished, packaged entertainers who performed perfectly pleasant but utterly commercial music that largely failed to address the pressing issues of contemporary culture.

The basic characteristics of punk style must be laid out carefully as movement insiders quickly commodified this subcultural look, and commodification changed the street style in pronounced ways. Furthermore, there is plenty of controversy to be found by exploring the autobiographies of seminal figures of this era (Richard Hell, John Lydon, Vivienne Westwood), and more than one person has often taken credit for particular innovations. Early punk style, which can be understood from fanzines, snapshots taken in clubs like CBGB, and the personal accounts of innovators like Hell all indicate that early punk style involved a great deal of self-modification and was a style rooted in the necessity of invention and the desire for an authentic form of personal expression. Taking as a given that punk was a rejection of the mainstream culture, then it was also a rejection of mainstream sartorial trends, which at the time included the last vestiges of psychedelic and bohemian hippie style and the influence of highly theatrical glam rock, as well as the more traditional long-lived dress practices of women's and men's fashionable apparel. As punk emerged in a fashion marketplace suffused with color, glitter, flounces and flares, platform shoes, and studied artifice (wigs were incredibly popular in the early 1970s), punks sought ways to subvert such looks. Thus early punks shopped for secondhand clothes from earlier eras and purchased apparel from various tradespeople such as police and maintenance personnel as well as from military surplus. Additionally, dress practices subverted the boundaries of gendered clothes through crossdressing and sexually explicit dress, and brought to the street gear purchased from stores that catered to the fetish and bondage scene.

Shock value and the undermining of widespread notions of good taste were visible markers of early apparel selections. Coveralls, military boots, and leather jackets were among the most iconic pieces of basic apparel that were acquired through mainstream suppliers and the secondhand market. Basic blue jeans were ripped and bleach splattered. T-shirts were torn, with graffiti scrawled across their surfaces. Dog collars, safety pins, and links of chain replaced more traditional jewelry. Combat and motorcycle boots as well as dilapidated canvas athletic shoes were worn scuffed, stained, and with scribbles over their surfaces. Hair and makeup in the early waves of punk were also visibly different from the mainstream. Richard Hell wrote of making a calculated decision to distill the most "perverted elements" from the hairstyles of Elvis and the Beatles when he hacked his hair into a short, spiky, irregular cut. He noted that he was seeking to communicate transgression, defiance, and even criminality with this new take on hairdressing. Early in the evolution of spiked hairstyles, styling products were not specifically designed to create the type of hold that was desired, and petroleum jelly was used in lieu of the hair gels that came later. Early punks also dyed their hair in unnatural hues such as blue and green, though in the early 1970s hair dyes in such hues were not readily available, and products such as fabric dye were used to create the effect.

Early punk style was primitive in its "design" sensibilities as it eschewed design. Basic objects such as safety pins, which have become icons of punk style, were used from very early on, but their genesis in the style was pure practicality. Rips, tears, and stains also originated organically in a heroin-soaked social milieu that did not put a priority on hygiene or grooming. Punk style was nihilistic in its outlook and embraced both eclecticism and perversion. Looking strung out, dirty, or unkempt was not initially affected but was a byproduct of poverty and drug use. These elements never disappeared from punk style, but major additions and modifications became visible after mid-decade.

Beginning in the middle of the 1970s the punk scene that was emanating from London had a profound impact on punk sartorial style around the world. The British scene introduced ideas that carried on the do-it-yourself tendencies that were first seen in New York. For example, British punks seem to have been the first to wear garbage bags (bin liners) as apparel. Interestingly, trash bags in this period came in vibrant hues of pink and green as well as the more customary black as a lengthy trash strike had led bag makers to improve the aesthetics of the plastic sacks that were piling up on British streets. British punks also slashed and pinned apparel and used graffiti techniques. Perhaps the largest contribution from the British scene relates to commercial punk design, or punk design as fashion design. Malcolm McLaren and Vivienne Westwood opened a series of influential shops in the same location near World's End in London, changing the name and updating the inventory as social trends dictated. The major shop that is pertinent to the evolution of punk was Sex (opened in 1974), which became Seditionaries in 1975. Among the most iconic items featured were latex and rubber apparel, garments with bondage straps, apparel made in tartan fabric, and provocative silk-screened T-shirts. In 1977 the store sold blazers that were marketed as "anarchy jackets," an indication of the marketing savvy of the store's proprietors. Westwood and McLaren, who had previously had a shop called Let It Rock, which catered to the Teddy Boys and featured 1950s revival clothes, also sold apparel such as pegged pants and winkle picker (pointed-toe) shoes, which ultimately became part of the punk look.

Westwood created many of the clothes featured in the shop. In general, the local music scene inspired her work; however, it is the subject of contentious debate as to whether she or performers such as Sid Vicious or Johnny Rotten (Lydon) of the Sex Pistols came up with an idea first. These performers often wore the clothes she made in performance, and this stimulated sales of her designs. Furthermore, Malcolm McLaren, who helped to form the band Sex Pistols, is credited as an influential force in transporting aspects of American punk to England, further muddying the waters and clouding the story of who originated what. Richard Hell recalls in his autobiography that in the summer of

1976 a friend showed him a picture of the Sex Pistols and said, "Hey, Richard, you've got to see this. There are four guys who look exactly like you" (2015, chapter 22, paragraph 1). Hell, who had met the Sex Pistols' manager in New York City the previous year, took this as a sign that he had strongly impressed McLaren.

In addition to specialty apparel from shops like Seditionaries entering the punk sphere via the British punk scene, styling decisions including ultrahigh spikes, Mohawk haircuts, and vibrant hair dyes seem to also be attributable to London punks. Crazy Colors, which produces hair dye in vibrant and unnatural hues, was launched in the United Kingdom in 1977. British punk style traits contributed greatly to the stereotypical punk type that was very visible on streets around the world from the early 1980s onward.

The codified punk style also included the lavish use of metal studs on leather, Doc Marten boots, studded leather bracelets and collars, and the heavy use of cosmetics including pale foundation, dramatic eye makeup, and black lipstick and nail polish. Despite the fact that punk style became more outrageous in the 1980s, by the late 1970s the original punk scene was already losing some of its abrasiveness. Though dress practices were visually arresting, they became more uniform over time; and similarly, many bands, following the successful formulae developed in the earlier part of the decade, scored recording contracts with major labels. When Sex Pistols toured the United States in 1978, *Time* magazine described their debut as a "tame, almost respectable happening," and their histrionics, insults, and obscenities were described as "calculated" ("The Sex Pistols" 1978). Punk stores and brands also developed in the United States in the late 1970s including Manic Panic in New York City (which later catered to the Goth scene). Specific brands, including Alchemy jewelry, made products to appeal to the punk set. Richard Hell recalls seeing torn punk-inspired T-shirts in the windows of Macy's Herald Square in 1976 or 1977, a sure sign that aspects of punk style had already gone mainstream and thereby lost some of their shock value (Hell 2013). John Lydon of Sex Pistols recently noted, "The trouble is punk got coopted and distorted by the media. People find it hard to get away from the clichés, from the popularized eighties version of punk, and it became a stereotype" (Lydon 2013, 21). Being a stereotype does not make punk style any less of a street style; however, it is an indication that some of the rawness inherent in the style's inception was diluted from quite early on.

Mass media was instrumental in diffusing punk and concretizing the look. Punk style can be seen in films including the narrative films *Jubilee* (1978) and *Suburbia* (1983), the mockumentary *The Great Rock 'n' Roll Swindle* (1980), the documentary of the Los Angeles punk scene *The Decline of Western Civilization* (1981), and *The Filth and the Fury: A Sex Pistols Film* (2002). Fanzines abounded in this period as Xerox technology improved in terms of both speed and quality. American titles included *Punk, East Village Other, New York Rocker, Wet, Slash, Contagion, The Lowest Common Denominator,* and *Search & Destroy.* In the United Kingdom *Sniffin' Glu, Damaged Goods,* and *Ripped & Torn* were widely circulated titles that were generally priced between twenty-five cents and a dollar and a half and were retailed through the many independent record stores that existed at the time. Some fanzines were distributed internationally. Notably, fanzines included ads for mail ordering products such as silk-screened T-shirts and jewelry

It did not take long for punk style to trickle-up to high fashion. Zandra Rhodes seems to have been the first of many designers to interpret punk for the runway. In 1977 she sent apparel that featured safety pins and chains down the catwalk. A few years later Stephen Sprouse interpreted some of the grit of the early punk scene in his graffiti-covered collection from 1987. Versace famously designed apparel with a punk influence in 1994, including a black evening dress split almost entirely up the side and closed by oversized gold safety pins with his Medusa-head insignia. John Galliano for Dior haute couture included bondage straps, graffiti, and Mohawk hairstyles in 2002. In addition to runway presentations featuring punk influence, in the 1980s and early 1990s an international mail-order company called Bogey's Underground Fashion from London sold sophisticated and expensive designs laden with straps, skulls, spikes, and studs. In the 21st century mass-market retailers including Hot Topic and Top Shop regularly sell elements of the look.

Punk style has never completely disappeared. It has been incorporated into fashionable dress to varying degrees over the years. It has also developed and evolved as a subcultural style. For example, there are now (since the early 2000s) subsets of punk known as queer edge (queer straight edge) and queercore (queer hardcore) that have developed a new take on punk style that subverts heteronormative dress practices (see Ensminger 2010). In addition, there are legions of young people, generation after generation, who continue to gravitate to the ideas expressed in punk-rock music old and new as well as the messages that are still perceived to be part of punk dress practices. Despite the fact that the style has become a stereotype of sorts there is still room for individuals to explore unique interpretations of the style, and this is a source of great appeal for people in the 21st century.

Further Reading

"Anthems of the Blank Generation." 1977. *Time* 110 (2): 48.

Bolton, A., and R. Hell. 2013. *Punk: Chaos to Couture.* New York: Metropolitan Museum of Art.

Ensminger, D. 2010. "Redefining the Body Electric: Queering Punk and Hardcore." *Journal of Popular Music Studies* 22 (1): 50–67.

Hell, R. 2013. "'Punk' Couture: Insides Out." In *Punk: Chaos to Couture,* by A. Bolton and R. Hell. New York: Metropolitan Museum of Art.

Hell, R. 2015. *I Dreamed I Was a Very Clean Tramp.* New York: Harper Collins.

Lydon, J. 1994. *Rotten: No Irish, No Blacks, No Dogs.* New York: McMillan.

Lydon, J. 2013. "A Beautiful Ugliness Inside." In *Punk: Chaos to Couture,* by A. Bolton and R. Hell, 20–21. New York: Metropolitan Museum of Art.

McNeil, L. 1996. *Please Kill Me: The Uncensored Oral History of Punk.* New York: Grove Press.

Meadows, E. 1977. "The Zeitgeist: Pistol-Whipped." *National Review,* November 11, 1311–12.

Moore, R. 2004. "Postmodernism and Punk Subculture: Cultures of Authenticity and Destruction." *The Communication Review* 7: 305–27.

O'Connell, H. 2014. "(Re)Turning Money into Rebellion: Reification and Utopianism in Early Punk Production." *The Journal of Popular Culture* 47 (3): 591–612.

Pope, R. 2009. "Realizing the Scene; Punk and Meanings Demise." *International Journal of Zizek Studies* 3 (1): 1–24.

Savage, J. 1991. *England's Dreaming: Anarchy, Sex Pistols, Punk Rock, and Beyond.* New York: St. Martin's Press.

"The Sex Pistols Are Here." 1978. *Time* 111 (3): 62.

Westwood, V., and I. Kelly. 2014. *Vivienne Westwood.* Oxford, UK: Picador.

Rastafarianism (ca. 1970–Present)

The Rastafarian movement was started in Jamaica in the 1930s by poor Afro-Caribbean men (and to a lesser extent women) as a response to the oppressive culture implemented through white colonial rule that made native people and people descended from slavery a marginalized underclass. Variously labeled as a cult, a mentality, a way of life, and a unifying "gospel of African pride" (Lewis 1989, 28), Rastafarianism is not a "religion" in the traditional sense as it does not have a cast of saints and heroes nor does it have a unified central creed (Gandhar Chakravarty 2015, 158, 160); however, many of its widely held principles can serve as the underpinnings for a specific way of life. Rastafarianism seems to have found a foothold in the United States beginning in the late 1960s when waves of Jamaican immigrants settled along the East Coast of the United States, especially in large urban centers from Florida north to Massachusetts (Barnett 2008, 104). In their newfound homes, the Rastafari (also referred to as Rasta) were inclined to find similar problems of segregation and discrimination as in Jamaica, which is arguably part of the reason that Rastafarian culture flourished in the United States (Lewis 1989, 23).

At its heart, Rastafarianism is a set of core beliefs that celebrate the African roots of its constituents. The name *Rastafari* is derived from the term "Ras" (meaning head or leader) and the name Tafari Makonnen, who was crowned Haile Selassie I, emperor of Ethiopia, and ruled the nation from 1930 until 1974. Rastafarian principles propound that this former emperor of Ethiopia was an almighty leader, and many Rastafarians believe in the promise of a return to Ethiopia as a homeland. Additionally, many Rastafari practice a lifestyle that seeks a return to nature and righteous living in accord with the Earth, and they, therefore, eschew polluting substances including alcohol and salt. Many Rastafari observe a vegan diet and abstain from mainstream hygiene and beauty products that include chemically derived detergents and emollients. Some of the dress practices of the Rastafari, which will be discussed in detail, also embody the desire to return to nature and to celebrate Africa. Seeking a return to a simpler, purer, cleaner set of practices is often described as an attempt to flee "Babylon." This expression is a reference to a neo-Babylonian city described in the Old Testament that has come to be associated with sin and debauchery. The Rastafarian subculture and the hippie movement were somewhat intertwined intellectually and with regard to some practices of living into the middle of the 1970s, as both groups sought an escape from materialism and a return to myriad forms of spirituality (Barnett 2008, 105).

A great deal of variety exists over time and across populations of individuals who identify as Rastafari, and it is important to note that dress practices that evoke this movement (especially dreadlocks) do not necessarily denote adherence to the principles of living that are identified with Rastafarianism (Nettleford 1998, 311). At least four sects of Rastafarians have developed since the 1930s: Nyabinghi, Bobo Shanti, Twelve Tribes of Israel, and School of Vision. Each of these sects espouses slightly different values and practices: some sects regard the Bible highly, while others advocate for its destruction; some have specific identifying dress customs, while others dress according to taste and temperament. The fact that the movement has spread to places like Cuba, New Zealand, Canada, Ghana, and the United States of America has also facilitated the hybridization of Rastafarian dress.

It is important to note that the dress of the Rastafari was originally considered "outlandish" and markedly countercultural within the confines of Jamaica, and there was a time when faithful individuals conformed to mainstream standards in order to get work (Kitzinger 1969, 242). Early in the evolution of Rastafarianism, identity was largely concealed in public (Chevannes 1994, 131), but with the mainstreaming of reggae music in the 1970s Rastafarian culture was embraced first within Jamaica and then gradually throughout the Afro-Caribbean diaspora.

The most distinctive indicator of being a Rastafari is the widely adopted dread-lock hairstyle, which is achieved over time as individual strands of hair are allowed to entangle and interlock into thick clusters that are generally left uncut for the life of the person. Locked hairstyles with the aesthetics of dreadlocks seem to have originated among African chiefs thousands of years ago; however, sociologist Barry Chevannes's research indicates that the custom of wearing (and naming) *dreadlocks* emerged from an encampment of men living in Jamaica in the middle of the 20th century who were known as Youth Black Faith. This organization, founded in 1949, instituted the custom of wearing beards, a visual reference to both Haile Selassie and Jesus. Locks were institutionalized in the early 1950s and were named "dreadlocks" as a reference to the "dreadful," a group of particularly ascetic, disciplined, and forthright members of the Youth Black Faith. According to Chevannes, the decision not to comb the hair was a way to "declare oneself not merely antisocial but extra social like mad derelicts and outcasts." Chevannes went on to note, "Locks had a shock value, but they were also a way of witnessing faith with the same kind of fanaticism for which the prophets and saints of old were famous, men gone mad with religion" (Chevannes 1994, 154–58).

Over time, the wearing of locks has come to be associated with rich symbolic and spiritual potential by those who wear them. Dreadlocks may be read as a figurative locking or linking with Africa. They may also be interpreted as symbol of a lifestyle, path, or spiritual covenant. Dreadlocks are believed by some to posses spiritual strength and are deemed similar to a crown or a mane, and some Rasta have even suggested that their locks act as sensors to the vibrations in their surroundings (Van De Berg 1998, 167). Some Rastafari read the length of one's locks as a barometer of power and a feature that has the capacity to command respect (Van De Berg 1998, 167; Chevannes 1994, 145). Notably, some Rasta have claimed that hair is of "no import" (Gandhar Chakravarty 2015, 170), an indication of the diversity that exists among those who identify as Rastafarian. Originally worn in defiance of British colonial rule (King 1999, 78), they are generally indicative of a refusal to make accommodations with the mainstream (Chevannes 1994, 145), and Jamaican security forces persecuted individuals who wore them into the 1970s (King 1999, 84).

In addition to the wearing of dreadlocks, many Rastafarians adopt dress that is both symbolic of Africa and related to a natural approach to living. All types of apparel including T-shirts, tams, and shoulder bags are created in the sacred colors of the Ethiopian flag: red, gold, and green. Red is a symbol of the "church triumphant"; gold symbolizes the gold of Africa; and green symbolizes the rich and verdant lands of Africa. Black is also worn as a symbolic reference to the continent of Africa. Iconography and images that relate to the political dynasty of Ethiopia are also used, including the face of Haile Selassie I, the Lion of Judah, the Star of

David, the Empress Menon, and epigraphs of Amheric script. Additionally, an outline of the continent of Africa, images of standing drums, herb chalices, marijuana leaves, and dreadlocks are images that are commonly applied to apparel and accessories (Yawney 1994, 76–77). Symbolic association with Africa is also achieved through the wearing of traditional African apparel derived from many cultures across the continent. Typical garments include dashikis, vibrantly colored caftans, and traditional African headdresses including the Nigerian gele.

There also exist a variety of dress practices that are related to specific Rastafarian sects. For example, within the Bobo Shanti sect, men wear their locks wrapped in turbans and are customarily attired in long, flowing black or white robes that are commonly accented with red, gold, and green scarves. Among the Nyabinghi, women generally cover their hair and wear long dresses or skirts, while pants are not customarily worn. As with all cultural and subcultural forms of dress, these practices are open to interpretation and hybridization and are constantly evolving as beliefs and global dress practices evolve.

Dress is important as a marker of beliefs and identity for all kinds of people in both mainstream societies and subcultural milieu; however, Bibi Bakare-Yusuf has noted that among "New World Africans," "bodily practices" are able to function as "political manifestos in the struggle for freedom, agency, and assertion of cultural identity" and may also function as "a critique of the dominant culture" (2006, 463). This point highlights the deeply seeded communications that are possible within Rasta dress practices that subvert mainstream standards of propriety; however, scholar Stephen A. King has noted that the growing international popularity of reggae music has, since the 1970s, played a major role in spreading Rastafari culture and, consequently, in changing attitudes about the movement (1999, 79). Beginning in the early 1970s, Chris Blackwell, the president of Island Records, marketed the reggae sound to a wider audience. He accomplished this by melding pop and rock riffs with the traditional reggae sound and printing the lyrics on album jackets (King 1999, 45). As a result of the widespread interest and acceptance of reggae music, Rasta symbols increasingly became mainstreamed, first in Jamaica, then in the Rastafarian diaspora and beyond. These symbols have been increasingly appropriated and commodified over the years (Salter 2008, 11; Lewis 1989, 23). A term even exists to label individuals who adopt the look but not the principles of Rastafarianism: a "Rastafake-I" has been defined as "an individual who displays some of the symbols of Rastafari adherence but does not follow the strict behavioral code of the biblical Nazerite vow". It has also been suggested that for some Rastafake-I, dressing is just "one phase in the continuum" of the acceptance of Rasta (Van de Berg 1998, 172–73), a point that reinforces the tremendous cultural and psychological power that is potentially inherent in dress practices and points to the complex issue of determining authenticity among wearers of subcultural dress.

Rastafarian dress practices continue to be the subject of derision and misunderstanding as well as the object of restrictions and outright bans. Rastafarian hair has been banned in some Midwestern American public schools based on the belief that the dreadlocks were a symbolic declaration of gang affiliation. Bans have been upheld despite the assertion that their implementation infringes upon religious freedoms (Gereluk 2006, 107, 111). Some American companies including Federal Express and UPS (United Parcel Service) have demoted and fired employees who refused to cut their dreadlocks (France et al. 2001), and both the United States military and prison system continue to grapple with this countercultural hairstyle that is also an embodiment of religious principles.

In the 1970s and 1980s popular media, both narrative fiction and broadcast news, frequently depicted Rastafarians as an evil, drug-peddling cult of illegal immigrants (Barnett 2008, 105). The movie *Marked for Death* is an example of this kind of negative depiction. Films related to the reggae music scene including *Rockers* (1978) and *Babylon* (1980) presented Rastas in a more objective light, but one that undoubtedly disturbed individuals in the mainstream. In the 21st century American popular culture is more likely to present Rastas as a more positive stereotype, but as a stereotype nonetheless. One example of this can be found in the Disney movie *Shark Tale* (2004), which includes the characters Bernie and Ernie who are "Rasta" jellyfish.

Rastafari dress practices have been interpreted by both high-style and mass-market fashion brands. For example, Rifat Özbek included traditional Rasta colors and oversized tams in his Spring/Summer 1991 collection, while the House of Dior applied the colors to a line of logoed accessories and apparel for Spring/Summer 2004. More recently, Tommy Hilfiger used red, gold, and green stripes in crocheted separates that were styled with a decidedly countercultural appeal for his Spring/Summer 2016 runway. Internet retailers including rastaempire.com and rastagearshop.com offer a wide variety of products for individuals wishing to communicate an interest in Rastafarian culture and lifestyle. Sites of this kind offer a wide range of apparel and accessories color-blocked or trimmed in the traditional Ethiopian colors. Contemporary items like board shorts, miniskirts, baggy jeans, and high-top sneakers are also adorned with symbols like the Lion of Judah or an outline of the continent of Africa. Symbols are also combined in new and creative ways. For example, a lion's mane might be illustrated as a mane of marijuana leaves. Some items that are routinely for sale in the 21st-century marketplace test the boundaries of good taste and fidelity to the ideals of the movement. For example, red, green, and gold caps, visors, and tams can be purchased with a cluster of synthetic dreadlocks attached.

Other subcultural groups have co-opted many aspects of the Rastafarian look. For example, participants of the ecological movement have adopted dreadlocks as a testament to a back-to-nature ethos. Modern Dead Heads also routinely adopt dreadlocks as a way to connect with the natural principles espoused by their hippie predecessors. Once a clear marker of Rastafarian beliefs, "Throughout North America, dreadlocks now represent something of an Afrocentric fashion statement, and disentangling the genuine Rastafarians from their dreadlocked imitators requires extensive ethnographic research" (Hepner 1998, 204–5). In addition to dreadlocks, the traditional Rasta colors have been widely adopted by "pot" culture (which overlaps with the Dead Head scene). It has been suggested that in some circles in the United States, Rasta dress practices function as simple shorthand for counterculture (Salter 2008, 10).

Rastafari culture and dress practices continue to evolve in both the United States and throughout the world and will undoubtedly continue to do so. In the 21st century the alienation of and discrimination against individuals of African descent make the principles of Rastafarian culture as relevant as ever. Additionally, in the fast-paced, highly commercialized global marketplace, many individuals are seeking respite in spaces outside of the mainstream, and Rastafarian subculture offers that as well. The omnivorous nature of global street style also provides a context for the continued presence of Rasta dress practices in both mainstream fashion and more personal and individualized expressions. Thus there are likely still chapters to be written regarding the visual identity of Rastafari and those who mimic them.

Further Reading

Bakare-Yusuf, B. 2006. "Fabricating Identities: Survival and the Imagination in Jamaican Dancehall Culture." *Fashion Theory* 10 (4): 461–84.

Barnett, M. 2008. "The Globalization of the Rastafari Movement from a Jamaican Diasporic Perspective." *IDEAZ* 7: 98–114.

Chevannes, B. 1994. *Rastafari: Roots and Ideology.* Syracuse: Syracuse University Press.

France, D., E. Pierce, and J. Chong. 2001. "The Dreadlock Deadlock." *Newsweek* 138 (11): 54.

Gandhar Chakravarty, K. 2015. "Rastafari Revisited: A Four Point Orthodox/Secular Typology." *Journal of the American Academy of Religion* 83 (1): 151–80.

Gereluk, D. 2006. "'Why Can't I Wear This?!': Banning Symbolic Clothing in Schools." *Philosophy of Education,* 106–14.

Hepner, R. 1998. "Chanting Down Babylon in the Belly of the Beast: The Rastafarian Movement in the Metropolitan United States." In *Chanting Down Babylon: The Rastafari Reader,* edited by N. S. Murrell, W. D. Spencer, and A. A. McFarlane, 199–216. Philadelphia: Temple University Press.

King, S. A. 1998. "International Reggae, Democratic Socialism, and the Secularization of the Rastafari Movement 1972–1980." *Popular Music and Society* 22 (3): 39–60.

King, S. A. 1999. "The Co-optation of a 'Revolution': Rastafari, Reggae, and the Rhetoric of Control." *The Howard Journal of Communications* 10: 77–95.

Kitzinger, S. 1969. "Protest and Mysticism: The Rastafari Cult of Jamaica." *Journal for the Scientific Study of Religion* 8 (2): 240–62.

Lewis, L. 1989. "Living in the Heart of Babylon: Rastafari in the U.S.A." *Bulletin of Eastern Caribbean Affairs* 15 (1): 20–30.

Nettleford, R. 1998. "Discourse on Rastafarian Reality." In *Chanting Down Babylon: The Rastafari Reader,* edited by N. S. Murrell, W. D. Spencer, and A. A. McFarlane, 311–25. Philadelphia: Temple University Press.

Salter, R. 2008. "Rastafari in a Global Context: Affinities of 'Orthognosy' and 'Oneness' in the Expanding World." *IDEAZ* 7: 10–27.

Van de Berg, W. R. 1998. "Rastafari Perceptions of Self and Symbolism." In *New Trends and Developments in African Religions,* edited by P. B. Clarke, 159–75. Westport, CT: Greenwood Press.

Yawney, C. D. 1994. "Rasta Mek a Trod: Symbolic Ambiguity in a Globalizing Religion." In *Arise Ye Mighty People!: Gender, Class, and Race in Popular Struggles,* edited by T. E. Turner and B. J. Ferguson, 75–84. Trenton, NJ: Africa World Press.

Raver (Early 1990s–Early 2000s)

Ravers were a specific category of clubgoer who adopted colorful and often out-landish dress for the purpose of self-expression and subcultural demarcation while dancing to electronic music and partying at "raves." Raves began as pop up parties in the north of England in the late 1980s and spread to American cities including San Francisco, Los Angeles, Detroit, and New York City in the early 1990s before ultimately becoming organized commercial affairs from the latter half of the 1990s into the first decade of the new millennium. While parties and club nights that are referred to as "raves" are still held, and both electronic music and elements of rave dress practices live on in EDM (electronic dance music) festival dress, the dress worn by ravers from the 1990s through the early 2000s will be considered here as a unique category.

Before the commercialization of the scene, raves were held in locations such as basements, fields, warehouses, and abandoned buildings, and the events were communicated through flyers, via 800 numbers posted in record shops, by pager messaging, and by word of mouth. As the Internet came into more and more peo-ple's homes, ravers also used web-based communication to promote one-time-only parties that often began late on a Friday night, could last until Sunday morning, and could attract thousands of revelers. True raves were different from other kinds of dance parties for several reasons. First, alcohol was largely eschewed in favor of certain kinds of mood-enhancing drugs including Ecstasy (MDMA), Ketamine (widely known as Special-K), whippets (balloons filed with nitrous oxide), and

LSD. Caffeine and sugar were also heavily indulged, and ravers were among the early adopters of energy drinks like Red Bull and Psuper Psonic Psybertonic. Second, participants in the rave scene treated ecstatic dancing to various forms of electronic music, including techno, jungle, dub, and trance, as a vehicle to reach an aerobic high that was widely believed to have the potency to induce an existential awakening. Additionally, unlike many nightclub scenes where bouncers select clubgoers based on their conformity to mainstream beauty standards, rave organizers generally expressed a come-all attitude that created a heterogeneously mixed group that was racially and ethnically diverse and embraced myriad sexual orientations. While the majority of ravers were aged 15–25 the demographic of raves spanned generations, from young teenagers getting their first taste of nightlife to middle-aged (and older) Dead Heads seeking a new psychedelic scene.

Rave goers routinely enthused that a rave was more than a party. The throbbing electronic music, the strobes and pulsing multicolored-light shows, the seemingly endless sea of bodies engaged in unbridled freeform dancing, and the heady mixture of caffeine, sugar, and mind-altering drugs worked together to create the feeling of a communal ecstatic state. In fact, many ravers considered the rave a spiritual experience. Some ravers considered the DJ as a kind of "high priest" and drugs like Ecstasy a "holy sacrament" (Hutson 1999, 60). For others, the DJ was not just a person who played music but "a combination electrical engineer, neurologist, and artistic magician wielding aural and visual stimulae," which had the ability to create "aural streams of consciousness" and "collective trances" among partygoers (Holden 2000). The rave was conceived as a form of communal catharsis achieved through the primal power of collective dancing. So widespread was the notion that a rave could elevate the spirit and help individuals tap into higher forms of consciousness and spirituality that mainstream Christian churches and youth groups both melded rave elements into traditional religious services and sponsored church-sanctioned Christian raves (Hutson 1999, 60). Notably, the raver philosophy, known as PLUR (peace, love, unity, respect) does align well with the values taught in Christianity, though the hedonistic impulses to use mind-altering substances and engage in public sexual experimentation (Denizet-Lewis 2000) generally fall outside the boundaries of proper behavior delineated by mainstream Christian sects.

The dress of ravers was incredibly distinctive. First of all, rave dress was colorful. Fluorescent hues, rainbow-colored clothes, and both garments and accessories designed to glow when exposed to ultraviolet light were ubiquitous elements. Fabric tie-dyed in fluorescent hues was also typical. Many pieces of clothing were worn oversized. Long baggy shirts, big baggy jeans, and oversized rubber platform shoes played upon sartorial tropes that were worn by skateboarders in the early 1990s, and followers of hip-hop before them. Ravers, however, took the oversized phenomenon to previously uncharted extremes. Massive jeans with pant leg hems up to 60 inches in circumference marked one as a raver. The oversized phenomenon also impacted floppy, multicolored sock caps and Dr. Seuss–inspired hats (accessories that were briefly adopted by early professional snowboarders), novelty glasses, colorful plastic or candy pacifiers, and oversized rainbow-colored lollipops, which were both a stylish accessory and a vehicle for a sugar high. A raver could be so heavily adorned in voluminous fabrics that one *New York Times* reporter described rave-goers as looking like "swaddled scarecrows" (Israel 1993). Raver fashions could also be quite diminutive. Some raver girls wore miniskirts so short that they barely concealed their undergarments. Tiny tube tops or cropped shirts in metallic fabrics or vinyl textiles were often worn in conjunction with the tiny skirts. Backpacks were the hand luggage of choice among ravers since they allowed for unfettered dancing, and the taste for teeny-tiny knapsacks seems to have started among ravers and spread to the wider fashion marketplace in due course. Small backpacks could be made of colorful vinyl or could be fashioned to look like a small stuffed animal, an idea that may have been borrowed from Japanese Lolita street style. Colorful hair, typically in the form of a wig in a vibrant hue like blue or purple, was a popular aesthetic choice in the rave scene long before it was ever considered mainstream fashion, while ravers were also among the vanguard for mainstreaming lip, eyebrow, and nose piercings. Glow sticks, glitter, and face paint often completed the look.

The elements described in the previous paragraph outline the common sartorial tendencies among ravers. For many ravers, these elements could be mixed at will. However, there were some ravers who fashioned a more specific sartorial identity from the exaggerated, multihued apparel. One subgenre of rave aesthetics was the "candy raver." Candy ravers could be male or female but tended to adopt an effeminate and infantile aesthetic that included wearing and carrying various kinds of toys, dolls, and stuffed animals and adopting childish accent pieces—apparel and accessories adorned with Japanese characters such as Hello Kitty, Keroppi the frog, and Pippo the pig. "Polo ravers" similarly wore bright hues and body paint and carried accessories like glow sticks or lollipops but also sourced much of their wardrobe from preppy, mainstream brands like Nautica, Tommy Hilfiger, and Polo Ralph Lauren. Notably, all of these brands were making oversized apparel throughout much of the 1990s in response to trends coming out of the hip-hop scene. A final subcategory of raver was often referred to as the "techno-hippie." These ravers maintained connections to the Dead Head scene and its sartorial practices (Grateful Dead T-shirts, elements of Rastafarian dress, love beads) while also adopting some of the dress elements that were iconic indicators of the rave scene. Notably, followers of the Grateful Dead were drawn to the raver scene in perceptible numbers in the aftermath of Jerry Garcia's death in 1995. Many ravers and Dead Heads share an interest in mind-altering substances and communal, transformative music and dance.

The raver look that was adopted by partygoers throughout the 1990s was largely the product of contemporary mass-produced apparel, coupled with do-it-yourself and bricolage techniques through which ravers reworked existing clothes and appropriated things like toys and stuffed animals into their ensembles. Some manufacturers did step in to fill demand for things like backpacks shaped like stuffed animals, and retailers like Patricia Fields (whose target market was always cutting-edge youth culture) and record stores like Satellite Records on the Bowery did supply raver-specific apparel like oversized jeans. Some of the clothing labels that met raver demand in the 1990s were Mom and Me, Dreams, and Kikwear.

Neither the interest in electronic music nor a passion for unfettered dancing died with the dawn of the new millennium; however, rave culture and dress practices did begin to change within the closing years of the 1990s. As clubs, promoters, and record labels began to recognize the economic power of the electronic-music scene, raves became increasingly organized, commercial, and regulated. Circuit parties and electronic-music festivals including Electric Daisy Festival, the Ultra Music Festival, and the Global Dance Festival developed as sites where rave culture was transformed and dress practices evolved. Contemporary EDM-festival dress, especially for women, continues to embody influences from the 1990s, including the use of rainbow colors, neon hues, body paint, colorful hair, and glitter. However, EDM-festival dress also shows influences from Coachella festival dress in that bikini tops and bottoms function as street apparel, flower crowns (made of plastic neon flowers) are popular, and mainstream standards of sex appeal are exploited. EDM-festival dress may also owe some of its aesthetics, in particular the use of neon-hued faux-fur boots and leg warmers, to influences derived from Burning Man. Thus EDM dress does have some interesting stylistic attributes; however, photographic imagery shows incredible homogeneity across participants as well as a celebration of the mainstream beauty ideal, factors that did not impact raver dress of the 1990s in such a pronounced manner.

Media outlets in the late 1990s and early 2000s were instrumental in communicating rave culture. Websites like ravedata.com and raves.com helped to promote parties and communicate information about DJs and recordings of interest. Rave flyers were interesting works of art in their own right. Postcards, often of high-quality printing, sometimes incorporated psychedelic influences but were perhaps most memorable for drawing on the Pop Art tradition by manipulating corporate logos to comic effect. For example, the MasterCard name and logo could be morphed into a graphic reading MasterRave, or the iconic Rice Krispies packaging could be modified to become Rave Krisp-E's. Designs of this kind appealed to ravers and nonravers alike and influenced the design of T-shirts and inexpensive accessories like vinyl handbags in the 1990s. Documentary films including *Better Living through Circuitry* (2000) and *Rise* (2005), as well as narrative films including *Groove* (2000), also helped to promote interest in the rave scene. The commercial success of electronic-music performers who developed through the rave scene, most notably Moby, also facilitated interest in raves while mainstreaming and diffusing some of the stronger subcultural tendencies.

The development of rave clubs and clubs that held rave nights, including Twilo in New York City and Megatripolis in London and San Francisco, both facilitated popular interest in raves and impacted the inherent nature of the scene by institutionalizing it. Similarly large organized events like Fantasia, held at Randall's Island in New York City, One-der in Minneapolis, and Even Further in rural Wisconsin drew ravers from across the country to a single extended party, but such large events incurred increased regulation and corporate influence. By the late 1990s some raves were nationally advertised events that sold tickets in the thousands. Such events caused concern among local politicians and monitoring by the police. This was true of the ill-fated Waterfront Electronic Music Fest that was scheduled to be held in Brooklyn but was canceled by the mayor of New York City just days before the party was set to start (Blair 1999).

Although the popularity of electronic music and rave parties increased as the 1990s progressed, so too did mainstream animosity to their subcultural activities. In fact, parental consternation over the rave scene was evident in mass media from the early 1990s. For example, a *Newsweek* article from 1992 described a rave as a surreal event that evoked "nightmare symbolism of the worst kind" and described one partygoer in terms of the Mad Hatter "flailing around frantically and gorging on lollipops," and another raver was compared to a Dr. Seuss character "sucking on a balloon and churning his pelvis" (Zerman and Crandall 1992). Rave-related deaths, which were typically related to illegal drug use, were publicized and politicized in ways that truly demonized the scene and gave it true subcultural cachet of a kind not typically attached to a mere social or nightlife scene. Augmenting the notion that raves were more than parties, Benoit Denizet-Lewis, writing for *The Advocate,* noted that raves of the 1990s were "a subculture that border[ed] on a full-fledged social movement." Denizet-Lewis pointed to the fact that raves provided safe spaces for young gay and lesbian men and women to express their sexualities, and he suggested that the raver mantra of PLUR had real substance early in the evolution of the scene. Furthermore, there were many ways in which raves embodied themes that were culturally relevant in the 1990s. The accelerated pace of life was reflected in the manic dancing, the impact of new technologies was reflected in the techno music, and the artificiality of the colors, textiles, and synthetic drugs reflected wider sociocultural shifts. Raves provided a space to be part of a collective and to be anonymous within the pulsating spectacle, themes that were becoming socially relevant with the advent of the Internet.

By the late 1990s electronic music had become ubiquitous background noise in national commercials, a sort of "aural wallpaper" (Reynolds 1999). Claims to creating peace, love, harmony, and enlightenment had fallen by the wayside, and the rave scene changed as times changed and innovators of the subculture aged out of it. Neil Strauss, writing for *The New York Times* in 1996, made an apt comparison when he noted, "The rave scene, like the Deadhead scene is turning into an autonomous, self-referential and self-perpetuating culture with little desire to effect change on the outside world, just to escape it for a little while." Thus, while the vestiges of rave live on in EDM festivals and parties that are referred to as raves, a wide gulf of difference exists between the modern incarnation and the social scene that existed at the end of the 20th century.

Further Reading

Blair, J. 1999. "New York City Cancels a Music Event, and Some See a Link to Woodstock." *The New York Times,* July 31. Retrieved October 3, 2016, from www.nytimes.com.

Denizet-Lewis, B. 2000. "Riding the Rave Scene." *Advocate* (802/803): 60.

Farley, C. J. 2000. "Rave New World." *Time* 155 (23): 70.

Gegax, T. T. 1994. "Cyber-Tribal Trance-Dance." *Newsweek* 124 (10): 74.

Gordon, M. 1998. "It's Fitted Skater vs Baggy Raver." *The New York Times,* January 1. Retrieved October 3, 2016, from www.nytimes.com.

Holden, S. 2000. "The Synergy! The Ecstasy! The Biology!" *The New York Times.* Retrieved October 3, 2016, from www.nytimes.com.

Hutson, S. R. 1999. "Technoshamanism: Spiritual Healing in the Rave Subculture." *Popular Music & Society* 23 (3): 53–77.

Israel, B. 1993. "Rave at Close of Day? You Betcha." *The New York Times,* May 9. Retrieved October 3, 2016, from www.nytimes.com.

Kourlas, G. 1995. "'Hello Kitty' the Club Cat." *The New York Times,* July 23. Retrieved October 3, 2016, from www.nytimes.com.

Pareles, J. 1993. "Sensory Overload on the Dance Floor." *The New York Times,* November 1. Retrieved October 3, 2016, from www.nytimes.com.

Reynolds, S. 1999. "Electronica Goes Straight to Ubiquity." *The New York Times,* June 6. Retrieved October 3, 2016, from www.nytimes.com.

Samuels, S. 2000. "They Also Dance Who Party the Night Away." *The New York Times,* August 20. Retrieved October 3, 2016, from www.nytimes.com.

Strauss, N. 1996. "All-Night Parties and a Nod to the 60's (Rave on)." *The New York Times,* May 28. Retrieved October 3, 2016, from www.nytimes.com.

Zeman, N., and R. Crandall. 1992. "Through the Looking Glass." *Newsweek* 119 (17): 54.

Rockabilly (1970s–Present)

The word "rockabilly" is a portmanteau of the words "rock" and "hillbilly." The term was first used by the press in the late 1950s to refer to the nascent rock and roll music scene, which incorporated elements of rhythm and blues, bluegrass, western swing, boogie woogie, and country music (then frequently referred to as hillbilly music) into its sound. Many music aficionados regard the July 5, 1954, Elvis Presley recording of "That's All Right" as the genesis of the genre, though it is often remarked that the term was seldom used by insiders to the scene (Dregni 2011, 10). Although the term was popularized by the 1957 song "Rock-a-Billy," the term "rock and roll" was more typically used in its stead. Thus rockabilly sartorial style refers to the style of dress worn by early musicians working in this genre, musicians who were predominantly men. This manner of dressing was copied and interpreted by some young men of the 1950s, and there is evidence that the look had international appeal. However, the "British Invasion" and the designer-driven and very commercial modern ("mod") London Look of the middle 1960s soon outmoded rockabilly music and sartorial practices, both of which evolved as the youth music scene absorbed diverse and internationally inspired influences. However, in the latter half of the 1970s and into the 1980s, a revival of the rockabilly sound and an interpretation of its attendant look were both audible and visible in international popular music, and the revived interest in turn contributed to a long-lived revival and reinterpretation of mid-20th-century dress practices that continues into the 21st century in a dramatically altered form. The original rockabilly look borrows most strongly from the sartorial practices of the zoot suiters of the 1930s and 1940s; however, revivalist interpretations of rockabilly also draw from the dress practices of greasers and bobby soxers, while also interpreting the visual language of World War II pin-up girls. Thus what is contemporarily referred to as rockabilly style also addresses women's sartorial practices and may perhaps more accurately be labeled as a nostalgic midcentury revival style.

Rockabilly music was popularized in the 1950s by artists including Bill Haley, Buddy Holly, Jerry Lee Lewis, Carl Perkins, and perhaps most importantly by Elvis Presley, whose daring sense of style was truly revolutionary. All of these artists embodied dress practices that drew from disparate sources including evening formal wear and country and western casual clothes, but Presley undeniably pushed the sartorial envelope the furthest by selecting clothes that were made in vibrant colors and lustrous fabrics and often had a snug fit; many of these clothes, it must be noted, were designed and made with African American males as the target consumer demographic.

The original rockabilly look, which was most vividly represented by male rockabilly musicians, had little impact on women's dress practices. There were few female rockabilly performers, and those who did exist do not seem to have made major sartorial statements. Although girls of the 1950s, including the bobby sox-ers, did sometimes crossdress, no record has been uncovered that shows females of the 1950s dressing like a male rocker. The rockabilly look was defined in part by the bold use of color. Jackets, pants, shirts, and socks were made in vibrant hues and shiny fabrics. Pants were often worn baggy through the leg and tapered or pegged at the cuff, a stylistic attribute found in the pants worn by zooties, though the proportions were far less extreme in the 1950s. Tuxedo pants, which typically include a satin stripe down the side seam, were sometimes made so that the stripe contrasted with the base fabric. Tuxedo jackets were also worn, although every color seems to have been more prevalent than the traditional black. Written records indicate tuxedo-style jackets were made in colors including bright red, sapphire blue, pastel pink, and canary yellow. Lustrous fabrics would have heightened the visual impact of these colors. Western shirt-jacks (jackets cut like shirts that fasten in the front with a zipper, pearl-effect snaps, or buttons) were also popular and generally featured contrasting colors in the yoke and the body of the garment. Patterned and colorful shirts were often worn partially unbuttoned with the collar popped and the undershirt exposed, although skinny neckties and bow ties were also worn. Two-tone shoes in colorful hues completed the ensemble, while daring hairstyles completed the look. Long sideburns were often worn in conjunction with hair left long on the top of the head and upswept with Brylcream, Vaseline, or hair oil. Common names for these radical styles included the Pompadour and the D.A. (code for "duck ass," a reference to the similarity between the hairstyle and the wedge-shaped appearance of a duck's tail feathers). These hairstyles were not wholly original as they mimicked the conked hairstyles worn by African American men who processed their hair with lye and then styled it with pomade, and were also a stylistic feature that was adopted by the greasers.

The rockabilly look could be acquired in the 1950s in part through specialty retailers but also through the work of custom tailors. Evidence suggests that color-ful suits were best sourced by retailers and tailors who catered to the African American community. Perhaps the most noteworthy provider of this kind of ap-parel was Lansky Brothers in Memphis, Tennessee, a shop that was famously patronized by Elvis Presley, who stood out as a white client. Sigrid Arnott noted of the Lansky Brothers store that the owners "hand-picked and later hand-tailored the sharpest fashions to attract an African-American clientele that wanted to look hot on a Saturday night" (2011, 34). It must be highlighted that purchas-ing "sharp" black fashions in racially segregated Memphis in the 1950s was a very radical sartorial move that undoubtedly raised eyebrows in the day. In addi-tion to providers of sharp, fashionable apparel, stores that catered to agricultural workers and cowhands would have also readily supplied items like shirt-jacks, while undershirts and socks could have been purchased from a wide variety of retailers.

Although the rockabilly look was fairly short-lived in its first incarnation, there is evidence that the look spread as far as Japan. Masaki Hirao was a Japanese singer who mimicked Elvis's dress, dance, and vocals so effectively that crowds of screaming and swooning Japanese teens flocked to his performances. He was described in a 1958 article that appeared in *The New York Times* as wearing a "poodle haircut," a bright red shirt, a pastel-pink jacket, skin-tight pegged brown pants, and canary-yellow suede Oxford-style shoes. American popular culture in general was widely copied and adapted throughout Europe in the postwar period, and Ted Polhemus has noted that the rockabilly style was interpreted in the U.S.S.R. by stylish youths referred to as *styilyagi* (1994, 55).

By the early 1960s, rockabilly music and style had become largely outmoded in mainstream circles, replaced by commercial, popular music that was performed by clean-cut, sweater-wearing crooners like Frankie Avalon, Fabian, and Bobby Darin. However, a revival of rockabilly music and style was in evidence by the latter half of the 1970s and has remained a musical and sartorial presence since then. Numerous rockabilly bands experienced success and acclaim from the late 1970s into the early 1980s. The most famous rockabilly band of this period was the Stray Cats, fronted by Brian Setzer. Other rockabilly bands included the Rockats, the Blue Cats, and the Polc Cats. Critics of the rockabilly revival have noted that neither the sound nor the look is genuine. Writing for *The New York Times* in the early 1980s, Robert Palmer referred to these musical acts as "cartoon rockabillies," and while Palmer took issue with both the look and the sound, perhaps the exaggerated mode of dress deserved this label. The more-modern iterations of rockabilly style often include heightened interpretations of 1950s dress practices. Colors are brighter, fabrics are shinier (and may include sequins for men), and pompadours and D.A.s tower precariously above men's heads. Additionally, modern rockabilly broadly interprets and incorporates 1950s visual references derived from motorcyclists and greasers. Elements include dark blue jeans with the cuffs turned up, black leather motorcycle jackets and boots, and Converse high-top canvas sneakers. Thus the reinterpretation of men's rockabilly is in actuality a broad-based 1950s revival.

In the late-20th-century and contemporary parlance, the term "rockabilly" is applied to a women's style of dress. However, close inspection of the ensembles reveals that they are in actuality an amalgam of visual references derived from roughly World War II through the 1950s. Some of the sartorial gestures are derived from World War II–era pin-up girls. Items like halter tops, high-waisted shorts, hosiery held up with garter belts, bright red lipstick, and hair styled into perfect, cylindrical curls (often called victory rolls or banana rolls) are worn to recreate a mid-century bombshell effect. Additionally, the visual language of the WPA (Works Progress Administration) is sometimes co-opted, with women adopting items like denim work shirts and bandanas over their hair to recall war-era factory workers like "Rosie the Riveter." Alternatively, women engaged in the rockabilly scene also recreate the bobby soxer in her tight sweater, ankle socks, Oxford or saddle shoes, poodle skirt or peddle pushers, with her hair styled into a ponytail. Visual references from both of these archetypes are sometimes mixed together, while women dressing in the rockabilly style may also adopt elements of men's apparel, including black leather motorcycle jackets.

Further complicating the categorization of rockabilly revival styles is the fact that they may also show visual evidence of elements of punk and new wave dress practices. Thus some recent interpretations of rockabilly are true hybrids. Since the latter part of the 1980s some people have identified subsets of rockabilly style such as punkabilly, thrashabilly, and gothabilly, which borrow from punk, heavy metal, and Goth, respectively.

The revival and development of rockabilly dress styles has much to do with the revival and reinterpretation of the sound. This in turn is related to the launch of record labels like Rock-a-Billy Record Company and Rollin' Rock Records, which are devoted to the sound. Concurrent with the release of records and the proliferation of bands has been the development of festivals such as the Viva Las Vegas event, the Rockabilly Festival held in Memphis, Tennessee, and the Rockabilly Ball held in Seattle, Washington. Many of these events incorporate classic car rallies, furthering the connection to the 1950s. Magazines including *Blue Suede News* and *Grindstone Magazine* (now defunct) have also been instrumental in spreading rockabilly music, culture, and dress practices.

Nostalgia for the 1950s and revivals and reenactments of the era have potentially normalized the sartorial impact of the rockabilly look. However, it is important to note that the original rockabilly aesthetic was initially perceived as a collection of strange and shocking juxtapositions worn by wild youths performing an unorthodox new style of music. The look transgressed widely recognized boundaries of gendered dress (largely through the use of color and print), while it also appropriated and paid homage to African American "cats"—men who were both undeniably cool and unabashedly sexy. Elvis, who was named the "worst dressed man on television" in 1957 (Arnott 2011, 36), emanated the "working class rebel," which in the 1950s had the ability to push "sex into the nation's consciousness" (Rockwell 1977). Additionally, rockabilly style repositioned iconic rural American dress practices, that had theretofore not really been considered hip or fashionable, into the realm of hip street style. Sigrid Arnott summed it up succinctly when she described this kind of rockabilly cool: "Elvis was a white boy wearing black cat clothes in women's colors with eye makeup and hick sideburns"

(2011, 36). The combination of these elements in conjunction with all the hip wiggling, the foot stomping, and the hard-driving rock and roll music created a perfect storm of rebelliousness on par with the punk rockers who followed in his footsteps roughly 20 years later.

Reinterpretations of 1950s dress practices are ubiquitous in both high-style and mass-market fashions in the 21st century; however, periodically there are runway presentations that specifically recall elements of rockabilly. For example, the Versace Spring and Summer 2011 menswear collection included strong visual references to rockabilly apparel and hairstyling. There are also a substantial number of retailers who specifically cater to individuals wishing to dress in a mode that recalls the 1950s. Online retailers like Rebel Circus, Atomic Cherry, and Pinup Girl Clothing offer items like halter-top dresses with circle skirts, high-waisted shorts and pants, and skin-tight pedal pushers. Many elements of the rockabilly look are wardrobe staples in the 21st century; motorcycle jackets and blue jeans exude the rockabilly aesthetic only when styled in specific combinations, thus individuals seeking out this look may also rely on mainstream retailers for many of their apparel purchases.

In the 1950s rockabilly or rock and roll was an emerging, revolutionary, iconoclastic genre of music, and both the individuals who performed it and the teenagers who reveled in its fresh, riotous, liberating rhythms sought ways to express their identification with this new youth culture. Adopting a sartorial style that broke with accepted conventions, codes, and barriers in American culture was a meaningful expression of the spirit of this scene. The fact that punks, metal heads, and Goths have adopted and interpreted the look speaks to the essence of rebelliousness that is still perceptible in rockabilly despite the fact that over time the look has been intermixed with a variety of mainstream influences from the 1950s. Individuals who adopt the rockabilly look today may do so out of nostalgia for the 1950s or because they wish to channel the rebelliousness of an early rocker or the brazen sexuality of a mid-century pin-up girl. Dressing up to go to a vintage car show or a performance of classic rock and roll also enables individuals to get into the spirit of an event. However, the adoption of this retro style may also be read as symptomatic of the widespread reliance on sampling, reworking, and reinvention of historical dress practices, a phenomenon that calls into question how, where, and why the next great, rebellious, revolutionary American subcultural style will emerge.

Further Reading

Arnott, S. 2011. "Cat Clothes." In *Rockabilly: The Twang Heard Round the World,* edited by M. Dregni, 32–37. Minneapolis: Voyageur Press.

Burgess, S. 2011. "Foreword." In *Rockabilly: The Twang Heard Round the World,* edited by M. Dregni, 13–14. Minneapolis: Voyageur Press.

Dregni, M., ed. 2011. *Rockabilly: The Twang Heard Round the World.* Minneapolis: Voyageur Press.

Neumaier, J. 1998. "Happy Days: Greasers, Sock Hops, Poodle Skirts—Those Were the Days." *Entertainment Weekly,* 132. Retrieved June 11, 2016, from http://search.ebscohost.com/login.aspx?direct=true&db=rch&AN=54516217&scope=site.

Palmer, R. 1981. "The Pop Life: Rockabilly, a Genre That Has Found Chic." *The New York Times,* June 3. Retrieved September 5, 2016, from www.nytimes.com.

Polhemus, T. 1994. *Streetstyle: From Sidewalk to Catwalk.* London: Thames and Hudson.

"A Presley of Its Own." 1958. *The New York Times,* April 20. Retrieved September 4, 2016, from www.timesmachine.nytimes.com.

Rockwell, J. 1977. "Presley Gave Rock Its Style: He Didn't Invent Form, but Did Bestow Image." *The New York Times,* August 17. Retrieved September 5, 2016, from www.nytimes.com.

Skateboarding (Mid-1970s–Present)

The first skateboards were recreational toys made in the late 1950s and originally consisted of homemade wooden planks with metal roller skate wheels attached, though by 1959 companies such as Roller Derby were making and selling skateboards. The first wave of widespread adoption of skateboarding came in the middle of the 1960s when surfboard companies like Hobie and skateboard specialists like Skate Gun began to mass-produce boards, but by 1967 the fascination with this form of skating plummeted. Interest was renewed again in about 1973, but the sport faded from popularity once again in the early part of the 1980s. A third renaissance of skateboarding culture began in about 1995 when ESPN launched the Extreme Games (which became the X Games). This final wave of enthusiasm has largely remained unabated. Each wave of skate culture has a distinct style, which will be discussed in detail.

Skateboard culture was initially a subculture born of southern California surf culture. Surf towns like San Diego and Los Angeles had large surfing communities situated within an urban milieu. In areas like Venice Beach, Santa Monica, and Long Beach, urban developments push right up to the coastline, and miles of sidewalks, boardwalks, as well as countless staircases and berms, abut the beachfront. This unique urban landscape provided the perfect topography for the development of a surf-like activity that could be done when the waves were not favorable. Skateboarding, which was originally referred to as sidewalk surfing, was somewhat limited in the 1960s by the technology of the boards, which were made with clay or metal wheels that were mounted to devices that limited the ability to turn and pivot. Despite these limitations, by the middle of the 1960s the sport of skateboarding had enough cultural traction to spawn a small industry of board manufacturers including Makaha, Surf Skater, and Bun Buster and enough enthusiasts, many of whom were accomplished surfers, to merit an international competition in Anaheim, California (Newell 1965, 87). In that early meet both men and women competed in events such as flatland and downhill slalom and the "figure eight." There was also a "tricks" category that included moves like the "coffin" (a pose that involved the skater laying prone on his or her back), drop knee turns, tandem riding, and hanging five and ten.

The sartorial style that was associated with early skateboarding is closely related to surfing. Early photographs show boys and girls wearing shorts or swim trunks coupled with a T-shirt that could be screened with the name of a surf shop or brand. Boys often skateboarded bare-chested. Button-up shirts with Hawaiian or Tahitian prints were also worn, sometimes with jeans. Many early pictures show skateboarders riding barefoot, but thin-soled tennis shoes such as Keds were also worn. The style associated with skateboarding in the 1960s is not especially distinct. It was a street style related to practicality that utilized existing pieces of apparel. In the 1960s there were only limited commercial products produced for skateboarders. Skateboards were largely available through mail order or at surf shops, and mail order offers did not include apparel options. The widespread popularity of skateboarding in the 1960s was fairly short-lived, and the limited possibilities that the board allowed undoubtedly led to the demise in popularity of the activity. Thus the style associated with skateboarding did not have time to develop. Furthermore, it seems that skating was largely recreational, not yet subcultural, in the 1960s and, therefore, did not necessitate the development of a distinct visual identity.

In the final years of the 1960s it was virtually impossible to buy a new skateboard; however, despite the crash of the fad, development of skateboard technology continued (thanks in part to the sustained interest in roller skating), and in 1972 urethane wheels were introduced along with specialized trucks (the wheel mounts) that facilitated mobility and agility for the rider. By mid-decade decks made of fiberglass and polyurethane were available along with wooden decks, and shapes and sizes became more varied. In the early 1970s competitive groups including the Zephyr Skateboarding Team (featuring Tony Alva, Stacy Peralta, and Jay Adams) were formed, which pushed techniques and tricks to new levels at meets, including the pivotal competition at Del Mar, California, in 1975. In the wake of that meet, skateboarding exploded in popularity and became more professional, and a commodity culture emerged in the wake of this newfound enthusiasm. In addition, the sport itself became infinitely more dynamic in the latter half of the 1970s as vertical moves were developed and aerial tricks were perfected. A drought that plagued southern California in the latter half of the 1970s meant that swimming pools could not be filled, and both public and private pools were left empty. Skateboarders, realizing the potential of this newly available urban topography, began to skate the basins and gradually developed tricks that allowed them to fly over the lip of the pool. Massive pipes, built to carry water to arid parts of the Southwest, including Arizona, were also co-opted by self-proclaimed "skate rats" who stole onto private property in hopes of catching air and who guarded the stellar spots like a surfer guards a newfound break (Barbish 1979, 27). In the middle of the 1970s skate parks were built across the United States, a phenomenon that both developed the sport and increased the importance of personal appearance while participating.

As the new, more physical style of skating developed, so too did the gear and apparel worn by skaters. A *Time* magazine article from 1975 noted that new boards (and by extension new techniques) "have fueled a satellite industry manufacturing accessories," including T-shirts, shoes, and bathing suits (Wheel Crazy). Kneepads, wrist guards, and helmets became a new part of the skateboarder look in the latter half of the 1970s. First acquired from hockey outfitters like Cooper, by the end of the decade manufacturers were catering to the safety needs of the skate scene and branding items with their logos. Shorts were still a key feature of skate style, and swim trunks and board shorts were still worn. However, specialty skate shorts, with hidden compartments for padding, were also made by companies such as High Rider. Vans "Off the Wall" shoes became a staple of skate apparel (they were worn by the Zephyr skate team), and the company also forayed into the realm of protective gear, offering ankle guards with Vans branding in 1978. Skateboard manufacturers also entered the apparel marketplace. Hobie sold a leather high-top sneaker in addition to a variety of shirts. *Skateboarder* magazine diversified their apparel offerings as the decade progressed, moving from an array of T-shirt styles to offerings that included high knee socks, shorts, and headbands. Skateboard stars also began to enter the commercial marketplace in the 1970s. Tony Alva sold both decks and apparel that featured his name in a stylized typeface. Notably, skateboard specialty apparel was retailed largely through surf shops and through mail order, as the style was largely adopted by individuals who actually skated. Skateboard jewelry was sometimes listed as an item available through mail order in the 1970s, though it is not clear exactly what kind of jewelry was available. Skateboard magazines also indicate that there were a handful of specialty boutiques that catered to skateboarders. For example, the 360° boutique in San Diego advertised sportswear as well as skate gear targeted to the skate scene.

Much was done to popularize and mainstream skateboarding in the 1970s. The United States Skateboarding Association was founded in 1975, and the International Skateboard Association followed in 1976. Mainstream media, including the film

Freewheelin' (1976) and the airing of the World Professional Skateboard Championships on ABC's (American Broadcast Corporation) *Wide World of Sports* program in 1977 also helped to spread the sport. However, despite the appearance of mainstream popularity, it is clear from the accounts of notable skaters who lived this scene that skateboarding was perceived as subcultural (surfing in the 1970s was also viewed as a fringe scene). It was a sport that was embraced in large numbers by self-proclaimed misfits. Kids with broken homes and kids who didn't fit in were often the ones who practiced for hours in illegally co-opted pools. Skate rats were outsiders who created a specialized "reject culture" (Mortimer 2008, 11). This fact reinforces the idea that skateboarder style was initially largely the domain of actual skateboarders.

By 1982 skateboarding had again lost some of its mainstream popularity. Skateboarding parks closed, and meets were often held on homemade backyard ramps. *Skateboarder* magazine ceased publication. As a result, skate culture contracted into an underground network of sorts. Stacy Peralta, who in 1979 had formed the skateboarding team the Bones Brigade with a new generation of misfit heroes including Tony Hawk, Steve Caballero, Lance Mountain, and Rodney Mullen, was an influential force who nurtured the skateboarding subculture. Powell Peralta, a maker of skateboards since the late 1970s, continued to produce boards in the 1980s but altered its approach to advertising. Under the art direction of Craig Stecyk, advertisements became more about the skate rat attitude and the personalities of Bones Brigade members. Thus while Powell Peralta aimed to sell boards, they also sold a lifestyle through their quirky, offbeat advertisements that spoke to the countercultural cool of skating. Skateboarding videos, many of them made under the direction of Stacy Peralta, also helped to perpetuate a subculture of skateboarding. Movies such as the *Bones Brigade Video Show* (1984), *Bones Brigade Search for Animal Chin* (1987), and *Gleaming the Cube* (1989) showed freestyle street-skating, which made the sport more accessible and promoted an aura of independence and free-spiritedness. Skateboarding videos were generally viewed on newly available home entertainment systems that included VCRs (video cassette recorders). Home viewing, rather than auditorium screenings, further helped to promote skateboarding as a subcultural practice rather than a mainstream sport.

The independent spirit associated with skateboarding in the 1980s is likely a factor that contributed to the diversification of skateboarding street style. There are two genres of 1980s skate style: style derived from surf culture, and style derived from the California punk-rock scene. The 1980s surf-inspired skate style continued the tradition of wearing graphic T-shirts with both surf and skate logos, but the proliferation of brand names and ostentatious logos was markedly increased, with companies like Pacific Sunwear and Ocean Pacific being highly visible examples. New skateboard magazines such as *Thrasher* also created branded apparel that was widely worn. Board shorts continued to be worn with high knee socks and protective gear by skaters who performed vertical tricks, but street-style skaters were often inclined to wear long pants and forgo much of the padding. Colorful Converse sneakers became a mainstay alongside Vans, which developed a slip on style that was popular in a checkerboard pattern. Painter hats briefly replaced baseball caps, and bold graphic patterns and vibrant colors, which were trending in mainstream fashion throughout much of the decade, were desirable in the skateboarding scene as well.

Skate punk was a distinct genre of skateboarding style in the 1980s. Skateboarders who listened to punk music, including artists coming out of suburban California such as the Germs and Black Flag, influenced skaters to adopt a hard-rock edge that was personified in part by professional skateboarder Christian Hosoi. Skate punks often wore T-shirts that promoted punk bands. In general, the punk-inspired look eschewed most color and trendy patterns. Apparel with Asian-inspired graphics including Chinese characters and Japanese rising-sun imagery were partially inspired by Hosoi, whose branding utilized those tropes, but were also related to a widespread fashion fad that was visible in mainstream apparel at mid-decade. Skate punks adopted graffiti graphics and could be seen wearing motorcycle jackets to a skating location, though heavy, restrictive leather is generally not conducive to skating.

Beginning in the late 1980s a new skate style emerged that included oversized T-shirts, baggy shorts or low-slung baggy jeans, hooded sweatshirts, high-top sneakers, visible boxer shorts, and backward baseball caps—a style that was markedly similar to contemporary urban hip-hop style and that communicated an updated version of the outsider status that both traditional surf and punk styles were losing as they were gradually mainstreamed. In the 1990s differences between vertical and street style skaters continued; however, individuals who wore the style as street wear did not generally discriminate. In the 1990s many brands were launched to cater to the growing popularity of the skate scene including Stussy, Raw Vibes, Stoopid, Supreme, and Fuct. Surf brands such as Billabong and Quicksilver catered to the skate scene by making collections of clothes in dark colors, as opposed to the higher-key hues that were more typical in surf apparel (Cocks 1988). The overall presentation of a skateboarder in the 1990s was crafted to present an "outsider" or "doomsday" aesthetic; however, by this period it was also clear that a sort of "uniform" had developed, which led *Vogue* writer Ralph Rugoff to note that the $300 million industry might "already be suffering the fate of punk: it's being institutionalized and marketed for a mass audience" (1992, 212).

A mass audience for skateboarding was being vigorously developed by the middle of the 1990s through a great array of promotional events, many of which were (and still are) annual, such as the X Games, the Vans Triple Crown Series, the MTV

Sports and Music Festival, and the NBC Gravity Games. In September 1998 *Details* magazine hosted a "field day" in New York City that featured "extreme" skateboarding demonstrations and promotions by mainstream companies like Foot Locker, Macy's, Perry Ellis, and Union Bay. The event was an effort to connect brands with the lifestyle of skateboarding and forge a connection between sport and fashion. Furthermore, apparel brands were launched in the 1990s that channeled the skateboarder lifestyle into fashionable apparel. Fresh Jive (founded by Rick Klotz) was an early example of a fashion-apparel brand that was modeled on skate style but designed for the street. In the 1990s some long-lived skate brands also sought to expand their markets. For example, Vans shoes, long favored by skateboarders, spent $25 million on marketing its "Team Vans" in 1997 as part of an effort to "mainstream" their brand for consumers who were "merely interested in the sports lifestyle look" (Jensen 1997). Skateboarding stars also entered the apparel industry in large numbers and for large dollars in the 1990s. For example, Steve Caballaro began collaborating with Vans for shoes that bear his name in the early 1990s, and in 1998 Tony Hawk inked a $120,000 shoe-endorsement deal with Adio.

By the early 2000s skateboarding style was an incredibly commercial street style that was a highly lucrative portion of the apparel market. Dozens of brands have launched internationally in the first decades of the new millennium, offering skate-inspired styles that echo larger trends in fashion. Skateboarder style in the new millennium often samples from both hip-hop and hipster aesthetics. Graphics and branding continue to develop as important markers of skate style. Jeans and cargo pants are worn more fitted than they were in the 1990s. Flannel shirts, knit caps, and camouflage textiles are among the trending items that have been incorporated into skateboarding style. Notably, the line between skateboarder apparel for skaters and followers of the lifestyle has become increasingly blurred in the first decades of the new millennium. Justin Porter, writing for *The New York Times* in 2008, commented that most sports equipment prioritizes function over fashion, but in the sport of skate, that is not always true. Porter spoke with professional skater Mike Vallely who suggested that a skateboarder's performance is related to his appearance and noted that a skater's important connection with his feet was augmented by good-looking shoes. Vallely stated, "I think skateboarding is more fashion than function. It's more aesthetic than anything else. It's more rock 'n' roll than athletics." Skate continues to develop as a lifestyle category, with famous skateboarders endorsing a wide range of products including video games, movies, books, toys, and food (Layden 2002).

Skateboarding style, both on and off the board, is an important part of 21st-century fashion. Its aesthetics and brands are promoted through skateboard magazines including *Thrasher, Transworld Skateboarding, Concrete Wave,* and *Skateboarder*. Both narrative films like *Grind* (2003) and documentaries such as

Dogtown and Z-Boys (2001) and *Bones Brigade: An Autobiography* (2012) are also influential vehicles for communicating skateboarder style and culture.

In addition to the numerous surf and skate brands that produce collections that facilitate the skateboarder look, high-style collections also periodically interpret the style. This was a pronounced phenomenon in the wake of the first X Games in 1995 when Donna Karan, Ralph Lauren, and Tommy Hilfiger all showed collections inspired by snowboarding and skateboarding. High-tech nylon, neoprene, and mesh were among the fabrics that were featured to create an extreme-sport aesthetic. Given the size of the skateboarding industry today, it seems unlikely that a quick collapse in the popularity of the sport and its style will happen again as it did in the 1960s. Skateboarder style continues to be important in the new millennium. It is an evolving style worn by practitioners of the sport, and it is also a highly visible street style worn by people who appreciate the athleticism of the sport and identify with the lifestyle.

Further Reading

Barbish, R. 1979. "Secret Pipes." *Breakout Magazine* 1 (3): 26–27.

Black, K. 1996. "Xtreme Prejudice." *Rolling Stone* (742): 52.

Cocks, J. 1988. "The Irresistible Lure of Grabbing Air." *Time* 13 (1): 90–91.

Fitzgerald, K. 1998. "'Details' in the Field: Men's Magazine Links Lifestyle with Sports via Fall Activities." *Advertising Age* 69 (37): 54.

Greenfeld, K. T. 1999. "Killer Profits in Velcro Valley." *Time* 153 (3): 50.

"Here Come the Sidewalk Surfers." 1964. *Life,* June 5. Retrieved February 28, 2016, from books.google.com.

Jacobs, A., and D. Pener. 1996. "Extreme Cool." *Entertainment Weekly* (333/224): 64.

Jensen, J. 1997. "Vans Readies $25 Mil Brand Blitz." *Advertising Age* 68 (9): 30.

Layden, T. 2002. "Making Millions." *Sports Illustrated* 96 (24): 80.

Mortimer, S. 2008. *Stalefish: Skateboard Culture from the Rejects Who Made It.* San Francisco: Chronicle Books.

Newell, S. 1965. "Surfing Stars Dominate the International Skateboard Championship." *Surfer* 6 (4): 87.

Rugoff, R. 1992. "Vogue's View: Get Big!" *Vogue* 182: 191, 194, 207, 212. Retrieved February 22, 2016, from http://search.proquest.com/docview/911902712?accountid=130772.

"Wheel Crazy." 1975. *Time* 106 (17): 60.

Skinhead (Late 1970s–Present)

Skinhead street and subcultural style is a manner of dress that is characterized in part by a shaved or buzzed hairstyle, the feature that gives this sartorial style its name.

The skinhead mode of dress developed in the United States in the late 1970s and is largely derived from a street style that was first seen in Great Britain in the late 1960s. In Great Britain the look first emerged out of the social milieu of disenfranchised youths in a variety of subcultural groups including the "hard mod" scene, a subcultural group called the Teddy Boys, the rocker scene, and the Jamaican "rude boys." Skinheads were first recognizable in England circa 1967 in the East End of London where working-class youths who shaved their heads were known as spy boys, lemons, peanut boys, and crop heads prior to the adoption of the name skinhead (Ryan 1981, 5). Originally, the look, which utilizes the staples of working-class clothes, developed around the reggae and ska music scenes (which were racially mixed) but was also closely associated with football (soccer) hooliganism that included starting fights for fun (Ryan 1981, 5–6). The look, which came to be adopted by both men and women, was first seen in the United States in urban centers like New York City and Los Angeles, which had developing punk-music scenes in the late 1970s and 1980s and, therefore, had connections to British youth culture. Both skinheads and punks shared notions of disaffection, nihilism, and victimization, sentiments that unify skinheads around a music scene and sometimes provide the impetus for the formation of gangs or membership in racist organizations. Ultimately, the sartorial style spread throughout the United States in the 1980s, especially through the northwestern and southeastern parts of the country. In the United States the skinhead dress style is strongly associated with the intertwined hardcore punk scene and skateboarding scene, and many skinheads identify also as punks and/or skaters. Since the latter part of the 1980s, in both the United Kingdom and the United States, skinhead style has also become strongly associated with the neo-Nazi, white power, and white supremacy movements, but it is important to note that the style did not originate in conjunction with any hate group, and not all skinheads identify with racist ideologies. Skinheads may be categorized in four distinctive ways: racist, nonracist, separatist, and political (Haenfler 2013, 22; Wooden and Blazak 2001, 146). As with all subcultural styles, the reasons that individuals have for adopting the look are highly varied, and the degree to which any ideology affiliated with a look is adhered to by a style adopter exists on a dramatic spectrum.

The racist aspect of skinhead style must be addressed, as their ideology is represented in variations on the essential skinhead dress style. Some skinheads are organized into cohesive regional gangs and belong to national organizations that are related to racial segregation and violence against racial minorities. The first indications that skinhead subculture was being shaped by hate groups were apparent in both the United States and the United Kingdom around the same time, during the administrations of Ronald Reagan (1981–1989) and Margaret Thatcher (1979–1990). Criminologist Mark Hamm assessed the historical context: "In sum, the social and political contentions of the Reagan era seemed to have produced conditions conducive to extreme alienation among white working class youth in the United States" (1993, 6). Sociologists Wooden and Blazak categorized the catalyst for becoming a racist skinhead as a "response to blocked opportunity" (2001, 144). Disenfranchised, angry youth were easy targets for preexisting white supremacy groups such as WAR (White Aryan Resistance), a national organization that recruited skinheads in the 1980s and purposefully targeted the skinhead population because of their social, emotional, and political characteristics (Wooden and Blazak 2001, 145). The first neo-Nazi skinhead gang in the United States was a group that called itself Romantic Violence. It formed in Chicago in 1984 (Hamm 1993, 5). The Detroit Area Skinheads (DASH) and the Chicago Area Skinheads (CASH) were two additional long-lived racist skinhead gangs (Covey 2003, 53). Dominant among organized skinhead groups is the belief that other individuals, including racial and ethnic minorities, are benefitting from the "oppression" of Caucasians (Covey 2003, 53). Not all skinhead gangs are racist. Skinheads Against Racial Prejudice (SHARP) is an antiracist group made up of racially and ethnically diverse members.

The primary hallmark of skinhead style is hair that is cut very short or shaved away entirely. Individuals with heads shaved bald are often referred to as "smooths." Smooths wear a "zero-zero cut," a reference to the setting on a barber's electric razor. Skinheads whose hair is shorn with the electric razor set above the number one, up to a number three, are sometimes referred to as "suedeheads," an indication that their skulls are covered with a short, velvety stubble. Male skinheads were traditionally clean shaven; however, contemporary men may wear an exaggerated goatee. Female skinheads traditionally wear their hair in a style called the Chelsea, which consists of hair closely cropped over the top and back of the head, but with bangs in the front and long locks over the ears. A variation of this style, called the Fringe, includes long locks that extend down the back of the neck. The origin of the closely shorn head is steeped in historical references. Nick Knight's influential 1982 book that is simply entitled *Skinhead* noted, "In Victorian times, the shaved head was the mark of the institution" (1982, 27): schoolmasters and orphanages shaved the heads of children to prevent infestations. Closely shorn hair is also the mark of working-class men whose labors preclude the maintenance of carefully styled hair. For many individuals, the adoption of a closely shorn hairstyle is elective, related to a personal choice about self-presentation, and a choice that is subject to whimsical change; however, skinheads who become associated with racist gangs may be "shaved in" to membership (Travis and Hardy 2012, 6).

The apparel of an American skinhead has its roots in the sartorial practices of British skinheads and is largely based on the apparel worn by the working class. Most any kind of apparel is acceptable for a skinhead as long as it isn't "fashion" (Knight 1982, 33). Ostentatious, obviously expensive, or trendy clothes are not typically adopted by skinheads, whose identity is grounded in outsider ideology and who, therefore, elect to wear apparel that does not conform to mainstream notions of status or style. Some of the basic components of skinhead apparel, which are worn by both men and women, have been fundamental to the look since the first British skinheads were a visible presence. Doc Marten or other combat or steel-toed boots were originally adopted for their utility in street fights; thus a scuffed toe box may be read as a symbol of toughness (Wooden and Blazak 2001, 133). Doc Marten boots are often styled with colorful contrasting shoelaces threaded horizontally through the eyelets. According to some writers, the shoelaces have a coded meaning: white indicates the wearer supports the white pride movement; red implies that the wearer supports a white power movement; yellow means the wearer is antipolice (Wooden and Blazak 2001, 133; Covey 2003, 55); and blue implies an interest in extreme violence (Travis and Hardy 2012, 2). The extent to which the color coding is used is unclear; however, the Southern Poverty Law Center, a group that tracks hate groups, notes the potential symbolism in their current literature, also suggesting that the red laces indicate that the wearer has shed blood for the movement ("Racist Skinheads"). To some skins, wearing color-coded shoelaces to send a message may be meaningful; "still other skinheads think giving such meaning to laces is a stupid myth concocted by law enforcement and media" (Haenfler 2013, 24). Images of skinheads of myriad racial and ethnic backgrounds wearing white shoelaces is also an indication that the meaning implied by color coding is not always acknowledged. Ample evidence of multiracial, multiethnic skinheads from around the world can be seen in the images that were collected and published by Estrella (see Estrella 2006; Estrella 2007).

Blue jeans, often red-tab Levis, have long been a staple of the skinhead look. Jeans are often worn with the legs rolled up over the boots "in order to show the boots' full menace" (Ryan 1981, 7). American skinheads also wear camouflage cargo pants, as well as Dickies and Ben Davis work pants (two styles that are notably favored in the cholo subculture). Skinny suspenders (measuring one-half to three-quarters inches wide are preferred). These are also derived from the original British look and may have a coded meaning. Suspenders worn hanging down may indicate the wearer is ready to fight (Wooden and Blazak 2001, 133), whereas yellow suspenders may be interpreted as an antipolice sentiment, and green may be decoded as an anti-gay communication (Covey 2003, 55). Skinheads around the world also wear shirts with the brand name Lonsdale, London. T-shirts that include imagery from the Stanley Kubrick film *A Clockwork Orange* (1971) have similarly enjoyed long-lived popularity. The most iconic jacket style is a satin flight jacket. Olive green is the most common color, but jackets of this kind are also worn in hues such as navy blue, burgundy, or black. Denim jackets are also a preferred type of outerwear.

Intermixing with the punk scene influenced the skinhead sartorial style. In some ways the groups were socioculturally similar: disaffected and known for physical abandon achieved through fist fighting and slam dancing. Punk music was a medium for communicating frustrations, and T-shirts imprinted with graphic designs that represented punk bands served as a way to communicate interests and tastes. Punk-rock band T-shirts became a common staple of the skinhead wardrobe from the latter part of the 1970s onward. Punk band shirts from groups such as the Buzzcocks, Cockney Rejects, Skrewdriver, Cock Sparrer, Black Flag, The Germs, Dead Kennedys, and Agnostic Front were worn when the bands were active and are worn currently by modern skinheads. The punk scene in general, especially in the United States, also impacted the overall aesthetic of the skinhead look. Whereas British skinheads had been meticulously neat in their dress, American skinheads incorporated elements such as ripped and graffiti-covered clothes, disheveled flannel shirts, and motorcycle jackets. The connection of skinhead style to the punk-rock scene meant that many American skins adopted the skinhead look as part of the music and fashion of the scene but did not necessarily embrace the politics and "hardcore skinhead manner" that began to evolve in the 1980s. However, as publicity surrounding the activities of racist skinheads was disseminated, it became increasingly difficult to adopt the look alone (Moore 1993, 74–75).

The difference between a racist and nonracist skinhead is most clearly demarcated through insignia. Racist skinheads wear a variety of political symbols that take the form of screened images on T-shirts, embroidered patches, and tattoos. Skinheads who elect to pay homage to the culture of Nazi Germany wear Nazi insignia including swastikas, SS lightning bolts, and the numbers "88" (code for "Heil Hitler," as H is the eighth letter of the alphabet). Some punks wore Nazi insignia in the middle of the 1970s, prior to the development of a racist skinhead subculture, but in that period it was done for shock value rather than to attest a belief in fascism. National insignia including German, British, American, and Confederate flags are also commonly worn and may have both nationalist and racist symbolic value. Celtic crosses (an allusion to white European ancestry), anarchy signs, and the numbers "666" (a reference to Satanism) are commonly occurring symbols and indicate the range of interests embraced by disaffected youths. Many of the aforementioned symbols, as well as a crucified skinhead and Celtic and Viking imagery are also commonly adopted as tattoos by racist skinheads. The laurel wreath, a symbol associated with the British brand Fred Perry (a brand favored by skinheads in the United Kingdom), is also adopted as a tattoo by skinheads around the world of varied beliefs. Inner-lip tattoos are common among skinheads and often feature racist symbols or text. Racist skinhead gangs use the tattoos and patches to mark their affiliation in the same way that motorcycle gangs use their "colors" to show membership. Skinheads who do not identify with the racist branch of the subculture may wear antifascist symbols (Haenfler 2013, 22).

Female skinheads (sometimes called "skinchicks") wear all of the aforementioned apparel and tattoos but also wear gender-specific clothes. Among the most common articles of apparel are short plaid miniskirts, fishnet stockings, and T-shirts with slogans like "Skingirls." Lip and nose piercings are far more common among skinhead females than they are among males. Skinchicks typically wear makeup, especially black eyeliner and dark-colored lipstick.

Among the items worn by British skinheads that were not adopted by Americans were Ben Sherman button-down shirts, white work or lab coats, Sta-Prest pants, apparel made of Prince of Wales check, and umbrellas with a sharpened tip (Ryan 1981, 32–34). Fred Perry sport shirts with laurel leaves were also typical for British skinheads but were not adopted in the United States. Some American skinheads wore Ralph Lauren, Lacoste, and Gant shirts as an alternative. Many of the iconic elements of British skinhead style are markedly more formal than classic American skinhead style, a phenomenon explained by the fact that early on the look was "firmly entrenched in working class values." The look was extremely tidy, and "the clothes served a dual purpose; they identified the wearer as a skinhead but also, they were clothes that could be worn to work" (Ryan 1981, 22). This latter point seems to have been largely irrelevant in the American scene where skinhead apparel seems to have been more commonly associated with leisure activities.

Although there are differences between British and American skinheads and there has been some change in the style over time, skinhead street and subcultural style is generally quite fixed. Professor J. B. Moore has noted, "Skinheads often resemble clones of some standard model. This is ironic since many skinheads avow that the course they have taken was set to protect their unique identity in a world generally populated by mindless de-individualized followers of some enemy dictatorship" (1993, 83). While the similarity of appearance among skinheads may be interpreted as clone-like behavior, it is also important to note that regimented behavior and shared visual indicators also function as ways to unite individuals, and the purchase and wearing of clothes and music that are similar to those owned and worn by one's confreres are ways of forging both individual and group identities. Purchasing symbols of belonging such as Doc Marten boots and suspenders allows skinheads to embody their beliefs and show belongingness.

Although skinheads are varied in their interests and ideology, the association between the dress style and violent white-supremacy advocates became indelibly linked in the minds of a generation of Americans beginning in the 1980s. In the late 1980s popular television talk-show hosts including Sally Jessie Raphael (June 1987), Oprah Winfrey (February 1988), and Geraldo Rivera (November 1988) had racist and antiracist skinheads as guests on their respective eponymous shows.

Many of these skinhead participants kept television censors busy as hate speech and cursing frequently ran afoul of daytime obscenity standards. In the case of Geraldo Rivera's program, incendiary speech escalated to an all-out brawl that left Rivera with a broken nose at program's end. Mainstream publicity of this kind undoubtedly negatively impacted the adoption of skinhead style by individuals who were not interested in white supremacy, as the social ramifications of visually identifying with hate groups cannot be understated.

Skinheads have decreased in numbers and in visibility in the 21st century. Crime legislation that imposed stiffer penalties for bias crimes may have led to reduced membership and visibility of skins in the 1990s (Wooden and Blazak 2001, 131). In the early 2000s many of the bands that performed music with white-supremacy themes broke up, causing the social scenes surrounding the music to evaporate (Travis and Hardy 2012, xxxii). The impact of a diminished music scene is important. "Skinhead music is thought to support a political belief system and a subcultural style that allows skinheads to display their resistance to cultural hegemony in visual terms for the general public to see: shaved heads, Nazi regalia, stormtrooper boots, and violence against blacks and other disenfranchised groups" (Hamm 1993, 116). However, organizations including the Southern Poverty Law Center do still track racist skinheads, who are estimated to number in the thousands. Individuals who dress in the skinhead manner but do not align with racist organizations can also still be seen in small numbers in hard-rock clubs and bars throughout the United States, Europe, and South America.

Skinhead style has been disseminated in a variety of ways including a myriad of punk-rock fanzines of the 1980s, the racist skinhead fanzine *Carry No Banners,* which was published from 1990 to 1992, and pamphlets published by both SHARP and WAR. A variety of specialty shops throughout the United States have also helped to perpetuate the style. Among the stores are NaNa in Santa Monica, 99X in New York City (closed), and Crash N Burn in Atlanta (closed) (Travis and Hardy 2012, xxix). Contemporary skinheads use the Internet for both communication of interests and recruitment into hate groups. Stormfront.org is the most prominent example of the latter type of skinhead web presence. Narrative films have also been influential in terms of disseminating information about skinhead dress and subculture. Films of this kind include *Skinheads* (1989), *Romper Stomper* (1992), and *American History X* (1998). The HBO documentary film *Skinheads USA: Soldiers of Race War* (1993) was also influential. The novel *American Skin* (1998) offers a vivid depiction of the skinhead lifestyle.

Skinheads are incredibly diverse in their ideology and behavior. At their worst they are drug-using sociopaths who dabble in Satanism and engage in intergang and racial violence. However, in many cases past and present skinheads are simply fans of music who have adopted a minimalist, British working-class–inspired sartorial pose. Nick Knight aptly noted, "Real skins are much less coherent than their stereotype" (1982, 33).

Further Reading

Covey, H. C. 2003. *Street Gangs throughout the World.* Springfield, IL: Charles C. Thomas Publisher, Ltd.

Estrella. 2006. *Skinhead Girls around the World* vol. 1. N.p.: Applanqued Productions.

Estrella. 2007. *Skinhead Girls around the World* vol. 2. N.p.: Applanqued Productions.

Haenfler, R. 2013. *Goths, Gamers, and Grrrls* 2nd ed. New York: Oxford University Press.

Hamm, M. S. 1993. *American Skinheads: The Criminology and Control of Hate Crime.* Westport, CT: Prager.

Knight, N. 1982. *Skinhead.* London: Omnibus Press.

Moore, J. B. 1993. *Skinheads: Shaved for Battle.* Bowling Green, OH: Bowling Green University Press.

"Racist Skinheads." n.d. Southern Poverty Law Center. Retrieved May 7, 2016, from www .splcenter.org.

Ryan, C. 1981. *Skinheads.* N.p.

"The Skinhead Fad Shows No Sign of Fading." n.d. Southern Poverty Law Center. Retrieved May 15, 2016, from www.splcenter.org.

Travis, T., and P. Hardy. 2012. *Skinheads: A Guide to an American Subculture.* Santa Barbara, CA: ABC-CLIO.

Wooden, W., and R. Blazak. 2001. *Renegade Kids, Suburban Outlaws: From Youth Culture to Delinquency* 2nd ed. Belmont, CA: Wadsworth.

Snowboarding (Late 1980s–Present)

A recreational activity resembling snowboarding has existed since the late 1960s. The Snurfer (a small surfboard with a rope attached to the nose of the deck), the Snow Skate (two polystyrene skis attached to a skateboard deck), and the SkiBoard (a skateboard deck with straps that lashed over a pair of shoes or boots) were all attempts to marry surfing, skateboarding, and skiing into one perfect snow sport, but it was not until the late 1970s when board designers like Jake Burton, Chuck Barfoot, and Tom Sims began making substantial improvements in board and bindings designs that a true sport and sporting subculture began to develop in remote, backcountry destinations on both the East and West Coasts of the United States.

Although meets and competitions began to be held in the first few years of the 1980s (an indication that the sport was garnering a substantial number of followers), photographs of the period largely reveal that early snowboarders wore existing ski apparel and other contemporary articles of clothing: traditional sweaters, snug-fitting jackets, both tight ski pants and loose snow pants, Bermuda shorts, jeans, T-shirts, wetsuits, typical hats and gloves, and Sorrel or other heavy winter boots. Early West Coast snowboarders also frequently wore skateboard-company branded apparel. In the early stages of the sport, before a unique sartorial identity had formed and before a marketplace had developed to cater to the sport's practitioners, there was little evidence of a unique snowboarding style of dress. In fact, Susanna Howe, author of *Sick: A Cultural History of Snowboarding,* noted, "Each group of back-country hikers had its own version of snowboarding shaped by local climate and terrain, equipment, and roots (e.g., skiing, skateboarding, BMX biking, mountaineering, and surfing)" (1998, 28), and each of these influences manifested itself in different parts of the country. It was only in the last years of the 1980s that a unique snowboarder dress style, worn on and off the slopes, became visible because of the increased mixing of the isolated scenes and the development of snowboarding media.

The development of snowboarding style and the development of the sport itself went hand in hand. Makers like Sims and Burton improved board designs by adding metal edges and developing both camber and side cuts to facilitate speed and agility and essentially make the boards easier to control. Improved maneuverability made the sport appealing to larger numbers of participants. Additionally, the sport itself developed to include both downhill (alpine) and freestyle (half-pipe) snowboarding, and as the improvements and developments gained traction, the sport grew. The growth of the sport ultimately led many ski resorts to allow snowboarders to use ski lifts and slopes, thereby bringing the sport out of the backcountry and eliminating the need to hike to the top of the slope to catch a ride down. Situating snowboarding within the domain of the ski resort created tensions between traditional skiers and young iconoclastic snowboarders, facilitated interaction among boarders, grew the number of participants, and resulted in the development of a more coherent and identifiable culture.

It is well documented that tensions existed between skiers and snowboarders from early on, and the dress selected by snowboarders across the first decade of the development of the sport may be read as a rejection of the more traditional sport and its followers. In the 1980s skiing was a sport that was largely practiced by upper-middle-class, middle-aged people. The costs of boots, skis, lift tickets, and resort fees meant that lower-income and younger individuals were excluded by default. Skiers generally dressed in snug-fitting, color-coordinated outfits that reflected mainstream fashion trends with regard to things like color schemes and branding. Early snowboarders, who came from diverse backgrounds and who had originally dressed for the sport by wearing whatever was available, entered the resorts as outsiders to skiing culture, and their antics on the slopes, which infuriated many skiers, pushed them further away from the established mainstream. Snowboarder style developed in the ensuing decade to mark that outsider status (see Fry 2010; Rosenberg 1998).

Increased numbers of participants in the sport of snowboarding also led to the development of the first professionals including Shaun Palmer, Damien Sanders, and Craig Kelly. Along with the rise of professional athletes came a surge in mass media in the form of magazines devoted to snowboarding, print advertisements, and some television exposure. Media exposure led to increased attention to image and style among snowboarders. In the late 1980s, the mix-and-match, antistyle elements that had been visible earlier in the decade were amped up to create a recognizable sartorial statement that expressed the oppositional relationship between snowboarders and skiers. Snowboarders eliminated traditional ski sweaters and tight ski pants from their wardrobes, opting instead for loose-fitting snow pants and boxy jackets. Beginning around 1987, surf companies began to get involved in the snowboarding-apparel marketplace, and companies like O'Neill, Body Glove, and Ocean Pacific began to make cold-weather apparel with huge logos and bold graphic patterns. The wearing of branded apparel was a notable marker of sport affiliation that aligned itself with both surfing and skateboarding, two sports that were not of the same social status as skiing in the 1980s and early 1990s. Brilliant neon hues were ubiquitous in both ski and snowboarding apparel at this time; however, snowboarders favored clashing combinations and riotous graphic patterns as opposed to primly coordinated ensembles. Snowboarders often sported piercings, tattoos, and spiky hairstyles. Perhaps most noteworthy was the wearing of colorful, outrageous hats likes those worn by ravers, jesters, and Dr. Seuss's Cat in the Hat. Snowboarder style in this period was also a matter of attitude. Professional snowboarder David Alden noted that by the end of the 1980s, "sponsors [had] quickly learned all they had to do was dress us up in Day Glo and catch somebody on camera saying 'Gnarly air dude,' and they were guaranteed 15 seconds on the evening news" (Howe 1998, 56). This comment speaks to the fact that snowboarders set themselves apart from the mainstream by using a subcultural argot that was not used (or understood) by skiers, who were generally dismayed by the shredding (riding), the jibbing (riding over unconventional surfaces), and the pulling of fakies (riding backward) that the young practitioners of this new sport did in their midst. The comment also speaks to the fact that garish late-1980s snowboarding style was at least partially constructed by commercial interests.

By the early 1990s snowboarding culture was gaining in popularity and was becoming a packaged commodity for the mainstream to consume. Professional snowboarders like Scott Schmidt, Glen Plake, and later in the decade Terje Haakonsen were making six figures and were actively involved in personal-image development and product promotion. As a result, the sartorial image of snowboarders became increasingly important. The wearing of neon diminished in the first years of the decade as the mainstream fashion for that color faded away and as snowboarders sought to further position themselves as subcultural. A mixture of punk, skate, grunge, and hip-hop dress practices, a cocktail of stylistic devices that produced a unique "alternative" look, replaced the aesthetic aggressiveness of clashing colors and patterns. Alterity, extremity, and authenticity were emphasized as guiding ideas both within the subculture of snowboarding and then within the marketing that increasingly surrounded the sport. The apparel that came to be associated with snowboarders moved them markedly further away from traditional snow-sport apparel as individuals sought to mark themselves as distinct from the mainstream. Giant cut-off jeans, wallets worn on large, dangling chains, hoodies, backward baseball caps, and exposed boxer shorts were key features borrowed from hip-hop, raver, and skateboarding culture. Some snowboarders would wear multiple pairs of long underwear under jeans rather than wear ski pants or snow pants. Beanies and flannels were stylistic elements selected out of the grunge music scene. Clashing colors, punk-rock band T-shirts, spiky or vibrantly colored hair, and piercings marked affiliations with punk rock and the subgenre of skate punk. The look that came to define snowboarding in the early 1990s was purposefully and graphically in opposition to mainstream dress practices. Holly Thorpe noted, "By aligning themselves with the styles of underclass groups, the mostly white, middle-upper class snowboarder was attempting to make authentic the claim to being marginal, abnormal, and poor, and most importantly, distinctly different from the upper class skier" (2004, 186).

The development of an identifiable snowboarding style contributed to the development of snowboarding-apparel companies. For example, Droors began to make snow clothes that mimicked the look of oversized jeans by creating items like waterproof nylon pants that looked like jeans. Surf companies like O'Neill entered the snowboarding marketplace with oversized clothes that featured pronounced branding. Mainstream brands associated with alpine snowboarding like Burton and Kemper became uncool in the eyes of some snowboarders, and the door was opened to a wave of product development. Brands like Type A, Special Blend, and Joyride were launched and positioned themselves as "tri-sport" (surf, skate, snowboard) lifestyle brands. Some companies like Volcom developed street apparel rather than sport apparel to reflect these lifestyles. So many companies of this kind were positioned in Orange County, California, that the nickname "Velcro Valley" was ascribed to the region. The label, a riff on Silicon Valley, was coined because tri-sport lifestyle brands often utilized the convenient fabric fastener.

By the end of the 1990s the "alternative look" had become so popular that it had lost its impact and was abandoned by core members of the snowboarding scene. Once rebellion against the mainstream became the mainstream, a change was required. The shift in the latter part of the 1990s marked a reversion to understated, largely unaffected apparel. While a loose fit was still favored, the dramatic oversizing of apparel was abandoned. Colors became more muted, and logos were downplayed. Cold-weather apparel that looked like normal street wear, including hoodies, flannel shirts, plaid jackets, and jeans, were made, thereby making snowboarding style less distinct in contrast to street apparel while maintaining its aesthetic distance from ski style. Over the course of the early 2000s some snowboarding apparel also reverted to old aesthetics but achieved them through the use of high-tech and expensive fabrics like Gore Tex. For example, the 2010 Olympic snowboarding uniforms attempted to rekindle aesthetics from the 1990s. Baggy snow pants were made of fabric that was printed to look like faded and distressed jeans, and they were coupled with plaid hooded jackets. Some observers critiqued the uniforms as an attempt to bring subcultural style into the formal setting of the Olympic Games, failing to realize that the subcultural impact of that style had long since faded. Snowboarding apparel in the second decade of the new millennium is not without controversy. As the sport has become increasingly professionalized, some snowboarders have sought to move away from the traditional loose snow pants and have adopted snug-fitting race suits similar to those worn by skiers. This has caused some alarm and objections from American snowboarders like Nate Holland, who remarked, "It betrays the antiestablishment culture that gave birth to snowboarding" (Fry 2010, 46). While Holland is correct about the history of snowboarding dress practices, his comment belies the fact that snowboarding has become a professional, mainstream sport that surpassed skiing in popularity in the early 2000s. Holland's comment also points to the fact that snowboarding style has become relatively fixed. While subtle changes evolve through the seasonal offerings of apparel manufacturers, new and noteworthy aesthetic ground has not been broken since the 1990s.

Snowboarding style and subculture was diffused to the mainstream, including to individuals who never set foot in the snow, through a variety of outlets in the late 1980s and 1990s. Magazines, both mainstream and niche, including *International Snowboarding* (1985–1991), *Transworld Snowboarding* (1987–present), and *Blunt* (1993–present) have communicated information about professional athletes, competitions, and brands. Videos, which were largely released as VHS cassettes, with titles such as *Snowboarders in Exile* (1990), *New Kids on the Twock* (1990), and *The Hard, the Hungry, and the Homeless* (1992) were set to hard-rock music and featured high-speed downhill snowboarding and daredevil tricks. Videos of this kind fueled both interest in the sport as well as the rebel imagery that was increasingly becoming associated with it. "Extreme" action sports coupled with music and other entertainments were also a common marketing tool in the 1990s, and the SnoCore Music Tour (1997) and the Winter X Games (1997–present) and Après X concerts are just a few examples of this phenomenon. The Nagano Olympics (1998) debuted snowboarding as an Olympic event, further helping to facilitate mainstream acceptance of the once subcultural activity and mode of dress.

Snowboarding style was not just a style seen on the slopes or in the half-pipe. Athletic apparel in general was evolving from the early 1990s onward. Companies like Fila, Nike, Adidas and Reebok as well as snow-sport companies were continually improving technical and aesthetic elements of athletic apparel, while designers like Ralph Lauren, Donna Karan, Calvin Klein, and Christian Lacroix were being inspired by the evolution of these specialty designs and moving them directly to the runway and the streets. *Vogue* writer Pamela Kaufman noted in 1991 that "sports clothes have gotten so sleek and high-tech that you may never want to come in from the cold" (90). The fit of athletic apparel designed for athletic use was also being dramatically improved for women at this fairly late stage in the history of fashion (see Schiro 1996), further facilitating their transition to the street. Finally, the connection between urban, hip-hop style and athletic apparel and the crossovers among hip-hop, skateboarding, and snowboarding styles further promoted the wearing of athletic apparel and apparel inspired by sport as street style, a fact noted in *Entertainment Weekly* in 1996: "As extreme sports go mainstream, they're spawning a whole new category of clothing: extreme sportswear. From snowboard boots to racing suits, the garb once reserved for competition is now hitting the streets" (Jacobs and Pener 1996). This kind of apparel was embraced for its comfort and also facilitated indulgence in "a form of acceptable fantasy" (Schiro 1996) as individuals who might never drop into a half-pipe could dress for the experience of "catching air" or "shredding powder." Designer collections continue to explore sports as a source of inspiration. Snowboarding informed the design of menswear collections for Byblos Fall/Winter 2000 and Michael Bastian Fall/Winter 2002. Burton partnered with Japanese street-wear label Neighborhood to create apparel for both on and off the slopes for the 2015–2016 winter season.

The future of snowboarding is in question. Drought, climate change, and a series of warm winters have impacted sales of snowboarding equipment and apparel, and businesses big and small have suffered. Sporting-goods giant Nike closed its snow-sports division in 2014. Furthermore, enthusiasm for and interest in snowboarding seem to have peaked in the winter of 2010–2011, and the market for goods and media has become saturated (see Higgins 2016). Live streaming has impacted the consumption of media and methods of advertising, and the sponsorship of professional riders has decreased, a fact that curtails the development of the sport as well as its stylistic attributes. It remains to be seen if a further stage of development of the sport will begin in winters to come, bringing with it new developments in style.

Further Reading

Black, K. 1996. "Xtreme Prejudice." *Rolling Stone* (742): 52.

Fry, J. 2010. "Fashion Police." *Ski* (75) 4: 46.

Greenfeld, K. T. 1999. "Killer Profits in Velcro Valley." *Time* 153 (3): 50.

Heino, R. 2000. "What Is So Punk about Snowboarding?" *Journal of Sports and Social Issues* 24 (2): 176–91.

Higgins, M. 2016. "Snowboarding, Once a High-Flying Sport, Crashes to Earth." *The New York Times,* March 6. Retrieved March 16, 2016, from www.nytimes.com.

Howe, S. 1998. *Sick: A Cultural History of Snowboarding.* New York: St. Martins Griffin.

Jacobs, A., and D. Pener. 1996. "Extreme Cool." *Entertainment Weekly* (333/224): 64.

Lane, R. 1995. "The Culture That Jake Built." *Forbes* 155 (7): 45–46.

Lopez, P. 1994. "Vogue's View: Gearing Up." *Vogue* 184 (October 1): 118, 120. Retrieved from http://search.proquest.com/docview/879293461?accountid=130772.

Rosenberg, D. 1998. "All Aboard." *Newsweek* 131: 72.

Schiro, A. 1996. "Chic Scales the Heights, or Walks the Dog." *The New York Times,* December 3. Retrieved March 16, 2016, from www.nytimes.com.

Schube, S. 2016. "Snowboard Gear That Gets the Tokyo Drift." *GQ,* January, 22.

Thorpe, H. 2004. "Embodied Boarders: Snowboarders, Status, and Style." *Waikato Journal of Education* 10: 181–201.

Steampunk (Late 1990s–Present)

Steampunk is a style of dress that melds a variety of historical or "retro" features with elements that have a distinctively futuristic, often times apocalyptic, feel. The "steam" in steampunk may be interpreted as a reference to the "age of steam," a label that is a synonym for the Industrial Revolution and evokes the understanding that many early machines were powered with steam engines. While the aesthetics of steampunk do not generally sample from the sartorial vocabulary of punk (items like leather motorcycle jackets or graphic T-shirts are not hallmarks of this style), steampunk does evoke an edgy and rebellious sartorial statement, albeit using apparel that is often quite formal and refined. The term "steampunk" was not originally applied to dress practices. The term was coined by science fiction author K. W. Jeter in April 1987 in a letter that he wrote to *Locus Magazine* that discussed anachronistic, Victorian-inspired science-fiction novels. The term "steampunk" is actually a play on the term "cyberpunk," which is also a genre of science fiction that features cyborgs as characters. Since the late 1980s the retrofuturistic genre has developed and expanded to impact literature, music, film, gaming, theater, fashion, and the design of everyday objects. It is a mode of expression that revels in the power of the imagination. Steampunk is fanciful and arguably a form of escape from the mundane aspects of workaday life in the slick, technological 21st century. Steampunk is considered a subculture by those writing and commenting from within the scene, but steampunk is different from many subcultures given its emphasis on craftsmanship, creativity, and problem solving rather than rebellion and expressions of antiestablishment sentiments.

Steampunk dress is a style that is worn both in the "con" (convention) scene and as regular street apparel. In this regard, steampunk shares an overlapping characteristic with cosplayers, with whom they sometimes cohabit cons. Steampunk ensembles exist on a continuum that may include incredibly outlandish features including prop weapons or machines but may also be composed to make a noteworthy street-style statement. Steampunk dress practices seem to date to the late 1990s when artists like Kit Stolen first took sartorial cues from literary sources by interpreting the aesthetics described in retrofuturistic science fiction, and applying the "steampunk" term itself, to the clothes they created and wore (Vandermeer 2011, 132). The aesthetic of steampunk is highly varied; however, some general concepts and a list of iconic pieces of apparel and accessories may be elucidated. First, steampunk typically has a strong historical component, which is often a mash-up of apparel and accessories from the Victorian (1837–1901) and Edwardian (1901–1910) Periods. Some steampunks also derive historical references from medieval Europe. Steampunk historical references are often derived from high-style fashion (tailored jackets and vests, elaborate dresses and hats) but may also be interpreted from historical working-class or sporting apparel; thus steampunk sometimes recalls the aesthetics of the "wild west" of the 19th-century American frontier. The widespread use of sepia tones is an additional way in which steampunks connect their clothes to the past. By restricting the color palettes of their ensembles to hues of brown, steampunks recall 19th-century cabinet photographs. As steampunk has evolved, some devotees have also incorporated paranormal elements that recall the aesthetics of zombies, mummies, and vampires. The style gains visual and discursive impact by highlighting contradictions through juxtapositions and explorations of time periods, genders, social classes, sexuality, formality, and informality. Incorporating paranormal aesthetics is one more way to achieve such contradictions and juxtapositions.

In *The Steampunk Bible* Jeff Vandermeer suggests that steampunk style can be grouped into four categories (2011, 138–41). His first category is the "street urchin." This interpretation of steampunk may include stained, torn, or worn, distinctly working-class apparel in hues of blue and brown such as simple pants worn with suspenders, untailored shirts, and dresses styled with an apron. Vandermeer's second category is the "tinker." Here working-class clothes may be slightly more refined and are accented with sleeve garters, bow ties, functional tools, and goggles. The "explorer" genre includes many iconic elements derived from the military and from 19th-century sport. Combat helmets, pith helmets, aviator apparel, jodhpurs, and goggles are among the iconic elements that are included in this aesthetic. Finally, there is a version of steampunk that relies heavily on high-style fashion—the "aesthete." Herein, men wear Victorian and Edwardian high-style clothes including frock coats, tailcoats, tailored vests, pocket watches, and spatterdashers. Women wear long dresses with elaborate decorations including bustles, lace, and feathers. Visible petticoats are often included, and corsets are typically worn as an exterior layer. Tiny hats, fingerless gloves, and beaded reticules often complete this kind of steampunk ensemble. Across all of these categories, accessories and decorations often feature mechanical aesthetics. Cogs, gears, bolts, screws, wires, and other features that recall mechanical technologies are affixed to accessories like hats and eyeglasses, stitched onto corsets, and fashioned into pieces of jewelry and serve as a concrete reference to the age of steam-powered technologies.

While Vandermeer's categories are useful for discussing the basic outlines of steampunk dress, it is important to note that these categories are far from rigid. Elements from each group are intermingled at will, and ensembles are highly personalized. Do-it-yourself garment design, creation, and decoration are an important part of steampunk culture. Handcrafting is also applied to the creation of pseudo-technologies. Guns and small handheld cannons with otherworldly powers are often incorporated into steampunk outfits worn to conventions. The sharing of knowledge and technique is also an important part of the culture. Books, blogs, and websites are all repositories for steampunk maker culture. In addition to do-it-yourself, steampunk apparel and accessories are also created through custom order. Designers, tailors, and dressmakers who specialize in steampunk can be found across the United States, especially in large metropolitan areas like Seattle, Los Angeles, and New York City. Vintage apparel is also an important source for the creation of a steampunk ensemble. Nineteenth-century accessories are worn, while apparel (which is often too fragile to wear) is often copied.

Part of the motivation for embracing the do-it-yourself ethos is the ability to create highly personalized apparel and accessories, while part of the motivation may also relate to the failure of the marketplace to meet each and every steampunk's needs and desires; however, the maker ethos that is embraced by steampunks is also a rebuke of mass production and the consumer ethos. The modern global apparel marketplace is understood as an engine of pollution, waste, and homogeneity. Steampunk designers often upcycle or recycle materials and strive to create objects of lasting value to their owners. Steampunk is, ultimately, a positive subculture, but its outlook is informed by a nihilistic, dystopian view of the future in which the speed of communication, transportation, globalization, pollution, and social change outpaces some of the finer aspects of human life. Notably, this understanding of the

21st-century social context is viewed and understood as an historical parallel to life in the Victorian Period (Thompson 2011, 67–68).

The steampunk response to the shortcomings of modern society is also manifested in the development of characters or personae (sometimes referred to as "steamsona"). This character may be embodied only in the context of a convention or in everyday life. The creation of a character is a link to the literary origins of steampunk and functions as a way to turn a regular day into an exciting adventure. The development of a character in conjunction with a distinctive dress style is another point of convergence between steampunks and cosplayers.

Steampunk culture is developed and conveyed through a variety of media. First of all, the genre of literature continues to develop, with writers such as Cherie Pot, Ekaterina Sedia, and George Mann developing new literary trends, while classics by H. G. Wells and Jules Verne continue to find new readership. Steampunk writers have also published a variety of books about the subculture. How-to and informational books include *Steampunk Gear, Gadgets, and Gizmos* (2011) and *1000 Steampunk Creations* (2011). *Steampunk* magazine (2006–2016) served until recently as a vehicle for sharing contemporary literature as well as articles, interviews, and visual culture. The huge variety of blogs, including "Beyond Victoriana" and "Steampunk Scholar," constitute vital web-based sources of information and community. Conventions are also important to steampunk culture, and events have occurred across the United States including Clockwork Alchemy, which was held in Chicago, and Salt City Steamfest, which was held in Salt Lake City, Utah. Steampunk conventions continue to be held, while maker fairs, Renaissance fairs, and other kinds of cons often have what are referred to as "alternate history" sections where steampunks often congregate. Steampunk fashion shows have become a common feature at conventions.

Various kinds of performance arts have also developed in relation to steampunk. Steampunk popular music groups include Abney Park, The James Gang, The Dresden Dolls, and Marquis of Vaudeville. Although the musical styles of these groups vary, each is known for a visually arresting steampunk manner of dress. The performance art group League of S.T.E.A.M., which had a web series called *The Adventures of the League of S.T.E.A.M.,* has also functioned as an important way to spread steampunk culture. Steampunk aesthetics have informed major Hollywood motion pictures including *Wild Wild West* (1999), *The Golden Compass* (2007), and *Sherlock Holmes* (2009). Theater productions of *Jekyll and Hyde, My Fair Lady, Titus Andronicus,* and *Hamlet* have all been designed with steampunk aesthetics. Designers for the stage have capitalized on the "rebellious, swaggering attitude that the style conveys" (Wren 2013, 31).

A peak in the mass appeal of the steampunk aesthetic was in evidence at the end of the aughts when a "steampunk treehouse" was exhibited at the Burning Man

Festival in 2007 and then at Coachella in 2008. Further evidence of mainstream interest in steampunk may be derived from the incredibly popular art exhibit that was presented at Oxford University from late 2009 until early 2010. A steampunk video game for Xbox and PlayStation called *Edge of Twilight* was developed from the middle of the aughts into the twenty teens, further evidence of the mass appeal of the steampunk aesthetic, but the game seems to have been withheld from release due to licensing issues.

Professionally made steampunk apparel and accessories have been part of the steampunk scene since the mid-aughts. Both brick-and-mortar boutiques like Gothic Renaissance and Berít in New York City and Clockwork Couture in Burbank, California, as well as Etsy and eBay retailers provide apparel and accessories. Ready-made steampunk apparel ranges from polyurethane and plastic items costing a few dollars to objects made of high-quality fabrics costing hundreds of dollars. Steampunk devotees as well as Goths (who are drawn to the Victorian and Edwardian aesthetics) and people who are simply interested in the style are among the customers who patronize these labels. Among the well-established and highly regarded brands are Spyder Designs, KVO by Karen van Oppen, Brute Force Studios, and Lastwear. High-style design has also taken cues from steampunk. Part of the Alexander McQueen Spring 2010 collection featured specific steampunk references including cogs and wheels adorning high-heeled shoes. Many collections from designers including Jean Paul Gaultier, John Galliano for Dior, and Ralph Lauren routinely include corsets, 19th-century references, and sepia tones and thereby play with some of the aesthetic tropes of steampunk.

The allure of steampunk style for some may simply be the visually arresting aesthetics of cogs and wheels or the elegance of tailored coats and ruffled dresses; however, the rich visual language of steampunk allows for manifold expressive possibilities. In the "Foreword" to *Anatomy of Steampunk: The Fashion of Victorian Futurism,* K. W. Jeter noted that the point of dressing as a steampunk is to "unnerve the onlooker" (Gleason 2013, 6), and he wrote of this capacity as being a liberating experience—dress that challenges the mainstream, marks the wearer as apart from the masses, and frees the wearer from the confines of mass culture. Jeter also wrote that steampunk style exhibits a "relentless push and mad rush toward mutation and a furious inventiveness" (7). Thus, developing a wardrobe in the steampunk style allows the wearer to create and innovate, expressing his or her unique perspectives and tastes while dressing in a manner that typically embodies a refinement not regularly seen in 21st-century dress practices.

Writing of the psychology of steampunk, Gail Gray suggested that people participate in steampunk in part because it is pleasurable and in part because they are disenfranchised by contemporary culture. Again, the wearing of steampunk dress marks one as separate from the mainstream. It is a visible sign of the refusal of a culture of alienation and disappointment. Gray further suggested that steampunk allows individuals to produce "a more aesthetically pleasing and less disposable future" (2011, 55, 56) than the one offered by mainstream society. This is accomplished in part through the act of imagining, designing, and handcrafting and through the community of apprenticeship and cooperation that is an important part of making in the steampunk subculture.

The discursive potential of steampunk is also a facet of these dress practices that has been considered by some individuals within the subculture. The symbolic and narrative potential of apparel is informed in part by science-fiction literature that describes heroes and heroines dressed in the steampunk manner. Thus, for some steampunks, dress is not just about appropriating historical fashion; it is about "safely and triumphantly" playing with and transgressing the boundaries of the past and interpreting and recreating cultural constructs, including gender roles (Taddeo 2013, 45). For example, the steampunk's use of corsetry reimagines its use and meaning. Whereas it was traditionally worn beneath one's clothes as an undergarment that restricted the wearer, steampunks often wear the corset on the outside of the garment; Taddeo regards this restrictive device as a kind of armament that functions as "an announcement of a woman's place in the public sphere, clad for battle." Taddeo considers the wearing of a corset to be a source of power (2013, 45, 49). Barber and Hale see steampunk dress as a form of "referential discourse that blends multiple temporalities into a single form." Mixing and juxtaposing diverse elements from across time, place, and socioeconomic class enable the wearer to create a visual narrative about culture, time, and place. Steampunk dress has the ability to allow the wearer to speculate about the culture in which he or she lives and perform a role or narrative (Barber and Hale 2013, 166–67). Steampunk can also be viewed as a form of self-expression and as a response to the wastefulness and frivolity of the mainstream fashion industry, a stance that aligns with the design reformers of the latter half of the 19th century (Huxtable 2013, 221–22).

Steampunk continues to evolve as the culture is influenced by new devotees who incorporate aspects of their unique selves into their interpretation of the subculture. Notably, the country in which a steampunk lives is influential, as the Victorian Period in France, Germany, or the United States all had different visual language and cultural references. Steampunk culture has spread all around the globe from Brazil to China, and Internet retailing facilitates the diffusion of new dress practices. While the commercial, mainstream popularity of steampunk seems to have peaked in the late aughts, the aesthetic and the attitude of steampunk live on. Ruth La Ferla, writing for *The New York Times,* noted, "If steampunk has a mission, it is, in part, to restore a sense of wonder to a technology-jaded world," and in its expression of history and formality it provides some relief from the mundane

(LaFerla 2008). If steampunk can truly provide such reprieves, then it seems safe to say that it is likely that the subculture will continue to grow and evolve.

Further Reading

Barber, S., and M. Hale. 2013. "Entering the Never Was: Upcycling the Past, Present, and Future in Steampunk." In *Steaming into a Victorian Future: A Steampunk Anthology,* edited by J. A. Taddeo and C. J. Miller, 165–83. Plymouth, United Kingdom: Rowman and Littlefield.

Gleason, K. 2013. *Anatomy of Steampunk: The Fashion of Victorian Futurism.* New York: Race Point Publishing.

Gray, G. 2011. "An Overview of the Psychology of Steampunk." In *Presentations of the 2010 Upstate Steampunk Extravaganza and Meetup,* edited by G. Teague, 55–64. Newcastle-upon-Tyne: Cambridge Scholars Publishing.

Huxtable, S. 2013. "Steampunk Design and a Vision of a Victorian Future." In *Steaming into a Victorian Future: A Steampunk Anthology,* edited by J. A. Taddeo and C. J. Miller, 213–33. Plymouth, United Kingdom: Rowman and Littlefield.

La Ferla, R. 2008. "Steampunk Moves between 2 Worlds." *The New York Times,* May 8. Retrieved August 26, 2016, from www.nytimes.com.

Taddeo, J. A. 2013. "Corsets of Steel: Steampunk's Reimagining of Victorian Femininity." In *Steaming into a Victorian Future: A Steampunk Anthology,* edited by J. A. Taddeo and C. J. Miller, 43–63. Plymouth, United Kingdom: Rowman and Littlefield.

Teague, G., ed. 2011. *Presentations of the 2010 Upstate Steampunk Extravaganza and Meetup.* Newcastle-upon-Tyne: Cambridge Scholars Publishing.

Thompson, R. P. 2011. "Commentary under Corsets: Steampunk's Underlying Message." In *Presentations of the 2010 Upstate Steampunk Extravaganza and Meetup,* edited by G. Teague, 65–71. Newcastle-upon-Tyne: Cambridge Scholars Publishing.

Vandermeer, J. 2011. *The Steampunk Bible.* New York: Abrams Image.

Wren, C. 2013. "You've Been Steampunked." *American Theatre,* February, 30–33.

Surfing (1960–Present)

The sport of surfing is ancient. Scholars estimate that it existed for 500 to 1,000 years before it was first seen by Western explorers. Captain Cook, who observed surfers at Kealakekua Bay in Hawaii in the late 18th century (Finney and Houston 1966, 24) may have been the first Westerner to witness surfing. Contact between European explorers, Calvinist evangelicals, and native people who surfed in places like Hawaii and Tahiti caused a drastic decline in surfing throughout the late 18th and duration of the 19th centuries, as disease from foreign pathogens decimated the native populations and religious proselytizing discouraged survivors from participating in this activity, which was generally done in a state of undress. Fortunately, the art and sport of surfing rebounded in the 20th century thanks in part to the efforts of Hawaiian native Duke Kahanamoku and Californian Tom Blake. Twentieth-century surfing is a sport, a street style, and for a happy minority a lifestyle that may also be categorized as a subculture, for those who set their agendas according to wind and waves eschew many of the mainstream expectations concerning work and family life. Although this article is largely concerned with the sartorial aesthetics of surfer dress, it is important to highlight that a core contingency of surfers believe that surfing is a spiritual and physical quest, a way to discover oneself in nature, and "a special kind of madness" all rolled into one (Wardy 1967, 18). For some surfers the practicality and durability of apparel are undoubtedly of far greater importance than aesthetics and fashions.

The development of surfing from a Polynesian sport to a widespread American street style has a great deal to do with the evolution of the sport itself, for it seems logical to argue that if surfboards had not evolved from being handcrafted wooden objects measuring 16 to 18 feet in length, 2 feet in width, and weighing about 150 pounds, then the sport would not have been accessible enough to catch on (Finney and Houston 1966, 33). Board design began to evolve in the 1930s, when native tropical woods such as koa and wiliwili were abandoned in favor of lightweight balsa that was then lacquered for water repellence. Beginning in the 1940s, experiments were done with fiberglass, a material that was being developed by the aerospace industry during World War II. Fiberglass became the material of choice by the 1960s, and its use ultimately made boards lighter and less expensive and facilitated rapid mass production. In fact, prior to the use of fiberglass, boards were cut to order depending on the user's height, weight, and skill and cost twice as much as the ready-made models ("Surf's Up!," 51). In addition to modifications that changed the weight of surfboards, avid surfers also helped to innovate board design to facilitate new riding techniques; thus as the decades went by, both the nose and tail of a surfboard were reshaped, one or more skegs (fins) were added, and ultimately the length of the board was shortened (Finney and Houston, 74–76). These modifications generally allowed for faster riding and for riding through the tubes of a cresting wave, thus making the sport more exciting and more appealing to large populations of Americans.

In addition to how the board design helped to proliferate the sport and culture of surfing, mass media, including popular music, film, and serial publications helped to promote both the sport and the lifestyle surrounding it. California pop rock bands such as the Beach Boys (formed 1961) and the Surfaris (formed 1962) were instrumental in conveying a sense of the carefree, endless summer of the California coast as well as the specifics of catching waves in tunes like "Surfin'

U.S.A.," "Surfer Joe," and "Murphy the Surfie." Films, which often included popular surf tunes, were also influential. *Gidget* (1959), *Beach Party* (1963), *Muscle Beach Party* (1964), and *Beach Blanket Bingo* (1965) are just a small sample of the scores of films that promoted surfing as a sport, lifestyle, and street style. In addition to these narrative films, there has existed since the early 1960s a culture of documentary filmmaking that produced films, which could be rented via mail order and played in community centers and gyms. Perhaps the most famous film of this genre is *Endless Summer* (1964). American magazines that catered primarily to the surfer community by documenting wave breaks, printing articles about technique, and running advertisements for board shops and wetsuit makers, also appealed to a large audience by printing page after page of illustrations depicting perfect waves, sandy beaches, and swaying palms and did much to promote the idea that surfing was a sport for the rebellious, independent spirit, thereby attaching a countercultural component to surfing in the United States. Both *Surfer* and *Surfing Illustrated* commenced publication in the 1960s. Mainstream publications also contributed to America's fascination with surfing. A *Time* article reporting on the International Surfing Championships in Makaha, Hawaii, quoted Ernest "Mud" Werner, a competitor, as follows: "When you crack through a tunnel, beat it across the face of a wave, and come out the other side—why man, it's a great thrill. You feel five or six emotions at once. It's better than sex. You own the world" ("Wall of Water" 1962, 38). Guidebooks and how-to manuals were available in the 1960s, though most were once again available only through mail order. However, in the 1970s a boom in publishing helped to spread surfer culture. Publications such as *Thrill Sports Catalogue* (1977), *The Surfer's Almanac: An International Guide* (1977), and *Surfing: Basic Techniques* (1979) represent just a small sample of the mainstream publications that helped to spread surfing beyond a geographically constrained subculture. Initially, the epicenter of surf culture in the United States was situated along the coast of California, but by the 1970s there were surf scenes on the East Coast, especially on Long Island and along the New Jersey shoreline.

Surfer style prior to the 1960s consisted largely of contemporary styles of bathing suits and sportswear, and there is no clear indication that any companies were making apparel that was directly targeted at surfers. William Finnegan mentioned in his memoir, *Barbarian Days,* that he recalled people selling apparel to surfers from the back of station wagons before it was available elsewhere, but he provided no other details in his recollections. The emergence of a fashionable American surfer style seems to have arisen in the first half of the 1960s for the surfer community and seems to have become a fashionable street style quite quickly. An article in *Surfer* from 1964 entitled "How to Shoot the Big Surf (and What to Wear While You're Waiting)" depicted apparel from a variety of surf-centric companies including Hang Ten and Duke Kahanamoku and noted for the reader, "Consciousness of surf wear reaches an all time high this year with more suits and styles available than ever before. It's a sign of maturity in the sport" (43). The article went on to note that 1964 marked the point when surfing was passing out of it's "bum" stage, a further indication that clothing aesthetics were being upgraded. Among the notable features of the clothes depicted was the use of "Tahitian" prints, madras plaid, and "competition" stripes—large vertical stripes that spanned the front of windbreaker jackets and trunks. Also notable were techniques to brand the apparel as appropriate for a surfer. Hang Ten called their bikini the "Surfette," and mainstream swimsuit maker Jantzen called their men's swim trunks the "Surfrider style."

In addition to swimming trunks with drawstring closures for men in both long (referred to as "baggies") and short cuts, and bikinis for women, early surfer apparel included nylon jackets (called surf jackets), striped T-shirts (called surf shirts), white Levis jeans, Keds canvas sneakers, bell-bottom slacks (some of which were advertised as unisex), and graphic T-shirts with printed surfing imagery, slogans, or branding. *Surfer* magazine offered two-dollar T-shirts with a cartoon image of Murphy, a character featured in a monthly cartoon about surfing, as well as shirts that simply bore the name of the magazine. Similarly, a T-shirt with an image of a surfer and text stating "cowabunga" could be had via mail order. Sweatshirts were also part of early surfer style, though most were of very ordinary design. In 1964 Jantzen offered a sweatshirt through mail order that featured the names of surfing spots like Makaha, Sunset, and Rincon screened on the fabric, but this kind of surf-centric product from a large mainstream brand seems to have been quite rare in the 1960s. Mexican imports including "safari" sandals, vests (called "gaucho jackets"), and ponchos were available both through mail order from surf magazines and in surf shops. Neoprene wetsuits for men and women were also marketed for surfing, and they were made in fashionable colors commencing in 1966.

Early advertising of surfer apparel was consistent in its approach: an air of authenticity was always perceptible, and a connection to the act of surfing was always made, except in advertisements that featured only women's apparel. Although there were a handful of accomplished female surfers including Margo Godfrey, the notion that surfing was a "man's sport" was regularly raised, and a great deal of women's surf apparel was for the female observer of surfing. To promote the connection between product and surfer culture, a 1964 advertisement for Central Skindivers, a company that retailed wetsuits for scuba diving and surfing, used the tagline, "Wipe Out in Style," thereby using surfer slang as a form of appeal. Advertisements for Hang Ten that ran in 1965 were even more direct, noting, "The styling of Hang Ten has become a symbol of the authentic surfer from the Hawaiian chain to the Atlantic coast." Kanvas by Katin, a maker of cotton canvas trunks and jackets, used the tag line "Surfwear Designed by Surfers," whereas Birdwell Beach Britches used a cartoon illustration of a surfer with his board as their logo. Advertisements also routinely used surfers as models for apparel, thereby endorsing and authenticating the product.

The basic components of surfer style that were visible in the 1960s remained in use throughout most of the 1970s with only minor changes in evidence. Notably, through most of the 1970s, true surfer apparel could still be obtained only by mail order or in specialty shops that also sold boards, racks, and wax to surfers. However, apparel that aped the surfer aesthetic was increasingly available through retailers like Sears and its catalog and was most typically designed for junior customers. Surfer-inspired apparel was marketed using surfing nomenclature (i.e., surf trunks, surf shirts) but was made with materials like cotton plain weave and polyester and utilized elastic, none of which was used in authentic surfing apparel. Patterns, colors, and design details showed evidence of change as style and use parted ways. The fact that clothing manufacturers had been hanging around surfing spots like La Jolla and studying the apparel of surfers like John Severson and Hobie Alter in the hopes of picking up surfing styles for mass production was noted by Tom Wolfe in his short story "The Pump House Gang," which seems to have been informed by events he witnessed at mid-decade (1968, 25). Thus while the styles seen at the beach changed only modestly throughout much of the 1970s, styles seen on the street began to reflect the modifications of designers and manufacturers and the intended use of the clothes.

Bold changes in the aesthetics of surfer style as well as a mass migration of surfer style from wave break to main street occurred beginning in the late 1970s and was a very visible phenomenon throughout much of the 1980s. Brands old and new repositioned themselves as lifestyle companies (companies that trade on an idea of a lifestyle) and began to produce diverse collections of apparel for men, women, and youths. Some notable brands that had tremendous traction in the 1980s included OP Swimwear and Sunwear, Rip Curls, Quicksilver, Hobie Apparel, Boogie Body Wear, Jimmy'z, and Corky. Apparel in this period often featured large, colorful graphics such as sunsets, palm trees, and tropical birds, and large logos were also often featured. Some of the companies that entered the lifestyle marketplace were brands that had long served the surfer community, including Body Glove, a maker of wetsuits since 1956, which started to make neoprene apparel suitable for dry land as well as other kinds of clothing and accessories. Other companies, which had long been a staple of the surfing scene, entered mainstream fashion while making few changes to their products. For example, Jams, a style and a brand of colorful and baggy rayon board shorts that have a drawstring waist and a small pocket designed for holding surfboard wax, were invented in Hawaii in 1964 by surfer David Rochlen. Jams were put into mass production in 1964 and soon became a staple of the surfer and skater scenes. Between 1984 and 1988 Jams were a fashion fad that swept the United States, and men wore the unmodified board shorts as street apparel.

Although the colorful aesthetics that dominated surfer fashions in the 1980s faded out before the end of the decade, the popularity of surf-inspired fashions did not, and the marketplace continued to develop and expand. In the 1990s surf brands from abroad, including Billabong from Australia, made major forays into the American marketplace as fashion brands and in some cases spawned secondary brands such as Roxy, Billabong's women's apparel label. Also in evidence from the 1990s onward was the launch of "heritage collections" or retro designs and the recasting of old surf labels as fashion brands. For example, O'Neill has been a maker of wetsuits since the 1950s but now retails men's, women's, and children's apparel and accessories. Diversification of product offerings, through the use of licensing agreements (design and manufacturing contracts that allow manufacturers to produce for a known brand), has also facilitated expansion of surf lines to include products such as luggage, eyewear, watches, and jewelry. This kind of expansion has moved a large portion of surfer apparel further away from the wave break and more comfortably into the realm of commodity culture. It is also notable that many of these brands cater to both the surfer and skater scenes, with some offering two distinct lines that are often largely differentiated by color and pattern rather than cut and concept.

Surfer style has developed into a subcategory of athleisure dressing (athletic apparel designed for leisure, not sport), and many of the dominant surf brands now make a disproportionate amount of apparel and accessories that are best suited for dry land. Surfer style has also found its way to the high-style runway. Karl Lagerfeld for Chanel showed wetsuit-inspired suiting in Spring/Summer 1991 along with Chanel-branded surfboards. More recently, for Spring/Summer 2012 both Michael Kors and Alexander Wang showed scuba suit–inspired dresses made with neoprene fabric in brilliant colors that recalled surfer trends from the 1980s.

Although surfer style and surfing had begun to splinter by the early 1970s, the allure of surfing and surfer style in its many incarnations is still strong. Television programs and movies periodically trend with surfing imagery, causing an uptick in interest; however, a contingency of people seem to consistently gravitate toward surfer style, regardless of whether or not they actually surf. A sentiment expressed in 1966 by a Midwestern teenager named Walter Wegman seems still to have resonance today. Wegman, reflecting on aspects of surfer dress, told a reporter at *Time,* "I'd like to be a surfer, but you can't do much on Lake Michigan. If you can't surf and you can't have a board, at least you can have something" ("Surfer's Cross"

1966, 97). Thus as long as surf brands can make the connection between their apparel and the dangerous and exhilarating sport of surfing, surfer aesthetics will continue to be an important style both on the beach and on the street.

Further Reading

Black, K. 1996. "Xtreme Prejudice." *Rolling Stone* (742): 52.

Finnegan, W. 2015. *Barbarian Days: A Surfing Life.* New York: Penguin Books.

Finney, B. R., and J. D. Houston. 1966. *Surfing: The Sport of Hawaiian Kings.* Johannesburg, South Africa: Hugh Keartland Publishers.

Greenfeld, K. T. 1999. "Killer Profits in Velcro Valley." *Time* 153 (3): 50.

"How to Shoot the Big Surf (and What to Wear While You're Waiting)." 1964. *Surfer* 5 (3): 42–43.

Jacobs, A., and D. Pener. 1996. "Extreme Cool." *Entertainment Weekly* (333/224): 64.

Siegel, J. 1966. "Surf, Wheels & Free Souls." *The Saturday Evening Post* 239 (24): 32–37.

"The Surfer's Cross." 1966. *Time* 87 (16): 97.

"Surf's Up!" 1963. *Time* 82 (6): 51.

"That Wall of Water." 1962. *Time* 79 (7): 38.

Wardy, F. 1967. "Surfing Is . . . ." In *Great Surfing: Photos, Stories, Essays, Reminiscences and Poems,* edited by J. Severson, 18. Garden City, NY: Doubleday and Company.

"Winter Surfwear for Surfers in the Know." 1965. *Surfer* 5 (6): 90–91.

Wolfe, T. 1968. "The Pump House Gang." In *The Pump House Gang,* 13–30. New York: Farrar, Strauss, & Giroux.

Zoot Suit (Late 1930s–Mid-1950s)

"Zooties" or "zoot suiters" were mostly male individuals who were identified by wearing a specific style of suit. Zoot suits may simply be defined as two-piece suits that were oversized. Suit jackets were cut so that hems often extended from about three inches above the knee to several inches past the knee. Pants were designed so that the waistband rose above the natural waistline and featured up to 10 pleats, the seat and legs were loose, and the ankle cuffs were tapered. On urban streets, suits of this kind were often referred to as "a solid set of threads," an indication that they were considered supremely stylish. The precise origin of the zoot suit is a matter of some debate; however, it is clear that the suits developed in an African American social milieu, and their use was connected to several facets of urban American life. Zoot suits, which broke markedly with mainstream sartorial trends in menswear, were a very visible part of cultural identification for African American and Latino

American men in the pre–civil rights era and may be read in part as a political statement and refusal of mainstream values, but they were also integral to followers of the swing-dance craze. In the context of jitterbug dancing, zoot suits facilitated movement and communicated sartorial swagger. For many men, the wearing of a zoot suit was an act of dressing to impress and an extravagant proclamation of success. Despite the fact that zoot suits were primarily a fashion statement, zoot suit wearers were frequently stereotyped as criminals, although there is only scattered evidence specifically connecting criminality to the wearing of this apparel (specifically individuals used the suits to subvert the law by concealing weapons or other paraphernalia in the oversized apparel). Those who wore zoot suits were united by their sartorial identity, and there were through-lines of common interest among wearers of zoot suits; however, zooties were not a unified sociocultural group.

Some historians mark the emergence of the zoot suit as early as the mid-1930s (see McClendon 2015), arguing that it gradually evolved from an existing kind of men's suiting known as drapes. English drapes were suits that had extra-wide shoulders and pants that were pegged at the ankles. This kind of suit was later referred to as a New York drape or Harlem drape (Peiss 2011, 24–25). These suits were adopted by jitterbug dancers and were made in Harlem shops such as Klein's on Lennox Avenue and Lew's Pants Store, stores that later came to be identified with zoot suits. There is also photographic evidence that clearly depicts young African American and Latino men wearing traditional suiting (presumably second-hand clothes) that was styled to create the oversized effect. Jackets were purchased several sizes too big; therefore, hems hung low on the leg. Pants were purchased oversized, hitched up high on the waist and cuffed at the ankle, creating a baggy effect. This phenomenon also seems to have emerged in the 1930s; however, applying a precise date to the first appearance of either phenomenon is challenging.

Two individual men are often credited with "inventing the zoot suit." Harold Fox, who was a big-band trumpeter and the proprietor of Fox Brothers Clothiers on Roosevelt Avenue in Chicago, is one. Fox gave inspirational credit for the style to teens he observed on the streets of Chicago but seemed to have elevated and diffused the aesthetic by hiring a manufacturer to put oversized suits into production. Accounts differ as to the year he hired the firm of Bill and Peanut Fuchs to do the cut and sew work; 1939 and 1941 are both cited. What is indisputable is that Harold Fox is credited with the nomenclature "zoot suit" (dictionaries that include the word derivation give him credit). In a 1988 interview for the *Sun Sentinel,* Fox noted, "In those days the highest compliment you could pay someone or something was to say it was 'the end to all ends.' I needed a word to rhyme with suit, so I used the letter of the alphabet that is the end to all ends—Z—and came up with zoot." Fox also took credit for the tendency of zoot suiters to wear an exaggerated watch chain. He claimed the first oversized chain was snapped from the tank of the toilet in his Chicago store and presented to a customer as an accessory.

In June of 1943 Meyer Berger, writing for *The New York Times,* credited the origin of the zoot suit to a Georgia busboy named Clyde Duncan. This account has a young Mr. Duncan approaching the staff of a Gainesville, Georgia, store called Frierson-McEvers and requesting a suit with extreme proportions. The specifications for the suit were sent to the Globe Tailoring Company in Chicago, and reports of the bizarre request circulated in the menswear industry. The exaggerated suit, worn by Mr. Duncan, was even depicted in the *Men's Apparel Reporter* about a year after the order was placed. Regardless of who is credited with the first zoot suit, it seems clear that the extreme style was rooted in tastes and attitudes that were circulating in urban youth culture of the day, and both the extreme style and the argot (slang) used to describe it caught on and spread.

Zoot suits—referred to in the slang as "killer dillers" with "reet pleats," "reave sleeves," "ripe stripes," "stuff cuffs," and a "drape shape"—were made for children as young as eight but were generally adopted by men in their teens through middle age. A female counterpart to this look also existed. Oversized jackets for women were often called juke jackets. Stuart Cosgrove has found evidence of female zoot suit gangs called the Black Widows and the Slick Chicks who wore their oversized jackets with short skirts and fishnet stockings (1984, 84). These suits were largely embraced by younger generations, and there is evidence to suggest that older generations of African Americans and Mexican Americans frowned on the extreme style that brought acute attention to ethnic and cultural difference (Alford 2004, 228). Zoot suits were made in traditional colors and fabrics but were also crafted in vibrant colors, including brilliant hues of yellow and green, and made in fabrics with bold patterns (including horizontal and vertical stripes, plaid, and houndstooth). Zoot suits varied in proportions, ranging from noticeably oversized to extremely oversized "superzoots." Some zoot suit pant legs were cuffed so tightly that a small zipper had to be included in the inseam to allow the wearer to slip his foot through the opening.

The zoot suit was visible in various forms of media and entertainment. It was worn with great panache by the jazz performer Cab Calloway in the Hollywood film *Stormy Weather* (1943) and was lampooned in the movie *Star Spangled Rhythm* (1943). Jazz musicians including Dizzie Gillespie, Duke Ellington, Stan Kenton, and Count Basie wore them in performance at venues such as the Cotton Club, and jitterbug dancers wore them at venues such as the Savoy Ballroom in Harlem and the Million Dollar Theatre in Los Angeles. Depictions of zoot suits even reached children's entertainment: Donald Duck was depicted in the 1943 cartoon *Spirit of '43* wearing a zoot suit, and a dapper wolf character created by Tex Avery appeared in several cartoons in a zoot suit beginning in 1943. Comics and cartoons often openly vilified and stereotyped zoot suiters as criminals and traitors; a serial called *Zoot Suit Yokum* by Al Capp helped to shape negative public sentiment toward wearers of these suits, as did satirical cartoons that ran in newspapers around the country (Webb 1999, 237).

Part of the motivation for the vitriol directed at wearers of zoot suits was related to the shortages and austerity measures that were a part of mainstream life in the United States during World War II. Conservative use of raw materials, reuse, repair, and recycling were ideas that prevailed in the culture and were reflected in publications such as *Make and Mend* that instructed Americans regarding ways to preserve their clothes and thereby limit their fabric consumption. Zoot suits flew in the face of these wartime social mores and, therefore, served as a catalyst for negative attitudes directed at their wearers. The wearing of zoot suits after government restrictions were placed on their manufacture surely exacerbated the negativity that was already percolating within American culture. A limitation order designed to cut wool consumption by 25 percent, issued in early 1942, seems to be the first government regulation to impact zoot suits. While it seems that most manufacturers complied with the order, the popularity of zoot suits did not abate. The War Production Board (WPB) effectively banned zoot suits by revising the limitation order to specifically stipulate jacket lengths, waist height, and pant leg width. At first, only suits made of wool were impacted (it was a textile that was in high demand given the war effort), but the War Production Board quickly revised the ban to include the use of cotton and rayon as well (Peiss 2011, 36–38). Zoot suits were considered incredibly wasteful and even unpatriotic, and during the war years the connection between zoot suits, criminals, slackers, and the avoidance of military service was routinely made in the press. An article from *The New York Times* entitled "Zoot Suit Models Rouse Ire of WPB" noted that the clothes of "jitterbug dancers" were seen to be interfering with the progress of the country's war effort. Governmental restrictions of zoots suits extended beyond the boundaries of the United States, and the suits were banned in Australia in 1943.

Riots between zoot suiters and servicemen and police, commonly referred to as "zoot suit riots," first erupted in June 1943 in Los Angeles, California. *The New York Times* reported that "zoot suit gangs" armed with homemade weapons such as lengths of rope weighted with wire and lead or other objects such as tire chains, wrenches, hammers, and heavy bottles (some with the tops broken off) skirmished with military personnel, resulting in the arrest of more than two dozen Mexican American zoot suiters, also known as Pachucos ("28 Zoot Suiters" 1943). Fighting spread to other cities along the coast and erupted in Chicago later that summer. Conflicts that took place between Pachucos and law enforcement the following March in Albuquerque, New Mexico, were still labeled as zoot suit riots. The conflicts that took place were not specifically about the suits the young men and women were wearing; rather, the conflict seems to have been more specifically about racial tensions between the white men in uniform and the zoot suiters, who were either recent immigrants or the children of immigrants. Douglas Henry Daniels has argued that calling the fights "zoot suit" riots was a euphemism. The riots were really about race and ethnicity. He notes that the use of the terminology is indicative of American society's "refusal to grapple with complex social issues and to attack symbols instead" (1997, 204).

Undoubtedly, wearing the zoot suit meant different things to different individuals. Zoot suits were a form of subcultural dress and marked some degree of refusal of the mainstream, but it is not clear that zoot suiters shared a strong enough affinity in terms of mindset and motivations for wearing the suits to be labeled a subcultural group. There do seem to have been gangs of Mexican American zoot suiters, groups of dancers at clubs, and packs of kids all hanging out on the corner, but for every loose affiliation of zooties there was likely a unique reason for uniting: to stir up trouble, to dance the lindy, to strut and preen. Alford noted that the zoot suit was "one of the first articles of clothing to cause a spontaneous youth movement" (2004, 226), and Daniels seems to agree that the suits were indicative of some larger, unified movement (1997, 215); however, this seems too strong of a statement both about the unity of the wearers and the power of the suit. The fact that no other form of cultural production can be ascribed to zooties undergirds this point. Although the natural inclination of the backward gaze of the historian or theorist is to search for metanarratives, such profoundly satisfying statements must be made with caution. If there was a youth movement at this point in history it may better be labeled as a precursor to the Civil Rights Movement of the 1960s as it is clear that zoot suits were a bold expression of pride surrounding cultural difference.

The visual power of the zoot suit was ultimately not contained within the boundaries of urban centers within the United States. French Zazous interpreted the look during the Nazi occupation of France, during World War II. The symbolism of refusal and the proclamation of cultural pride were just as inherent in their gesture as in the original implications of the suit in the United States. There was also evidence of zoot suits in Germany, Bulgaria, the United Kingdom, and the Soviet Union in the 1950s. Each of these nations, scarred by the destruction, deprivation, and political realignment in the wake of the war adopted and adapted the look as a way to cope with and overcome the social circumstances.

Zoot suits continue to be used to communicate difference and swagger. Some modern images include Janet Jackson in the *Alright* video (1989), characters in Spike Lee's biopic *Malcolm X* (1992), and Jim Carey in *The Mask* (1994). Zoot suits also are occasionally updated and interpreted in fashion design, with varying degrees of fidelity to the original and with varying degrees of success. Celine Dion infamously wore a white zoot suit ensemble to the 1999 Academy Awards and was almost universally panned for the look. More recently Yohji Yamamoto sent menswear with strong zoot suit references down the runway (Fall/Winter 2011) with far greater success. There are also modern companies that make and sell zoot suits that are fairly faithful to the original designs of the mid-20th century. Companies such as Zoots by Suavecito's and El Pachuco Zoot Suits direct their marketing to a Latino audience, while Internet retailer mensusa.com presents the suits as a fashion alternative for any man. The persistence of zoot suits in popular imagery and in contemporary dress practices is testimony to the strength of their sartorial symbolism.

Further Reading

Alford, H. 2004. "The Zoot Suit: Its History and Meaning." *Fashion Theory* 8 (2): 225–36.

"Australia Bans Zoot Suit, Puts Wearer in War Job." 1943. *The New York Times,* September 4. Retrieved February 4, 2016, from www.timesmachine.com.

Berger, M. 1943. "Zoot Suit Originated in Georgia; Bus Boy Ordered First One in '40: Known as 'Killer Diller' It Started as Joke in Trade—Tailors Surprised as Demand for It Spread from South to Harlem." *The New York Times,* June 11. Retrieved February 4, 2016, from www.timesmachine.com.

Cosgrove, S. 1984. "The Zoot-Suit Culture and Style Warfare." *History Workshop* 18 (Autumn): 77–91. Retrieved September 11, 2015, from www.jstor.org/stable/4288588.

Daniels, D. H. 1997. "Los Angeles Zoot: Race 'Riot,' the Pachuco and Black Music Culture." *The Journal of Negro History* 82 (2): 201–20. Retrieved September 19, 2015, from www.jstor.org/stable/2717516.

Grimes, D. 1988. "Creator Welcomes Zoot Suit Rebirth." *The Sun Sentinel,* September 22. Retrieved February 4, 2016, from http://articles.sun-sentinel.com.

McClendon, A. 2015. *Fashion and Jazz.* New York: Bloomsbury.

"Not a Race Issue, Mayor Says." 1943. *The New York Times,* June 10. Retrieved February 4, 2016, from www.timesmachine.com.

Peiss, K. 2011. *Zoot Suit.* Philadelphia: University of Pennsylvania Press.

Thomas, R., Jr. 1996. "Harold Fox, Who Took Credit for the Zoot Suit Dies at 86." *The New York Times,* August 1. Retrieved February 4, 2016, from www.nytimes.com.

"28 Zoot Suiters Seized on Coast after Clashes with Service Men." 1943. *The New York Times,* June 7. Retrieved February 4, 2016, from www.timesmachine.com.

Tyler, B. 2008. "Zoot Suit Culture and the Black Press." In *Men's Fashion Reader,* edited by Andrew Reilly and Sarah Cosbey, 381–92. New York: Fairchild.

Webb, S. 1999. "Masculinities at the Margins: Representations of the Malandro and the Pachuco." In *Imagination beyond Nation,* edited by Eva Bueno and Terry Caesar, 227–64. Pittsburgh: Pittsburgh University Press.

"WPB Bars 'Zoot Suit' Made in Any Material: 'Wasteful Garments' Ruled Out as a War Menace." 1942. *The New York Times,* September 12. Retrieved February 4, 2016, from www.timesmachine.com.

"Zoot Suit Fighting Spreads on Coast." 1943. *The New York Times,* June 10. Retrieved February 4, 2016, from www.timesmachine.com.

"Zoot Suit Models Rouse Ire of WPB: Agency Warns Industry These and 'Juke Jackets' of the Female Jitterbugs Waste Fabric." 1942. *The New York Times,* September 4. Retrieved February 4, 2016, from www.timesmachine.com.

Part III

Gallery of American Street Style

American street gangs are almost as old as the United States itself, and as American culture has developed and changed, so, too, have the ways in which street-gang members have marked their affiliations. Street-gang dress is related to the time and place in which a street gang operates, to the types of enterprises that the group engages in (i.e., petty crimes or lucrative drug trafficking), and to the racial and ethnic backgrounds of the members and the tastes that adhere to their cultural backgrounds. Despite the fact that street gangs are involved in criminal enterprises and street violence, and thus strive to avoid the attention of law enforcement, the need to publicly convey membership in this kind of affiliation is virtually universal, though methods of communicating membership range from the subtle use of color or the modification of basic apparel to the much more obvious use of nomenclature or insignia. This photograph depicts members of the Savage Nomads street gang, a group that controlled turf in the southern part of the Bronx in New York City. The image was taken in 1973. (AP Photo)

The "B" in b-boy is a reference to the "break" created by deejays manipulating record tracks on turntables, and in turn relates to the style of athletic dance that was innovated in response to the music in early hip-hop culture. From the middle of the 1970s into the middle of the 1980s, a wide variety of dance moves evolved including top rocking, floor rocking, popping, locking, freezing, and spinning, and this athletic style of dancing necessitated the wearing of apparel that facilitated and accentuated movement. B-boys and b-girls wore head coverings like beanies, caps, and bandanas to facilitate head spins and gloves to accentuate and protect their hands. Color-coordinated sweatshirts, T-shirts, and later nylon tracksuits (with the slippery fabric that enabled dancers to perform floor moves with ease) were the most typical staples of dress. The apparel of b-boys and b-girls in the 1970s through the middle of the 1980s was largely derived from the general mass market for clothing, as specialty hip-hop designers and labels did not exist until the latter half of the 1980s. Fit, color coordination, and customization served to differentiate the b-boy and b-girl. This image depicts b-boys from the early 1980s demonstrating some popping and locking moves while wearing coordinated nylon tracksuits, Nike shell-toe sneakers, and white cotton gloves. (Michael Ochs Archives/Getty Images)

The Beats, also known as members of the "Beat Generation," were a loosely unified group of post–World War II bohemians who generally eschewed the American "rat race" of the postwar period and upended conservative and conformist tendencies in dress. Artists, poets, and musicians of the Beat Generation affected a decidedly antistyle aesthetic composed of jeans, T-shirts, work shirts, sweatshirts, and imported indigenous dress including sandals and peasant blouses. The true Beat look was decidedly unstudied and existed in stark contrast to fashionable dress for men and women of the 1950s. The image depicted here shows acclaimed Beat author Lenore Kandel wearing a basic turtleneck and blue jeans, pants that were notably not fashionable for an adult woman of this era. Her long, natural hair, styled in a simple braid, is also in opposition to the meticulously styled and lacquered women's coifs of the 1950s. Kandel's companion is wearing a crisply ironed button-down shirt and apparel more commonly associated with "beatniks," individuals who attached themselves to the scene and strove to evoke an artsy persona. Wearing all-black apparel and donning a beret came to be associated with this bohemian scene, but this look seems to have evolved as part of a media stereotype. This image was captured on November 12, 1958, in a Los Angeles café. (AP Photo/Ed Widdis)

The Black Panther Party for Self-Defense was a grassroots organization that was formed by Huey Newton and Bobby Seale in Oakland, California, on October 16, 1966. The organization was primarily concerned with serving the needs of the poor and disenfranchised; however, aggressive tactics and violent clashes with the police ultimately overshadowed these social-service initiatives in the eyes of many observers and the press. The paramilitary style of dress that was adopted by members of the Black Panther Party undoubtedly contributed to negative perceptions about and fear of the members of the Black Panther organization by many mainstream observers. The severe aesthetic of black leather jackets paired with black pants, fitted shirts, berets, and sunglasses created an effect that could have been as ominous and imposing, especially when members of the Black Panther Party appeared as a group. This illustration depicts a protest that took place on April 11, 1969, at a New York City courthouse. The building is adorned with a portion of an Abraham Lincoln quotation, which reads, "The Ultimate Justice of the People"; the sentiment of justice for all echoes the mission of Black Panther Party activism. (David Fenton/Getty Images)

Bobby soxers is a name given to the young female fandom of the 1940s and 1950s. This youth style was curiously named for the short cotton socks that were typically worn with saddle shoes and circle skirts by teenage girls in this period, though these socks were not otherwise known by the "bobby" label. Bobby soxers were identified through apparel combinations that were neither entirely new nor completely revolutionary. Wearing cotton sport socks with a lace-up shoe had been acceptable practice for sporting since the 1930s; however, the combination of short socks against bare legs combined with regular street apparel marked a small breakdown in the rules of sartorial comportment. The categorization and labeling of young women who dressed in this manner evolved because it was perceived that many young women of this period embodied a new vision of young femininity, one that was generally frowned upon by adults. Noteworthy behavior of bobby soxers included gathering in large, loud groups, staying out late, dancing in stocking feet, and engaging in fanatic displays of fandom for popular musicians that included swooning, screaming, and wailing. This image depicts a gaggle of female fans of blue-eyed crooner Frank Sinatra as they wait for a glimpse of the star outside a venue in Los Angeles in 1944. One bobby soxer, overcome by her enthusiasm for the singer, has fallen in the street. (Bettmann/Getty Images)

The competition dress of a bodybuilder includes only limited apparel. Competition suits are cut similarly to bikini bathing suits for both men and women but generally feature leg openings that are cut high in order to better showcase the muscle groups of the upper leg. For women, string-bikini tops feature small panels that allow the muscles surrounding the breast to be showcased. The iconic dress of a bodybuilder also includes a deep mahogany tan, which may be achieved from natural or artificial ultraviolet rays but is more commonly sprayed on. Bronzed skin is then oiled to highlight the striations or cuts of muscle masses. The most important part of bodybuilder dress in both competition and on the street is the body itself. Through the maintenance of a strict diet and meticulous exercise regimen, bodybuilders modify their physiques to attain dramatic proportions that are markedly different from normative physiques and thus mark themselves as members of a unique subculture. In this image a group of men strike a pose during the middleweight competition at the annual Mr. & Ms. Muscle Beach Bodybuilding and Figure Championship that took place in 2006 in Venice Beach, California. (AP Photo/Ric Francis)

The Burning Man festival is an annual weeklong event that takes place in the desolate and arid Black Rock Desert in Nevada. Over the years, Burning Man has evolved into a subcultural phenomenon, a temporary society, and for some, a belief system that informs daily life beyond the event in the desert. The dress that is embodied at Burning Man is incredibly eclectic and is designed to express the Burning Man principle of "radical self-expression." Attendees create, wear, and share unconventional, unique, and imaginative assemblages. Costume elements like masks, body paint, and headdresses are commonly used to express an alternative sense of self. Practical items that are also worn to help "burners" adapt to the dusty desert landscape include goggles and bandanas to curtail the dust and broad-brimmed hats to shield an individual from the sun. Various states of undress are common during daytime hours when temperatures in the desert soar to 100 degrees or more and are also evocative of a wholly unbridled attitude toward self-presentation. Burning Man dress often challenges cultural standards of propriety and established gender norms and seems to have contributed to evolving standards of street style that have transcended the festival in the desert. (David McNew/Newsmakers/Getty Images)

The cholo street style is one that is largely adopted by marginalized Latino populations and is especially common in parts of the United States that include large Mexican immigrant groups, including the greater Los Angeles area. The largely unisex style is used as a means of sociocultural bonding within a peer group of the disenfranchised but may also be indicative of street-gang membership. Elements of the look include pieces of apparel that are commonly associated with working-class dress or that are assigned to people who have been incarcerated. Dickies or Ben Davis work pants, undershirts or work shirts, and work boots, as well as tattoos and shaved heads, are common markers of the cholo look. These apparel basics are styled in specific combinations, worn in atypical fashions (like buttoning only the top button of a work shirt), and worn oversized so as to expose the waistband of an underpant. Notably, there are strong links between this socioculturally based style and versions of hip-hop dress that also feature elements of working-class apparel. Both the cholo street style and hip-hop style share similar impulses: to express and celebrate marginality through the use of apparel basics. This image depicts three members of a group who identified as the Dog Patch Gang. Dog Patch is a reference to a part of the Los Angeles *barrio* (neighborhood) of Paramount. (PYMCA/UIG/Getty Images)

Many music scenes, including punk, heavy metal, and jam-band music (typified by the now-defunct Grateful Dead), have evolved a specific sartorial style that is associated with the social scene and is an expression of identity connected to each music genre. The Coachella Music and Arts Festival similarly has evolved a recognizable dress style, but this music scene is notable for the fact that the Coachella festival features different performers each year, showcases a variety of musical styles, and is, therefore, not a unified cultural milieu but rather a gathering of generally young partygoers. The Coachella look is typified by bohemian, neo-hippie influences including crochet, fringe, and beads, and often includes body-revealing apparel for women such as short shorts and cropped tops. The presence of celebrities and high-fashion models at Coachella has helped to transform the event into a fashion incubator and a marketing vehicle. This image depicts festival-goers Regine Lahrkamp (left) and Julia Gilles (right) of Germany at the 2015 Coachella Music and Arts Festival in Indio, California. The dress of these European visitors conforms strongly to an established type— evidence of the power of mass media and the fashion industry to promote a distinctive Coachella festival style. (AP Photo/Rich Fury/Invision)

Cosplayers are part of a subcultural group that embody characters from comic books, movies, and cartoons or of the player's own design. The act of crafting a dress aesthetic and enacting aspects of a character is a form of fandom, a creative outlet, a means of socializing with like-minded individuals, and a means of embodying interesting and inspirational character traits. Many cosplayers make their own apparel, accessories, and props; however, a burgeoning industry exists that supports people's desire to dress in character. While individuals who cosplay typically wear their ensembles only to specific events like Comic Con, fashion designers have long taken cues from the fantastic worlds of superheroes and supervillains and have brought aspects of fantasy to the runway. In recent years a category of street apparel that reflects an interest in cosplay has also begun to develop, and this allows cosplayers to embody aspects of a beloved character virtually all the time. This image depicts contestant Meisha Monk performing as Warrior Arcanine from *Pokemon* during the 41st Annual Comic-Con Masquerade Costume Competition in San Diego, California, in 2015. (AP Photo/Chris Pizzello/Invision)

Dead Heads, followers of the long-lived jam band the Grateful Dead, have, since the 1980s, embodied a distinctive sartorial style. The Dead Head aesthetic is comprised of components that clearly evoke the bohemian lifestyle of the hippie subculture of the 1960s. Tie-dyed apparel including T-shirts, skirts, and dresses are commonplace, and blue jeans (especially tattered and worn examples) are standard elements of dress. Apparel derived from foreign cultures in Africa, Asia, and South America is also meant to evoke the hippie ethos that eschewed American commodity culture in favor of homespun and handmade items. Simple leather sandals, fabric and sisal *huaraches*, embroidered peasant blouses, cotton tunics or caftans, floppy hats, and hand-woven satchels are all staples of the look. Symbolism is also used to mark Dead Head identity: peace signs, marijuana leaves, and icons like skulls with flowers or lightning bolts and colorful dancing bears, symbols which originally appeared on album covers, are routinely worn as designs printed on T-shirts and embroidered on patches. Many elements of the Dead Head look could be purchased near concert venues at a makeshift marketplace called Shakedown Street. Here, some avid followers of the Grateful Dead set up stalls that sold apparel, drug paraphernalia, and collectibles as a means to financially support regular concert attendance and participation in the Dead Head lifestyle. (Steve Schapiro/Corbis/Getty Images)

The emo look is typically comprised of an amalgam of modernized punk characteristics. These are adopted along with a mixture of elements of Goth, hipster, and skater sartorial choices and trendy youth fashions. Spiky jet black or colorfully dyed hair with long, greasy bangs interprets punk influences, while preripped leggings reflect the commodification and modernization of 1970s punk stylistic innovations that are now widely available in the mass market. Many emo characteristics are unisex. Both males and females adopt hair, makeup, and apparel choices in similar fashion, and men who dress in emo style may wear items that are commonly deemed feminine. Shrunken polo shirts or hoodies, skinny jeans, diminutive cardigans, nail polish, teased hair, and eyeliner are examples of male sartorial practices that challenge the normative gendering of dress. This photograph demonstrates the similarity of hair cut, color processing, and styling as well as the similarity of fit and fabric treatment on both figures' pants. (PYMCA/UIG/Getty Images)

Gay pride events are an opportunity for LGBTQ (lesbian, gay, bisexual, transgender, queer) people to openly and proudly express personal identity and are a showcase for sartorial expressions that challenge cultural norms. The first gay pride event was held in New York City in 1970, but the celebrations quickly spread to other cities in North America and Europe. The five-decade history of these events and their interpretations around the globe ensure both variety and change over time; however, gay pride celebrations function as a microcosm for exploring the myriad ways in which gender identity and sexuality may be expressed through dress. Dress practices that are perceptible at gay pride events include the wearing of flamboyant, colorful costumes; exposing parts of the body that are routinely concealed by dress; wearing sexually provocative costumes (especially apparel with fetish and bondage references); donning apparel that reflects the gay pride rainbow flag; and wearing ensembles that confront the stereotypes of gendered clothing by exploiting the masculine/male and feminine/female binaries. The ways in which these tendencies may be combined are seemingly limitless. The two young gay pride attendees depicted here have both bared their toned, hairless chests. The person on the left offsets his bare skin with leather straps and chains, while the person on the right wears a flowing wig, sparkly accents, and makeup. (Picklesaddle/Dreamstime.com)

292

The Goth scene and sartorial style emerged out of the punk scene and dress practices that had developed especially in the United Kingdom. Thus the Goth look may include aesthetic hallmarks that are important to the punk look. Spiky hair dyed black or a vibrant hue is common. Numerous piercings of ears, lips, and nose are also common and an obvious aesthetic link to punk. The wearing of a preponderance of black apparel, combat boots, leather, studs, and chains is also commonly incorporated into the Goth look. However, Goth dress practices also frequently embody romantic, dramatic, and historical flourishes as a means of expressing disaffection, alienation, and otherness. Anachronistic elements of Gothic dress include apparel like corsets, capes, and frock coats, and luxurious textiles like velvet and lace. Symbols that express an affinity for the occult including pentagrams, crucifixes, and skulls are also markers that differentiate Gothic style from its punk roots. Overall, a sense of theatricality pervades Goth style. Makeup applied to create extreme pallor may be contrasted with darkly colored lips and heavily outlined eyes. Some Goths also adopt colored contact lenses and prosthetic teeth to create an otherworldly or undead aesthetic, a tendency that reflects an interest in classic Romantic literature like *Dracula* and *Frankenstein*. (Erica Echenberg/Redferns/Getty Images)

What has come to be known as the "greaser" look was visible on American streets since at least the 1950s; however, the fact that the term "greaser" was not used to describe this style of dress until the middle of the 1960s makes dating the advent of this look problematic. Furthermore, individuals who wore this look varied in terms of their sartorial intentions. For some young men, the wearing of blue jeans, T-shirts, and Converse sneakers in tandem with a highly stylized greased and upswept hairstyle communicated youthful rebellion, while there is also evidence to support the assertion that some greasers were members of American street gangs who engaged in criminal endeavors including street fights. Popular culture, especially television and film of the 1970s, has codified a look that was far less uniform in its original form at midcentury. Similarly, individuals who identify with the rockabilly scene of the late 20th century onward have contributed to the aesthetics of this evolving look. This image depicts five boys, all wearing blue jeans and the same dark shirt, standing in front of the booking officer at the West 47th Street police station in New York City in 1954. The youths were among some 90 persons picked up by police in the Times Square area in an effort to crack down on juvenile delinquents and "generally undesirable characters," an indication that in 1954 this mode of dress communicated at least a modicum of rebelliousness. (AP Photo/Chris Daly)

The look that came to be referred to as "grunge" originated in the Pacific Northwest, especially in Seattle, Washington, and its surrounding suburbs. The sartorial assemblage, which was associated with a local hard-rock scene, originally relied heavily on old or secondhand apparel basics like jeans, T-shirts, and Converse sneakers, worn in used and abused condition. The grunge look was also inspired by the cool, wet climate that is typical in Washington and Oregon; thus layers of clothes including thermal undershirts, plaid flannel shirts, and knit beanies were staple apparel pieces that were worn by the original followers of this music scene. Before the grunge look had a label it was a largely unaffected, organically developed youth style. However, as the music of bands like Nirvana and Pearl Jam gained national popularity, and the press seized upon grunge as a cultural commodity, the look quickly traversed geographical boundaries and was rapidly turned into fashionable commodities. Jeans could be purchased preripped, flannel could be acquired prefaded, and knit caps were worn regardless of climate or weather. Even high-style designers attempted to turn this thrift-shop look into pricey merchandise for consumers far removed from an interest in 1990s hard rock. This photograph was taken in the autumn of 1994 and shows iconic components of this sartorial style. (ZUMA Press, Inc./Alamy Stock Photo)

The fan of heavy metal rock music, who is often referred to as a "metal head" or "headbanger," is often identifiable in large part through the wearing of long, often slightly disheveled hair. The look, which is generally unisex, is typically composed of lived-in band T-shirts, worn or ripped blue jeans, tough black boots or scuffed Converse sneakers, and leather jackets or vests. Heavy chrome jewelry including thick chains, studded leather bands, skull rings, pentagram necklaces, and crucifixes complete the look. The heavy metal street style shares commonalities with the sartorial aesthetics of motorcyclists, punk rockers, and the grunge look. All of these street styles strive to communicate countercultural sensibilities and a tough outsider status. The heavy metal image has evolved over the past 50 years and has undergone stylistic trends in line with the imagery promoted by artists; however, the look is largely concretized, and a great deal of similarity exists between the heavy metal aesthetic of the 1970s and the look that is visible in the early 21st century. This image depicts heavy metal fans at the 2014 Rock on the Range Festival in Columbus, Ohio. (ZUMA Press, Inc./Alamy Stock Photo)

Hip-hop style has probably undergone more aesthetic evolutions than any other American street style. The look has used and interpreted inexpensive mass-market as well as high-end luxury apparel and accessories. Clothes have been worn forward, backward, and angled to the side, dramatically oversized as well as carefully fitted, bedecked with bold and colorful logos as well as with understated aesthetics. Although hip-hop street style has evolved over the past 40 years, some staples of the look have persisted. The heavy use of athletic apparel, especially the wearing of crisp, clean sneakers, has been a long-lived standard. Signature jewelry, made of both real and fake gold or diamonds, has also served to distinguish this street style. However, much of the hip-hop look consists of elements that words may fail to capture. The way something is worn, the swagger that the wearer imparts to otherwise ordinary clothes, and an ineffable quality of coolness that is better expressed in a photograph are signatures of this street style. The men in this undated photograph are wearing a version of hip-hop street style that was most popular in the 1980s. Among the signature features are the baseball cap worn with the brim to the side, the thick dookie rope necklaces, and the partially laced sneakers. The graffiti-covered boom box also relates to the early days of hip-hop; however, nostalgia for the past and the revival of early aspects of the culture make it difficult to date the image with surety. (Luz Martin/Alamy Stock Photo)

The original "freaks," who came to be widely referred to as hippies, were decidedly un-*hip* with regard to their dress practices. Unified by a desire to live outside of the rat race of American culture, determined to abstain as much as possible from commodity culture by living off the land, and galvanized by an interest in peaceful and harmonious living, the original hippies dressed in a manner that was inexpensive, sustainable, and largely outside of commodity culture. Durable denim, secondhand and homemade clothes, and mass-market staples like T-shirts, sneakers, and sandals were embraced for their practicality, comfort, and durability. Hair was worn long and unkempt (and sometimes unwashed) in keeping with an attitude best described as embracing "back-to-nature" practices. Considered in light of late 1960s standards of fashionable dress, the hippie look was decidedly sloppy and indicative of countercultural impulses. Over time, as the hippie subculture gained broader appeal, elements of imported ethnic dress and a wide variety of commercially produced products were adopted by individuals who expressed interest in the hippie lifestyle. This image depicts hippies and other antiwar demonstrators protesting the Vietnam War in People's Park, which is located in Berkeley, California—a locale that was an important incubator for the hippie subculture in the 1960s. (Bob Kreisel/Alamy Stock Photo)

A hipster by definition is one who is "hip" or "hep" to the coolest, most interesting currents in contemporary culture. Although the label "hipster" has been used since the early 20th century, more recently the term has been applied to reference a specific yet amorphous group of young urbanites whose raison d'être seems to be acquiring cultural capital by locating the next frontier of novelty. The eternal search for the next iteration of hipness necessitates the fact that hipster sartorial style is a moving target; however, a few key points of reference have remained in play over the years. Hipsters test the boundaries of gendered dress and long-lived standards of good taste. Hipsters play with the distinctions between high-style fashion and low-brow or working-class dress and explore anachronistic sartorial practices as much as they also appropriate items from foreign cultures. The couple depicted here was photographed in 2015 in Williamsburg, Brooklyn, a site long considered an important incubator for hipsterdom. The two individuals are dressed in a mash-up of working-class elements including their jeans and T-shirts, elements of ethnic dress including the black and white kafiya scarf, sleeves of tattoos and various piercings, and "retro" elements including the cat-eye sunglasses. (Ethel Wolvovitz/Alamy Stock Photo)

Leather subculture emerged among gay men in the United States in the wake of World War II. It evolved in conjunction with the motorcycle club scene that was also developing at that time, and some leathermen are members of gay motorcycle clubs. There are sartorial similarities between both styles as well as overlapping motivations for adopting the hypermasculine dress. Dressing in leather may be viewed as a refusal of and release from social and cultural codes of propriety as well as a way of upending stereotypical cultural constructions of gay masculinity—that is, gay men construed as effeminate or weak. Leathermen adopt a strong, dominating appearance and attitude as a way to confront and upend that stereotype and also use their appearance as a way of expressing specific sexual proclivities. Black leather jackets, jeans or leather pants, black leather vests, Muir caps, and motorcycle boots, as well as leather harness straps with accents of shiny chrome, are long-standing features of this dress style. This image depicts a leatherman posing in iconic leather apparel after earning the title of Mr. Fire Island Leather in 2003. (LHB Photo/Alamy Stock Photo)

Self-proclaimed modern primitives are individuals who live in the modern, industrial world but who adopt dress and other practices from a wide variety of preindustrial tribal cultures, which are broadly referred to as "primitives." The dress practices that modern primitives adopt are largely related to body modifications including piercing, gauging, scarification, and tattooing. In some instances modern primitives carefully copy the "primitive" practice, inscribing or otherwise altering their bodies just as a member of a tribal culture might have done. In other instances modern primitives modify tribal practices and imagery or adopt wholly new aesthetics and techniques to the existing cannon of body modifications. Modern primitive body modifications may function as a boundary mechanism; the shock value of a heavily tattooed or pierced face may serve to keep others at a distance. These body modifications may also allow like-minded individuals to identify one another within the broader social milieu; however, modern primitives are not a tightly unified subculture. For many individuals who identify as a modern primitive, the act of transforming the body is as important as the indelible change that is made to the body. Slow, self-inflicted modification of the flesh, which may push the practitioner to experience intense and prolonged pain, is embraced by some as an important, transformative experience that has the ability to energize the spirit in a way not found in mainstream modern industrialized culture. (Ron Chapple/ Dreamstime.com)

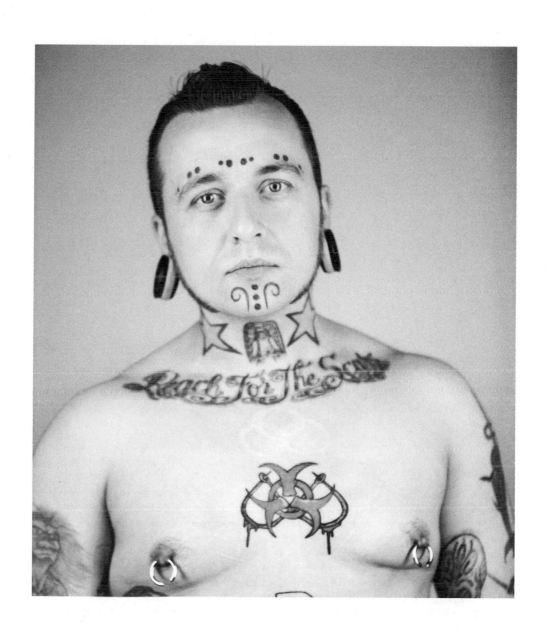

Motorcyclists, both those who belong to raucous gangs and those who belong to social riding clubs, adopt a similar look that is derived partially from functionality and partially to convey an attitude. Denim and leather are dominant materials that resist wear, conceal soiling, protect the wearer, and have long histories of conveying outsider status. Jackets, vests, pants, and chaps are signature elements of a motorcyclist's wardrobe, while T-shirts with branding or other slogans are also apparel staples. The wearing of "colors," insignia that indicate group membership, was innovated in the post–World War II period when motorcycle riding clubs, composed in large part of veterans returning from the war, experienced a period of important development in which marking camaraderie was an important facet. Large back patches and other smaller crests are used to indicate membership and rank or function in gangs as well as social clubs and are also mimicked by companies like Harley Davidson that produce branded apparel. Notably, American street gangs also adopted the wearing of colors, especially in the 1970s. This image shows a group of riders on Memorial Day weekend 2009 at the annual Rolling Thunder Rally Ride for Freedom around the Mall in Washington, D.C. (Huguette Roe/Dreamstime.com)

The term "new wave" has been used over the years to refer to a variety of movements in the arts that were *new* in their time. However, the "new wave" label is also used to describe a style of music and dress of the early 1980s. New wave was a successor of the punk scene and maintained some of the spirit of punk's unbridled, unstudied innovation while embracing the tradition of uninhibited juxtapositions. However, new wave departed from much of the calculated shock value of its hard-edged progenitor and developed both a look and a sound that were far more playful, upbeat, and accepting of a wide variety of influences. Individuals who were part of the new wave scene shared obvious sartorial links with the punks, especially through the adoption of uneven, spiky haircuts, but whereas the punk look evoked a spontaneous, brutally hacked effect, the new wave style was often big, complex, and the result of numerous commercial styling products and tools. New wave is also linked to the heritage of punk through its use of anachronistic dress elements, but while the punks sampled from the world of fetish and adopted latex and choke chains to shock the public, new wavers sampled from the dustbins of past fashions to create a sort of ironic pageantry. This undated photograph shows two youths embodying the new wave style, which was often colorful and eclectic. (PYMCA/UIG/Getty Images)

American punk of the middle 1970s was in some ways a sartorial amalgam of the many subcultural groups that preceded it, including early rockers, Beats, and hippies. The early American punk look was typified by a decidedly disheveled, sometimes dirty aesthetic that impacted both apparel and grooming. Clothes could be ripped by accident or by design and similarly scribbled upon or splattered with intention or as a matter of living out a rough-and-tumble lifestyle. These widely used aesthetic tropes marked punks as dissenters from the mainstream. Over time, as punk music developed and the scene spread to other cities, the look associated with punk became more refined and more specific to the punk subculture with chrome studs, silk-screened T-shirts, and colorful spiked hair developing as iconic markers that set punk apart from other rock and roll subcultures. This image depicts a group of young people outside a crucible of the New York City punk scene. CBGB, which was located on the Bowery near flophouses, cheap restaurants, and secondhand clothing dealers, provided a platform for many early punk acts including Richard Hell and the Voidoids. (Ebet Roberts/Redferns/Getty Images)

Like all street styles, the sartorial markers of the Rastafari may indicate that the wearer has specific principles and beliefs, which are communicated through the adoption of specific dress practices that hold deeply felt significance. Conversely, the adoption of these cultural markers may indicate only a loose interest in or affiliation with a certain way of life. Rastafarianism is, for some, a creed that governs beliefs, diet, and dress, and one important marker of this affiliation is the wearing of dreadlocks. These entangled clusters of hair may be construed as a symbolic linking with Africa and as a marker of the lifestyle path that the wearer has chosen to take. Many individuals who follow the Rastafarian creed also commonly wear the colors green, gold, and red—the colors of the Ethiopian flag—as a marker of identification with Haile Selassie I and the notion of a return to the African homeland of Ethiopia. Some aspects of Rastafarian culture, including the smoking of *ganja* and reggae music, have made the Rastafari look popular among individuals who identify superficially with some aspects of the culture. Thus Rastafari dress practices have become extensively commodified and incorporated into the dress practices of a great many people who do not practice the tenets of the creed. (Steve Skjold/Alamy Stock Photo)

The dress of electronic music partygoers (also known as ravers) in the 1990s and early 2000s was incredibly distinctive and is related to the fact that many rave-goers conceived of the experience as more than a night of dancing; it was also an immersive experience and a bonding opportunity in which the creed of PLUR (peace, love, unity, respect) was adopted. Considering the rave as a special, experimental space for self-expression provides a context for understanding the wildly colorful and incredibly creative clothes that were unique, quirky, and often the product of do-it-yourself initiative in the first decade or so of this scene. Dramatic proportions, vivid colors, fluorescence, childish effects, and wacky juxtapositions were general features of the look that was interpreted with countless nuances. The two young women depicted here were photographed at a rave in Los Angeles, California, in the 1990s. Their dramatic makeup, oversized plastic jewelry, and quirky hairstyles evoke the carefree spirit of this lively party scene. The uniqueness of these looks, which include found objects and toys, marks them as distinctively different from the colorful dress practices of the electronic music scene of the 21st century in which a great deal of homogeneity exists among the colorfully dressed participants. (Photograph by Michael Tullberg)

The style that is commonly associated with the term "rockabilly" is largely a construction of the late 20th century and a vivid sartorial expression of the nostalgia for the music and culture of midcentury America. The rockabilly dress style includes tendencies in dress that existed during World War II and styles that were iconic in the postwar period, including the style of early rock and roll artists. Although rockabilly artists of the 1950s did dress in a discernible manner that included colorful shoes and socks that coordinated with shiny blazers, it does not seem that their sartorial mode was referred to as rockabilly style in the 1950s. From the 1970s onward an international interest in the culture of midcentury America caused a wave of nostalgia, revivalism, and reinterpretation that included renewed interest in music and dance styles as well as a mode of dress that selectively sampled from sources including 1940s pin-up girls, 1950s teen fashions, the greaser look, and the stage clothes of early rockabilly artists. Each of these sources was reenvisioned in a heightened manner: bigger hairstyles, bolder colors, more lustrous fabrics. Thus while there is an historical American rockabilly, the style illustrated here is an amalgam of dress practices gleaned from across roughly two decades and reinterpreted internationally for the late 20th and early 21st centuries. (Neville Elder/Redferns/Getty Images)

Skateboarding, originally referred to as "sidewalk surfing," emerged in the environs surrounding the California surfing scene. Originally conceived as an alternative to surfing the waves and as a way to pass the time when there were no wave breaks worth riding, the pursuit has emerged over time into a fully commoditized industry. Early skateboarding dress practices (like those depicted here) were largely derived from surf and beach attire but evolved to include skateboarding-specific products and aesthetics as companies like Powell Peralta produced decks, trucks, wheels, accessories, and branded apparel specifically for the scene and with the input of their skateboarding team members. Skate style has also evolved in response to other popular culture phenomena and street styles. Skateboarder style has reflected the influence of hip-hop brands as well as the grunge music scene. This image depicts Lance Mountain, an early star of the nascent skateboarding scene. He is shown riding for team Powell Peralta, doing a frontside handplant invert above the keyhole pool during competition at the 1985 National Skateboarding Association event at the Del Mar Skate Ranch in Del Mar, California. (Doug Pensinger/Getty Images)

The American skinhead street style is derived from a look that was originated in the United Kingdom among working-class youths who, taking great pride in their dress despite financial hardships, created a clean, neat, polished look that often included a closely cropped or shaved hairstyle. American skinheads interpreted the British aesthetics. However, over time the look has come to be interpreted as a marker of two intertwined sets of values. Some American skinheads are involved in the hardcore punk-music scene, a genre that is typified by hard-driving instrumentation but that includes a great deal of variety in terms of lyrical content. Some hardcore punk bands do sing about racist themes, but lyrics related to positive and clean living are also part of the genre. The American skinhead look is also used as a declaration of white supremacy. Some skinheads belong to neo-Nazi organizations and actively seek to promote white power, which may include enacting violence against a variety of minority groups identified through their race, ethnicity, or sexual orientation. Interestingly, the skinhead look is also adopted by individuals who disavow bigotry and violence, thus making this street style one of the most difficult to decode, despite the very specific, largely unchanging aesthetics. This image depicts a demonstrator at the 1996 Texas Skinheads March against Desegregation. (Buck Kelly/Gamma Liaison/Getty Images)

The dress of snowboarders reflects an interesting array of influences. As practitioners of a snow sport that began with outsider status, barred from well-maintained slopes designed for skiing, snowboarders, in turn, developed an outsider sartorial aesthetic, eschewing prim, tailored, and coordinated ski ensembles in favor of street apparel with links to the skate, grunge, and hip-hop scenes. By adopting these dress aesthetics, snowboarders bucked the established traditions of the slopes, electing to express attitude in lieu of wearing warm and dry clothes. Early snowboarders would do their runs wearing oversized jeans, T-shirts, and hoodies or flannel shirts—cotton clothes to which snow would adhere and melt and to which ice would cling. Over time, snowboarding has become a sport that is embraced by most ski resorts and has become professionalized as well. As the sport has changed, so too has the apparel. This image depicts American skateboard and snowboard superstar Shaun White after he competed for the United States in the snowboard men's half-pipe final at the 2010 Winter Olympics, which were held in Vancouver, British Columbia, Canada. His clothes are made of a kind of performance fabric that is engineered to withstand cold and moisture; however, his jacket is designed to reflect the aesthetics of a flannel shirt, and his snow pants have been printed so that they look like denim jeans. (Streeter Lecka/Getty Images)

The steampunk style of dress is an incredibly creative amalgam of historical and fantastical, antiquated and futuristic features that are combined to create a look that melds past and future in an aesthetically distinct manner. Individuals who dress in this style generally have interest in some form of steampunk cultural production such as literature, film, or gaming. The steampunk genre generally explores a form of science fiction that considers alternative versions of history—thus the interest in historical references. The execution of the steampunk dress aesthetic exists on a continuum ranging from highly theatrical costumes that include props, such as fantastical weapons that are worn to conventions, to regular street apparel that includes elements of historical dress combined with modern apparel juxtaposed to create a striking impact. Individuals who are interested in steampunk generally value the maker ethos that eschews mass production; however, there are professional designers and retailers that sell apparel that caters to the steampunk aesthetic. This image depicts a young woman dressed in the steampunk style while posing in the wheelhouse on the *Belle of Louisville*. (Daniel Dempster Photography/Alamy Stock Photo)

The ancient art, skill, or sport of surfing first gained widespread popularity in the United States in the 1960s, and along with the growth of participation came the development of a wide variety of consumer products to facilitate catching waves and to help individuals act the part of the consummately cool wave rider. This image depicts a group of guys and gals and their surfboards gathered around a Ford Mustang on the beach in 1964, a year in which many American songs, movies, and magazines were dedicated to surfing. By 1964 a number of national companies devoted to selling surfing suits and beach apparel had been established, and specific aesthetic elements came to define the surfer look. Among the common tropes were bold floral prints, madras plaid, and "competition" stripes—large stripes that dominated the design of shirts, jackets, and trunks. Many basic pieces of apparel were given surf-centric nicknames in the 1960s to market clothes to a public eager to tap into the freewheeling lifestyle. Nylon jackets were marketed as "surf jackets," T-shirts were offered as "surf shirts," and specific apparel designs were given style names like "the Surfette." Over time, not only has the apparel market related to surfing grown, but the marketplace for the clothing and accessories has moved further and further away from the beach, testimony to the powerful allure of this exciting, dangerous, and exceedingly difficult pastime. (Tom Kelley/Getty Images)

"Zooties" or "zoot suiters" were mostly male individuals who were identified by wearing dramatically oversized suits that consisted of a jacket with a hem that extended well past the fingertips and pants that were wide through the upper leg and knee but tapered dramatically toward the ankle. Worn largely as leisure clothes by disenfranchised youths including African Americans and Latinos, these voluminous suits were in part related to the joyous celebration and athleticism of swing dancing and the sartorial swagger of youths who participated in it. However, zoot suits may also be viewed as gestures of defiance when viewed in light of mainstream dress practices. Whereas the fashionable elite wore slim, tailored suits, and the dominant culture embraced these proportional clothes as indicative of status and taste, these ethnic and racial minorities, who in the pre–civil rights era were by default largely excluded from this fashionable mainstream, dressed in a way that refused these standards. Zoot suits and the people who wore them consequently became the target of derisive linguistic attacks and physical violence. The two young men depicted here were photographed in 1943. The figure to the left wears a mix-and-match, possibly secondhand assemblage styled on the body to create the oversized effect, while the figure on the right wears a suit that was cut and sewn to achieve the oversized proportions. (Bettmann/Getty Images)

Conclusion

What is the future of American street style? If we walk the incredibly diverse streets of the United States or scrutinize endless pages of social-media posts, what we will see are a wide variety of dress practices that, given the use of the term today, all may be labeled "street style," but we must ask if the current dress practices and the commentary and commerce surrounding them are moving fashion and style in a positive direction. In this conclusion to our exploration of American street style I would like to give final consideration to the state of American street style: how it is construed, how it is labeled, how it is communicated, and how it is commodified. I believe all of these issues may impact and reorient the future of fashion at large.

The facts that street-style photography has become commercialized (Rodic 2013, 8) and that brands send the latest apparel and accessories to "street style darlings" (Rodic 2013, 9) certainly are points that muddy the meaning of contemporary street style as personal style and reorient much of the street-style commentary to function as simple advertising. Additionally, the fact that fashion professionals invest so much merit in "personal street style" may ultimately be to the detriment of fashion *design*. The topical entries in this book demonstrate that fashion designers throughout the 20th century have taken inspiration from the streets, especially from radical subcultural styles and have thereby reoriented mainstream dress practices. By interpreting subcultural dress practices, producers of apparel and accessories have modified tastes, beauty standards, and notions of propriety. Designers continue to look to the streets; however, there is evidence that designers in the early 21st century are looking with a different kind of gaze. Now there is a culture of catering to the street, of presenting on the runway what youths want to see, and of simply reflecting how youth culture already sees itself. Maya Singer, writing for *Vogue,* presented one recent example of this as she reflected on the spring 2016 collections. She observed that while they reflected relevant forms of dressing, "relevance did not always equate to originality," nor did the collections offer "fashion *qua* fashion"—meaning that while the clothes were technically fashion, in that they were designed for a selling season, their stylistic innovativeness was not significantly present. This phenomenon is also seasonally evident in the celebrity-designed collections of individuals like Kanye West, which offer mundane basics of similar cut and color season after season, but which are heralded by some important fashion professionals as important expressions of the celebrity's taste, personality, and street style.

This tendency is widespread though not universal. Fashion at its worst has become a swirling vortex in which seasonal collections highlight tried and true ideas that are already the current state of dress rather than developing a vision of the future. The big business of modern fashion makes risk-taking a threat to the financial bottom line; thus designing to satisfy the desires that already exist is far safer than designing to create new desires. The street-style phenomenon is not solely to blame for the current state of affairs, but placing these kinds of fashions in street-style contexts functions as a means to legitimize their stylishness, creativity, novelty, and contemporaneity. Furthermore, the fact that street-style commentary often extolls the virtues of the most mundane ideas ultimately reinforces incredibly flexible standards of taste and originality. This flexibility sets the aesthetic bar low for both designers and consumers. Given the right spin, the right context, the right spokesperson, virtually anything may be presented as a means for expressing one's best, most creative self.

In the modern milieu of the street and the photographs that capture it there are individuals who exercise tremendous individuality and creativity. This incredibly innovative segment of the population has been especially visible since the latter half of the 20th century and is an important contingent of fashionable dressers in the 21st century. Unlike the stylish milieu of the early 20th century, which eschewed such unbridled individualism, we celebrate it today. However, the erosion of standards of taste, originality, and stylishness that are part and parcel of the contemporary street-style phenomenon have also impacted creative expression and iconoclasm in a way that is potentially negative. There is ample evidence today of individuals using personal style statements solely as a means to stand out in the crowd, rather than to truly make a personal statement of aesthetic sensibilities or identity. Shock for the sake of shock, rule breaking for the express purpose of garnering attention, adopting ungainly, ostensibly ugly apparel and accessories simply to be different are part of an array of tactics that are especially apparent among young urban men and women who are interested in style and design. Making a sartorial scene in the hopes that someone will take a picture seems to be the point of distinction sought by individuals who adopt odd juxtapositions of apparel that were never meant to be personal style statements. We must ask ourselves, is the wearing of a polyester housedress and plastic shower shoes inspiring? Is it meaningful? Is this a source from which we may want to take future sartorial cues?

Certainly it is demonstrative of the fact that many people in the early part of the 21st century thrive upon the rush of seeing themselves online and having other people "like" or repost images of them, but again this kind of style, which falls under the umbrella of street style in the United States, muddies our conceptualizations of what it means to be stylish in America today.

Many of the street styles that are discussed in the entries in this text are true subcultural styles—modes of dress that developed outside the bounds of fashion, within social groups, used to mark dissent, difference, and a loose unification around an idea or interest. Virtually all of these styles were, for a time, completely and truly subversive and outside of the fashion system. Subcultures and their dress practices had the luxury of time and physical space to incubate, percolate, and develop in their unique social contexts before widespread dissemination of the scene led to the impact of diffusion and commercial interests. One thing that seems to be lacking in the current state of American street style is the presence of a true subculture—a group of iconoclasts, incubating new ideas off the radar of the mainstream. Perhaps it is the case that there is no "off the radar" anymore. It is clear from the historical record that *groups* of individuals who challenge normative dress practices are important. Their absence is notable.

A review of the entries shows that as the 20th century marched on, the window of time and space in which subcultures develop contracted. Communication and socialization are crucial aspects of subcultural style development, and in the years since the demise of grunge in the 1990s, common modes of interactivity have drastically shifted, and we have not seen a new, unified subcultural style develop from the street. It does seem that the immediacy of communication that is facilitated by the Internet in general, but particularly by social-media portals like Snapchat, Pinterest, and Facebook, has made the communication of niche interests, local trends, obscure products (some of the building blocks of subcultural interests) points of common knowledge. Everything can be immediately shared; everyone can be in the know. It is virtually impossible to have a set of interests and a form of expression that are off the grid. Writing in *100 Ideas That Changed Street Style*, the author reflected that due to globalization, "it is hard to imagine a new street style embraced with the passion and conviction—such that it becomes a way of life as much as a way of dress" (Sims 2014, 7). True subcultural styles represent important forms of dress. They are expressive and creative, a form of communication indicative of shared ideas and evocative of the sociocultural context in which they developed. Subcultural forms of dress have eroded old rules of comportment, re-oriented the gendering of dress, opened the gateways to creative juxtapositions, and directly inspired the work of fashion designers. Writing in 1994, Ted Polhemus posited that were it not for subcultural groups like punks, b-boys, and surfers, "most of us would be left without anything to wear" (10). A look at the streets reveals that *new* cliques of people united around *new* shared interests are either absent or aesthetically indistinct; thus we may question from where new forces of change will come.

It is clear that declarations of countercultural group affiliations have given way to declarations of unbridled individuality—street style as personal style. This shift to a full focus on individual expression can perhaps be interpreted as emblematic of broader shifts in cultural currents in the United States and beyond. Cyberculture has in many ways made us more isolated, and the street as a site of social interaction is not as relevant as it once was. Local boutiques that offer the products of youth culture have been replaced by Internet portals in which we shop alone, and perhaps we share the experience of a new product with only a tweet or a post to Facebook. For some 21st-century style-conscious people, the street is no longer the optimal place to make a declaration of personal style; the preferred platform is the planned, filtered, cropped, and edited realm of street-style photography, which can live on indefinitely in the realm of social media. The "Introduction" to *Street: The Nylon Book of Global Style* aptly noted, "The Internet means that people can, through the use of clothing, invent themselves" (Jarrett 2006, 9). Inventing oneself online is a facet of life in the 21st century, but if what is invented online does not fully translate to offline reality, then the scope of the *invention* is limited in a meaningful way. The prevalence of inauthenticity that is evident in social-media posts of personal style complicates both the theorization of 21st-century personal style and its evolution.

What Is the Future of the Street-Style Phenomenon?

As long as there is variety in terms of the types of clothes that are available in the marketplace, it seems likely that personal style will continue to be an important part of getting dressed. The variations in our clothes and how we move in them help to communicate subtle aspects of taste and character. This is true of the person who preens before going shopping on Madison Avenue and the farmhand who selects one baseball cap over another before beginning a long day of work. However, the widespread focus within popular culture and the commercial constructions within the fashion industry surrounding the conceptualizations of "street style" seem unlikely to persist for several reasons. First, the fashion industry thrives on novelty, whether it is real or imagined; thus the street-style verbiage will undoubtedly run its course in due time. Whether it will be replaced by an entirely new concept or will simply be rebooted in a new guise remains to be seen. Additionally, youth culture, though markedly different now than it was before the proliferation of social-media portals, is a constantly evolving phenomenon. It is best not to let nostalgia for an era of record shops, fanzines, and mail order cloud a view to the future. There is no precedent for the stagnation of youth culture and no reason to believe that changes in technology and human interactivity have permanently and irrevocably impacted the evolution of dress practices. Whether this current period in which the focused interest in street style as personal style will create a backlash that leads to something radically new or whether it is merely a step in a path of gradual evolution remains to be seen.

Further Reading

Barberich, C., and P. Gelardi. 2014. *Refinery29: Style Stalking.* New York: Potter Style.

Cocks, J., D. Worrell, and M. Smiglis. 1982. "Rock Hits the Hard Place." *Time* 119 (7): 74.

Hill, A. 2005. "People Dress So Badly Nowadays: Fashion and Late Modernity." In *Fashion and Modernity,* edited by C. Breward and C. Evans, 66–77. Oxford, UK: Berg.

Jarrett, M. S. 2006. *Street: The Nylon Book of Global Style.* New York: Universe Publishing.

Polhemus, T. 1994. *Streetstyle: From Sidewalk to Catwalk.* London: Thames and Hudson.

Polhemus, T. 1996. *Style Surfing: What to Wear in the 3rd Millennium.* London: Thames and Hudson.

Rodic, Y. 2010. *Face Hunter.* New York: Prestel.

Rodic, Y. 2013. *Travels with Facehunter: Street Style from around the World.* Philadelphia: Running Press.

Schuman, S. 2009. *The Sartorialist.* New York: Penguin Books.

Sims, J. 2014. *100 Ideas That Changed Street Style.* London: Laurence King Publishing.

Singer, M. 2015. "Fashion in the Age of the Selfie: Looking at the Spring 2016 Collections from a New Angle." www.vogue.com, October 14. Retrieved October 21, 2015, from www.vogue.com.

Taschen, A., and A. von Hayden. 2014. *Berlin Street Style: A Guide to Urban Chic.* New York: Abrams Image.

Thomas, I., and F. Veysset. 2012. *Paris Street Style: A Guide to Effortless Chic.* New York: Abrams Image.

Woodward, S. 2009. "The Myth of Street Style." *Fashion Theory* 13 (1): 83–102.

Bibliography

Adam, T. 2012. "It's Not Just About the Music, Retailers Are Cashing In on Coachella's Fashion Parade." *The Hamilton Spectator,* April 20. Retrieved June 2, 2016, from http://search.ebscohost.com/login.aspx?direct=true&db=rch&an +q4k053964205012&scope=site.

Advertisement for Diana's. 1983. *Creem,* March, 24.

Advertisement for Incognitos's. 1980. *Creem,* October, 9.

Alford, H. 2004. "The Zoot Suit: Its History and Meaning." *Fashion Theory* 8 (2): 225–36.

Alford, S., and S. Ferriss. 2007. *Motorcycle.* London: Reaktion Books.

Alkebulan, P. 2007. *Survival Pending Revolution: The History of the Black Panther Party.* Tuscaloosa: University of Alabama Press.

Amon, M. P. 2014. "Performance of Innocence and Deviance in Disney Cosplaying." *Transformative Works and Cultures* 1/1. Retrieved March 3, 2016, from http:// dx.doi.org/10.3983/twc.2014.0565.

Andrews, E. 2013. "7 Infamous Gangs of New York." History.com, June 4. Retrieved November 21, 2016, from www.history.com.

Anspach, K. 1967. *The Why of Fashion.* Ames, IA: The Iowa State University Press.

"Anthems of the Blank Generation." 1977. *Time* 110 (2): 48.

Aranza, J. 1983. *Backward Masking Unmasked: Backward Satanic Messages of Rock and Roll Exposed.* Shreveport, LA: Huntington House.

Archer, A. 1933. *The Secrets of Smartness and the Art of Allure.* N.p.: N.p.

Arnold, R. 1999. "Heroin Chic." *Fashion Theory: The Journal of Dress, Body & Culture* 3 (3): 279–95.

Arnott, S. 2011. "Cat Clothes." In *Rockabilly: The Twang Heard Round the World,* edited by M. Dregni, 32–37. Minneapolis: Voyageur Press.

Aspelund, K. 2009. *Fashioning Society: A Hundred Years of Haute Couture by Six Designers.* New York: Fairchild Books.

"As Seen by Him." 1908. *Vogue,* February 27, 288.

"As They Wear It—Seen by Him." 1933. *Vogue,* November 1, 32.

Atkinson, M., and K. Young. 2001. "Flesh Journeys: Neo Primitives and the Contemporary Rediscovery of Radical Body Modification." *Deviant Behavior: An Interdisciplinary Journal* 22: 117–46.

"Australia Bans Zoot Suit, Puts Wearer in War Job." 1943. *The New York Times,* September 4. Retrieved February 4, 2016, from www.timesmachine.com.

"Back to Twiggy." 1993. *Newsweek* 121 (5): 64.

Bakare-Yusuf, B. 2006. "Fabricating Identities: Survival and the Imagination in Jamaican Dancehall Culture." *Fashion Theory* 10 (4): 461–84.

Baker, G. 2007. "Pride-Flyin' Flag: Rainbow Flag Founder Marks 30 Year Anniversary." *Metro Weekly,* October 17. Retrieved September 8, 2016, from www.metroweekly.com.

Barbeau, C. C. 1960. "The Plight of the Beat." *America* 104 (7): 210–12.

Barber, S., and M. Hale. 2013. "Entering the Never Was: Upcycling the Past, Present, and Future in Steampunk." In *Steaming into a Victorian Future: A Steampunk Anthology,* edited by J. A. Taddeo and C. J. Miller, 165–83. Plymouth, UK: Rowman and Littlefield.

Barberich, C., and P. Gelardi. 2014. *Refinery29: Style Stalking.* New York: Potter Style.

Barbish, R. 1979. "Secret Pipes." *Breakout Magazine* 1 (3): 26–27.

Barger, R., and K. Zimmerman. 2002. *The Life and Times of Sonny Barger and the Hell's Angels' Motorcycle Club.* New York: William Morrow.

Barker, T. 2011. "American Based Biker Gangs: International Organized Crime." *American Journal of Criminal Justice* 36: 207–15.

Barnett, M. 2008. "The Globalization of the Rastafari Movement from a Jamaican Diasporic Perspective." *IDEAZ* 7: 98–114.

Baruch, R. M., and P. Jones. 2002. *Black Panthers 1968.* Los Angeles: Greybull Press.

Baudrillard, J. 2005. *The Intelligence of Evil or the Lucidity Past.* Translated by James Benedict. New York: Verso.

Bean, J. W. 1994. *Leathersex: A Guide for the Curious Outsider and the Serious Player.* Los Angeles: Daedalus Publishing Company.

Bellezza, S. M., F. Gino, and A. Keinan. 2014. "The Red Sneaker Effect: Inferring Status and Competence from Signals of Nonconformity." *Journal of Consumer Research* 41 (2): 35–54.

Bender, S. 2003. *Greasers and Gringos: Latinos, Law, and the American Imagination.* New York: New York University Press.

Berelian, E. 2005. *The Rough Guide to Heavy Metal.* London: Rough Guides.

Berger, M. 1943. "Zoot Suit Originated in Georgia; Bus Boy Ordered First One in '40: Known as 'Killer Diller' It Started as Joke in Trade—Tailors Surprised as Demand for It Spread from South to Harlem." *The New York Times,* June 11. Retrieved February 4, 2016, from www.timesmachine.com.

Bernierè, V., and M. Primois. 2012. *Punk Press: Rebel Rock in the Underground Press, 1968–1980.* New York: Abrams.

Beshears, L. 2010. "Honorable Style in Dishonorable Times: American Gangsters of the 1920s and 1930s." *Journal of American Culture* 33 (3): 197–206.

Bešić, N., and M. Kerr. 2009. "Punks, Goths, and Other Eye-Catching Peer Crowds: Do They Fulfill a Function for Shy Youth." *Journal of Research on Adolescence* 19 (1): 113–21.

Black, K. 1996. "Xtreme Prejudice." *Rolling Stone* (742): 52.

Blair, J. 1999. "New York City Cancels a Music Event, and Some See a Link to Woodstock." *The New York Times,* July 31. Retrieved October 3, 2016, from www.nytimes.com.

"#Blogchella: Introducing Fashion's Newest Website, blogchella.fashion at Coachella." 2015. *PR Newswire US,* April 9. Retrieved June 2, 2016, from http://search.ebscohost.com/login.aspx?direct=true&db+bwh&AN=201504090800pr.news.uspr.enuk201504094028&scope=site.

Blumenthal, E. 2016. "Festival Fashion without Fringe or Feathers." *The New York Times,* April 13. Retrieved May 30, 2016, from www.nytimes.com.

Bolton, A. 2008. *Superheroes: Fashion and Fantasy.* New Haven: Yale University Press.

Bolton, A., and R. Hell. 2013. *Punk: Chaos to Couture.* New York: Metropolitan Museum of Art.

Bourdieu, P. 1984. *Distinction: A Social Critique of the Judgment of Taste.* New York: Routledge.

Breines, W. 1992. *Young, White, and Miserable: Growing Up Female in the Fifties.* Chicago: University of Chicago Press.

Breakdancing: Mr. Fresh and the Supreme Rockers Show You How to Do It. 1984. New York: Avon Books.

"Bringing Paris Fashions Down to the Mass Market." 1960. *Business Week,* August 20, 72–77.

Brokaw, L. 1994. "The Dead Have Customers, Too." *Inc.* 16 (9): 90.

Brotherton, D. C., and L. Barrios. 2004. *The Almighty Latin King and Queen Nation: Street Politics and the Transformation of a New York City Gang.* New York: Columbia University Press.

Brown, E. 1992. *A Taste of Power: A Black Woman's Story.* New York: Pantheon.

Browne, D. 2012. "Business Booming for the Dead." *Rolling Stone* 1149: 15–18.

Buckley, D. "New Wave (II)." *Grove Music Online. Oxford Music Online.* Oxford University Press, accessed October 13, 2016, http://www.oxfordmusiconline.com.ez-proxy.brooklyn.cuny.edu:2048/subscriber/article/grove/music/49689.

Burgess, S. 2011. "Foreword." In *Rockabilly: The Twang Heard Round the World,* edited by M. Dregni, 13–14. Minneapolis: Voyageur Press.

Burroughs, W. S. 1959. *Naked Lunch.* New York: Grove Press.

Caplan, J. 2005. "Messengers of Cool." *Time* 166 (17): 98.

Carr, J. R. 2012. "Shakedown Street: A Benjamin Approach to the Grateful Dead." In *Reading the Grateful Dead: A Critical Survey,* edited by N. Meriwether, 163–80). Toronto, ON: The Scarecrow Press, Inc.

Carrillo-Vincent, M. 2013. "Wallflower Masculinities and the Peripheral Politics of Emo." *Social Text* 31 (3): 35–55.

Casino, K. 2010. "Why Lesbians Hang On to the Hipster." *The Gay and Lesbian Review,* September/October, 25–27.

Cateforis, T. 2011. *Are We Not New Wave?: Modern Pop at the Turn of the 1980s.* Ann Arbor: The University of Michigan Press.

Cerio, G., and P. Rogers. 1993. "Goodbye, G Word." *Newsweek* 121 (20): 8.

Chevannes, B. 1994. *Rastafari: Roots and Ideology.* Syracuse: Syracuse University Press.

Clay, A. 2003. "Keepin' It Real: Black Youth, Hip-hop Culture, and Black Identity." *American Behavioral Scientist* 46 (10): 1346–55.

Cleaver, K., and G. Katsiaficas, eds. 2001. *Liberation, Imagination, and the Black Panther Party: A New Look at the Panthers and Their Legacy.* New York: Routledge.

Clemente, D. 2014. *Dress Casual: How College Students Redefined American Style.* Chapel Hill: University of North Carolina Press.

Cocks, J. 1988. "The Irresistible Lure of Grabbing Air." *Time* 13 (1): 90–91.

Cohen, A. 1955. "A General Theory of Subcultures." In *The Subcultures Reader* 2nd ed., edited by K. Gelder and S. Thornton, 50–59. New York: Routledge.

Cohen, L. 2003. *A Consumer's Republic: The Politics of Consumption in Postwar America.* New York: Alfred A. Knopf.

Cohen, N. 2000. "Introduction." In *The Grateful Dead: The History of a Folk Story,* by G. H. Geroule. Chicago: University of Illinois Press.

Cole, S. 2000. *Don We Now Our Gay Apparel.* New York: Berg.

Cole, S. 2013. "Queerly Visible: Gay Men, Dress, and Style." In *A Queer History of Fashion: From the Closet to the Catwalk,* edited by V. Steele, 135–65. New York: Fashion Institute of Technology.

"Combating the Victory Girl." 1944 *Newsweek* 88 (March 6): 91.

Cook, J. 1959. "Teen-age Fashions Represent a Major Business Today." *The New York Times,* July 6. Retrieved April 4, 2016, from www.timesmachine.nytimes.com.

Cooke, C. 2012. "Right Turn on the Open Road." *National Review,* April 30, 36–38.

Cooper, M. 2004. *The Hip-hop Files.* New York: From Here to Fame.

Cosgrove, S. 1984. "The Zoot-Suit Culture and Style Warfare." *History Workshop* 18 (Autumn): 77–91. Retrieved September 11, 2015, from www.jstor.org /stable/4288588.

Covey, H. C. 2003. *Street Gangs throughout the World.* Springfield, IL: Charles C. Thomas Publisher, Ltd.

Crazy Legs. 2011. "Introduction." In *B-Boy Championships: From Bronx to Brixton,* by D. J. Hooch, 6–9. London: Virgin Books.

"Crime Gangs Organized as Big Business." 1926. *The New York Times,* April 4. Retrieved June 7, 2016, from www.timesmachine.nytimes.com.

"Cult of Personality." 1997. *Vogue,* January, 108–21.

Dalbow, T. A. 2015. "Grunge Is Good." *Footwear Plus Magazine,* April/May, 44–45.

Daniels, D. H. 1997. "Los Angeles Zoot: Race 'Riot,' the Pachuco and Black Music Culture." *The Journal of Negro History* 82 (2): 201–20. Retrieved September 19, 2015, from www.jstor.org/stable/2717516.

Daves, J. 1967. *Ready-Made Miracle: The Story of American Fashion for the Millions.* New York: G. P. Putnam's Sons.

Davis, R. A. 1994. "Urban Outback Puts Hip-hop on a Hanger." *Advertising Age,* March 21, 12.

De La Haye, A., and V. Mendes. 2014. *The House of Worth: Portrait of an Archive.* London: V&A Publishing.

DeMello, M. 1995. "Not Just for Bikers Anymore: Popular Representations of American Tattooing." *Journal of Popular Culture* 29 (3): 37–52.

Denizet-Lewis, B. 2000. "Riding the Rave Scene." *Advocate* (802/803): 60.

Dery, M. 2005. "Brown Power." *Print,* September/October, 94–101.

DiMartino, D., and C. Greyshock. 1990. "A Seattle Slew." *Rolling Stone* (587): 23.

Dimitriades, G. 1996. "Hip Hop: From Live Performance to Mediated Narrative." *Popular Music* 15 (2): 179–94.

DiPrima, D. 1969. *Memoirs of a Beatnik.* New York: Penguin Press.

Dragseth, D. 2012. "The Rally Ritual." *South Dakota Magazine,* June/July, 84–90.

Dregni, M. 2011. *Rockabilly: The Twang Heard Round the World.* Minneapolis: Voyageur Press.

Dr. Lizard. 2003. "Why People Dress Funny at Burning Man." burningman.com, October 17. Retrieved June 9, 2016, from www.burningman.com.

Dr. Rock. 1987. "Silent Night, Troglodyte (or Corporate Metal, Yo Mama)." *Creem,* December, 30–31.

Dunn, J. 1999. "How Hip-hop Style Bum-Rushed the Mall." *Rolling Stone* 808: 54.

Eisenman, L. 2002. "Educating the Female Citizen in a Post-war World: Competing Ideologies for American Women, 1945–1965." *Educational Review* 54 (2): 133–41.

"The Emergence of S.D.S." 1968. *Time* 91 (21): 59.

Ensminger, D. 2010. "Redefining the Body Electric: Queering Punk and Hardcore." *Journal of Popular Music Studies* 22: 1, 50–67.

Entwistle, J. 2000. *The Fashioned Body: Fashion, Dress and Modern Social Theory.* Cambridge, UK: Polity Press.

Estrella. 2006. *Skinhead Girls around the World,* vol. 1. N.d.: Applanqued Productions.

Estrella. 2007. *Skinhead Girls around the World,* vol. 2. N.d.: Applanqued Productions.

"Extreme Individualism." 2016. WGSN, April 27. Retrieved May 1, 2016, from www.wgsn.com.

Farley, C. J. 2000. "Rave New World." *Time* 155 (23): 70.

Feldman, R. H. 2013. "Sleeping in the Dust at Burning Man." *Tikkun* 28 (3): 17–20.

Ferrier, M. 2014. "The End of the Hipster: How Flat Caps and Beards Stopped Being So Cool." *The Guardian,* June 21. Retrrieved June 21, 2016, from www .theguardian.com.

Finnegan, W. 2015. *Barbarian Days: A Surfing Life.* New York: Penguin Books.

Finney, B. R., and J. D. Houston. 1966. *Surfing: The Sport of Hawaiian Kings.* Johannesburg, South Africa: Hugh Keartland Publishers.

"A First Look: H&M Coachella." 2015. *Women's Wear Daily 209* (32). Retrieved June 3, 2015, from www.wwd.com.

Fitzgerald, K. 1998. "'Details' in the Field: Men's Magazine Links Lifestyle with Sports via Fall Activities." *Advertising Age* 69 (37): 54.

"Flash: TNT." 2014. *Vogue* 204 (June 1): 94. Retrieved May 26, 2016, from http:// search.proquest.com/docview/1540295053?accountid=130772.

Fleishmann, W. B. 1959. "Those 'Beat' Writers." *America* 101 (26): 766–68.

Flugel, J. C. 1932. *The Psychology of Clothes.* London: Hogarth.

Foner, P. S. 1970. *The Black Panthers Speak.* Cambridge, MA: Da Capo.

"For Gamines' Gams, It's Grunge Gear." 1993. *Newsweek* 121: 65.

France, D., E. Pierce, and J. Chong. 2001. "The Dreadlock Deadlock." *Newsweek* 138 (11): 54.

Freeman, T. 1999. "Post-war America Hitches Up and Heads for the Burbs." *NREI,* 20–26.

Fry, J. 2010. "Fashion Police." *Ski* (75): 4, 46.

Garcia, P. 2015. "Instagram Star Quits Social Media, Says It's Not Real Life." *Vogue,* November 2. Retrieved Novber 15, 2015, from www.vogue.com.

Gaddis, J. L. 2005. *The Cold War: A New History.* New York: Penguin Books.

Gandhar Chakravarty, K. 2015. "Rastafari Revisited: A Four Point Orthodox/ Secular Typology." *Journal of the American Academy of Religion* 83 (1): 151–80.

Gass, L. 2008. "Radical Self-Expression: The Costumes of Burning Man." *Fiberarts* 34 (4): 34–39.

Gegax, T. T. 1994. "Cyber-Tribal Trance-Dance." *Newsweek* 124 (10): 74.

Gereluk, D. 2006. "'Why Can't I Wear This?!': Banning Symbolic Clothing in Schools." *Philosophy of Education,* 106–14.

Gillette, F. 2015. "Occupy Burning Man." *Bloomberg Businessweek* (4414): 60–63.

Ginsberg, A. 2001. *Howl and Other Poems.* San Francisco: City Lights Publishers.

Ginsberg, M. 2014. "The New Dirt Carpet." *Hollywood Reporter* 420 (14): 30–31. Retrieved June 2, 2016, from http://search.ebscohost.com/login.aspx?direct=tru e&db+bth&AN=95584225&scope=site.

Gleason, K. 2013. *Anatomy of Steampunk: The Fashion of Victorian Futurism.* New York: Race Point Publishing.

Gn, J. 2011. "Queer Simulation: The Practice, Performance and Pleasure of Cosplay." *Continuum: Journal of Media & Cultural Studies* 25 (4): 583–93.

Goldberg, M. 1983. "Ric Ocasek: Worms on a String." *Creem,* March, 24–25.

Goldstein, R. 1966. "Drugs on the Campus." *The Saturday Evening Post* 239 (11): 40–62.

Goodland, L., and M. Bibby, eds. 2007. *Goth: Undead Subculture.* Durham, NC: Duke University Press.

Goodman, F., and T. Whiteside. 1990. "The End of the Road?" *Rolling Stone* (585): 21.

Greenberg, J. 2007. "Hip-hop's Fashion Evolution." *WWD,* April 5, 11. Retrieved April 30, 2016, from www.condenast.com.

Gordon, M. 1998. "It's Fitted Skater vs. Baggy Raver." *The New York Times,* January 1. Retrieved October 3, 2016, from www.nytimes.com.

Graves, S. 2013. "New Wave Music." In *St. James Encyclopedia of Popular Culture* 2nd ed., edited by T. Riggs, vol. 3, 748–50). Detroit: St. James Press.

Gray, G. 2011. "An Overview of the Psychology of Steampunk." In *Presentations of the 2010 Upstate Steampunk Extravaganza and Meetup,* edited by G. Teague, 55–64. Newcastle-upon-Tyne: Cambridge Scholars Publishing.

Greenfeld, K. T. 1999. "Killer Profits in Velcro Valley." *Time* 153 (3): 50.

Greenwald, A. 2003. *Nothing Feels Good: Punk Rock, Teenagers, and Emo.* New York: St. Martin's Griffin.

Grief, M. 2010. "What Was the Hipster?" *New York Magazine,* 43 (35: November 1): 32–37.

Grief, M. 2010. "The Hipster in the Mirror." *The New York Times,* November 12. Retrieved June 21, 2016, from www.nytimes.com.

Grimes, D. 1988. "Creator Welcomes Zoot Suit Rebirth." *The Sun Sentinel,* September 22. Retrieved February 4, 2016, from http://articles.sun-sentinel .com.

Grimes, W. 1992. "1992: The Year in Style." *The New York Times,* December 27. Retrieved October 15, 2015, from www.nytimes.com.

Grossberg, L. 1986. "Is There Rock after Punk?" *Critical Studies in Mass Communication* 3: 50–74.

Grushkin, P. 1983. *Grateful Dead: The Official Book of the Dead Heads.* New York: William Morrow & Company, Inc.

Haddow, D. 2012. "Hipster: The Dead End of Civilization." In *The Meanings of Dress* 3rd ed., edited by K. Miller-Spillman, A. Reilly, and P. Hunt Hurts, 74–77. New York: Fairchild Books.

Haenfler, R. 2013. *Goths, Gamers, and Grrrls* 2nd ed. New York: Oxford University Press.

Hager, S. 2014. *Hip Hop: The Complete Archives.* Wilmington, DE: CreateSpace Independent Publishing Platform.

Halbersberg, E. 1987. "Black and Decker Meets Miss Clairol: Poison vs. Mötley Crüe." *Creem,* December, 4–11.

Hale, M. 2014. "Cosplay: Intertextuality, Public Texts, and the Body Fantastic." *Western Folklore* 73 (1): 5–37.

Hamm, M. S. 1993. *American Skinheads: The Criminology and Control of Hate Crime.* Westport, CT: Prager.

Harkness, G. 2014. *Chicago Hustle and Flow: Gangs, Gangsta Rap, and Social Class.* Minneapolis: University of Minnesota Press.

Hawes, E. 1954. *It's Still Spinach: How American Men and Women Can Have More Satisfying Lives by Dressing to Suit Their Individual Personalities.* Boston: Little Brown and Company.

Hazelhurst, K., and C. Hazelhurst. 1998. *Gangs and Youth Subcultures.* New Brunswick, NJ: Transaction Publishers.

Hebdige, D. 1979. *Subculture: The Meaning of Style.* New York: Routledge.

Heinmann, J. 2006. *70s Fashion: Vintage Fashion and Beauty Ads.* Los Angeles: Taschen.

Heinmann, J. 2007. *60s Fashion: Vintage Fashion and Beauty Ads.* Los Angeles: Taschen.

Heino, R. 2000. "What Is So Punk about Snowboarding?" *Journal of Sports and Social Issues* 24 (2): 176–91.

Hell, R. 2015. *I Dreamed I Was a Very Clean Tramp.* New York: Harper Collins.

Henderson, P. 1993. "With the U.S. New Wave Ascendant, Is It Over for U.K.'s Old Guard and Poodle-head Bands?" HM4, May 22.

Hepner, R. 1998. "Chanting down Babylon in the Belly of the Beast: The Rastafarian Movement in the Metropolitan United States." In *Chanting Down Babylon: The Rastafari Reader,* edited by N. S. Murrell, W. D. Spencer, and A. A. McFarlane, 199–216. Philadelphia: Temple University Press.

"Here Come the Sidewalk Surfers." 1964. *Life,* June 5. Retrieved February 28, 2016, from books.google.com.

Higgins, M. 2016. "Snowboarding, Once a High-Flying Sport, Crashes to Earth." *The New York Times,* March 6. Retrieved March 16, 2016, from www.nytimes.com.

"High School Fads: The Ever-Changing Fashions and Language of Youth Indicate a Healthy Spirit of Rebellion." 1944. *Life,* May 15, 65–71. Retrieved April 8, 2016, from www.books.google.com.

Hilfiger, T., and P. Knobler. 2017. *American Dreamer: My Life in Fashion & Business.* New York: Ballantine Books.

Hill, A. 2005. "People Dress So Badly Nowadays: Fashion and Late Modernity." In *Fashion and Modernity,* edited by C. Breward and C. Evans, 66–77. Oxford, UK: Berg.

Hill, W. 2015. "A Hipster History: Towards a Post-critical Aesthetic." *Critical Studies in Fashion and Beauty* 6 (1): 45–60.

Himes, G. 2014. "What New Wave Brought to Rock 'n' roll." *Smithsonian* 45 (5): 1.

Hinton, S. E. 1967. *The Outsiders.* New York: The Penguin Group.

"Hip-hop Fashion." 1992. *Essence* 23 (7: November): 26.

"Hipitaph." 1961. *Time* 77 (7): 50.

"The Hippies." 1967. *Time* 90 (1): 22.

Hoare, P. 2014. "The Rise and Fall of Emo: Why You Shouldn't Be Ashamed for Liking Emo Music." www.mtv.com, May 24. Retrieved August 16, 2016, from www.mtv.com.

Hochswender, W. 1996. "Prep Urban." *Esquire,* 125, 131–32.

Hoff, V. D. 2014. "'The Coachella Diet' Is Now a Thing." *Elle,* April 2. Retrieved June 8, 2015, from www.elle.com.

Hogan, R. 1987. "Cinderella Be A'happenin'." *Creem,* December, 12–15.

Holden, S. 2000. "The Synergy! The Ecstasy! The Biology!" *The New York Times.* Retrieved October 3, 2016, from www.nytimes.com.

Holgate, M. 2010. "View: All Dressed Up: When Did Chic Get So Cool?" *Vogue* July 1, 60–62. Retrieved May 26, 2016, from http://search.proquest.com/docview /879327447?accountid=130772.

Hollander, E. P. 1958. "Conformity, Status, and Idiosyncratic Credit." *Psychological Review* 65 (2): 117–27.

Holmes, C. 1952. "This Is the Beat Generation." *The New York Times,* November 16. Retrieved February 16, 2016, from www.timesmachine.com.

Hooch, D. J. 2011. *B-Boy Championships: From Bronx to Brixton.* London: Virgin Books.

Howe, S. 1998. *Sick: A Cultural History of Snowboarding.* New York: St. Martins Griffin.

Howell, J. C. 2015. *The History of Street Gangs in the United States.* Lanham, MD: Lexington Books.

Howell, J. C., and J. P. Moore. 2010. "History of Street Gangs in the United States." *National Gang Center Bulletin* (4: May): 1–25.

"How to Shoot the Big Surf (and What to Wear While You're Waiting)." 1964. *Surfer* 5 (3): 42–43.

Hutson, S. R. 1999. "Technoshamanism: Spiritual Healing in the Rave Subculture." *Popular Music & Society* 23 (3): 53–77.

Huxtable, S. 2013. "Steampunk Design and a Vision of a Victorian Future." In *Steaming into a Victorian Future: A Steampunk Anthology,* edited by J. A. Taddeo and C. J. Miller, 213–33. Plymouth, UK: Rowman and Littlefield.

Iacob, I. F. 2010. "Rethinking Goth Identity as Style." *The Scientific Journal of Humanistic Studies* 2 (2): 13–25.

Israel, B. 1993. "Rave at Close of Day? You Betcha." *The New York Times,* May 9. Retrieved October 3, 2016, from www.nytimes.com.

Ives, A. 2015. "Cool-girl Outfits to Copy This Summer." *Refinery29,* April 17. Retrieved May 31, 2015, from www.refinery29.com.

Jackson, B. 2003. *Grateful Dead: The Illustrated Trip.* London: DK Publishing, Inc.

Jacobs, A., and D. Pener. 1996. "Extreme Cool." *Entertainment Weekly* (333/224): 64.

James, F. 1985. "Postmodernism and Consumer Society." In *Postmodern Culture,* edited by Hal Foster. London: Pluto Press.

Jarrett, M. S. 2006. *Street: The Nylon Book of Global Style.* New York: Universe Publishing.

Jenkins, S. 2015. *Fresh Dressed.* United States of America: Samuel Goldwyn Films.

Johnson, F. 2012. "Burning Man, Desire, and the Culture of Empire." *Tikkun* 27 (3): 20–63.

Johnson, J. 1983. *Minor Characters.* New York: Simon & Schuster.

Jones, B. 2015. "Fannish Tattooing and Sacred Identity." *Transformative Works and Cultures,* 181. Retrieved March 3, 2016, from http://dx.doi.org/10.3983 /twc.2014.0626.

Kantrowitz, A. 2001. "Swastika Toys." In *Leatherfolk: Radical Sex, People, Politics, and Practice,* edited by M. Thompson, 193–209. Los Angeles: Alyson Books.

Karen, T. 2003. "Cholo Is Bursting Out of the Barrio." *USA Today,* October 9. Retrieved April 19, 2016, from Canadian Reference Center.

Katz, J. D. 2013. "Queer Activist Fashion." In *A Queer History of Fashion: From the Closet to the Catwalk,* edited by V. Steele, 219–32. New York: Fashion Institute of Technology.

Kerouac, J. 1957. *On the Road.* New York: Penguin Press.

Kerouac, J. 1958. *The Dharma Bums.* New York: Penguin Press.

Killer, M. 1971. "What It Means to Be a Homosexual (Continued)." *The New York Times,* October 10. Retrieved September 10, 2016, from www.nytimes.com.

King, S. A. 1998. "International Reggae, Democratic Socialism, and the Secularization of the Rastafari Movement 1972–1980." *Popular Music and Society* 22 (3): 39–60.

King, S. A. 1999. "The Co-optation of a 'Revolution': Rastafari, Reggae, and the Rhetoric of Control." *The Howard Journal of Communications* 10: 77–95.

Kilpatrick, N, 2004. *The Goth Bible.* New York: St. Martin's Press.

Kirby, R. J. 2011. "The Revolution Will Not Be Televised: Community Activism and the Black Panther Party." *Canadian Review of American Studies* 41 (1): 25–62.

Kitwana, B. 1994. *The Rap on Gangsta Rap.* Chicago: Third World Press.

Kitzinger, S. 1969. "Protest and Mysticism: The Rastafari Cult of Jamaica." *Journal for the Scientific Study of Religion* 8 (2): 240–62.

Kleese, C. 2000. "'Modern Primitivism'": Non-mainstream Body Modification and Racialized Representation." In *Body Modification,* edited by M. Featherstone, 15–38. London: Sage Publications.

Klein, A. 1985. "Pumping Iron." *Society,* September/October, 68–75.

Klein, A. 1987. "Fear and Loathing in Southern California: Narcissism and Fascism in Bodybuilding Subculture." *The Journal of Psychoanalytical Anthropology* 10 (2): 117–37.

Klein, A. 1993. *Little Big Men: Bodybuilding Subculture and Gender Construction.* Albany: State University of New York Press.

Klein, M. W. 1995. *The American Street Gang: Its Nature, Prevalence and Control.* New York: Oxford University Press.

Klein, M. W., and C. Maxson. 2006. *Street Gang Patterns and Policies.* New York: Oxford University Press.

Klosterman, C. 2002. "Paradise City." *Spin*, September, 70–78.

Knight, N. 1982. *Skinhead.* London: Omnibus Press.

Kobel, P. 1993. "Smells Like Big Bucks." *Entertainment Weekly,* April 2. Retrieved February 22, 2016, from www.ew.com.

Kolker, A. 2012. "What Are Dead Heads? An Informal Survey." In *Reading the Grateful Dead: A Critical Survey,* N. Meriwether, 181–92. Toronto, ON: The Scarecrow Press, Inc.

Kourlas, G. 1995. "'Hello Kitty' the Club Cat." *The New York Times,* July 23. Retrieved October 3, 2016, from www.nytimes.com.

Kozinets, R. V. 2002. "Can Consumers Escape the Market? Emancipatory Illuminations from Burning Man." *Journal of Consumer Research* 29 (1): 20–38.

Kurutz, S. 2013. "Caught in the Hipster Trap." *The New York Times,* September 14. Retrieved June 21, 2016, from www.nytimes.com.

Kuznick, P. J., and J. Gilbert. 2001. "U.S. Culture and the Cold War." In *Rethinking Cold War Culture,* edited by P. J. Kuznick and J. Gibert, 1–13. Washington, D.C.: Smithsonian University Press.

Lacayo, R. 2008. "A Piece of Our Time." *Time* 171 (14): 64.

Lacayo, R., and G. Bellefonte. 1994. "If Everyone Is Hip . . . Is Anyone Hip?" *Time* 144 (5): 48.

La Ferla, R. 2008. "Steampunk Moves between 2 Worlds." *The New York Times,* May 8. Retrieved August 26, 2016, from www.nytimes.com.

Lane, R. 1995. "The Culture That Jake Built." *Forbes* 155 (7): 45–46.

Langton, J. 2009. *Fallen Angel: The Unlikely Rise of Walter Stadnick and the Canadian Hell's Angels.* Ontario, CA: John Wiley & Sons Canada, Ltd.

Lamerichs, N. 2014. "Costuming as Subculture: The Multiple Bodies of Cosplay." *Scene* 2 (1&2): 113–25.

Laura, A. 2013. "How Hipster Lost Its Cool." *Sunday Telegraph Magazine,* 16.

Laura, C. 2013. "Why You'll Be Wearing What They're Wearing." *The Times,* April 17. Retrieved June 2, 2016, from http://search.ebscohost.com/login.aspx?direct=true&db=nfh&an=7eh71445663&scope=site.

Lavigne, Y. 1996. *Hells Angels: Into the Abyss.* New York: Harper Collins.

Lawson, D. 1974. *Superjeans: Easy Ways to Recycle and Decorate Your Jeans.* New York: Scholastic Book Services.

Layden, T. 2002. "Making Millions." *Sports Illustrated* 96 (24): 80.

Levi's Denim Art Contest: Catalogue of Winners. 1974. Mill Valley, CA: Squarebooks.

Lewis, L. 1989. "Living in the Heart of Babylon: Rastafari in the U.S.A." *Bulletin of Eastern Caribbean Affairs* 15 (1): 20–30.

Lewman, M. 1993. "Grunge Shopper Mike Watt." *Entertainment Weekly,* March 26. Retrieved February 22, 2016, from www.ew.com.

Linder, L. R. 1999. *Public Access Television: America's Electronic Soapbox.* Westport, CT: Greenwood Publishing Group.

Lipovetsky, G. 1994. *The Empire of Fashion.* Translated by C. Porter. Princeton: Princeton University Press.

Lipton, E. 2000. "Politicians March in a Racy Celebration of Gay Progress." *The New York Times,* June 26. Retrieved September 10, 2016, from www.nytimes.com.

Lipton, L. 1959. *The Holy Barbarians.* (Kindle version). Retrieved from Amazon.com.

Lisanti, T. 2014. "Jam-On." *License Global* 17 (6): 35–42.

Lloyd, B. 1996. "Extreme Sports; in Newport, a Grunge Grand Prix." *The New York Times,* June 29. Retrieved October 15, 2015, from www.nytimes.com.

Lodder, M. 2011. "The Myths of Modern Primitivism." *European Journal of American Culture* 30 (2): 99–111.

Lopez, P. 1994. "Vogue's View: Gearing Up." *Vogue* 184 (October 1): 118, 120. Retrieved from http://search.proquest.com/docview/879293461?accountid=130 772.

Lydon, J. 1994. *Rotten: No Irish, No Blacks, No Dogs.* New York: McMillan.

"Made for You: Made to Order by a Great House, Made Your Own by Your Own Ideas." 1948. *Vogue,* October 1, 136–41.

Maffesoli, M. 1996. *The Times of the Tribes: The Decline of Individualism in Mass Society.* London: Sage.

"Mail: Letter from Em J. Zee." 1980. *Creem,* October, 6, 8.

Mains, G. 1984. *Urban Aboriginals: A Celebration of Leathersexuality.* Los Angeles: Daedalus Publishing Company.

Majewski, L., and J. Bernstein. 2014. *Mad World: An Oral History of New Wave Artists and Songs That Defined the 1980s.* New York: Abrams.

Marin, R. 1992. "Grunge: A Success Story." *The New York Times,* November 15. Retrieved October 15, 2015, from www.nytimes.com.

Marks, J. 1997. "Burning Man Meets Capitalism." *U.S. News & World Report* 123: 46–47.

Massoni, K. 2006. "'Teena Goes to Market': *Seventeen Magazine* and the Early Construction of the Teen Girl (as) Shopper." *Journal of American Culture* 29 (1): 31–42.

Mataillet, D. 2015. "From Zazous to Hipsters." Translated by A. Uff. *France-Amérique,* November, 76.

McClendon, A. 2015. *Fashion and Jazz.* New York: Bloomsbury.

McGuire, K., and C. Serres. 2016. "Gang Clothing Ban: Deterrent or Discrimination? Some Shoppers Say the Rule Is Leading Security Guards at Maplewood Mall to Unfairly Target Youths." *Star Tribune* [Minneapolis], April 11. Retrieved June 22, 2016, from *Business Insights: Essentials.*

McKinney, J. 2002. "Rags to Riches." *Black Enterprise* 33 (2): 98–104.

McNeil, L. 1996. *Please Kill Me: The Uncensored Oral History of Punk.* New York: Grove Press.

Meadows, E. 1977. "The Zeitgeist: Pistol-Whipped." *National Review,* November 11, 1311–12.

Meehan, T. 1965. "Where Did All the Women Go?" *The Saturday Evening Post* 238 (18): 26–30.

Menkes, S. 1993. "Vogue's Point of View: What's Modern Now?" *Vogue* 183 (January 1): 91–101. Retrieved February 22, 2016, from http://search.proquest .com/docview/879295463?accountid=130772.

Mercury, M. 2000. *Pagan Fleshworks: The Alchemy of Body Modification.* Rochester, VT: Park Street Press, 2000.

Merritt, G. 2013. "The Life of Joe Weider—The Man Who Transformed Bodybuilding and Fitness." *Joe Weider's Muscle and Fitness,* April, 108–25.

Meyerowitz, J. 1994. "Introduction: Women and Gender in Postwar America 1945–1960." In *Not June Cleaver: Women and Gender in Postwar America 1945–1960,* edited by J. Meyerowitz, 1–16. Philadelphia: Temple University Press.

Meyerowitz, J. 1994. "Beyond the Feminine Mystique: A Reassessment of Postwar Mass Culture." In *Not June Cleaver: Women and Gender in Postwar America 1945–1960,* edited by J. Meyerowitz, 229–62. Philadelphia: Temple University Press.

Miklas, S. 1999. "The Extraordinary Self: Gothic Culture and the Construction of Self." *Journal of Marketing Management* 15: 563–76.

Millard, A. 2012. *Beatlemania: Technology, Business, and Teen Culture in Cold War America.* Baltimore: Johns Hopkins University Press.

Miller, C. 1993. "Marketers Tap into Rap as Hip-hop Becomes 'Safe.'" *Marketing News,* January 18, 10, 15.

Miller, J. 1979. "Jim Miller on Pop Music: Some Future." *The New Republic,* March 24, 25–28.

Miller, T. S. 2012. *The Hippies and American Values.* Nashville: University of Tennessee Press.

Millstein, G. 1960. "Rent a Beatnik and Swing." *The New York Times,* April 17. Retrieved February 16, 2016, from www.timesmachine.com.

Mirabella, G. 1995. *In and Out of Vogue.* New York: Doubleday.

Moore, J. 2015. *Fashion Fads through American History: Putting Clothes into Context.* Santa Barbara: ABC-CLIO.

Moore, J. B. 1993. *Skinheads: Shaved for Battle.* Bowling Green, OH: Bowling Green University Press.

Moore, R. 2004. "Postmodernism and Punk Subculture: Cultures of Authenticity and Destruction." *The Communication Review* 7: 305–27.

Morehead, J. W. 2009. "Burning Man Festival: An Alternative Interpretive Analysis." *Sacred Tribes Journal* 4 (1): 19–41.

Morris, B. 1970. "Java's Gift to Seventh Avenue—Fabrics with a Tie-Dyed Look." *The New York Times,* February 16. Retrieved January 17, 2016, from timesmachine.nytimes.com.

Mortimer, S. 2008. *Stalefish: Skateboard Culture from the Rejects Who Made It.* San Francisco: Chronicle Books.

Mosher, C., H. Levitt, and E. Manley. 2006. "Layers of Leather: The Identity Formation of Leathermen as a Process of Transforming Meanings of Masculinity." *Journal of Homosexuality* 51 (3): 93–123.

Moskowitz, E. 1996. "It's Good to Blow Your Top: Women's Magazines and a Discourse of Discontent." *Journal of Women's History* 8 (3): 66–98.

Muggleton, D. 2000. *Inside Subculture: The Postmodern Meaning of Style.* New York: Berg.

Mulloy, D. J. 2010. "New Panthers, Old Panthers and the Politics of Black Nationalism in the United States." *Patterns of Prejudice* 44 (3): 217–38.

Murphy, M. 2013. "The Rise of Hipster Sexism." *Herizons* 27 (1): 16–19.

Murray, W. 1965. "Hell's Angels." *The Saturday Evening Post* 238 (23: November 20): 32–39.

Musafar, F. 1996. "Body Play: State of Grace or Sickness?" In *Bodies Under Siege: Self-Mutilation and Body Modification in Culture and Psychiatry,* edited by A. R. Favazza, 325–34. Baltimore: Johns Hopkins University Press.

Musafar, F. 2002. *Spirit and Flesh.* Santa Fe, NM: Arena Editions.

Musafar, F. 2015. "Fakir.org." Retrieved February 12, 2016, from www.fakir.org.

Myers, J. 1992. "Nonmainstream Body Modification: Genital Piercing, Branding, Burning, and Cutting." *Journal of Contemporary Ethnography* 21 (3): 276–306.

Neely, K. 1992. "Alternative Music." *Rolling Stone* (645/646): 43.

Nettleford, R. 1998. "Discourse on Rastafarian Reality." In *Chanting Down Babylon: The Rastafari Reader,* edited by N. S. Murrell, W. D. Spencer, and A. A. McFarlane, 311–25. Philadelphia: Temple University Press.

Neumaier, J. 1998. "Happy Days: Greasers, Sock Hops, Poodle Skirts—Those Were the Days." *Entertainment Weekly,* 132. Retrieved June 11, 2016, from http://search.ebscohost.com/login.aspx?direct=true&db=rch&AN=54516217&scope=site.

Newell, S. 1965. "Surfing Stars Dominate the International Skateboard Championship." *Surfer* 6 (4): 87.

Newfield, J. 1967. "One Cheer for the Hippies." *Nation* 204 (26): 809–10.

"New Trends in Urban Style." 1999. *Ebony* 54 (6): 48.

Nir, S.M. 2015. "Burning Man's Fashion Is Wild, but There Are Rules." *The New York Times,* August 21. Retrieved June 12, 2016, from www.nytimes.com.

Norris, H. (1927). *Medieval Costume and Fashion.* Mineola, NY: Dover Publications.

Norwich, W. 2006. "Features: Euroflash!" *Vogue* 196 (December 1): 390–97, 423, 424. Retrieved May 25, 2016, from http://search.proquest.com/docview/879325741?accountid=130772.

"Not a Race Issue, Mayor Says." 1943. *The New York Times,* June 10. Retrieved February 4, 2016, from www.timesmachine.com.

O'Connell, H. 2014. "(Re)Turning Money into Rebellion: Reification and Utopianism in Early Punk Production." *The Journal of Popular Culture* 47 (3): 591–612.

Ogbar, J. 2004. *Black Power: Radical Politics and African American Identity.* Baltimore: The Johns Hopkins University Press.

Ongiri, A. A. 2009. "Prisoner of Love: Affiliation, Sexuality, and the Black Panther Party." *The Journal of African American History* 94 (1): 69–86.

"Open Up, Tune In, Turn On." 1967. *Time* 89 (25): 61.

Orejuela, F. 2015. *Rap and Hip Hop Culture.* New York: Oxford University Press.

Palladino, G. 1996. *Teenagers: An American History.* New York: Harper Collins.

Palmer, R. 1981. "The Pop Life: Rockabilly, a Genre That Has Found Chic." *The New York Times,* June 3. Retrieved September 5, 2016, from www.nytimes.com.

Pareles, J. 1993. "Sensory Overload on the Dance Floor." *The New York Times,* November 1. Retrieved October 3, 2016, from www.nytimes.com.

Pareles, J., B. Ratliff, and J. Caramanica. 2016. "Why We're Not Making Plans for Coachella and Bonaroo." *The New York Times,* March 18. Retrieved June 3, 2016, from www.nytimes.com.

Peiss, K. 2011. *Zoot Suit.* Philadelphia: University of Pennsylvania Press.

"Personal Style." 1972. *Vogue,* March, 91.

Pieri, K. 2016. "The 19 Fashion Blogger Instagrams You Should Follow Now." *Harpers Bazaar,* June 13. Retrieved November 12, 2016, from www.harpersbazaar.com.

Pitts, V. 2003. *In the Flesh: The Cultural Politics of Body Modifications.* New York: Palgrave McMillan.

Polhemus, T. 1994. *Streetstyle: From Sidewalk to Catwalk.* London: Thames and Hudson.

Polhemus, T. 1996. *Style Surfing: What to Wear in the 3rd Millennium.* London: Thames and Hudson.

Polhemus, T. 2011. *Fashion and Anti-fashion: Exploring Adornment and Dress from an Anthropological Perspective.* Lexington, KY: Open Source.

"Police Drive on 'Bobby Socks' Girls Will Curb Teen-age Night Owls." 1944. *The New York Times,* February 15. Retrieved April 4, 2016, from www.timesmachine.nytimes.com.

Poneman, J. 1992. "Features: Grunge & Glory." *Vogue* 182 (December 1): 254–63, 313. Retrieved February 22, 2016, from http://search.proquest.com/docview/879295203?accountid=130772.

Pope, R. 2009. "Realizing the Scene; Punk and Meaning's Demise." *International Journal of Zizek Studies* 3 (1): 1–24.

"A Presley of Its Own." 1958. *The New York Times,* April 20. Retrieved September 4, 2016, from www.timesmachine.nytimes.com.

"The Psychedelicatessen." 1967. *Time,* 96.

"The Punk Rock and New Wave Movements." 2001. In *American Decades* vol. 8, edited by J. S. Baughman, V. Bondi, R. Layman, T. McConnell, and V. Tompkins. Detroit: Gale. Retrieved from http://go.galegroup.com.ez-proxy.brooklyn.cuny .edu:2048/ps/i.do?p=GVRL&sw=w&u=cuny_broo39667&v=2.1&it=r&id= GALE%7CCX3468302577&sid=exlibris&asid=c95d7019efef50d2a9b13 3bc11067515.

Quant, M. 1966. *Quant by Quant.* London: Cassell and Company, Ltd.

Queen, W. 2007. *Under and Alone: The True Story of an Undercover Agent Who Infiltrated America's Most Violent Outlaw Motorcycle Gang.* New York: Ballantine Books.

Quant, M. 1966. *Quant by Quant.* London: Cassell and Company, Ltd.

Quinn, J. F., and C. J. Forsyth. 2009. "Leather and Rolexes: The Symbolism and Values of the Motorcycle Club." *Deviant Behavior* 30: 235–65.

"Racist Skinheads." n.d. Retrieved May 7, 2016, from www.splcenter.org.

"Real Gone Garb for Fall, Beat but Neat." 1959. *Life,* August 3, 48–49.

Reeves, M. 2008. *Somebody Scream: Rap Music's Rise to Prominence in the Aftershock of Black Power.* New York: Faber & Faber.

Reinhold, R. 1988. "In the Middle of L.A.'s Gang Wars." *The New York Times,* May 2. Retrieved June 21, 2016, from www.nytimes.com.

Remsberg, R. 2000. *Riders for God: The Story of a Christian Motorcycle Gang.* Chicago: University of Illinois Press.

Reynolds, J. 2014. *Blood in the Fields: Ten Years Inside California's Nuestra Familia Gang.* Chicago: Chicago Review Press.

Reynolds, S. 1999. "Electronica Goes Straight to Ubiquity." *The New York Times,* June 6. Retrieved October 3, 2016, from www.nytimes.com.

Reynolds, T. 2000. *Wild Ride: How Outlaw Motorcycle Myth Conquered America.* New York: TV Books.

Rhodes, N. 2014. "Foreword." In *Mad World: An Oral History of New Wave Artists and the Songs That Defined the 1980s,* edited by L. Majewski and J. Bernstein, 6–9. New York: Abrams.

Ridinger, R. 1998. "Children of the Satyrs: Naming Patterns of Leather and Levi Clubs." *Names* 46: 2, 97–111.

Ridinger, R. 2002. "Things Visible and Invisible: The Leather Archives and Museum." *Journal of Homosexuality* 43 (1): 1–9.

Riggs, M. 2008. "Emo Rescue." *Reason* 40 (6): 72.

Ringen, J. 2006. "Emorexia." *Rolling Stone,* October 19, 84.

"Rival for Dinah?" (1947). *Time* 50 (2): 70.

Robbins, I. A. 1983. *The Trouser Press Guide to New Wave Records.* New York: Charles Scribner's Sons.

Roche, D. 1994. *The Culture of Clothing: Dress and Fashion in the Ancien Regime.* Translated by Jean Birrell. Cambridge, UK: Cambridge University Press.

Rockwell, J. 1977. "Presley Gave Rock Its Style: He Didn't Invent Form, but Did Bestow Image." *The New York Times,* August 17. Retrieved September 5, 2016, from www.nytimes.com.

Rodic, Y. 2010. *Face Hunter.* New York: Prestel.

Rodic, Y. 2013. *Travels with Facehunter: Street Style from around the World.* Philadelphia: Running Press.

Rodriguez, M. G. 2014. "'Long Gone Hippies in the Desert': Counterculture and 'Radical Self-Reliance' at Burning Man." *M/C Journal* 17 (6): 1.

Rohrmeier, K., and S. Bassett. 2014. "Planning Burning Man: The Black Rock City Mirage." *California Geographer* 54: 23–46.

Rohrmeier, K., and P. F. Starrs. 2014. "The Paradoxical Black Rock City: All Cities Are Mad." *Geographical Review* 104 (2): 153–73.

Romero, E. 2012. *Free Styling': How Hip Hop Changed the Fashion Industry.* Santa Barbara: Praeger.

Rosen, C. 1994. "Labels Raid New Wave Vaults as 'Valley Girl' Makes Charts." *Billboard* 106 (13): 14.

Rosenberg, D. 1998. "All Aboard." *Newsweek* 131: 72.

Rosenblatt, D. 1997. "The Antisocial Skin: Structure, Resistance, and 'Modern Primitive' Adornment in the United States." *Cultural Anthropology* 12 (3): 287–334. Retrieved November 11, 2015, from www.jstor.org/stable/656555.

Roshco, B. 1963. *The Rag Race: How New York and Paris Run the Breakneck Business of Dressing American Women.* New York: Funk and Wagnalls Company, Inc.

Roskind, R. 2001. *Memoirs of an Ex-hippie: Seven Years in the Counterculture.* Blowing Rock, NC: One Love Press.

Rothman, L. 2015. "Motorcycle Culture's Long History of Image Problems." *Time .com.* Retrieved March 13, 2015, from www.time.com.

Royal, L. E. (2000). "Hip Hop on Top: Urban Fashion Designers Rule." *Black Enterprise* 30 (12): 91–94.

Rugoff, R. 1992. "Vogue's View: Get Big!" *Vogue* 182 (September 1):, 191, 194, 207, 212. Retrieved February 22, 2016, from http://search.proquest.com/docview /911902712?accountid=130772.

Ryalls, E. 2013. "Emo Angst, Masochism, and Masculinity in Crisis." *Text and Performance Quarterly* 33 (2): 83–97.

Ryan, C. 1981. *Skinheads.* N.p.: N.p.

Salter, R. 2008. "Rastafari in a Global Context: Affinities of 'Orthognosy' and 'Oneness' in the Expanding World." *IDEAZ* 7: 10–27.

Salisbury, H. E. 1958. *The Shook-Up Generation.* New York: Harper & Row.

Samuels, D. 1991. "The Rap on Rap." *The New Republic,* November 11, 24–29.

Samuels, G. 1958. "Why They Rock 'n' roll—and Should They?" *The New York Times,* January 12. Retrieved September 30, 2016, from timesmachine.nytimes .com.

Samuels, S. 2000. "They Also Dance Who Party the Night Away." *The New York Times,* August 20. Retrieved October 3, 2016, from www.nytimes.com.

Sanders, W. B. 1994. *Gangbangs and Drive-bys: Grounded Culture and Juvenile Gang Violence.* New York: Aldine de Gruyter.

Sandy, C. 2015. "With Runway Shows and Pop-Up Shops, Fashion Aims to Share Spotlight with Music at Coachella." *The Canadian Press,* September 4. Retrieved June 3, 2016, from http://search.ebscohost.com/login.aspx?direct=true&db+rch &an=myo020707085515&scope=site.

Sanford, D. 1967. "The Hippie Business." *New Republic* 156 (23): 7–8.

Sanneh, K. 2013. "Harlem Chic." *The New Yorker* 89 (6: March 25): 52.

Savage, J. 1991. *England's Dreaming: Anarchy, Sex Pistols, Punk Rock, and Beyond.* New York: St. Martin's Press.

Savage, S., and E. Marlow. 2011. *Focused Fandom: Cosplay, Costuming and Careers.* Seattle: Create Space Independent Publishing Platform.

"Says Bobby Socks Invite Illness." 1945. *The New York Times,* February 3. Retrieved April 4, 2016, from www.timesmachine.nytimes.com.

Schecter, L. 1989. "Vogue's View: Antifashion Fashion." *Vogue,* June, 59.

Schiro, A. 1996. "Chic Scales the Heights, or Walks the Dog." *The New York Times,* December 3. Retrieved March 16, 2016, from www.nytimes.com.

Schloss, J. 2009. *Foundation: B-boys, B-girls and Hip-hop Culture in New York.* London: Oxford University Press.

Schmidt, G. 2016. "Narrowing a Gap in the Sci-Fi Universe: One Fangirl Giving Voice to Others." *The New York Times,* January 17. Retrieved March 3, 2016, from www.nytimes.com.

Schouten, J. W., and J. H. McAlexander. 1995. "Subcultures of Consumption: An Ethnography of the New Bikers." *Journal of Consumer Research* 22 (1): 43–61.

Schrum, K. 2004. *Some Wore Bobby Sox: The Emergence of Teenage Girls' Culture 1920–1945.* New York: Palgrave Macmillan.

Schube, S. 2016. "Snowboard Gear That Gets the Tokyo Drift." *GQ*, January, 22.

Schumach, M. 1956. "The Teen-age Gang—Who and Why." *The New York Times,* September 2. Retrieved June 7, 2016, from www.timesmachine.nytimes .com.

Schuman, S. 2009. *The Sartorialist.* New York: Penguin Books.

Scott, D. M., and B. Halligan. 2010. *Marketing Lessons from the Grateful Dead: What Every Business Can Learn from the Most Iconic Band in History.* Hoboken, NJ: John Wiley & Sons.

Seliger, M. 1993. "Normal Weirdness in Seattle." *Rolling Stone* (652): 34.

Serwer, A. E., E. Schonfeld, and W. Woods. 1992. "The Hells Angels Devilish Business." *Fortune* 126 (12): 118–22.

"The Sex Pistols Are Here." 1978. *Time* 111 (3): 62.

Shabaz, J. 2001. *Back in the Days.* New York: Power House Books.

Shakur, A. 1987. *Assata: An Autobiography.* Westport, CT: Hill.

Shames, S. 2006. *The Black Panthers.* New York: Aperture Foundation.

Shaw, G. H. 1945. "Let's Do Less for Youth." *America* 73 (25): 489–90.

Shields, D. 2012. "The Infamous 'One Percenters': A Review of the Criminality, Subculture, and Structure of Modern Biker Gangs." *Justice Policy Journal* 9 (1): 4–33.

Shilling, C. 1993. *The Body and Social Theory.* London: Sage Publications.

Siegel, J. 1966. "Surf, Wheels & Free Souls." *The Saturday Evening Post* 239 (24): 32–37.

Silva Laughlin, L. 2015. "The Hipster Trend Going Flat?" *Fortune,* 12.

Simmons, S. 1987. "Bon Jovi: Can They Bake a Kidney Pie?" *Creem,* December, 40–43.

Simon, L., and T. Kelly. 2007. *Everybody Hurts: An Essential Guide to Emo Culture.* New York: Harper Entertainment.

Sims, J. 2014. *100 Ideas That Changed Street Style.* London: Laurence King Publishing.

"Sinatra Fans Pose Two Police Problems and Not the Less Truancy." 1944. *The New York Times,* October 13. Retrieved April 4, 2016, from www.timesmachine.nytimes.com.

Singer, M. 2015. "Fashion in the Age of the Selfie: Looking at the Spring 2016 Collections from a New Angle." *Vogue,* October 14. Retrieved October 21, 2015, from www.vogue.com.

Singer, S. 2010. "Fashion & Features: Second Acts: Bird of Britain." *Vogue,* 200 (August 1), 196–99. Retrieved May 26, 2016, from http://search.proquest.com/docview/879326040?accountid=130772.

"The Skinhead Fad Shows No Sign of Fading." n.d. Retrieved May 15, 2016, from www.splcenter.org.

Smil, V. 2011. *Made in America: The Rise and Retreat of American Manufacturing.* Cambridge, MA: MIT Press.

Smith, D. 2005. "An Outsider, Out of the Shadows." *The New York Times,* September 7. Retrieved October 1, 2016, from www.nytimes.com.

Snelson, T. 2012. "From Juke Box Boys to Bobby Sox Brigade." *Cultural Studies* 26 (6): 872–94.

Sommers, J., and S. Chean. 2011. *Hip-hop: A Cultural Odyssey.* Los Angeles: Aria Multimedia Entertainment.

Spiegler, M. 1996. "Marketing Street Culture: Bringing Hip-hop Style to the Mainstream." *American Demographics* 18: 28–34.

Spindler, A. 1993a. "Patterns." *The New York Times,* September 7. Retrieved October 15, 2015, from www.nytimes.com.

Spindler, A. 1993b. "How Fashion Killed the Unloved Waif." *The New York Times,* September 27. Retrieved October 15, 2015, from www.nytimes.com.

Spooner, C. 2007. "Undead Fashion: Nineties Style and Perennial Return of Goth." In *Goth: Undead Subculture,* edited by L. Goodland and M. Bibby, 143–54 Durham, NC: Duke University Press.

Spooner, C. 2008. "Goth Boys in the Media: Femininity and Violence." In *Men's Fashion Reader,* edited by A. Reilly and S. Cosbey, 145–59. New York: Fairchild.

"Squirrels, Beads, and the Hippie-Bead Fad Give Navajos a Lift." 1968. *The New York Times,* September 7. Retrieved March 27, 2015, from timesmachine .nytimes.com.

Steele, V. 2013. "A Queer History of Fashion: From the Closet to the Catwalk." In *A Queer History of Fashion: From the Closet to the Catwalk,* edited by V. Steele, 7–75. New York: Fashion Institute of Technology.

Steele, V., and J. Park. 2008. *Gothic: Dark Glamour.* New Haven: Yale University Press.

Stern, M. 2014. "Coachella, Oasis for Douchebags and Trustfund Babies Should Be Avoided at All Costs." *The Daily Beast,* April 11. Retrieved June 2, 2016, from www.thedailybeast.com.

Stewart, M. L. 2005. "Copying and Copyrighting Haute Couture: Democratizing Fashion, 1900–1930." *French Historical Studies* 28 (1): 103–30.

Strauss, N. 1996. "All-Night Parties and a Nod to the 60's (Rave On)." *The New York Times,* May 28. Retrieved October 3, 2016, from www.nytimes.com.

Styles, J. *The Dress of Everyday People: Fashion in the Eighteenth Century.* New Haven: Yale University Press.

Sullivan, J. 2006. *Jeans: A Cultural History of an American Icon.* New York: Gotham Books.

"The Surfer's Cross." 1966. *Time* 87 (16): 97.

"Surf's Up!" 1963. *Time* 82 (6): 51.

Taddeo, J. A. 2013. "Corsets of Steel: Steampunk's Reimagining of Victorian Femininity." In *Steaming into a Victorian Future: A Steampunk Anthology,* edited by J. A. Taddeo and C. J. Miller, 43–63. Plymouth, UK: Rowman and Littlefield.

Taschen, A., and A. von Hayden. 2014. *Berlin Street Style: A Guide to Urban Chic.* New York: Abrams Image.

Taylor, A. 1974. "Shoes That Make You Waddle Like a Duck—and They Sell." *The New York Times,* February 25. Retrieved January 17, 2016, from http:// timesmachine.nytimes.com/timesmachine.

Teague, G. 2011. *Presentations of the 2010 Upstate Steampunk Extravaganza and Meetup.* Newcastle-upon-Tyne: Cambridge Scholars Publishing.

"Teen-age Girls: They Live in a Wonderful World of Their Own." 1944. *Life,* December 11, 91–99. Retrieved April 8, 2016, from www.books.google.com.

"Telling the Story behind the Story behind *West Side Story.*" 2012. *The Los Angeles Times,* February 27. Retrieved October 1, 2015, from latimesblogs.latimes.com.

"That Old Sweet Song." 1943. *Time* 42 (1): 78.

"That Wall of Water." 1962. *Time* 79 (7): 38.

Thomas, I., and F. Veysset. 2012. *Paris Street Style: A Guide to Effortless Chic.* New York: Abrams Image.

Thomas, R., Jr. 1996. "Harold Fox, Who Took Credit for the Zoot Suit Dies at 86." *The New York Times,* August 1. Retrieved February 4, 2016, from www.nytimes .com.

Thompson, H. S. 1967. *Hell's Angels: A Strange and Terrible Saga.* New York: Ballantine Books.

Thompson, R. P. 2011. "Commentary under Corsets: Steampunk's Underlying Message." In *Presentations of the 2010 Upstate Steampunk Extravaganza and Meetup,* edited by G. Teague, 65–71. Newcastle-upon-Tyne: Cambridge Scholars Publishing.

Thornton, S. 1997. "The Social Logic of Subcultural Capital." In *The Subcultures Reader* 2nd ed., edited by K. Gelder and S. Thornton, 184–92. New York: Routledge.

Thornton, S., and W. P. Cassidy. 2008. "Black Newspapers in 1968 Offer Panthers Little Support." *Newspaper Research Journal* 29 (1): 6–20.

Thorpe, H. 2004. "Embodied Boarders: Snowboarders, Status, and Style." *Waikato Journal of Education* 10: 181–201.

"Timeline." Retrieved June 9, 2017, from www.burningman.com.

Torbet, L. 1973. *Clothing Liberation: Out of the Closets and into the Streets.* New York: Praeger Publishers.

Tortura, P. G., and K. Eubank. 2015. *Survey of Historic Costume.* New York: Fairchild Books.

Travis, T., and P. Hardy. 2012. *Skinheads: A Guide to an American Subculture.* Santa Barbara: ABC-CLIO.

Trunk, E. 2011. *Eddie Trunk's Essential Hard Rock and Heavy Metal.* New York: Abrams Image.

Tuttle, W. M. 2001. "An Era of War, Hot and Cold." In *Rethinking Cold War Culture,* edited by P. J. Kuznick and J. Gibert, 14–34. Washington, D.C.: Smithsonian University Press.

"28 Zoot Suiters Seized on Coast after Clashes with Service Men." 1943. *The New York Times,* June 7. Retrieved February 4, 2016, from www.timesmachine.com.

Tyburczy, J. 2014. "Leather Aanatomy: Cripping Homonormativity at International Mr. Leather." *Journal of Literary and Cultural Disabilities Studies* 8 (3): 275–93.

Tyler, B. 2008. "Zoot Suit Culture and the Black Press." In *Men's Fashion Reader,* edited by A. Reilly and S. Cosbey, 381–92. New York: Fairchild.

Tysk, G. 2013. *Breaking All the Rules: Cosplay and the Art of Self-Expression.* Berkeley, CA: Edition One Books.

Vale, V., and A. Juno. 1989. *Modern Primitives: An Investigation of Contemporary Adornment and Ritual.* San Francisco: Re/Search Publications.

Van de Berg, W. R. 1998. "Rastafari Perceptions of Self and Symbolism." In *New Trends and Developments in African Religions,* edited by P. B. Clarke, 159–75. Westport, CT: Greenwood Press.

Vandermeer, J. 2011. *The Steampunk Bible.* New York: Abrams Image.

Vigil, J. D. 1988. *Barrio Gangs: Street Life and Identity in Southern California.* Austin: University of Texas Press.

Vigil, J. D. 1990. "Cholos and Gangs: Culture Change and Street Youth in Los Angeles." In *Gangs in America,* edited by C. R. Huff, 116–28. Newbury Park, NJ: Sage Publications.

Vigil, J. D., and J. M. Long. 1990. "Emic and Etic Perspectives on Gang Culture: The Chicano Case." In *Gangs in America,* edited by C. R. Huff, 55–68. Newbury Park, NJ: Sage Publications.

"Vogue Point of View: Daring to Be Different." 1991. *Vogue,* October, 259.

"Vogue's View: Close-ups, Personal Style." 1984. *Vogue,* July, 168, 170.

Voight, J. 2000. "The Consumer Rebellion." *Adweek* 50 (2): 46.

Voltaire. 2004. *What Is Goth?* York Beach, ME: Weiser Books.

Waldman, A. 1999. "30 Years after Stonewall, Diversity Is Shown in Gay Pride Parade." *The New York Times,* June 28. Retrieved September 10, 2016, from www.nytimes.com.

Walpita, S. 2016. "Coachella 2016: Young Men's Apparel." *WGSN,* April 25. Retrieved May 30, 2015, from www.wgsn.com.

Ward, J. 2013. *Running the Gauntlet.* San Francisco: Re:Ward, Inc.

Wardy, F. 1967. "Surfing Is . . ." In *Great Surfing: Photos, Stories, Essays, Reminiscences and Poems,* edited by J. Severson. Garden City, NY: Doubleday and Company.

Webb, S. 1999. "Masculinities at the Margins: Representations of the Malandro and the Pachuco." In *Imagination beyond Nation,* edited by E. Bueno and T. Caesar, 12–22. Pittsburgh: Pittsburgh University Press.

"Week's Best Promotions." 1948. *The New York Times,* March 21. Retrieved April 4, 2016, from www.timesmachine.nytimes.com.

"The Well-Dressed Man: Some Observations on the Ways of Smart Men." 1900. *Vogue,* November 15, 334–35.

Welters, L. 2008. "The Beat Generation: Subcultural Style." In *Twentieth Century American Fashion,* edited by L. Welters and P. Cunningham, 145–67. New York: Berg.

Westwood, V., and I. Kelly. 2014. *Vivienne Westwood.* Oxford, UK: Picador.

"What Is a Bobby Sock?" 1944. *The New York Times*, March 5. Retrieved April 4, 2016, from www.timesmachine.nytimes.com.

"Wheel Crazy." 1975. *Time* 106 (17): 60.

"Where Have All the Flowers Gone?" 1967. *Time* 90 (15): 40.

Whittaker, J. 2007. "Dark Webs: Goth Subcultures in Cyberspace." *Gothic Studies* 9 (1): 35–45.

Wienzierl, R., and D. Muggleton. 2003. "What Is Post-subcultural Studies Anyway?" In *The Post-subcultures Reader,* edited by R. Wienzierl and D. Muggleton, 3–26. New York: Berg.

"Wild at Heart." 1991. *Vogue* 181 (September 1): 484–99. Retrieved March 28, 2016, from http://search.proquest.com/docview/879297547?accountid=130772.

Williams, S. 2007. "A Walking Open Wound: Emo Rock and the 'Crisis' of Masculinity in America." In *Oh Boy! Masculinity and Popular Music,* edited by F. Jarman-Ivens, 145–60. New York: Routledge.

Willis, R. 1945. "Among the New Words." *American Speech* 20 (3: October): 223.

Wilson, E. 1992. "Fashion and the Postmodern Body." In *Chic Thrills,* edited by J. Ash and E. Wilson, 3–16. London: Pandora.

Wilson, E. 2013. "What Does a Lesbian Look Like?" In *A Queer History of Fashion: From the Closet to the Catwalk,* edited by V. Steele, 167–91. New York: Fashion Institute of Technology.

"Wilting Flowers." 1968. *Time* 91 (19): 37.

Winge, T. M. 2003. "Constructing 'Neo-tribal' Identities through Dress: Modern Primitives Body Modifications." In *The Post-Subcultures Reader,* edited by D. Muggleton and R. Weinzierl, 119–32. Oxford, UK: Berg.

"Winter Surfwear for Surfers in the Know." 1965. *Surfer* 5 (6): 90–91.

Wolfe, T. 1968. "The Pump House Gang." In *The Pump House Gang,* 13–30. New York: Farrar, Strauss, & Giroux.

Wong, J. 2015. "13 Beauty Lessons from the Streets of NYC." *Refinery29,* May 15. Retrieved May 31, 2015, from www.refinery29.com.

Wood, J. 2003. "Hell's Angels and the Illusion of the Counterculture." *Journal of Popular Culture* 37 (2): 336–50.

Wooden, W., and R. Blazak. 2001. *Renegade Kids, Suburban Outlaws: From Youth Culture to Delinquency* 2nd ed. Belmont, CA: Wadsworth.

Woodward, S. 2009. "The Myth of Street Style." *Fashion Theory* 13 (1): 83–102.

"WPB Bars 'Zoot Suit' Made in Any Material: 'Wasteful Garments' Ruled Out as a War Menace." 1942. *The New York Times,* September 12. Retrieved February 4, 2016, from www.timesmachine.com.

Wren, C. 2013. "You've Been Steampunked." *American Theatre,* February, 30–33.

Yarrow, K. 2014. *Decoding the Consumer Mind: How and Why We Shop and Buy.* San Francisco: Jossey Bass.

Yawney, C. D. 1994. "Rasta Mek a Trod: Symbolic Ambiguity in a Globalizing Religion." In *Arise Ye Mighty People!: Gender, Class, and Race in Popular Struggles,* edited by T. E. Turner and B. J. Ferguson, 75–84. Trenton, NJ: Africa World Press.

Yee, V. 2014. "With Rainbow Neckerchiefs, Celebrating Pride and Progress at Parade: Boy Scouts Make Provocative Statement at Gay Pride Parade." *The New York Times,* June 29. Retrieved September 10, 2016, from www.nytimes.com.

"Yield from High Fashion Is Low." 1957. *Business Week,* February 16, 69–71.

Zeman, N., and R. Crandall. 1992. "Through the Looking Glass." *Newsweek* 119 (17): 54.

"Zoot Suit Fighting Spreads on Coast." 1943. *The New York Times,* June 10. Retrieved February 4, 2016, from www.timesmachine.com.

"Zoot Suit Models Rouse Ire of WPB: Agency Warns Industry These and 'Juke Jackets' of the Female Jitterbugs Waste Fabric." 1942. *The New York Times,* September 4. Retrieved February 4, 2016, from www.timesmachine.com.

Index

Page numbers in **bold** indicate main entries in the text.

About the Author

JENNIFER GRAYER MOORE, PhD, is an art and design historian who lives and teaches in New York City. She is a graduate of the Design Studies PhD program at the University of Wisconsin, Madison, and has taught art and design history, material culture studies, and fashion history to both undergraduate and graduate students for the past 14 years. Dr. Moore's research is largely focused on 20th- and 21st-century fashion, with a special interest in the intersection between design and the business of fashion. Her first text, *Fashion Fads through American History: Fitting Clothes into Context,* was published in 2015.